Cultural
Anthropology

Cultural Anthropology

Paul G. Hiebert

University of Washington

Edgar V. Winans

Consulting Editor

J.B. Lippincott Company   Philadelphia   New York San Jose Toronto

ISBN 0-397-47349-4

Library of Congress Catalog Card Number 75-33067

Printed in the United States of America
3 5 7 9 8 6 4

Library of Congress Cataloging in Publication Data

Hiebert, Paul G
  Cultural anthropology.

  Includes bibliographies and index.
    1. Ethnology. 2. Culture.   I. Title.
GN316.H53   301.2   75-33067
ISBN 0-397-47349-4

Photography Credits

The photos on pages 60 and 156 are courtesy of the Photography Collection,
Suzzallo Library, University of Washington, Seattle.

The photos on pages 88, 112, 138, 242, and 396 are courtesy of the Burke
Museum, University of Washington, Seattle.

The photo on page 176 is courtesy of UNESCO Courier; Bernheim/Unicef.

The photo on page 260 is courtesy of J.N.C. Hiebert.

The photos on pages 370 and 430 are courtesy of Vaughn Chapman.

The photo on page 410 is courtesy of Margaret Adams.

The Tlingit mask on the cover is courtesy of
Peabody Museum, Harvard University.

To E. Adamson Hoebel, true scholar, teacher, and friend

Contents

Foreword

One of the most fundamental characteristics which distinguishes man from other animals is the knowledge built up by each individual in interaction with others. Such knowledge is often faulty or partial, but it is the most central and difficult task each of us undertakes. In part this is an individual effort at self discovery, but most crucially, it rests upon a vast and cumulative effort in which each individual participates and contributes. Every society has highly systematic methods of channelling this process and insuring the transmission of the accumulated knowledge and beliefs which comprise its culture.

As I have read Professor Hiebert's book and reflected on the role of introductory courses and introductory texts, I have been struck again by how very important and institutionalized they have become in our society. Many of us take an array of "Introduction to . . ." courses in fields we have been curious about, thus slake what turned out to be a minor thirst, and go on to other things. We may never again attempt any systematic enquiry into that discipline, and will retain the image we gain in that first book for the remainder of our lives.

The scholarly disciplines jostle for the opportunity to gain our attention in this process, teach us their central ideas, their methods and a bit of their history. Yet in one sense there is no beginning to any scholarly discipline; all are simply aspects of our effort to know ourselves and our world. At the same time each is characterized by a distinctive array of concerns, approaches and techniques of investigation. In this sense, anthropology has its formal historical beginnings in the efforts of certain scholars of the last century to apply the methods and perspectives of science to the study of culture and society.

What contribution anthropology has made in this on-going effort at knowledge has come primarily from the provision of systematic information about different modes of life in the various parts of the world. Professor Hiebert has had this consideration strongly in mind in preparing this book. Throughout he utilizes information from other cultures to illuminate our own culture, while thus extending our grasp of other ways of life simultaneously. It is extremely difficult to gain an insider's view of some other society; to avoid imposing at least some part of one's own values on another's culture may be close to impossible. Yet we must, as Hiebert has done here, attempt this kind of understanding.

It is not for the purpose of holding up a mirror for our inspection of ourselves that other societies exist. As Hiebert uses anthropological findings to aid in our understanding of ourselves, so at the same time he seeks to advance our knowledge of others in their terms. For if there is one lesson that anthropologists have learned, it is that a conception of "natural man" stripped of some artificial overlay of culture leads to no man who now exists or has ever existed. Thus if it is illusory to seek the "real" animal by penetrating some gaudy layer of cultural embellishments, then we must seek to understand man-in-culture.

This is not to say that the universal experience of language, and the commonalities of conception, birth, growth and death are not powerful shapers of all societies. Rather it is to stress, as Hiebert has in this text, that anthropology seeks to understand both differences and commonalities by taking human life as it is in all its diversity. Anthropologists may have as their goal the growth of some sense of social responsibility, the desire to ameliorate human suffering or the aim of effective social planning in the face of constant social change. Whatever the goal or combination of goals, we can agree with Hiebert's aim of making a contribution to the lessening of those kinds of errors that follow from ignorance and misunderstanding of other cultures.

Edgar V. Winans
Seattle, Washington
October 1975

Preface

Knowledge is doubling every five years, we are told. The quantity of information produced each year is overwhelming. Add to this the fact that much of what we now know will become obsolete within our lifetime, and the futility of trying to learn even a fraction of the sum of the known becomes apparent. Nevertheless, we continue to equate learning with memorizing large quantities of information, with heaping up facts that may be unrelated to each other and often irrelevant to our own interests. Acquiring factual information becomes an end in itself, stifling the excitement of learning, the thrill of new experiences, the discovery of fresh insights and meanings, and the pleasures and pains of intellectual growth.

If we are to recapture the exhilaration of learning, it must become less a matter of acquiring information (though the need for accurate and relevant information with which to work will remain) and more the acquisition of methods of thought, adaptive attitudes, critical reactions, and ways of applying available knowledge to human life and environment. The notion that we can acquire a body of knowledge that will be valid for our whole existence has itself become a myth. We must learn *how* to learn, how to *select* what should be learned, and how to *use* what has been learned. Only then will we be able to adapt to the rapid changes we face.

It is the assumption of this book that learning can be exciting and meaningful, but only if we are aware of its intrinsic value and of its relevance to ourselves. This assumption leads to several consequences. First, we must be aware not only of the data to be learned but also of how we affect such data. Thus, rather than focusing on the great body of data that makes up the field of anthropology, this text emphasizes the ways in which anthropologists approach and handle their data. In this manner, learning a new discipline helps us to break out of the confines of our old knowledge. It opens up new experiences to explore and reveals new ways to analyze and interpret old experiences. There is the danger, however, that we will be so caught up in acquiring the new information the discipline has to offer that we overlook the new ways of thinking it provides. Such a loss is to be avoided, for it is precisely these new ways of thinking—the novel questions the discipline poses; its concepts, assumptions, methods, and theories—that are the tools we need most to acquire to permit us to find new meaning in our experiences.

This text is not intended to be a comprehensive introduction to the field of cultural anthropology, nor does it attempt to cover all the information a beginning student of anthropology should have. Rather, it is a *core* text that introduces the student to anthropological ways of thought. It is, therefore, most effective when complemented with other books, methods, or materials. If the purpose of a course is to develop insights into specific cultures, it can be supplemented with several ethnographies. The text is designed to adapt well to ethnographies of varying lengths and should serve equally well regardless of the culture or region covered. If the focus of the course should be on anthropological theory, the text can be paired with one of the many books of readings in cultural anthropology.

If the instructor prefers to teach anthropological methods through field studies within the student's own culture, the text may be combined with one of the field manuals designed for introductory courses. Another choice can be to supplement the book with a case study in applied anthropology, to show how anthropology can be effective in programs of community development and planned culture change.

A second consequence of our assumption is that we learn best when new knowledge is linked to existing experiences and understandings. Thus, when a concept, method, or theory is introduced in the text, it is first illustrated with reference to experiences common to most Americans, so that its meaning can be grasped through appreciation of its application. Once its meaning is clear, the new concept can be applied to the analysis of new data from other parts of the world. A summary then links it to the concepts previously presented.

A third consequence is that we must learn to apply to ourselves and to anthropology the same methods we use to study others. The anthropologist knows that the insights gained in studying others are also insights into study of his or her own self, for anthropology is above all a human activity. It is subject to constant change, as new information is gathered and new concepts and theories are formulated. Obviously, anthropological statements do not reflect absolute, unchanging knowledge but instead convey current insights.

While anthropology asserts no claim to complete and final knowledge, it is unique in a significant way. Its holistic approach offers a conceptual framework sufficiently broad to accommodate all human experience. Like a backpack frame, anthropology provides a support for a wide range of data and information. This is to say that anthropologists recognize that human beings are biological, psychological, social, economic, political, religious, and historical beings — and even more; and that all of these factors must be taken into account when we try to understand them. Obviously, no individual or discipline can incorporate all that is known about humankind; but by providing us with a sufficiently broad conceptual framework, anthropology can help us to integrate what we do know into a growing understanding of human beings, including our personal selves.

Acknowledgments

I cannot conclude without expressing my appreciation to the authors and publishers who permitted me to quote from their materials, to those who helped produce this volume, and to my colleagues and students who have stimulated and broadened my thinking. As is so often the case in such ventures, there are a few whose contributions are so significant that the least one can do is express a personal word of thanks. This I would like to do to Professor E. V. Winans, who was kind enough not only to critically review the material but also to provide a great deal of constructive advice. I also want to thank Mr. A. Richard Heffron and Ms. Gale C. Schricker, who by careful attention to editing and format transformed a rough manuscript into clear English. But they were more than editors; they helped a great deal in uncovering areas of muddled thinking and writing. A great deal of the credit for clarity and readability of the material must go to them. However, I only am responsible for any shortcomings displayed herein.

Finally, I would like to thank Frances, Eloise, Barbara, and John for their patience with all the inconveniences this project created at home and for their encouragement and assistance when the task became tedious and the end was not in sight.

Paul G. Hiebert
Seattle, Washington
October 1975

What are human beings?
What is knowledge?

Introduction to cultural anthropology

Anthropology is the study of people. But, of course, it is not alone in this endeavor; psychology, sociology, history, human physiology, medicine, and many other arts and sciences also study people. How, then, is the knowledge about human beings sought by anthropologists different from that sought by other students of humankind? Before we consider this question, we must ask two others, namely: What are human beings? and, What do anthropologists mean when they talk about "knowledge"?

What are human beings?

On the surface, the answer to this question seems obvious; we have little difficulty pointing to people around us. But a little reflection raises some serious problems in our attempt to formulate a precise definition of the term, "human being." Some of these problems have been the basis of a great deal of scientific and philosophical debate. As with most definitions, difficulties arise not in including or excluding the things that clearly belong inside or outside of the category, but in distinguishing the things that are on the boundaries—in this case, beings that might be considered human or nonhuman.

The question explored through fiction

Jean Bruller, a French novelist writing under the pseudonym Vercors, raises some of these questions by means of science fiction. In his novel *You Shall Know Them* (1953), a team of scientists discovers creatures in New Guinea that are neither fully man nor fully ape. These creatures feed on roots, fruits, insects, and some meat, which they smoke over fires. They fashion simple stone tools and communicate by means of grunts, but they have no language for discussing abstract ideas and are incapable of higher reasoning. In short, the creatures resemble a form of protohuman that, anthropologists believe, preceded man in the evolutionary sequence.

Vercors poses the dilemma of how people should relate to these beings. The scientists in the novel capture "specimens" for experimentation and find that they can be cross-bred with both apes and men. A priest is uncertain whether they have souls and need baptism. Neighboring Papuan tribesmen kill and roast the creatures, and industrialists want to raise them like domestic animals to perform simple tasks in their textile mills.

A crisis is precipitated when a man kills his child, born of one of the protohuman females, in order to force the courts to rule on the legal status of the creatures. Are they or are they not human? Can they be killed and domesticated, or do they have human rights and responsibilities? Implicit in the story are the fundamental questions of when in the process of evolution there developed beings we consider human and what it is that makes them unique.

The boundaries of personhood

The problem of defining what it means to be human becomes more contemporary if we try to determine when a fetus becomes a "person." (See Figure 1.1.) Is the fertilized egg a human being? May a pregnancy

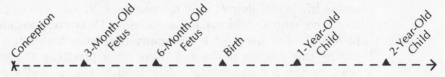

Figure 1.1 When do you become a human being?

be terminated, if it is the result of rape or if the embryo is malformed, without destroying a person? Is abortion permissible to save the life of the mother, to prevent her undue mental anxiety, or simply to comply with her request? How late in pregnancy may fetal life be terminated, what are the legal and moral rights of the unborn, and when does the taking of fetal life become murder?

In our society, there is no generally accepted answer to many of these questions. Some groups define "persons" in terms of biological life, beginning at conception. Others hold that certain levels of biological development must be reached before the fetus becomes a human being. Still others define a person in terms of birth or in terms of a social identity developed after birth in interaction with other people. Obviously, our attitudes toward abortion are closely linked to our ideas about the nature of human beings.

People in other societies look at life in different ways. For example, the Ashanti of West Africa believe that spirits play pranks on people by being born as babies but also that within a few days, the spirits lose interest in the game and leave the body. Only infants that live more than eight days are considered human beings and given names and places in the society. In a society where infant mortality is high, this belief helps mothers explain and accept the deaths of so many of their young.

The problem of defining personhood arises also in the areas of biological experimentation and human engineering. For instance, should scientists generate human fetuses in test tubes in attempts to control or prevent birth defects, develop easier methods for reproduction, or create better strains of human beings? Is the destruction of test-tube embryos different from abortion? Should scientists alter the genetic structures of human life or mix human and other animal genes to create new forms of life that are especially well adapted to specific jobs or climates?

Similar to the problem of determining when life begins is determining when it ends. Suppose a brilliant woman injured in an automobile accident becomes a human vegetable, with no hope for recovery, whose life is maintained only by machines. Should she be permitted to die? If so, who should make the decision? Or is every expense justified in maintaining her life? Is there any difference between a society allowing this woman to die and these other practices: the aged Eskimo who, during a bitter winter when food is scarce, walks out into the snow to die, in order to leave food for the young and the strong, or the Eskimo who abandons an infant born too soon after a previous child, who threatens the lives of both through undernourishment?

Our ideas about people and ourselves are closely tied to our ideas of what it means to be human. Religion, philosophy, and science have each offered answers to this basic question, but before we examine how anthropologists view people, we must see how social scientists view knowledge.

What is knowledge?

Anthropology is one of the youngest of the social sciences, but it shares with the others certain basic assumptions about the nature of knowledge. These assumptions have been the object of a great deal of debate over the years and, as a result, have undergone some radical changes.

From laws to models

Until the turn of this century, science was thought to be a process by which laws existing in nature were revealed and recorded by systematic use of the human senses. We can illustrate this by a brief look at the phenomenon of gravity. You might observe that when you throw a ball into the air, it falls back to earth. Repeating the experiment several times, you conclude that if you throw the ball up again, it will come down. After testing this hypothesis, you accept the law of gravity as a fact. There is, however, another question. Under what conditions does this law operate? At this point, you test your findings in the next room, on the top of a mountain, in a vacuum, under water, and in space, thus exposing the limitations of the law.

This early view of science assumed a real world outside the observer, which he could accurately perceive and describe. It also assumed that the observer had little or no bias, that is, that he did not influence or impose any order on his observations. Any order he perceived was thought to exist in the real world.

The process was sometimes compared to building a house of knowledge by means of experimental data and scientific laws that were be-

Figure 1.2   One way we select experiences is by picking out one thing we see and rejecting the others. These illustrations show how the same scene might appear to three people in different situations: left, to a young man "on the town"; center, to a person needing to cash a check; right, to someone late for an appointment.
Source: Adapted from Don Fabun, *Communications: The Transfer of Meaning*. Copyright © 1968, Kaiser Aluminum & Chemical Corporation. Reprinted with permission of Macmillan Publishing Company, Inc.

lieved to be true statements of reality. To challenge any of these was to threaten the total structure of science and truth, itself.

The role of the observer

In recent years, scientists have become increasingly aware of the part the observer plays in the scientific process. In the first place, the observer can work only with his experiences, and these are limited by his senses and the instruments he uses to extend his senses. Ultraviolet light, electromagnetic fields, and atomic particles, for example, became known to us only as we devised tools whereby we could observe their effects. Consequently, our picture of the real world is always incomplete.

Secondly, the observer is highly selective in choosing his data. Life

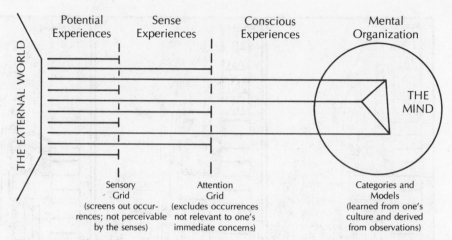

Figure 1.3 The selection and organization of sense experiences occurs both through the senses and in the mind.

is a narrative of ever new and often unpredictable events. At any given moment, an individual is bombarded with sense experiences and can, if he desires, expose himself to more. But he is really interested or concerned with only a few of these. Other experiences are consciously or unconsciously screened out as irrelevant to the task at hand. (See Figure 1.2.) For example, as we read a book, we are often surrounded by sounds and activities that we ignore, but by turning our attention to them, we become conscious of their presence. What a scientist discovers depends, to a great extent, on what he is looking for—on the questions he is asking. Thus, academic disciplines differ in their study of human beings in large part because they ask different questions.

Human beings live, as it were, in a house with only a few windows of tinted and curved glass, through which we can see the outside world. The glass colors and distorts our observations, but its effects can be determined only with much difficulty. Scientists are increasingly aware of the fact that they work with sense data, not with the world itself. (See Figure 1.3.)

GENERALIZATION The ever-changing, immensely varied kaleidoscope of our experiences must be reduced to manageable proportions if we are to make sense out of them. Life and nature are infinitely varied. When we look at two apples, we automatically look at those features they share with other apples we have seen: their roundness, their redness, and their appeal to our appetite. On closer examination, however, we find many differences: one has a bruise and wormhole; another is overripe. No object in nature is identical to another object or even to itself over a period of time. The object ages or is acted upon by an outside force. There are changes in the interests and understandings of the observer, as well.

The ability to generalize or, in other words, to reduce a great many varied experiences to a single category on the basis of certain shared structural characteristics, is the foundation of human reasoning. Without this deceptively simple ability of grouping things which are not identical into sets, a person could not reduce his experiences to manageable proportions or use them to predict future events. And without predictability, life as we know it would be impossible.

Generalizations are based on empirical observations. Nature and life are crystallized in forms and structures, but without ever exhausting their possibilities. Despite their fundamental differences, for example, apples show certain structural similarities to one another, and although any particular apple constantly changes, it has a basic continuity over time. Science is, in part, an exploration of the basic structures and order of the perceived world.

Generalizations also involve logical processes—the mental ability to create abstract concepts by noting certain similarities and overlooking others. For example, in some ways, small apples resemble large ones, but in other ways, such as size, they more nearly resemble small oranges and plums. We could distinguish fruit according to size (smalls, mediums, larges, and jumbos) or according to color (reds, yellows, greens, and purples), rather than by kind (apples, oranges, and plums). In reducing experiences to ideas, only a few of all possible similarities are used, and a great deal of information about the unique nature of specific things must be ignored. (See Figure 1.4.)

There are many levels of abstraction, and at each ascending level we sacrifice detail to gain a simpler, more comprehensive view of the world. For example, Muggayya is a farmer living in a South Indian village with his wife, two children, and mother. Conceivably, at the most detailed level, a biography and precise description can be made of him, or one could learn to know him as a friend. We may speak of him and certain other fellow human beings as "Indians"; we refer to certain characteristics that they all share, such as national identity, or that are common to many of them, such as eating practices and religious beliefs.

At a broader level, defining Muggayya and other Indians as "people" conveys little information other than the dictionary definition of "human beings as distinct from lower animals," which, as we have already seen, raises more questions than it answers. Finally, to classify Muggayya as a "male" is to lump him in a category with a great many creatures, both human and nonhuman.

Generalizations are useful and necessary to organize our experi-

SIGNS	I	II	III	IV	V
□	Yes	Yes	Yes	Yes	Yes
△	Yes	Yes	Yes	Yes	No
○	No	Yes	Yes	No	Yes
□ □	Yes	No	Yes	Yes	No
□ over □	Yes	No	No	Yes	Yes
△ △	Yes	No	Yes	Yes	No
△ over △	Yes	No	No	Yes	Yes
○ ○	No	No	Yes	Yes	No
○ over ○	No	No	No	Yes	Yes
△ □	Yes	No	Yes	Yes	No
△ ○	No	No	Yes	No	Yes
△ over ○	No	No	No	No	No
△○□	No	Yes	Yes	No	Yes
8	No	Yes	No	Yes	No
PRINCIPLES	Yes = only straight line figures; No = a round figure present.	Yes = an odd number of signs; No = an even number of signs.	?	?	?

Figure 1.4 Human thought depends on the ability to discover structural similarities and relationship between different experiences. On the left is a set of signs. Each column of yes/no responses is related to these signs in a systematic way. The principles behind these systems are given for the first two columns. What are they for the last three? Other response patterns can readily be formulated using still other principles.

ences, and little is lost if the information ignored is irrelevant to the study at hand, but there is always the danger of leaving out critical details. The danger of generalization is oversimplification. (See Figure 1.5.) When Leslie Stephen, one of the great alpinists, was asked if it were safe to climb the Matterhorn, he replied:

> There is no mountain in the Alps which may not become excessively dangerous if the climbers are inexperienced, the guides incompetent, the weather bad and the snow unfavorable. . . . There are circumstances under which the Righi [a smaller peak] is far more dangerous than the Matterhorn under others. (Chase 1954:144)

ORDER Concepts are creations of human languages and cultures, and different cultures organize their conceptual sets in different ways. A person who speaks English learns to describe a certain color as "green" and to differentiate it from "blue," which in English is a different color. Within each of these colors there are numerous shades, such as "light green," "emerald," and "olive," or "azure" and "ultramarine," but these shades are perceived as variations of a single color. English speakers distinguish six or seven colors in the rainbow, depending on whether they classify "indigo" as a separate color or as a shade of blue or violet. In other languages, the color spectrum is divided differently, so that what we distinguish as shades are perceived as separate colors, and vice versa. (See Figure 1.6.)

The order which concepts such as color bring to our experiences is not the product of culture alone. At times, it is a reflection of an order that appears to exist in nature, for human thought enables man to change natural events in predictable ways. He can light fires to protect

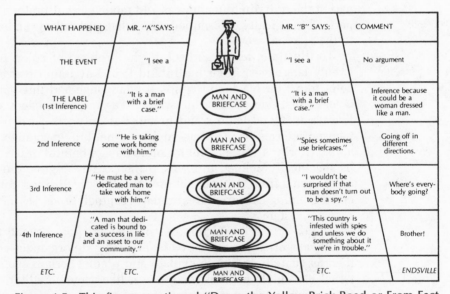

WHAT HAPPENED	MR. "A" SAYS:		MR. "B" SAYS:	COMMENT
THE EVENT	"I see a		"I see a	No argument
THE LABEL (1st Inference)	"It is a man with a brief case."	MAN AND BRIEFCASE	"It is a man with a brief case."	Inference because it could be a woman dressed like a man.
2nd Inference	"He is taking some work home with him."	MAN AND BRIEFCASE	"Spies sometimes use briefcases."	Going off in different directions.
3rd Inference	"He must be a very dedicated man to take work home with him."	MAN AND BRIEFCASE	"I wouldn't be surprised if that man doesn't turn out to be a spy."	Where's everybody going?
4th Inference	"A man that dedicated is bound to be a success in life and an asset to our community."	MAN AND BRIEFCASE	"This country is infested with spies and unless we do something about it we're in trouble."	Brother!
ETC.	ETC.	MAN AND BRIEFCASE	ETC.	ENDSVILLE

Figure 1.5 This figure, captioned "Down the Yellow Brick Road or From Fact to Fallacy," illustrates how two people can see the same thing and draw completely different inferences as to the meaning of what they are seeing.
Source: Adapted from Don Fabun, *Communications: The Transfer of Meaning.* Copyright © 1968, Kaiser Aluminum & Chemical Corporation. Reprinted with permission of Macmillan Publishing Company, Inc.

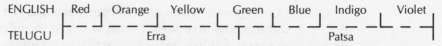

Figure 1.6 Differences in cultural color perceptions are seen in the two languages of English and Telugu.

himself against cold, build air conditioners to offset excessive heat, and calculate the trajectories necessary to place a man on the moon within a half mile of the target. These accomplishments would be impossible if there were no order in nature.

Order is also partly a product of the ways in which the human mind is formed and functions. The biological processes involved in human thought and perception seem to play an important role in determining the basic structure of human thought and language. For instance, while languages vary greatly in the sounds they employ and in words and grammars, all seem to rest on some basic processes of the human mind common to all individuals.

One of the most difficult problems facing anthropologists, and one which they are currently studying very carefully, is to determine what part of the order in human ideas and models is culturally molded, what part is biologically determined, and what part reflects an existing order in the external world.

To illustrate, let us go back to the problem of color. In a study of twenty languages, Brent Berlin and Paul Kay found that all had basic color terms for black and white. If a language had three or more basic color terms, one of these invariably was red. Languages with four or five terms added yellow and green. But only if a particular language had more terms were colors such as blue, brown, orange, and purple added (Berlin and Kay 1969). Colors have a natural order, for they can be specifically defined in terms of their wave lengths. But concepts of color result from a combination of culturally learned categories and certain biological structures and perceptual processes of the human nervous system.

The order a scientist imposes on his data goes beyond the observational categories provided by his language. He organizes concepts into theories that allow him to explain and predict certain events in the external world. He acts, in some ways, like a movie editor, who selects strips of film taken at many different times and places and arranges them in a logical sequence to tell a story . However, as we shall see, the same data can often be organized in different ways to "explain" what is going on. (See Figure 1.7.) Light, for example, can be described as electromagnetic waves or as small quantums or bundles of energy.

Kitchen wares are popular market items at Cuernavaca, Mexico.

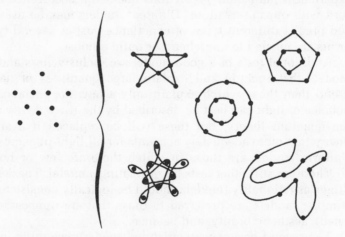

Figure 1.7 Sense experiences can be interpreted in many different ways. The five figures to the right represent various ways of organizing the set of dots to the left.

Evaluating models

While theories were formerly considered as accurate statements of reality (as true descriptions of the order and laws that exist in the universe), we now recognize that they are *models* that we construct in our minds to organize our experiences and replicate the outside world. They are our maps of the world, and just as a map itself is not the actual land but a simplified way of showing the structural arrangements of cities, roads, rivers, and mountains, so also is a model a means by which the basic structure and operation of the real world is portrayed. But to be useful, maps must accurately reflect their geographical counterparts. A map full of errors may lead us to San Francisco when we set out for New York. Similarly, models must replicate our experiential world if they are to help us to understand and function within it.

Models have several basic characteristics. First, because they are ways of seeing things rather than declarations about the real nature of things, themselves, we cannot speak of models as being ultimately true or false. Instead, we talk of their usefulness and their fit. This does not mean that the scientist is not interested in pursuing truth, but rather reflects his awareness that his understandings of reality are always limited, incomplete, and only approximations.

By usefulness, we mean that models help us organize our experiences meaningfully and that they can be used to solve the problems with which we are concerned. By fit, we mean that they conform to our experiences, and their predictions about the occurrence of events accord with our observations. Different models may be used to describe and predict different types of experience, just as several types of blueprints are needed to apprehend or build a house.

Additional tests of a good model are inclusiveness and uniformity. Models that include and explain large quantities of data are more useful than those which explain only a few. For instance, some phenomena of light can best be described by the wave theory and some by the quantum theory, but these will be replaced if a single unified theory that more adequately accounts for all light phenomena is found. Uniform models are those in which there are few or no exceptions.

There are still other tests for evaluating a model. These include such things as rationality (models should be logically consistent), simplicity (simpler models are preferred to those that are unnecessarily complicated), aesthetic beauty, and balance.

The second basic characteristic of modern scientific models is that they are open models; they do not claim to explain all known phenomena. Some early scientists, such as the astronomer and mathematician

La Place, believed we would be able to predict the future accurately if we knew all the laws of nature and the present state of all things. These early thinkers saw the world as a closed, determined system, to which science could ultimately give a complete explanation. The hard fact is that we can never know the present completely, for science is restricted by the limitations of observation, and can deal only with those parts of the world that are observable. No reliable assertions can be made about phenomena that may exist outside of our experience.

Third, models are ways of looking at the world; therefore, they are tentative and subject to change and improvement. The scientist starts with observational data and forms concepts and models by the processes of induction—by making systematic wholes of separate parts. His models enable him to organize and explain his data. They also help him, by the processes of deduction and projection, to predict how the objects of his analysis will behave under different circumstances and to test his predictions by further experimentation. These experiments, in

---

Savages, we call them
Benjamin Franklin (1784)

Savages we call them, because their manners differ from ours, which we think the perfection of civility; they think the same of theirs.

Perhaps, if we could examine the manners of different nations with impartiality, we should find no people so rude as to be without rules of politeness; nor any so polite as not to have some remains of rudeness.

The Indian men, when young, are hunters and warriors; when old, counselors; for all their government is by the counsel or advice of the sages; there is no force, there are no prisons, no officers to compel obedience, or inflict punishment. Hence they generally study oratory; the best speaker having the most influence. The Indian women till the ground, dress the food, nurse and bring up the children, and preserve and hand down to posterity the memory of public transactions. These employments of men and women are accounted natural and honorable. Having few artificial wants, they have abundance of leisure for improvement in conversation.

Our laborious manner of life, compared with theirs, they esteem slavish and base; and the learning on which we value ourselves, they regard as frivolous and useless. An instance of this occurred at the treaty of Lancaster, in

Source: As quoted in Charles C. Hughes, ed., *Make Men of Them: Introductory Readings for Cultural Anthropology* (Chicago: Rand McNally, 1972), p. vii.

Pennsylvania, anno 1774, between the government of Virginia and the Six Nations. After the principal business was settled the commissioners from Virginia acquainted the Indians by a speech, that there was at Williamsburgh a college, with a fund, for educating Indian youth; and that if the chiefs of the Six Nations would send down half a dozen of their sons to that college, the government would take care that they should be well provided for, and instructed in all the learning of the white people.

It is one of the Indian rules of politeness not to answer a public proposition the same day that it is made: they think that it would be treating it as a light matter, and they show it respect by taking time to consider it, as of a matter important. They therefore deferred their answer till the day following: when their speaker began by expressing their deep sense of the kindness of the Virginia government, in making them that offer.

"For we know," says he, "that you highly esteem the kind of learning taught in those colleges, and that the maintenance of our young men, while with you, would be very expensive to you. We are convinced, therefore, that you mean to do us good by your proposal; and we thank you heartily. But you who are wise must know, that different nations have different conceptions of things; and you will therefore not take it amiss, if our ideas of this kind of education happen not to be the same with yours. We have had some experience of it; several of our young people were formerly brought up at the colleges of the nothern provinces; they were instructed in all your sciences; but when they came back to us they were bad runners; ignorant of every means of living in the woods; unable to bear either cold or hunger; knew neither how to build a cabin, take a deer, or kill an enemy; spoke our language imperfectly; were therefore neither fit for hunters, warriors or counselors; they were totally good for nothing. We are not, however, the less obliged by your kind offer, though we decline accepting it; and to show our grateful sense of it, if the gentlemen of Virginia will send us a dozen of their sons, we will take great care of their education, instruct them in all we know, and make men of them."

---

turn, become the basis for expanding, modifying or rejecting the original model.

Because models are not statements of ultimate reality, the true scientist is not dogmatically committed to them. He is willing to alter them to fit his experiences more closely or reject them if newer models are found which describe the world more adequately. The scientific process is a continuous cycle of observation, formulation, prediction, and reobservation. (See Figure 1.8.)

Finally, as Clifford Geertz (1926–   ) points out (Lessa and Vogt

Meditation is a common sight in south India.

eds. 1972:168–169), models have two sides. On the one hand, they are models *of* reality—that is, they describe and explain the nature of things. But they are also models *for* action, providing us with maps which guide our decisions and behavior. In this sense, models have an implicit normative or ethical dimension, in that the knowledge they

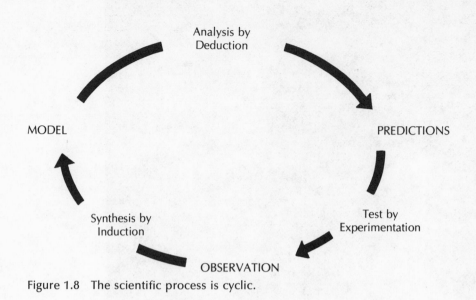

Figure 1.8   The scientific process is cyclic.

provide becomes the power which permits men and women to plan their courses of action.

Summary

Anthropologists are aware of the fact that the methods and assumptions of the social sciences are themselves products of a certain historical time and cultural setting. For example, science is based on the assumption that observation and reason can be used to give meaning to human experiences. Science also assumes that the order in nature continues uniformly over time. Unpredictable changes in the natural order would undermine our ability to project beyond the present.

We will return to these and other assumptions later when we examine the ways different cultures view their worlds.

Suggested readings

Chase, Stuart
    1954   Power of Words. New York: Harcourt, Brace. (A useful introduction to the way concepts and generalizations are made.)
Hayakawa, S.I.
    1972   Language in Thought and Action. 3rd ed. New York: Harcourt Brace Jovanovich. (An excellent analysis of levels of abstraction.)

Ross, Ralph
    1962   Symbols and Civilization. New York: Harcourt Brace Jovanovich. (Discusses science as a self-correcting process involving the interaction of observation and reason.)

VanPeursen, Cornelis
    1972   Phenomenology and Analytical Philosophy. Pittsburgh: Duquesne University Press. (A difficult but valuable discussion on the nature of two contemporary schools of philosophical thought and their implications for the philosophy of science.)

White, Leslie A.
    1938   Science is 'Sciencing'. Philosophy of Science 5:369–389. (An early but important analysis of the nature of modern science.)

A holistic view of humanity
The concept of culture
Cross-cultural comparison

Anthropological points of view

Scholars in a great many disciplines focus their studies on human beings. The main differences between the disciplines are not the objects of their study nor even the methods they use, but the points of view that guide their inquiries. Modern atomic physicists, for example, might view a person as a perpetual dance of atomic particles. Engineers working with automobile safety are concerned with the effects of mass and inertia on the human body in accidents; and microbiologists see the human being as a mass of corpuscles, cells, and bacterial organisms.

The questions scholars ask of their data are based in part on their own interests and experiences and in part on the kinds of questions other scholars in their fields are asking in conjunction with the theories that have developed within their disciplines. In short, a discipline is a point of view, a way of looking at things.

What kinds of questions do anthropologists ask? What are their primary interests and theoretical orientations? Anthropology shares with other disciplines many general interests in the nature of human beings and borrows heavily on the insights of others. Furthermore, the range of specific interests among anthropologists is so broad that it is virtually impossible to find a single common denominator that characterizes them all. Nevertheless, there are a few basic viewpoints that characterize much of the field.

A holistic view of humanity

Anthropologists take a comprehensive approach to the study of humanity. They assume that no understanding of human beings is complete without study of the full range of the human phenomenon. As individuals, anthropologists may concentrate their studies on a specific society or aspect of the human being, but they put their findings into a broad theoretical perspective that seeks to include all of human experience. This "holistic" approach is reflected both in an interest in the broad *variety* of human beings and in a *comprehensive approach* to the study of human beings.

The variety and unity of humankind

Most scholarly studies of people have dealt with "modern, civilized humankind," with those people who have lived in the great literate civilizations of the past four or five millenia. And within this frame, the focus has been on Western civilization. This emphasis can be seen in any catalogue of courses offered in an American college or university. There are few courses on the literature of sub-Sahara Africa, the South Sea Islands, or tribal South America. China and India have fared little better, even though they have extensive literatures, much of which is available in translation or was originally written in English.

The study of history has also focused its attention on Western society. Until recently, comparatively few courses on the history of black Africa, North America prior to 1492, or preliterate societies were taught in colleges. Moreover, the histories that were taught were essentially records of the elite and powerful, with little reference to the common man or woman and to their everyday lives.

In their search for a comprehensive understanding of humankind, anthropologists have emphasized the need to look at the full range of human variety, to study people in all parts of the world, at all times, and at all levels of society. Anthropology's hallmark has been to gather data on nonliterate societies, peasants, common people, and others who seldom have been objects of scientific study.

Behind this effort is the assumption that any general theory of humanity must account for this variety. For example, from a study of Western society, we might conclude that early child rearing is largely in the hands of mothers. However, until we test this hypothesis in societies around the world, we cannot be sure whether this is a Western custom or a characteristic of mankind. The result is an emphasis in anthropology on the "comparative method," in which theories based on data from one part of the world are tested against data from other areas to test their validity. (Only rarely is the anthropologist able to conduct experiments in which he controls the variables, but with the world as a laboratory, he can often find situations where his hypotheses may be tested.)

But anthropologists are interested not only in human variety; they are also concerned with human universals. Are there properties and processes—biological, psychological or social—that are characteristic of all males, all females, all adults, all people? Do all digest food in the same way, have the same psychological drives, make tools, organize families, or believe in a god? Are human languages based on the same principles of thought, and is human reasoning universally logical? If there are no human universals, how is it possible for human beings to communicate with one another or from one language or society to another?

Questions of human variety and unity and the extent to which they can be explained in terms of man's biological or social nature have remained central issues in anthropology since its inception.

A comprehensive model of humanity

A person can be studied from many points of view. The body consists of matter that is subject to the physical laws of nature. It can, for instance, be studied as a machine, composed of levers such as arms and legs and of a data-processing system linked to sensory receptors. Or, one can analyze the stress on a body when it is shot into space.

But a person can also be studied as a biological creature whose life processes, including the assimilation of food, reproduction, and excretion of wastes, are similar in many ways to those observed in other animals. Biological investigation yields insight into the nature and operation of the human being and helps anthropologists see how such factors as diet, climate, aging, hormone balances, and sexual differences affect people's behaviors.

People can be viewed as psychological beings, as products of conscious and subconscious drives, feelings, and ideas. They can be looked on as social beings, as parts of interactional systems and social groups, or as creators of culture. Each of these models is useful in understanding particular *aspects* of human beings.

MULTIPLE MODEL APPROACH Anthropology has taken a "multiple model approach" to its study of people; this accounts for the wide scope of the field. "Physical anthropologists" examine the physical and biological processes of the human body and the relationship of these to cultural and historical factors. "Paleontologists" and anthropologically oriented "archaeologists" are concerned with the origins and evolution of the human body and of culture. "Cultural anthropologists," for the most part, analyze contemporary sociocultural systems around the world, while anthropological "linguists" specialize in studies of language, a major area of culture.

The breadth of anthropological studies is both its strength and its weakness. Through use of multiple complementary models, the anthropologist is able to gain an understanding of humanity which no single model can provide. But when discussing a problem, the anthropologist may display the disconcerting habit of switching from one model to another in an attempt to throw more light on the issue. The weakness of the multiple model approach is its potential for fragmentation resulting from the rapid growth of information and specialization and from the impossibility of keeping up with all areas of the discipline. How, then, is it possible to bring together all knowledge of humanity into a single, broad, analytical scheme?

Two common pitfalls must be avoided in a search to provide a broad analytical scheme that integrates a number of different approaches to the study of humankind. The first, which Clifford Geertz calls the "stratigraphic approach" (Hammel and Simmons 1970:50), simply stacks independent models, one on another, without any serious attempt to interrelate them. Each remains autonomous and self-contained. The result is a collection of fragmentary understandings gathered at various levels of analysis. Human beings, however, are more than collections of bits and pieces, and this approach fails to provide an integrated view of them. To state it graphically, people cannot be understood simply as sums of models:

$$\text{Understanding of the person} \neq \text{Physical models} + \text{Biological models} + \text{Psychological models} + \text{Social models} \ldots$$

A second error is "reductionism," the attempt to interpret all observations by reducing them to a single level of analysis. By this process, for instance, ideas are explained purely in terms of electron flows in the brain; life is defined only in terms of chemical equations; and human culture is described only by biological needs and instincts.

Obviously a person is a physical creature, whose body can be analyzed in terms of physical equations; he also has a life which can be studied in biological terms. However, the biological concept of "life" cannot be reduced to purely physical terms and chemical equations without changing its meaning. Likewise, "ideas" can be thought of as electrical impulses within the nervous system; but in other contexts, it is meaningful to speak of them as "concepts" and as ways of thinking that are something more than electrical pulses. For instance, a young man does not say to his fiancée, "I love you. My heart rate is up forty beats a minute, and my adrenalin secretion is up 15 percent."

At another level of analysis, social institutions are composed of individuals, but they also retain an existence apart from any specific set of individuals and cannot be reduced to purely psychological processes. A school, for example, continues to operate in normal fashion when one group of students and faculty has been replaced by another.

One danger of reductionism is that it defines the essential nature of a person in physical and biological terms and treats his social and cultural behavior as mere accretions or modifications of this nature. Each man or woman is seen as a noble beast burdened with social and cultural restrictions. Reductionism fails to take into serious account the fact that at each level of mankind's development, new and more complex syntheses are found which cannot be fully explained by an analysis of their parts at a lower level. To study humanity as we know it today, we must have meaningful definitions for such concepts as "life," "reason," "personality," "society," and "culture." Reductionism, in the end, negates the meaning of human thought, including that of the scientists and scholars.

TOWARD A SYNTHESIS Any holistic approach to humankind must integrate various models into a broader framework without the loss of understanding that each model can bring. Anthropology tries to achieve this by accepting multiple models and then showing the interactions between them. (See Figure 2.1.) For instance, people's physical characteristics obviously affect the kind of culture they build and the ways in which they relate to fellow human beings. To see this, you

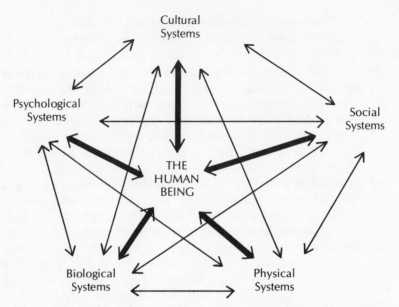

Figure 2.1 Anthropology seeks to discover the interrelationships between various scientific models of the human being.

need only imagine what the world would be like if even slight changes were made in the body. What types of buildings, furniture, cars, and cities would people build if they were ten feet tall, had a tail, or reached sexual maturation at twenty-four instead of twelve? What would social relationships be like if there were three sexes?

You do not have to depend only on your imagination to see the impact of physical characteristics on the way people view their world. We all too quickly forget how the outside world looks to a little child, to whom stairs may be mountains and toy counters wonders beyond his reach.

On the other hand, a person's culture influences his physical being. People are remarkably imaginative in molding their bodies to fit their tastes. They drill holes into their ears, lips, cheeks, and teeth to support ornaments; bind heads and feet to change their shapes; put on glasses and hearing aids to improve their perceptions; and ingest chemicals of all sorts to alter their minds. Even diets are influenced in part by ideals of health and beauty. In the West, where slim figures are thought to be attractive, women diet to stay slender; in Togo in the South Pacific, where beauty is measured by bulk, a woman eats to maintain her shape.

Similarly, the interaction of models must be studied in order to determine how a person's biological system affects him psychologically, how his psychological system affects him physically, and how both affect and are affected by his culture.

Finally, a comprehensive model of people must go beyond showing the interaction of various systems by which a person can be analyzed and their role in his formation. It must take into account the individual's responses to the pressures and constraints of these systems and the ways in which he alters and manipulates the systems to gain his own ends. In one sense, the integration of systems lies in each individual and in his responses to the world around him.

The concept of culture

Just as each discipline has its own points of view, each also develops its own concepts, which become the tools it uses to analyze data. A second characteristic or viewpoint of anthropology is its development of the term "culture."

As commonly used, the word "culture" is defined in terms of the behavior patterns of the rich and elite, a meaning derived from the German *Kultur*. It denotes the proper, sophisticated, refined way of acting. Because of their interest in all of humankind, anthropologists have broadened the definition of culture and freed it from value judgments, such as good or bad. There has been considerable debate about a precise definition of the concept, but for our purposes we can define culture as *the integrated system of learned patterns of behavior, ideas, and products characteristic of a society.*

Patterns of learned behavior

The first operational part of this definition is "learned behavior patterns." In describing a culture, the anthropologist begins by observing and listening to people in the society and by discerning patterns of behavior. He may note, for example, that American men shake hands in greeting, Mexican men embrace, and the Siriano of South America spit on one another's chests. Americans have another form of greeting between men and women, described by a Waunana tribal chief as "sucking mouths." (The accompanying extract, "The Natural History of a Kiss," takes a humorous look at this custom.)

Not all behavior is learned. A boy, touching a hot stove, jerks his hand away and yells "Ouch"! His physical reaction may be instinctive,

The natural history of a kiss

E. Royston Pike

What's so strange about a kiss? Surely kissing is one of the most natural things in the world, so natural indeed that we might almost ask, what are lips for if not for kissing? But this is what *we* think, and a whole lot of people think very differently. To them kissing is not at all natural. It is not something that everybody does, or would like to do. On the contrary, it is a deplorable habit, unnatural, unhygienic, bordering on the nasty and even definitely repulsive.

When we come to look into the matter, we shall find that there is a geographical distribution of kissing; and if some enterprising ethnologist were to prepare a "map of kissing" it would show a surprisingly large amount of blank space. Most of the so-called primitive races of mankind, such as the New Zealanders (Maoris), the Australian aborigines, the Papuans, Tahitians, and other South Sea Islanders, and the Esquimaux of the frozen north, were ignorant of kissing until they were taught the technique by the white men who appeared among them as voyagers and explorers, traders and missionaries. The Chinese have been wont to consider kissing as vulgar and all too suggestive of cannibalism, and, as we shall see in a moment, they have not been alone in this. The Japanese have no word for it in their vocabulary, and the practice is tabooed as utterly immodest and revolting, except of course among those who have made a point of adopting Western ways. But it is Africa which "has the sad distinction of being the largest non-kissing area in the world."

Such at least was the conclusion of the young English traveller Winwood Reade, and (to meet the objections of those who speak out of present-day experience) it should be explained that he was writing of a time when the natives of Equatorial Africa were still savages. The words are taken from his book *Savage Africa* (1863), in which he describes his travels in the unknown "Gorilla country" of the Upper Gaboon in West Africa. Alone save for a few native attendants, he penetrated farther upcountry than a white man had ever been before, and for some time he remained in a kind of honourable captivity as the guest of Quenqueza, the "king" of the Rembo tribesfolk. It was then that he met Ananga. She was beautiful—"full and finely moulded, hands and feet exquisitely small, complexion a deep warm colour, her eyes large and filled with a melancholy expression"—no wonder that, in one of

Source: Reproduced by permission of The Hamlyn Publishing Group, Limited, from *The World's Strangest Customs*, by E. Royston Pike.

those unguarded moments "in which the heart rises to the lips, and makes them do all sorts of silly things," he made to kiss her. . . .

Not on first meeting, of course, but when for weeks they had been for hours each day in one another's company. He had gone to Africa to study the gorilla in his native haunts, but he found "this pretty savage" a much more delicious study. At first she was timid, very timid, for she had never seen a white man before, but she tried to keep this from him lest she should hurt his feelings, "and I could read it only in her fluttering eyes and in her poor little heart, which used to throb so loudly when we were alone. I found her as chaste, as coquettish, and as full of innocent mischief, as a girl of sixteen would have been in England. In a little while I found myself becoming fond of her." So the thought came to him of a "new and innocent pleasure." To bestow a kiss upon lips which tremble with love for the first time—that (he reflected) was certainly an epoch in a man's existence; but just imagine what it must be to kiss one who has never conceived the possibility of such a thing, who has never dreamt that human lips could be applied to such a purpose! "And so, I kissed Ananga, the daughter of the king." And what happened? "She gave a shriek, and bounded from the house like a frightened fawn." What Winwood Reade had forgotten, or perhaps had never realized, was that "this mode of salutation is utterly unknown in Western Africa. Ananga knew that the serpent moistens its victim with its lips before it begins its repast. All the tales of white cannibals which she had heard from infancy had returned to her. The poor child had thought that I was going to dine off her, and she had run for her life!"

---

hence does not derive from culture, but his exclamation is learned, for in other societies different expletives are used.

Nor is all behavior patterned. A teacher dropping his book or a student slipping on ice are events that may be important to the individual but, in most cases, are not part of learned behavior. Moreover, even when behavior is patterned, some of it is characteristic of a single individual and has no significance or meaning in the society. One person develops a taste for sour foods, another for brown ties. To the extent that these are personal styles with which an individual performs culturally defined behavior, they are part of his or her personality.

The terms "culture traits" and "customs" are used for simple behavior patterns that are transmitted by a society and to which the society gives recognition and meaning. The practice of some culture traits, however, is restricted to a single person at a given time. A king, for example, is unique in some of his actions, but these may be transmitted to his successors. It is important to note that all the subjects know what the king should do. So, in a sense, they all possess the cultural trait; they just do different things with it. Other traits are characteristic of smaller or larger segments of the society. Baseball players, secretaries, and students each have their own cultural behavior patterns. So do women and men in a particular society. At times, people must choose between "cultural alternatives," for instance between single and married life, between various occupations, or between life on a farm or in a town or a city.

There also exist "cultural universals"—traits that are characteristic of most or all of the people in a given society. For example, in the United States, all people are expected to wear clothes in public and to respect the private property of others. A man in a city does not take the car closest to hand nor the best; from among hundreds in the parking lot, he takes the one that is his personal property.

It is not always easy to distinguish between patterned and unpatterned behavior, because cultures are constantly changing. Incidental or innovative activities become culturally accepted, and existing traits are dropped. The process can be illustrated by the American abroad who decided to treat the American children in his area to a Christmas celebration. Dressed as Santa Claus and riding a bicycle, he went to their homes with gifts, but on the way, he slipped in the mud while crossing an irrigation ditch. Each year thereafter, the children waited at the ditch to see him fall, and each year he did not disappoint them.

Just as people develop habits in life, so individual families, schools, and other institutions develop customs that are distinctly their own. So do societies, ethnic groups, and social classes.

Culture molds much of human behavior, and individual variations are permitted and tolerated only within limits set by a society. Even when a person rejects his society, he does so in the culturally accepted way, such as adopting certain styles of dress, hairdos, and actions. Suicide, the ultimate antisocial act, is also culturally patterned. American men seldom slash their wrists, nor do American women drown themselves in large open wells, which is the practice of women in South Asia.

Form and meaning

The second part of our definition of culture is "ideas." In addition to patterns of behavior, culture is made up of systems of shared *concepts* by which people carve up their worlds, of *beliefs* by which they organize these concepts into rational schemes, and of *values* by which they set their goals and judge their actions. Viewed in this way, culture is the model that provides the people in a society with a description and an explanation of reality. Obviously, there are many differences among the mental images people have of the world; nevertheless, there must be a great deal of consensus within a society if communication and organization are to be possible.

The relationship between ideas and behavior is complex. In the first place, as children, we learn the cognitive schemes of our society in behavior contexts. But in time these models become the maps whereby we set our goals and plan our courses of action. Patterned behavior takes on meaning only as it is linked to ideas, and learning to live in a culture involves not only learning new patterns of behavior but also the idea systems that lie behind them.

While behavior is linked to concepts and beliefs, the correspondence between them is by no means perfect. On the one hand, people do not always live up to their own ideals or to other people's expectations of them. On the other, they may acquire behavior patterns without learning their meanings or adopt patterns whose meanings have been lost. Cultures constantly change as new meanings are assigned to existing behavioral forms or as old meanings are forgotten. An illustration of this is the lapel buttonholes on men's business suits, which once served the useful function of buttoning up the collar. Nowadays, they are almost meaningless and are often omitted altogether. The result of such changes is often "cultural lag," in which forms and meanings change out of phase with one another.

Material culture

A third part of our definition of culture is "products." Human thought and behavior often lead to the production of material artifacts or tools. In this people are not alone; other forms of life also make and use simple tools. Birds make nests; some ants use sticks as prods; caged monkeys use sticks to get bananas. But in transmitting knowledge to successive generations so that it becomes cumulative, humans are distinctive. And as human knowledge and technology grow, human tools become increasingly complex, and growing bodies of information stimulate an even more rapid rate of expansion.

Human artifacts are of particular importance to archaeologists. Since they deal with cultures long extinct, they cannot observe the behavior of those who developed the culture nor study their ideas, except as these may be left behind in writing and material artifacts. Archaeologists must reconstruct past cultures as best they can from those physical remains that have survived the ravages of time and nature. We are surprised not by the scantiness of their cultural descriptions but rather by the large amount of information that can be gleaned from the little that remains.

Cultural configurations and integration

Culture is an "integrated system," not a random assortment of quaint customs. Ideas, behavioral patterns, and material products are related to one another in cultural traits, and these are linked to each other in broader patterns called "cultural configurations."

PLATFORMS VERSUS FLOORS An illustration of cultural configurations is American sitting and sleeping habits. In an auditorium, Americans find small platforms on which to sit, while latecomers stand along the walls or leave. In their homes, Americans spend a great deal of money and effort on acquiring platforms suitable for the various rooms and occasions: couches, recliners, rockers, dining room chairs, bar stools, and lawn chairs. At night, they are lost without their beds and privacy. If delayed at an airport at night, slumping in a chair is preferred to the indignity of lying on the floor. In short, platforms are everywhere. We build our houses on them, store our goods on them, and put fences around them to protect our babies.

Why this obsession with platforms? Our normal response is to say that this is the "natural" way for people to sit, given the shape of their bodies. But most people of the world are comfortable without chairs, and there is no evidence that chairs are a more healthful way of sitting. We might argue that using chairs is the civilized way to sit. But a little thought would show us that this is only a rationalization of a behavior pattern and not its original cause. The fact is that most of our cultural behavior is learned from our society and is not a product of reasoned planning.

Our concern for platforms is closely associated with certain of our basic assumptions about the nature of things, such as our notion that the ground, and its extension, the floor, are dirty, and that dirt is bad. Consequently, we get away from dirt floors to raised floors, and then off floors to sit and sleep on chairs and beds. Consequently, we scold a child who eats food that has fallen to the floor, and we keep our shoes on when we enter a room.

However, like the Japanese, we might have started with the assumption that the floor is clean, in which case we would leave our shoes at the door, and sit and sleep on small pads on the floors.

INTEGRATION AND REINTERPRETATION At the highest level of analysis, configurations in a culture are integrated into a broad cultural system. (See Figure 2.2.) At the center are basic assumptions and values about the world and the behavior patterns most closely associated with

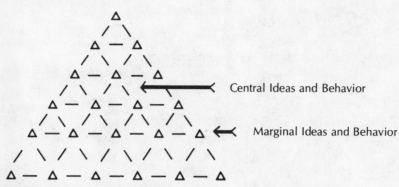
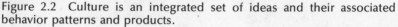

Figure 2.2 Culture is an integrated set of ideas and their associated behavior patterns and products.

them. Because they are considered very important, and because they are linked to and underlie a great many other traits, it is often difficult to change them. Marginal traits, those that are only loosely tied to the culture and to which people have little commitment, are more easily changed. For example, styles in Western dress change rapidly, but the idea that certain parts of the body must remain covered in public has persisted over long periods of time.

The concept of integration is crucial to the study of cultural change. New customs cannot be plugged into the system or old ones changed without affecting other traits to which they are linked and the system as a whole. An illustration of this is the automobile, which has had a profound effect on the organization of American life. Today we can only speculate on the ultimate impact of computers and nuclear energy.

On the other hand, new customs are not left unchanged as they are absorbed by a culture. They are selected on the basis of how well they fit the values and beliefs of the culture, and they are modified and reinterpreted to fit its patterns. An example of this is the identification, by the blacks in the Catholic countries of the New World, of African deities with the saints of the Church. Legba, a West African trickster who wanders around as an old man clad in tatters, reappears as Saint Anthony, patron of the poor. Damballa, the West African rainbow-serpent, is reinterpreted as Saint Patrick, who is portrayed with serpents around him.

Other examples of reinterpretation are umbrellas and pajamas. The umbrella was originally used in South Asia to shade kings from the sun and, as a symbol of royalty, was forbidden to commoners. Today they

An Egyptian traveling with his camels.

are used by everyone, more often than not as a shelter against rain. Pajamas were invented in the Near East for daytime wear, but Westerners have adopted them for use at night.

All cultures are changing constantly, some rapidly, some more slowly. New traits are being added, and in time, their impact is felt in other areas of the culture, while other traits are being dropped. Change is *continual;* no culture ever arrives at a state of perfect integration or internal harmony. Inconsistencies as well as conflicting and competing life-styles often exist side by side, but so long as minimal integration exists, organized social life is possible.

Culture and society

The final part of our definition of culture is the phrase "characteristic of a society." With few exceptions, people live together in groups and societies. Processes associated with such bodies and with the interaction of people are referred to as "social." Thus, for example, "social organization" refers to the ways in which people in a society structure their relationships. But social organizations are learned patterns of thought and behavior and, therefore, part of the culture transmitted from generation to generation. In short, *culture is the creation of a group of people,* and *society is the group of people, itself.*

It is obvious from these definitions that the boundaries of a particular culture are determined by the boundaries of the society of people who practice it, but this does not really solve the problem of what constitutes a single culture or society. In the parts of the world first studied by anthropologists, the people were divided into more or less autonomous tribes, each having a single culture and language. Although these were rarely completely isolated, they could for most purposes be treated as distinct societies.

In more complex peasant and urban areas of the world that are of interest to many contemporary anthropologists, there are generally no clear boundaries distinguishing relatively self-contained bodies of people who share a single culture. In such cases, the analyst must modify his use of the words "society" and "culture." Thus, he may speak of "American society," or "urban society," of the "culture of the elite," of the "culture of poverty."

Cross-cultural comparison

The third major contribution of the field of anthropology to the understanding of humankind is its use of the method of "cross-cultural comparison." This viewpoint springs from the anthropologist's concept of culture and from his interest in a holistic approach to people. As we have seen, this method is important in studying both the variety of cultures and the basic unity of humanity. There are, however, several problems stemming from cultural differences that anthropologists face when they deal with cross-cultural studies.

The fundamental nature of cultural differences

In their study of various cultures, anthropologists have become aware of the profound differences among them. Not only are there differences in behavior and material culture (encompassing foods, eating patterns, houses, dress and language) and in beliefs and values (such as religious, political and social views), but also in the ways people perceive and organize their worlds. Edward Sapir (1884–1939) pointed out that people do not simply live in the same world with different labels attached but in *different* worlds.

Time and space An illustration of just how deep cultural differences in behavior can be has been given by Edward Hall in his studies on the use of time and space (Hall 1959). All people live in time and in space, and you might, therefore, assume that in these areas, at least, there is a widespread agreement between cultures. Not so, says Hall.

Americans, for instance, place a premium on punctuality and define being "on time" as from five minutes before to five minutes after the set time. If someone arrives for an appointment fifteen minutes after the appointed hour, an apology is expected but does not require a detailed explanation. Arrival more than fifteen minutes after the appointed hour needs an apology and a credible excuse.

In Egypt, Hall points out, only servants are expected to show up at the time set for an appointment, and then as an act of obedience. The proper arrival time for men of equal rank who want to show their independence and social status is roughly an hour after the set time. Only after an additional half hour are they considered "late." (See Figure 2.3.)

There is no confusion when two Americans agree on a meeting or when two Egyptians do so, because they understand one another. But when an Egyptian and an American arrange a meeting, confusion often results. The American arrives "on time" at the set hour, the Egyptian "on time" an hour later. Meanwhile, the American is frustrated at having to wait and complains that Egyptians lack a sense of time, and

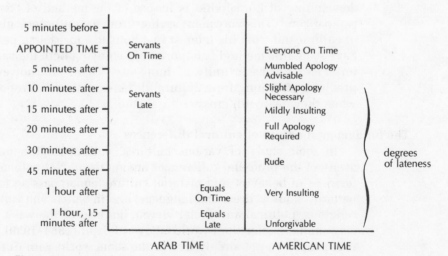

Figure 2.3   Use of time differs with cultures.

the Egyptian is perplexed by the subservient behavior of the American who arrived, as he sees it, an hour early.

Americans have different and complex concepts of punctuality for different occasions that often confuse foreigners in the U.S. To see this, one need only compare differences in concepts of punctuality for doctors' appointments, picnics, formal dinners, and concerts.

Space is another silent language that communicates ideas and feelings. According to Hall, people in the U.S. use physical distance to communicate social distance. In casual situations they feel free, even obliged, to speak to persons within about twelve feet of themselves; therefore, they readily introduce themselves to strangers next to them in buses and planes. On the other hand, people outside this "social zone" can be ignored as if they were merely part of the scenery.

Americans discussing general social matters stand about four or five feet apart, often at right angles to each other. It is important to avoid the smell of the other's breath. However, if they are discussing personal matters, they move closer to each other and drop their voices. Intimate communication takes place within the two foot zone.

Americans feel at ease in the company of their fellow countrymen, for subconsciously both parties take a distance and a stance appropriate to the type of conversation going on. In the presence of Latin Americans, however, Americans often feel vaguely uneasy, for Latin Americans have smaller zones and stand closer to each other when they talk. The Latin American steps closer until he is comfortable and the North American is in his social zone. The North American, however, is uneasy because the Latin American is in his personal zone, and since their discussion is of a general social nature, he takes a step back and places the Latin American in his social zone. But now the Latin American is ill at ease, for he finds his friend from the North out in his public zone. He therefore steps forward to set what is for him the right distance for general conversation. Neither is aware of the conflict in the use of space, and each has a vague feeling that something is wrong. The North American has the impression that Latin Americans are pushy, while the Latin American feels North Americans are cold and distant. (See Figure 2.4.)

REALITY AND MORALITY Cultural differences are found not only at the level of behavior but exist also in the basic assumptions people make about the nature of the world around them and in their concepts of right and wrong. An example of this is the differences between the American and Indian views of life. (See Figure 2.5.)

Many North Americans divide words for different forms of life (dogs, cows, demons, flies, people, sharks) into five or six general

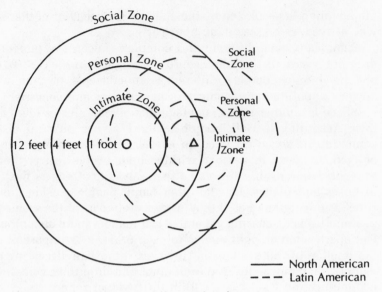

Figure 2.4   Use of space differs with cultures.

AMERICAN CONCEPT OF LIFE   INDIAN CONCEPT OF LIFE

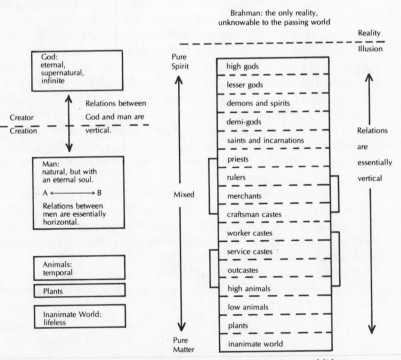

Figure 2.5   A comparison of American and Indian views of life.

categories. At the top are supernatural beings: gods, spirits, angels, demons, nymphs, and so on. Even though they may not believe in the existence of such beings, they have words and a place in their conceptual scheme for them. In other words, for some people, the set of supernatural beings is a null set.

The second general category is that of people. Scientifically, people may be treated as animal forms, but in everyday life a sharp distinction is made. People readily kill and eat lower animals or harness them to their carts or plows, but to do so to their fellow men and women would be a criminal offense. On the other side, a sharp distinction is also made between people and gods, and it is sacrilegious for the former to claim to be the latter.

Below supernatural beings and people, Americans have general categories for animals, plants, and inanimate objects. Broadly speaking, animals are mobile and eat plants or other animals, and plants are stationary and do not eat animals. (Plants that catch and eat insects are confusing, because they disturb our common sense categories.)

In the Indian/Hindu view of things, there is only one reality, Brahman, and the universe, so to speak, is only a dream or fantasy in the mind of Brahman. It is difficult, therefore, for people, who are a part of this illusory universe, to know about ultimate reality. Within the universe there is only one kind of life, and it is found in all things: gods, demons, people, animals, and plants. The differences among them are quantitative, not qualitative. Some have more of this life than others, but all life is of the same kind.

Given this assumption, it is clear why Indian villagers can worship saints as gods, for there is no categorical distinction between them, and gods are constantly visiting the earth in human forms to save mankind. On the other hand, one can understand why Indians oppose the killing of higher forms of life such as cows, particularly for food. Their response to an American expert who suggested that they slaughter cattle for consumption was similar to what our response might be if such an expert advised us to solve our poverty problem by shooting the poor.

One of the problems facing an anthropologist is to discover and comprehend the basic differences that exist between the behavior patterns, values, and conceptual categories between cultures. As you can see, that is quite a demanding task.

Cross-cultural misunderstandings

Cultural differences lead to misunderstandings, as people move from one culture to another, particularly when the same behavior has different meanings in the new setting. In the West it is not uncommon to see young men and women holding hands or putting their arms around each other in public. In other parts of the world, this is considered highly improper, even obscene. South Asian men, on the other hand, show their mutual friendship by walking down the street hand-in-hand, a practice often misinterpreted as a sign of homosexuality by Westerners. Actions that mean one thing to the performer may mean something else to observers from another culture. The result is often confusion or worse.

Misunderstandings can lead to unforeseen side effects, particularly as people are taught new ways of life. A missionary concerned with modesty introduced blouses into a society where the women wore none, only to find a marked increase in adultery. Only later did he discover that in this society prostitutes used blouses as a sign of their trade!

Ethnocentrism

Misunderstandings can often be resolved by careful analysis of the situation. It is more difficult to deal with our attitudes and with differences in learned and ingrained values and assumptions.

Human beings are at the center of their own perceptual worlds, resulting in a basic egocentrism in which everything is judged in terms of the self. As they grow up and interact with other members of their society, they generally acquire a broader view by learning to look at life from the perspectives of others and temper their actions accordingly.

On another level, people everywhere seem to look on their own culture as most suitable or best and on that of others as less civilized. This becomes the source of "ethnocentrism," the tendency of people to judge other cultures by the values and assumptions of their own culture. Of course, by one's own culture's criteria, all other cultures appear inferior. (See Figure 2.6.)

Ethnocentrism is a two-way street. We judge other peoples' customs as crude, and they feel the same about ours. Americans abroad frequently show contempt for those who eat with their fingers. On the other hand, a foreign student in an American restaurant expressed disgust at the idea of having to use spoons and forks that had been inside the mouths of others. Or, to take another illustration, Americans are often shocked at what they consider to be a lack of regard for human life in other societies. Foreigners, however, are struck by the American's inhumanity to the aged and the sick, who are sent away from friends and relatives and left to the care of strangers, and that even in death, the body and grave are prepared by strangers.

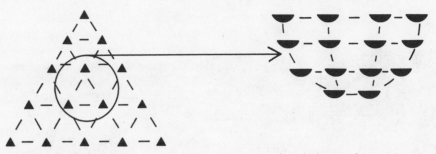

Figure 2.6   Ethnocentrism is judging other people's behavior by one's own values.

Ethnocentrism occurs wherever cultural differences are found. In times of rapid change, parents are raised in one culture and often are critical of their children who grow up in another, and vice versa. People from one ethnic or racial group set themselves above another; urban folk look down on their country cousins; and the upper classes are critical of the lower.

The solution to ethnocentrism is to try to understand another culture in terms of its own values and assumptions and its members as fellow humans. But cultural differences can be very great indeed, and when these are coupled with deep-seated attitudes and beliefs, change comes slowly, if at all. For anthropologists, the history of their discipline has been one of unearthing layers of ethnocentrism at the observational, conceptual, and theoretical levels.

Culture shock

Life in a foreign culture leads to misunderstandings and ethnocentric responses and also to culture shock. This is a period of confusion and cultural disorientation in which people who move from one culture to another may find it hard to cope with even the simple tasks required to stay alive.

The shock does not arise from sights of poverty or a lack of sanitation but stems rather from the fact that those in an unfamiliar culture do not know the language or even the simplest rules of social behavior. Suddenly, they have become children who must begin again to learn a whole new way of life. To add to the confusion, cultural landmarks that appear familiar may in fact be foreign, because the same behavior has a radically different meaning in a different society.

In time, a person learns to operate in a new society; his level of adjustment rises; and he is acculturated into the new culture (See Figure

Indian man and boy contemplating a "flat tire" on their oxcart.

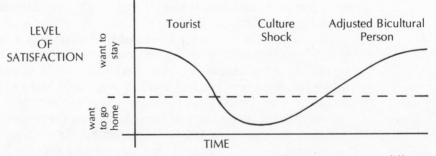

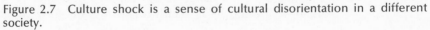

Figure 2.7   Culture shock is a sense of cultural disorientation in a different society.

2.7.) In the process, he becomes a bicultural person, who has come to grips with the issues of cultural parochialism and relativism.

Many people respond with contempt for the new society and separate themselves into their own cultural ghettos. Some, however, involve themselves in their new cultural surroundings, and learn to appreciate it, and in doing so, become more aware of their own cultural assumptions and of alternate life-styles. They acquire an international perspective and the ability to adapt to more than one culture, but at the price of being fully adjusted to none of them. They are often happiest when they are flying from one country to another.

The potential for culture shock is present each time a person changes cultures, and even the seasoned bicultural person, aware of the hazard, faces disorientation in a new society and a reverse culture shock when he returns to his parent culture.

Summary

Three approaches characteristic of anthropologists' study of people have been: 1) an emphasis on a holistic theoretical model of man, 2) the use of the concept of culture as an analytical tool, and 3) the use of the method of cross-cultural comparison.

One of the value assumptions behind these three approaches is the desire to understand all people as fully human. Alicia Iwanska, a Polish anthropologist, pointed out how difficult this can be. In a study of Americans of the Northwest coast, she concluded that they divide their world into three broad categories: "scenery," such as the mountains, weather, and strange places, which provide the staple for most conversations; "machinery," such as tractors, cars, books, pencils, and other items used to do a job; and "people." She found, however, that they tended to see American Indians as "scenery" and transient laborers as "machinery." Only friends and relatives were really "people."

But this ethnocentrism is not unique to Americans. Humans in a great many societies call themselves by words that can be roughly translated as "people" and refer to all other humans by terms that mean "enemy," "devils," or "evil spirits"—in other words, as something other than human beings.

A traveling band gives a performance in an Indian village.

Suggested readings

Hall, E.T.
 1959   The Silent Language. Greenwich, Conn.: Fawcett. (A pioneering work in the human uses of time and space.)
Henry, J.
 1963   Culture Against Man. New York: Random House. (An anthropologist uses his approach to make a critical study of American culture and society.)
Kluckhohn, Clyde and William Kelly
 1949   The Concept of Culture. *In* The Science of Man in the World Crisis. Ralph Linton, ed. New York: Columbia University Press. (An excellent discussion of various definitions of the concept of culture.)
Singer, M.
 1968   Culture: The Concept of Culture. International Encyclopedia of the Social Sciences, Vol. 3. (Summarizes various theories on the concept of culture and society.)

Fieldwork
Describing a culture
Ethnographic and comparative approaches

More on culture

The cultural anthropologist begins by studying human societies in depth. More than likely, he or she will investigate a society other than his own, and frequently he will choose one of the many non-Western, often nonliterate societies around the world.

Fieldwork

The anthropologist gathers his data by living among people, observing their behavior, listening to their words, and learning their ways. In many cultures, there are no books nor written records to supplement personal observations, so long months of fieldwork form the basic source of anthropological knowledge about the culture under study. No matter how abstract his models, the anthropologist must return to concrete human experience to test and verify his ideas.

Facing a foreign culture, the anthropologist must solve the immediate problems of living—arranging for food and shelter. At first he may depend on familiar items from his own culture that he considers essential to life, but slowly he becomes aware that it is possible for him to live as the people around him do.

A more serious problem is that of communication. Anxious to study the culture, the anthropologist is frustrated to find language barriers at every turn; he may have little or no knowledge of the language. Even when he speaks it fluently or has a good translator, there is the problem of building rapport, for he remains a stranger and a foreigner; people are uncertain how to treat him. He is stared at and questioned, and his odd customs provoke laughter. Above all, he is the topic of endless discussions. Some resent him as an intruder; others offer to teach him the right way to live, particularly if he shows a readiness to learn. At last, the novelty of his presence wears off, and he is accepted as a member of the community and drawn increasingly into the experiences of the society which he has come to observe.

What are the anthropologist's methods? The anthropologist is a scientist and hence must retain his role of observer. He studies each phenomenon in the widest possible range of its concrete manifestations. He gathers case studies, geneologies, descriptions of behavior, statistical information, and test responses. He develops close relationships with members of the society who become his informants and who interpret the meaning of what he sees and describe events which he is unable to witness. Immersed in the life around him, he begins to participate in the activities of the community as he tries to see life through the eyes of its members. This experience often makes him more aware of the assumptions of his own culture and of his own ethnocentrism.

Fieldwork has a profound effect on the anthropologist. In the field, he increasingly identifies with the society he is studying, thinking of the people as "his people." He cannot remain uninvolved in the study of human beings as he might with nonhuman beings and objects, but neither can he become a native member of another culture and erase his own cultural upbringing and still retain his role as a scientist. There is no alternative but to become a bicultural person.

Describing a culture

Using his field data, the anthropologist prepares a description of the culture, choosing his approach from several alternatives. Should he describe what he personally observes taking place and explain it in scientific terms? Or should he present the culture as the people themselves see it? If so, should he gather his information from the leaders and wise old men, or should he turn to the common people, to the young rebels, or to all these groups?

At the heart of his dilemma is the age-old question, "What is real?" Is reality only that which occurs in the thoughts of people, or does it exist outside the mind? If culture is, in part, in the minds of individuals, are there not as many cultures as there are people? As any judge knows when he tries to reconstruct the events surrounding an accident, there are no simple answers to these questions. Each witness has his own version of what occurred, and the judge must presumably try to determine what "in fact" happened.

Real cultures and folk systems

Field investigations quickly reveal a marked difference between what people do and what they think or say they do. The people's image of their own culture is made up of observations of their own behavior, interpreted and screened by means of the values and ideals of their society. The "is" is mixed up with the "ought."

Two concepts are needed to clear the confusion. "Real culture" consists of the patterns of actual behavior and the thoughts of the people—what, in fact, they do and think. A "folk system" is the people's description of their own culture—how they see and interpret it. Obviously, a study of both is needed for a comprehensive understanding of a culture.

Folk systems consist both of the people's ideas of what is "proper" and what is "acceptable" behavior and of their awareness of the ways in which their society deviates from these ideals. There are as many versions as there are participants in the society, because no person experiences the totality of his culture. There is, therefore, no single "right" folk system, and the formation of a composite picture of the people's image of themselves is difficult, if not impossible. On the other hand, unless the people of a society or a segment of that society share a great many perceptions, social behavior is impossible.

CULTURAL RULES Many of the shared understandings in a society are rules governing behavior that permit people to communicate and relate to one another. For example, in order to speak, people must put their ideas into sentences, in accordance with a great many rules governing what sounds they can use, how to group the sounds into meaningful words, and finally how to put the words together in meaningful sentences. In order to speak a language, a person must follow the generally accepted rules of that language. Similarly, in other areas of culture, there are a great many rules that enable people to interact in meaningful ways.

Just as people learn to speak largely by imitating others, so too they learn the rules of how to operate in their culture. In the process, they are often unaware of the rules that govern their behavior. These rules become a part of their thought patterns, without ever being explicitly formulated or learned; in other words, they are implicit or covert. On the other hand, some rules are formulated and consciously taught to children, who therefore become aware of them. For example, children learn to speak by the age of three or four, without ever becoming aware of the structure of the language. However, later in school, they are taught the rules of the language, such as the word order of a regular sentence: subject + verb + object. Likewise, a person learns how to eat with a fork by imitating others, and later he is told which fork to use when.

A study of the people's folk analysis is important, in that it is the world in which they live and make their decisions. Their actions are based on what they think has happened, rather than on what in fact may have happened. Real culture, on the other hand, is important in that it reflects behavioral realities and provides an overview of the total culture. It is greater than any of the individuals within it.

IDEAL VS. REAL IN MARRIAGE The difference between real and folk cultures can be illustrated by looking at North American marriage customs. Most Americans, when discussing these customs with foreigners, describe their cultural ideals: Americans are monogamous; they marry only one spouse and have sexual relations only with him and only after marriage. They also stress what they believe to be a fact—that Americans are free to marry whomever they choose—which is not true, of course.

A social scientist studying actual American behavior discovers that it is markedly different from the people's descriptions of it. In 1970, of all United States men and women over the age of twenty, 74 percent had been married at least once. Of those, one third were known to have been divorced or widowed. Moreover, 6 percent of all married couples were separated for a variety of reasons (Social and Economic Statistics Adminstration 1970:1–3). Furthermore, Alfred Kinsey found earlier (1953:330, 437) that 92 percent of all males and 50 percent of all females in his sample had engaged in premarital sexual relations and more than 50 percent of the males and 26 percent of the females had had extramarital sexual relations.

The ideal marriage for many Americans is monogamy; the accepted practice is serial monogamy—one may have as many spouses as he or she wishes, so long as they are had one at a time. But many people, in fact, do not even live up to this. Public reaction to such studies as the Kinsey reports show how deeply people believe their group behavior conforms to their accepted practices and how threatening it is when they discover that a great many of the people in their society do not so conform.

Culturally defined ideals and accepted behavior never fully fit real life. They provide the goals and limits for behavior, but deviations are frequent. Even so, there is a close relationship between goals and behavior. Behavior reflects, in part, the ideals of the culture *and* the people's perceptions of reality. On the other hand, people learn much of what is accepted behavior by observing the behavior of their fellow humans.

Cultural constructs

Another problem arises when anthropologists describe other cultures. Obviously, they can never give a complete and unbiased analysis of either real cultures or the folk analyses of these cultures. At best, they formulate cultural constructs, which are approximations of real or folk cultures, as seen by the anthropologists.

The limitations of cultural models or constructs appear on three levels. First, culture is too vast for anyone to see all of it. Some experiences are closed to an anthropologist because of his or her sex, foreignness, or assigned place in the society or because of the private nature of the experiences, themselves. Other events take place only after long intervals of time. The chance is remote that the anthropologist will be present at the right time, so he or she must depend on statements of informants to reconstruct the events. Finally, anthropologists cannot familiarize themselves with all the events taking place at any given time, let alone with all the changes that are constantly taking place.

On a second level, observers themselves act as filters, and we must check their accounts. Anthropologists are influenced by their personal values as well as those of science in their selection of events to record and in their interpretations of the data. They use the language and thought categories of their own culture to organize and describe their experiences and to communicate them to their fellow social scientists. They may use native terms for those essential ideas in a culture that lose too much meaning in translation. But they must limit their use of native terminology to avoid impairing communication with their anthropological colleagues.

The history of anthropology has been one of exposing levels of biases in the cultural constructs made by anthropologists. These constructs must be tested and retested against the cultural data in order to make them reflect the real culture and folk analyses with greater accuracy. However, as we will see later, not all biases can or should be removed. Some are inherent in the cross-cultural nature of anthropological studies, and others reflect the values and assumptions of the social sciences. It is important, however, that the scientist be aware of biases and their effect on interpreting the data.

On a third and possibly less obvious level, the presence of an anthropologist, in itself, causes changes in the culture being observed. The very fact that the anthropologist lives with the people, observing them, writing down or taping what they say, and photographing their activities affects their thoughts and behavior, no matter how hard the anthropologist tries to avoid it.

Etic and emic constructs

Should anthropologists describe the real culture or the folk systems? The answer is that generally they do both. Two terms, "etic" and "emic," are used to differentiate between the two types of constructs.

ETIC MODELS One of the goals of the social sciences is to predict human behavior. As anthropologists observe people and discover patterns in their behavior, they formulate models. These models are often in terms of the analyst's conceptual categories and basic assumptions. Such explanations may not correspond with the way the people themselves explain events, but they are useful, precisely because they account for observations in scientific terms. Thus, for example, the anthropologist may turn to germ theories to explain diseases in a society that attributes them to evil spirits or study the people's diets in order to determine their intake of protein.

Another goal for many anthropologists is to learn how to live and function properly in another culture. Now the anthropologist must

Children in a village in India are shy of their American visitors.

learn not only how to predict the people's behavior, but also how to re-produce the right behavior, himself. In other words, the anthropologist must learn "rules" that enable him to know what to do in a variety of new social situations. But even here, the anthropologist's model need not correspond with the people's view of the world. His model is suffi-cient if it enables him to live within the society.

In both of the above cases, the anthropologist's model is framed in terms of his own concepts and assumptions. In other words, it is an "etic" mode, the primary purpose of which is to predict and possibly control events.

EMIC MODELS Often anthropologists are not content only to predict human behavior; they want to see the world as the people they study see it. Descriptions of a culture from this perspective are called "emic" descriptions. There is only one small problem: How do you "get into people's heads" in order to find out what they are thinking?

One way is to ask people to describe their ideas and feelings and to explain their actions. By this means, one can learn much about a cul-ture, keeping in mind that people will tell only what they want to re-veal or what they want the observer to think.

But even if people are completely open and candid, there remains a much deeper problem. As we have already seen, cultures differ not only in the ideas people have, but also in the conceptual categories they use to convey their ideas. Moreover, people are generally unaware of the specific nature of these categories (they take them for granted), and therefore they are unable to describe them for the observer.

The new ethnography Recently, a new school of anthropological thought, sometimes known as the "new ethnography" or "ethno-science," has arisen, concerned with developing methods that help dis-cover how people think. One of these methods enables an analyst to chart the conceptual categories of a culture. By looking at the meanings and boundaries of words the people use and how these words are used in speaking, the categories implicit in the language can be mapped.

An example or two will show how the analysis of words and folk classification systems can help us see how people conceptualize their world. English speakers distinguish among hail, snow, sleet, frost, dew, and mist as different types of precipitation. Telugu speakers in tropical south India use a single word to describe all these phenomena. Again, English speakers name specific fruits and vegetables, such as apples, oranges, tomatoes, and beans, and qualify them with adjectives, such as ripe and green. Thus, they say "ripe apples" or "green carrots." Te-lugu speakers, however, distinguish between ripes and greens, and qualify them with modifiers like mango and tamarind. Thus, they speak of "mango ripes," "tamarind ripes," or "lime ripes" and of "mango greens" and "tamarind greens." (Generally speaking, ripes can be eaten raw, while greens are used in cooking.)

Even if we can discover, with a reasonable amount of accuracy, the categories people use to order their world, our problem is not solved. We must also discover what basic principles they use in forming these categories. Often, a number of different principles can be used to produce the same set of categories.

Look at the concept "father." What distinguishes a father from other male kinsmen? Someone may say that he is your biological progenitor and other males are not. Someone else may say that he is the man who lives in the same house with you and your mother and raises you, as, for example, in "stepfather." A third person, seeing the sentence, "George Washington was the father of our country," concludes that it means any male who starts or creates something. Which of these principles is, in fact, the way most Americans think of the term "father"?

In emic analyses, the answers to such questions are determined not by what principles most logically explain the people's use of the term but by what principles they themselves use. This we can discover only as we let the people discuss the ideas, but, as we already noted, people are not always aware of their own thought processes.

Finally, anthropologists seek to discover the basic existential and normative assumptions that underlie a culture, for only as they understand these do they begin to see the perceptual world of the people.

"Going native" Emic studies raise two prickly questions about how far one can or should "go native." First, since the native concepts are different from scientific ones, would it not be best to describe a culture in native terms? Carried to the extreme, of course, this implies that a truly adequate description of a culture can be made only in the language of that culture. There would be no loss of meaning nor subtle ethnocentrism due to translation; but how, then, can the anthropologist communicate his findings to others who do not know the language, and how can he compare one culture with another? For the most part, anthropologists have been content to use native terms for concepts that are central to the understanding of a culture and have no close English equivalents.

Second, if the anthropologist accepts basic assumptions of another culture that contradict those of science, is he still an anthropologist? To "go native" is not "bad," nor is it necessarily a less useful way of looking at things; but it does imply that the observer has shifted his basic premises for organizing the world.

COMBINED APPROACHES Can the emic and etic approaches be integrated into a single model? The best approach seems to be to use both, while remaining conscious that each presents a particular view of culture and answers certain types of questions. Moreover, one should make clear in each analysis which approach is being used.

The issue can be illustrated by looking again at our disease analogy. How does the anthropologist interpret a culture where disease is thought to be caused by demons which people claim to have seen? Should he, as the native does, accept as fact that disease *is* caused by demons? Should he say that the people in that culture *believe* disease is caused by demons, just as people in the West believed it to be linked to germs (an emic approach)? Or should he report the people's belief in demons as a cause of disease but use germ theory to explain outbreaks of illness among them (an etic approach)?

The answer lies in part in what the social scientist wishes to do with the information. If he wants to explain the people's responses to certain situations, he will use an emic approach. If he is trying to explain an outbreak of plague, he will probably use the etic model. However, if he is trying to eradicate a disease in that society, he will need to use both. The medical side of the campaign will most likely be designed with his own scientific knowledge of diseases in mind. But to gain the cooperation of the people, the anthropologist must explain his actions in terms they understand and accept. This may involve modifying the program to fit the cultural patterns.

Ethnographic and comparative approaches

Before we turn to an analysis of different cultural complexes and systems, some comment on the organization of materials is needed. Commonly, there are two approaches to the study of culture. The first is ethnographic—the in-depth analysis of a specific culture, based on field data. One of the advantages of this approach is that the student develops an appreciation of the holistic, integrated nature of culture. The interdependence of various traits and complexes, as well as the functions they serve in maintaining a society, are best seen in the studies of the different parts of a single culture. The approach also gives rise to theories dealing with cultural conflict and integration, the functional nature of culture traits, and processes of change. Because the analysis centers on a specific society and its people in all their different activities, we more readily see them as fellow human beings.

The weakness of the ethnographic approach is that it fails to expose the full range of human cultures around the world. In the extreme, we build our theories on the study of a single society and generalize our findings to all humankind. As ethnographers, we are in danger of seeing everything through the eyes of "our people."

The interests of most anthropologists are not limited to a single culture, although they depend on thorough ethnographies for their data. They are also interested in a comparative approach, which enables them to examine and compare cultures around the world. (See Figure 3.1.)

The advantage of the comparative approach is its ability to formulate and test general cultural theories. For example, it can examine how differences in variables, such as climate, type of family organization, or ideas of God, affect a culture as a whole. No general model of human beings or culture can be fully accepted until it is tested in a broad range of cultures.

But the comparative approach is not without shortcomings. Specific details are lost in classifying cultural traits into scientific categories and in the processes of comparison. This is the price we pay for any generalization. A greater danger, if the comparative approach is used alone, is that we lose sight of the holistic and integrated nature of a single culture. Since the focus is on analytical concepts rather than culture wholes, bits and pieces of cultures are often removed from their cultural contexts, for purposes of comparison. Thus, for instance, we might study types of families found around the world or the ways people dress or worship. In doing so, the relationships among family types, dress, and worship in a specific culture are blurred. In this approach, it

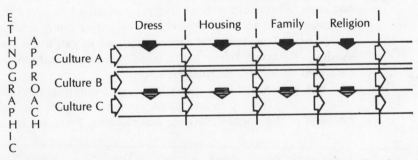

Figure 3.1 Approaches to the study of culture are many and can be classified as "ethnographic" or "comparative."

The feast of love

McKim Marriott

. . . I had entered Kishan Garhi for the first time in early March, not long before what most villagers said was going to be their greatest religious celebration of the year, the festival of Holī. Preparations were already under way. I learned that the festival was to begin with a bonfire celebrating the cremation of the demoness Holikā. Holikā, supposedly fireproofed by devotion to her demon father, King Harnākas, had been burned alive in the fiery destruction plotted to punish her brother Prahlāda for his stubborn devotion to the true god, Ramā. . . .

The celebration began auspiciously, I thought, in the middle of the night as the full moon rose. The great pile of blessed and pilfered fuel at once took flame. . . . A hundred men of all twenty-four castes in the village, both Muslim and Hindu, . . . marched around the fire in opposite directions and exchanged roasted grains with each other as they passed, embracing or greeting one another with "Rām Rām!"—blind in many cases to distinctions of caste. Household fires throughout the village had been extinguished, and as the assembled men returned to their homes, they carried coals from the collective fire to rekindle their domestic hearths. . . .

I was awakened . . . just before dawn by the crash of the old year's pots breaking against my outer door. Furious fusillades of sand poured from the sky. Pandemonium now reigned: a shouting mob of boys called on me by name from the street and demanded that I come out. I perceived through a crack, however, that anyone who emerged was being pelted with bucketfuls of mud and cow-dung water. Boys of all ages were heaving dust into the air, hurling old shoes at each other, laughing and cavorting "like Krishna's cowherd companions"—and of course, cowherds they were. They had captured one older victim and were making him ride a donkey, seated backward, head to stern. Household walls were being scaled, loose doors broken open, and the inhabitants routed out to join these ceremonial proceedings. Relatively safe in a new building with strong doors and high walls, I escaped an immediate lynching. . . .

I was summoned by a messenger from a family at the other end of the village to give first aid to an injured woman. A thrown pot had broken over her head as she opened her door that morning. Protected by an improvised helmet, I ventured forth. As I stepped into the lane, the wife of the barber in the house opposite, a lady who had hitherto been most quiet and deferential, also stepped forth, grinning under her veil, and doused me with a pail of urine from her buffalo. . . .

At noontime, a state of truce descended. Now was the time to bathe, the neighbors shouted, and to put on fine, fresh clothes. The dirt was finished. . . "What is it all going to be about this afternoon?" I asked my neighbor, the barber. "Holī," he said with a beatific sigh, "is the Festival of Love!" . . .

I happily bathed and changed, for my eyes were smarting with the morning's dust and the day was growing hot. My constant benefactor, the village landlord, now sent his son to present me with a tall glass of a cool, thick green liquid. This was the festival drink, he said; he wanted me to have it at its best, as it came from his own parlour. I tasted it, and found it sweet and mild. "You must drink it all!" my host declared. I inquired about the ingredients—almonds, sugar, curds of milk, anise, and "only half a cup" of another item whose name I did not recognize. I finished off the whole delicious glass, and, in discussion with my cook, soon inferred that the unknown ingredient—*bhang*—had been four ounces of juice from the hemp leaf known in the West as hashish or marijuana.

Because of this indiscretion, I am now unable to report with much accuracy exactly what other religious ceremonies were observed in the four villages through which I floated that afternoon, towed by my careening hosts. They told me that we were going on a journey of condolence to each house whose members had been bereaved during the past year. My many photographs corroborate the visual impressions that I had of this journey: the world was a brilliant smear. The stained and crumpled pages of my notebooks are blank, save for a few declining diagonals and undulating scrawls.

---

is also easy to lose sight of human beings who live out their lives within a single cultural web.

Students of culture need both ethnographic and comparative approaches. The former provides the roots from which data and theories of specific cultures are drawn; the latter presents the synthesis of general theories of humanity and culture. Since in this book we will deal with culture from a conceptual and comparative approach, the reader is advised to study several ethnographies, to obtain a balanced view of the discipline. Without such ethnographic study, our conceptual framework will have no practical application.

Motor transportation can be prohibitively expensive in many countries, even for hospital cases.

Summary

The basic data on which anthropologists build most of their theories is gathered by fieldwork, in which they spend many months living with a people, talking with them, participating in their activities, and observing their behavior. This means not only finding a way to live in that society, but also building a rapport with the people.

As they gather information, anthropologists are aware that there are often great gaps between what people say and what they do, between the people's folk analysis of their own culture and the real culture.

In analyzing the culture, anthropologists may choose an "etic" approach and use their own categories and assumptions to describe the culture; they may chose an "emic" approach and describe it in terms of the people's views of their own world; or they may use both approaches to form a composite picture. The approach any anthropologist opts to use is determined largely by the types of questions being asked, but in each case, the anthropologist must specify the approach being used.

Suggested readings

Casagrande, J.B. ed.
   1960   In the Company of Man: Twenty Portraits by Anthropologists. New York: Harper and Row. (Twenty leading anthropologists discuss key informants with whom they have worked and, in doing so, throw a great deal of light on the way anthropologists work.)
Spindler, George D. ed.
   1970   Being an Anthropologist: Fieldwork in Eleven Cultures. New York: Holt, Rinehart and Winston. (Eleven sketches of fieldwork by some of the best anthropologists of our day.)
Tyler, Stephen A. ed.
   1969   Cognitive Anthropology. New York: Holt, Rinehart and Winston. (Readings on the methods and results of ethnoscience.)

4

Description
Explanation

Material culture: description and explanation

Anthropologists, like other scientists, are confronted in their work with a bewildering variety of data from which they must try to derive some sense of order and meaning. And, like other scientists, anthropologists utilize "description" and "explanation" to do so. In early anthropological writings, description predominated, as detailed accounts were made of various cultural activities around the world. More recently, the emphasis has shifted to explanations of cultural events—that is to say, to the discovery of the order and causal relationships underlying human events.

As we have already seen, the relationship of observation to theories and models is a reciprocal one. On the one hand, observations provide the data from which concepts and theories are built; on the other, our concepts and theories mold what and how we observe and what we perceive in the world around us.

We can see some of the ways anthropologists have approached their data by looking at their treatment of material culture through description and explanation.

Description

The most obvious elements of a culture are its material products. One cannot walk through a tribal camp or peasant village without noting huts, clothes, crops, cooking pots, beds, hoes, plows, and many other items of material culture. It is not surprising, therefore, that until recent times, most anthropological ethnographies began with extensive descriptions of housing, tools, dress, and other human products. For example, in the mid-nineteenth century, Stephen Powers described the lodges of some California Indian tribes in the following terms:

> This wigwam is in the shape of the capital letter L, made up of slats leaning up to a ridge-pole and heavily thatched. All along the middle of it the different families or generations have their fires, while they sleep next to the walls, lying on the ground, underneath rabbitskins and other less elegant robes, and amid a filthy cluster of baskets, dogs, and all the wretched trumpery dear to the aboriginal heart.*

A more professional description is given a few years later by Lewis Henry Morgan (1818–1881), one of the first outstanding American anthropologists. Regarding the "long-houses" of the Iroquois (see Figure 4.1), who called themselves the Ho-de-no-sau-nee (People of the Long-House), he wrote:

> [The long-house] consisted of a strong frame of upright poles set in ground, which were strengthened with horizontal poles attached with withes, and surmounted with a triangular, and in some cases with a round roof. It was covered over, both sides and roof, with large strips of elm bark tied to the frame with strings or splints. An external frame of poles for the sides and of

---

* This and the following quotation are taken from L. H. Morgan, *Houses and House-Life of the American Aborigines* (Chicago: University of Chicago Press, 1965), pp. 109 and 126–127, respectively. Copyright 1965, University of Chicago.

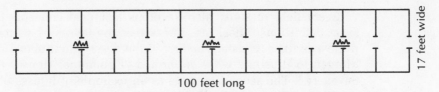

Figure 4.1 Floor plan of an Iroquois long-house shows the continuous inner passageway and the placement of fire pits to accommodate every four apartments.

rafters for the roof were then adjusted to hold the bark shingles between them, the two frames being tied together.

The interior of the house was comparted at intervals of six or eight feet, leaving each chamber entirely open like a stall upon the passage way which passed through the center of the house from end to end. At each end was a doorway covered with suspended skins. Between each four apartments, two on a side, was a fire-pit in the center of the hall, used in common by their occupants. Thus a house with five fires would contain twenty apartments and accommodate twenty families, unless some apartments were reserved for storage. They were warm, roomy, and tidily-kept habitations. Raised bunks were constructed around the walls of each apartment for beds. From the roof-poles were suspended their strings of corn in the ear, braided by the husks, also strings of dried squashes and pumpkins. Spaces were contrived here and there to store away their accumulations of provisions . . . Whatever was taken in the hunt or raised by cultivation by any member of the household, as has elsewhere been stated, was for the common benefit. Provisions were made a common stock within the household.

Here was communism in living carried out in practical life, but limited to the household, and an expression of the principle in the plan of the house itself.

Concepts

Descriptions such as the above involve little theory, but certain assumptions are implicit in the selection and ordering of the materials within the descriptions. Moreover, descriptions of any sort require the use of concepts and words. For the most part, scientists use words according to their common meaning, but even these can be weighted with assumptions about the way things are ordered. For example, the phrases, "filthy cluster of baskets, dogs, and all the wretched trumpery dear to the aboriginal heart" and, "Here was communism in living carried out in practical life," reflect the attitudes and beliefs of the writers.

Every field of study also develops technical concepts that require exact definitions. These are, in a sense, the lenses by which the discipline examines its data. The first of the descriptions above was used by Morgan to illustrate what he termed "Communal Houses in Tribes in Savagery." The second he gave as an example of houses of "Tribes in the Lower Status of Barbarism." These terms spring from Morgan's theory that all cultures evolve through three stages: savagery, barbarism, and, finally, civilization.

Concepts are arbitrary categories created by people to stand for certain kinds of experiences; therefore, they are true by definition. By definition, "X" could stand for cars, pencils, or dollars. We could, if we wished, classify potatoes as a kind of fruit or, for that matter, as a kind of animal or machine. But this does not mean that all concepts are useful ways of dividing and organizing experiences. The first task of any academic discipline is to create concepts that are efficient analytical tools, and a great deal of the history of any science deals with the definition and refinement of a few central concepts.

Definitions must stipulate those qualities that characterize a term. A "house" might be defined as 1) a structure 2) for the habitation 3) of human beings. Many things clearly belong in or out of the category of "house" when defined in this way. It would include houses of many colors, shapes, and types of construction, as well as apartments, hotels, and a wide variety of other structures. It would exclude tables, chairs, and a host of other things.

However, as in the case of most concepts, there is some fuzziness at the boundaries, and it is there that the problems occur. As it stands, the definition would exclude certain types of "houses," such as doghouses, dollhouses and greenhouses. If, however, we were to include these by dropping the phrase "of human beings" as a defining characteristic, questions might arise as to how we should classify barns, animal cages, and bird nests.

In a world of infinitely varied experiences, every definition draws a boundary around certain types of observations on the basis of certain shared characteristics. A good definition must also distinguish between the concept it denotes and other concepts closely related to it by the process of contrast. "Houses" must be differentiated from "hospitals," "stores," "offices," and other types of human structures and from oceanliners, trains, and spaceships, which "house" people for varying lengths of time.

Concepts vary in the levels of their generalization. It is obvious that no language can have a separate word for every human experience. Thought is possible only as we lump our experiences into a limited number of categories. On the one hand, the more general the concept, the more it overlooks the differences between the various experiences included within it. On the other, the more specific the concept, the more terms we must include in our vocabulary, and in the end, there is a limit to the number we can handle.

Classification systems

Concepts rarely exist apart, by themselves; generally, they are parts of larger classification systems. As we have already seen, for Morgan, concepts like "barbarism" and "savagery" were stages in a broader classification scheme.

One approach to classification is simply to define all of the categories within a single domain of study. For example, houses can be classified according to the materials used in their construction: rock, wood, concrete, and so on. Or they can be described as to shape: square, rectangular, or round.

A second approach is to arrange a set of categories along some continuum or hierarchy, such as from simple to complex, small to big, bad to good. While in some classification systems, categories may be unrelated to each other, in hierarchical classifications (sometimes called "taxonomies"), the order and relationships between categories are specified. For instance, rock houses are not necessarily better or more durable than wooden ones; they are only different. But $30,000 houses are more "valuable" than $10,000 houses or huts worth a few hundred dollars.

One of the problems with taxonomies is that there is often an implicit assumption that more costly, complex, modern, or higher ranked forms are somehow "better" than cheaper, smaller, traditional, or lower ranked ones. There is also a question of whether the units in the classification system are, in fact, comparable. What does it *mean* to compare mud huts with leaf shelters and suburban homes? Are not they all, perhaps, equally "valuable" to their occupants?

More complex classification schemes can be formed by using two or more taxonomies, for example, in descriptions such as, "single-family, stone houses," or by combining several levels of taxonomy into a single system. For instance, people are classified in the kingdom "animal," in contrast to "plants." Among animals, they belong to the phylum "chordate." Within this phylum, they are put into a class with other "vertebrates." Among vertebrates, they are "mammals"; among mammals, "primates"; among primates, "hominids"; among hominids, people belong to the genus "homo"; and within this genus, they belong to the species "sapiens." At each level, humans belong to one of a set of classes, and all of these are ranked into a single taxonomy.

There is no single "correct" classification system for any field of

Building styles differing as to
place and purpose: Top left,
American Indian teepees in the
Montana Rocky Mountains
(photo courtesy of Photography
Collection, Suzzallo Library,
University of Washington,
Seattle). Top right, a pagoda in
the Far East, a temple to the
gods. Left, a village tavern in
south India (photo courtesy of
J.N.C. Hiebert).

study. Turning again to houses as an illustration, we can form any number of taxonomies, depending on the organizing principles we chose. We could classify houses by type of construction (leaves, fabric, ice, wood, earth, cement), by occupants (single-family, multiple-family, community dwellings), by permanence (disposable windscreens and space capsules; transportable tents, trailers, and houseboats; immobile caves, houses, and skyscrapers), or by location (farm, village, city). Obviously, many other classifications could be added to this list.

As with concepts, all classification schemes are not equally useful to everyone. A surveyor assessing a city may not be interested in the number of houses with tile roofs; but to tile manufacturers, this information is essential in determining the size of a market.

Comparative taxonomies

Many anthropologists are not content to study just one culture. Some are interested in broader questions about the fundamental natures of cultures and human beings, for example: What is the range of cultural variation? What are the relationships between various kinds of cultural phenomena? And what, if any, are the characteristics common to all human beings or to all cultures? For instance, do all people possess a sense of modesty, reflected in wearing clothes? Or, to what extent are the clothes people wear determined by their environments? Underlying these questions are the assumptions that all human beings share similar biological and psychological characteristics and that all organized societies have in common basic activities, such as procuring food and shelter and raising the young.

Other anthropologists are concerned with the distribution or spread of cultural traits. For example, clothes can be classified into those that are draped on the body and those that are tailored to fit the body's form. The former are widespread, particularly in warm climates. The latter were originally found in a geographical band, running across North Asia to the Eskimos and Indians of the northern half of North America. During the Middle Ages, tailoring spread from the North to Europe, where form-fitted clothes replaced flowing Roman gowns, and then to the New World, via the colonists.

Concepts and taxonomies used in cross-cultural comparisons are on a higher level of abstraction than those dealing with single cultures. This does not mean, however, that they are better—only that they cover a broader range of human experience and, therefore, must be more generalized. Furthermore, while descriptions of single cultures may be either emic or etic in nature (see Chapter 3), concepts and classification schemes used in comparative studies must, of necessity, be etic in character.

Limitations of concepts and classifications

Concepts and classification systems are essential to any scientific description, but there are several dangers in their use. The first is overgeneralization. In dealing with the full range of culture, it is necessary to lump together a variety of objects, beliefs, or practices, to reduce the data to manageable proportions. But in doing so, one overlooks a great many specific differences among the data so grouped.

This process of simplification—of concentrating on certain characteristics of the things observed and of ignoring the rest—is, of course, characteristic of the generalization inherent in all thought and language. The danger, particularly as one deals with higher levels of abstraction, is that one can generalize to the point of saying nothing at all or stating the obvious. It is not particularly enlightening, for example, to say that some people wear clothes.

A more subtle objection is raised by critics of comparative studies. They point out that one cannot pull traits out of their cultural contexts without a great loss of meaning. Putting a ring in the nose of another person has different meanings for Americans (a sign of enslavement) and for the Gypsies of south India (a sign of marrage). Modern comparativists are well aware of this problem, but they contend that they are dealing with different types of questions at higher levels of abstraction and that, just as ethnographers overlook differences between individuals in the study of a culture, so compartivists overlook differences between cultures in a search for universal cultural theories.

A second danger is the tendency to reify concepts, that is, to regard concepts as material things. We create concepts to analyze our experiences, but in time we are lulled into thinking these concepts exist in the real world. Our categories harden, and our perception of the world becomes stereotyped.

A third danger, found particularly in comparative studies, is the use of culturally biased concepts. Most of the concepts currently in use in anthropology are specialized words used in the ethnographies of specific societies. If we take these terms and use them blindly for other cultures, we are in danger of putting together data that are not comparable or of falsely attributing to other cultures the biases implicit in the terms themselves. For example, even words like "house," "kitchen," "money," "family," and "caste," have different meanings in different societies. It is extremely difficult to formulate concepts and classifications that are free from cultural biases.

In the end, no matter how detailed and accurate our concepts and descriptions, we still have not given an *explanation* of things. For this we must turn to "hypotheses" and "theories."

Explanation

During the comparatively short life span of the science of anthropology, a number of major theoretical models have been used to explain human actions. Two of the important early ones, namely evolution and function, can help us to understand the place of explanation in science.

Evolutionary models

Many early anthropologists were interested in gathering and classifying information on strange customs from around the world and in explaining the bewildering variety of human activities they discovered. Classification schemes were developed for houses, dress, tools, families, kinship terminologies, religious systems, and other cultural traits and complexes. It was only a small step from these taxonomies to the assumption that there was a historical evolution of cultures, from the simple to the complex, from the "primitive," defined by the anthropologists in terms of tribal societies, to the "civilized," which anthropologists equated with modern Western cultures, of which, fortunately, anthropologists were a part.

An example of a theory of evolution is Morgan's, to which we have already referred. According to Morgan, all cultures evolved through the following stages:*

Savagery
  Older period: From the first humans to the domestication of fire and subsistence on fish.
  Middle period: From fishing to the invention of the bow and arrow.
  Later period: From the bow and arrow to the invention of pottery.
Barbarism
  Older period: From pottery to the domestication of plants and animals.
  Middle period: From the domestication of plants and animals to the invention of iron smelting.
  Later period: From iron to the invention of the alphabet.
Civilization From the alphabet to the present.

Morgan held that these stages could be traced in all major areas of culture, such as technology, family structure, and economic organization. In a classical study (1881), he described the houses of the North American Indians, from the simplest shelters of California to the pueblos of New Mexico and the palaces of the Aztecs. In conclusion he noted:

* The following listing is adapted from L. H. Morgan, *Houses and House-Life of the American Aborigines* (Chicago: University of Chicago Press, 1965), p. 43 *fn.* Copyright 1965, University of Chicago.

The Indian family, in its different branches, offered for our investigation not only the state of savagery, but also that of both the opening and of the middle period of barbarism in full and ample development. The American aborigines had enjoyed a continuous and undisturbed progress upon a great continent, through two ethical periods, and the latter part of a previous period, on a remarkable scale. (1965:308)

Models of cultural evolution, like Morgan's, provided more than a description of historical development; they supplied an explanation of this development in terms of man's increasing rationality and human progress. Stages of development for particular traits were not determined primarily on the basis of historical evidence, but on the assumption that there was a logical evolution of cultures from primitive to civilized and from simple to complex.

Early anthropological theories of cultural evolution appeared to provide social scientists with a grand scheme, into which they could fit data from all human societies, but some of their assumptions were soon called into question. The first to encounter doubt was the faith in the progressive rise of human rationality. Are modern people really all that logical, and did tribesmen think in simple, prelogical terms? The second assumption to be questioned was that cultural traits could be treated as autonomous units and studied apart from their cultural contexts. For example, the houses of the Eskimo, African Bushmen, European kings, and Arab nomads were compared, with little consideration of how the meaning and place of housing differed in each society.

Functionalism

In 1922, two new books introduced another approach to the study of culture. Bronislaw Malinowski (1884–1942) completed his first major report on fieldwork in Melanesia, titled *Argonauts of the Western Pacific,* and A.R. Radcliffe-Brown (1881–1955) published *The Andaman Islanders.* Both books treated societies as organic wholes, and both gave greater attention to the present *operations* of cultures than to their historical development.

In this new school of thought, cultural traits were explained in terms of their social significance, by the functions they served within the society. A general agreement developed that the basic function of all traits was to weld society together into an organic whole and that all cultural practices contributed to the maintenance of a social order. But there was sharp disagreement on the specific nature of the concept of function.

CULTURAL LINKAGE A holistic approach to the concept of culture meant that, at the simplest level, traits were thought to be linked to each other in a single, integrated, organic whole. A change in any one trait was assumed to produce a change in the others to which it was linked.

This concept of cultural linkage can be illustrated by comparing modern American suburban homes with those built before the first world war. Many houses built at the turn of the century faced sidewalks, to permit easy access on foot to all parts of a town or neighborhood. Generally, the houses included front porches, with swings for relaxing on hot summer evenings and for courting; parlors for hosting guests and for important family rituals, such as weddings and wakes; dining rooms for formal meals; and large kitchens for work and casual visiting. Backyards contained clotheslines, gardens, garbage cans, and small garages. All of these reflected—and in turn molded—the life-style of that era.

Modern houses are linked to contemporary ways of living. Sidewalks and picket fences are rare, having been replaced by carefully kept lawns that display the householder's pride in appearance. Gone are the porches and alleys. Instead, we have family rooms, patios, indoor bathrooms, two-car garages, and an occasional swimming pool. (See Figure 4.2.)

Houses reflect not only life-styles, but also levels of technology and ecological factors, such as climate and available materials. In many warm, dry countries, the "house" includes not only the roofed portions, which are used primarily for shelter, storage, and sleeping, but also an open courtyard, where a great deal of daily living takes place.

Ideas about the proper use of space and its orientation to the world at large are closely related to the arrangement of houses on the land. Maps of some American cities show how reference points have changed in the past century. Early colonists used a survey method known as the "metes-and-bounds" or "indiscriminate" system to demarcate their lands. A field would be bounded on two sides by a river and a road and on the third by a line that met the river at its fork and joined the road at the crest of the hill. When towns were planned, streets were laid according to the main typographical features in the area, such as rivers, mountains, or railroad tracks.

As the frontier expanded westward, a new survey method known as the "Township-and-Range" system, oriented to the North Pole, was introduced. Streets were laid out in a north-south, east-west grid, creating a disorderly pattern in relation to earlier street patterns, especially in some older cities. In the center of such cities, streets run at angles to

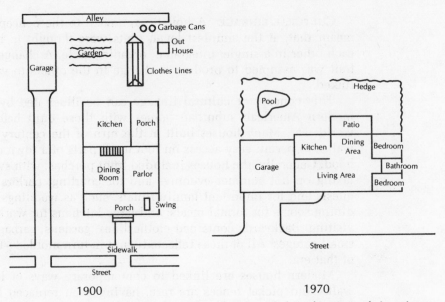

Figure 4.2 There have been many changes in the planning of American houses since the early part of this century.

those in outer areas, and the articulation of the two grids leads to irregularly shaped blocks and confusing intersections. (See Figures 4.3 and 4.4.)

Finally, housing is closely related to the values of a society. Thus, suburbs in the United States reflect America's strong sense of private ownership. Blocks are divided into individually owned lots and houses, and even within the house, certain rooms are seen as belonging to certain family members. The concept, "This is mine," is quickly learned.

We see similar values in the case of the American farmer. Unlike most farmers around the world, who live together in small hamlets for companionship and safety and who walk to their fields, American farmers traditionally live alone, in the manner of lords on their private land, traveling to town for supplies or social purposes.

In the Western world, ownership of land carries with it a great many rights, including the right of transfer of ownership. It does not, however, permit absolute control. A man living in an area of immaculately clipped lawns may decide to let his yard grow wild, but he will soon

Figure 4.3 This is a graphic portrayal of two different landscape patterns which have developed in two 100-square-mile sample areas in the state of Ohio, similar in physical features but surveyed by two different systems: the Township and Range survey system (top) and the so-called "metes and bounds" or indiscriminate system (bottom).

Source: Reproduced by permission of the Association of American Geographers from Monograph #4, "Original Survey and Land Subdivision," by Norman J.W. Thrower, 1966.

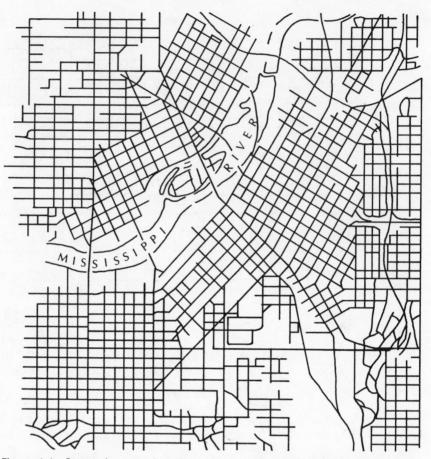

Figure 4.4 Streets in many American cities, such as Minneapolis, Minnesota, shown here, reflect a shift from the past in spacial reference points.

face an army of angry neighbors demanding that he conform to local custom by maintaining a lawn. Moreover, zoning laws prevent a man from building a barn in the middle of a housing tract, and the government retains the right to repossess land whenever it is needed for greater public good.

Other cultures have different ideas of ownership. In many tribal areas of the world, land is ultimately owned by the tribe or by groups of relatives and cannot be sold or alienated. Individuals are given the right to use certain tracts of land by their kin group. So long as a man tills the soil, he may "keep" it and pass it down as an inheritance to his sons. However, when the land is unused, it reverts to the kinship group, which then reassigns it to another member of the group. It cannot be sold. This concept of ownership, in which one has a right to use or rent land but not to sell the ultimate rights in it, is termed "usufruct."

Differences among concepts of land ownership have led to many misunderstandings. Most of us are familiar with the case of the American Indians, who "sold" the rights to use land to settlers, who in turn refused to relinquish these rights when the Indians expected and demanded their return. The colonists believed they had acquired permanent rights to the land, a cultural assumption they enforced with guns.

FUNCTION AND THE INDIVIDUAL While cultural linkage is implied in functional models, it is often merely a description of correlations between certain traits, rather than an explanation in which a causal relationship is assumed or shown. For instance, there may be a high correlation between eating bread and automobile accidents, but it is not assumed that the one causes the other. On the other hand, drinking hard liquor can be shown to be a cause of such accidents. The term function has generally been reserved for the latter types of linkage.

To Malinowski, all cultural practices served particular functions in a society. They were not there by accident but existed because they met some need. Moreover, he defined "need" largely in terms of the individual. He argued that people have biological requirements, such as food, shelter and reproduction, as well as psychological needs, such as a sense of security and the means to reduce anxiety in situations where an element of chance or hazard exists. By means of social organization and culture, people adapted to their environment and satisfied their personal needs.

Given this perspective, we can argue that people build houses for shelter against the weather and protection from other people and beasts. Moreover, houses also provide people with a sense of place, personal identity, and privacy.

The forms houses take will vary according to the ecological setting and a society's level of technology, but their functions may be much the same in different societies. We can see this in differing attitudes towards privacy. In the United States, front lawns are public but not for general use, and backyards are semiprivate. Walls provide privacy in the house, and there are different levels of permissible access, as well. Living rooms are public, although entry to them is regulated by a number of very complex and often subconscious customs. Kitchens and dens are semipublic and open to friends, while bedrooms and bathrooms are private.

By contrast, south Indians often entertain friends in the bedroom, but their kitchens are extremely private. It is a serious breach of etiquette for nonfamily members to enter the kitchen, and their presence may defile it, making elaborate purification rituals necessary. Thus, while the form privacy takes varies greatly between the two cultures, the need for it is present in both, and, in part, this need is satisfied in both by houses.

FUNCTION AND SOCIETY Radcliffe-Brown rejected the reduction of social processes to biological and psychological needs, instead holding that society had to be studied at its own level and explained in its own terms. He defined function in terms of social needs, as the way in which customs linked to and reinforced other customs and thereby strengthened social integration. Two illustrations may help us to understand Radcliffe-Brown's position.

American houses are closely linked to the American style of family. The permanent residents are generally members of a nuclear family, the parents and unmarried children. Relatives and friends may stay in the house for short periods of time, and family members stay away from the house for a while, but there is generally a clear understanding as to those who rightfully belong to the household and those who are outsiders.

The relationship between house and family style is more than coincidental. Given the American emphasis on individualism and the nuclear family, it is not surprising that houses are built to accommodate this type of family. On the other hand, because houses are built for nuclear families, changes in family style cause difficulties. When children marry, the facilities are poorly suited to their sharing the same house with their parents for any length of time, and pressures develop for them to move elsewhere. By contrast, the long-houses of the Iroquois (see page 63) reflected their pattern of extended families, in which daughters stayed with their mothers after marriage.

The relationship between housing and social stratification in the United States is a second illustration of Radcliffe-Brown's theory. On the one hand, differences in wealth, power, and social prestige often lead to differences in housing, not only relating to style and cost but also to location. In most towns of any size, certain areas are associated with well-to-do families, and in cities, the differentiation is likely to be more complex and elaborate.

It is not difficult to show that variations in housing are a product of social status. An individual's house is one of the important visible symbols whereby he can display his wealth and position, so much so that Lloyd Warner (1960) used the cost and location of a person's house as two of four measurements in his formula for assessing the rank of a person in the American society.

On the other hand, and perhaps less obvious, is the fact that wherever housing is stratified and segregated, social classes will be perpetuated. It can thus be asserted that housing differences function to maintain a system of social stratification and to support a particular type of social order.

CRITICISMS OF FUNCTIONALISM As a method for describing cultures, functionalism has inspired a great many detailed studies of particular societies, in which the internal relationships of cultural complexes have been carefully analyzed. Functionalism's emphasis on the study of cultures as wholes is now widely accepted in anthropology.

As an explanatory theory, however, functionalism has attracted strong criticism. For example, it has been accused of ignoring historical explanations. Every cultural trait is thought to serve some essential function in the society and is explained in terms of this function; but this does not explain why things are the way they are, only how they operate once they come into being. Referring once more to our example of social stratification, it is possible to show how segregated housing reinforces social differences, but this does not explain how social classes and segregated housing came to be in the first place.

Closely associated is a second criticism: that functionalism fails to adequately account for change. If societies are seen as harmonious functioning wholes, there is no room for internal discord or for traits that might undermine cultural integration and, therefore, no reason for societies to change. Change, when it occurs, must come from outside the culture. But this is obviously false. Cultures, particularly complex ones, have internal tensions and conflicts that may foster disintegration. For example, segregated housing may serve the interests of the rich, but it can create an explosive resentment among the poor. What is functionally useful for one part of a society may be disruptive for another part or for the whole of the society. Moreover, cultures do change and change constantly, in response to internal as well as external factors. The changes in American housing noted above are certainly not due primarily to forces outside the society.

A third criticism leveled at functionalism is that, in its extreme form, it allows for no value judgments and rejects such concepts as development. If each trait is essential to the maintenance of a culture and each culture is a unique expression of a group of people, there can be no universal standard of values or morals. Whatever is, is right.

It could then be argued that slavery, colonialism, racism, and facism are justified in particular cultural settings, because they help maintain those societies. Moreover, as social scientists in developing countries have pointed out, the same argument can be used to oppose national development. If, for example, a particular style of housing is found in a given society, why try to change it in favor of more modern housing?

In 1948, Max Gluckman (1911–   ), a British anthropologist, questioned whether functionalism, as a method, could be used for discovering universal social laws (Jarvie 1973:20). Functionalists have generally argued that while social forms may vary from society to society, the social processes behind these forms are common to all societies; therefore, a detailed study of one or two societies is sufficient to make valid generalizations about the nature of all societies. One might argue, for instance, that while housing varies greatly from society to society, in all societies it is closely linked to the way in which families are organized.

Other anthropologists, like Gluckman, however, argue that universal social laws can be discovered only by the methods of cross-cultural comparison. Only by a study and comparison of a great many societies can we know which processes are universal and which are peculiar to specific societies.

In 1963, Robert Brown, a philosopher, questioned the validity of the logic behind functional explanations. One of the dangers in arguments of cause and effect is to explain a process by its consequences and not its antecedents. For example, one might argue that it rains because rains bring good crops. But this logic is obviously false. However, functionalist arguments are in danger of falling into the same trap by arguing, for instance, that the function of segregated housing (what it does for the society and the reason for its existence) is to maintain stratification in the society. Although it may not be so obvious to us, the logic here is equally false.

The final criticism we will consider was raised by another philosopher, I.C. Jarvie, who feels that functionalists do not take seriously the content of the people's ideas and beliefs (1968). Why, for example, do Christians spend much money for churches, hospitals, and schools in other countries, that are of no apparent gain to themselves? If we inquire, they will explain their actions in terms of their faith in God and their desire that all people should hear about Him. A functionalist would, however, argue that such mission programs help maintain and integrate the Christian community by providing it with a common task that unites the people. In order to carry on such programs, the people must organize ways for raising the money, recruiting personnel, and spending the funds abroad. These tasks, in themselves, draw the people in the contributing churches together and strengthen their faith. To a strict functionalist, the content of the people's faith is irrelevant to the analysis.

MODIFICATIONS OF FUNCTIONAL THEORIES Criticisms have caused modern functionalists to modify their theories. Robert Merton (1910–   ), an American sociologist, did much to clear the air. He pointed out that human societies, like many biological organisms, can survive without some of their parts. They, particularly the complex ones, may be only loosely organized and may have dysfunctional traits (traits that tend to disrupt the society). But so long as the net balance of all the social processes in a society is integrative, it can survive. This position also leaves room for cultural survivals—customs that are perpetuated by tradition even after they have lost their functions, due to changes within a culture.

Merton also made a useful distinction between "manifest" and "latent" functions (1949).

Manifest functions Hearts and lungs serve vital functions in the survival of many organisms, but these functions are not the product of deliberate planning on the part of the organisms. However, on the level of culture, humans do consciously plan acts and organize institutions to achieve certain goals or ends. They hire police to maintain the peace, build houses for shelter, and establish schools to educate their children. It is this characteristic of intentionality that marks "manifest" functions. They are the functions intended and recognized by the people.

Let us look at the functions of clothing, by way of illustration. One of the common reasons given for dress is protection from inclement weather. Humans lack the body hair that protects other primates from the elements, so they depend on clothes and houses to create artificial environments for their bodies. These, in turn, enable them to survive almost everywhere on the earth, as well as in the sea and outer space.

Nevertheless, it is surprising how indifferent people are to the weather. The Yahgan of the southern tip of South America live in temperatures commonly below freezing, with snow and cold rain, yet they once wore almost no clothes at all. When they began to adopt Western dress, their level of health declined. To some extent, the same indifference to the weather is shown by Western men in their formal dress on hot summer evenings and by Western women, who wear short skirts in winter.

A second reason people give for wearing clothing is modesty. Certain parts of the body are exposed for public view and admiration; other parts are considered private, and their exposure in public may not only be considered immodest but also immoral. These feelings are

Body ritual among the nacirema

Horace Miner

. . . Professor Linton first brought the ritual of the Nacirema to the attention of anthropologists twenty years ago (1936:326), but the culture of this people is still very poorly understood. They are a North American group living in the territory between the Canadian Cree, the Yaqui and Tarahumare of Mexico, and the Carib and Arawak of the Antilles. Little is known of their origin, although tradition states that they come from the east. According to Nacirema mythology, their nation was originated by a culture hero, Notgnihsaw, who is otherwise known for two great feats of strength— the throwing of a piece of wampum across the river Pa-To-Mac and the chopping down of a cherry tree in which the Spirit of Truth resided. . . .

The fundamental belief underlying the whole system appears to be that the human body is ugly and that its natural tendency is to debility and disease. Incarcerated in such a body, man's only hope is to avert these characteristics through the use of the powerful influences of ritual and ceremony. Every household has one or more shrines devoted to this purpose. The more powerful individuals in the society have several shrines in their houses and, in fact, the opulence of a house is often referred to in terms of the number of such ritual centers it possesses. Most houses are of wattle and daub construction, but the shrine rooms of the more wealthy are walled with stone. Poorer families imitate the rich by applying pottery plaques to their shrine walls.

While each family has at least one such shrine, the rituals associated with it are not family ceremonies but are private and secret. The rites are normally only discussed with children, and then only during the period when they are being initiated into these mysteries. I was able, however, to establish sufficient rapport with the natives to examine these shrines and to have the rituals described to me.

The focal point of the shrine is a box or chest which is built into the wall. In this chest are kept the many charms and magical potions without which no native believes he could live. These preparations are secured from a variety of specialized practitioners. The most powerful of these are medicine men, whose assistance must be rewarded with substantial gifts. However, the medicine men do not provide the curative potions for their clients, but decide what the ingredients should be and then write them down in an an-

Source: Reproduced by permission of the American Anthropological Association from *American Anthropologist*, 58(3):503–506 (1956).

cient and secret language. This writing is understood only by the medicine men and by the herbalists who, for another gift, provide the required charm.

The charm is not disposed of after it has served its purpose, but is placed in the charm-box of the household shrine. As these magical materials are specific for certain ills, and the real or imagined maladies of the people are many, the charm-box is usually full to overflowing. The magical packets are so numerous that people forget what their purposes were and fear to use them again. While the natives are very vague on this point, we can only assume that the idea in retaining all the old magical materials is that their presence in the charm-box, before which the body rituals are conducted, will in some way protect the worshipper. . . .

In the hierarchy of magical practitioners, and below the medicine men in prestige, are specialists whose designation is best translated "holy-mouth-men." The Nacirema have an almost pathological horror of and fascination with the mouth, the condition of which is believed to have a supernatural influence on all social relationships. Were it not for the rituals of the mouth, they believe that their teeth would fall out, their gums bleed, their jaws shrink, their friends desert them, and their lovers reject them. They also believe that a strong relationship exists between oral and moral characteristics. For example, there is a ritual ablution of the mouth for children which is supposed to improve their moral fiber.

The daily body ritual performed by everyone includes a mouth-rite. Despite the fact that these people are so punctilious about care of the mouth, this rite involves a practice which strikes the uninitiated stranger as revolting. It was reported to me that the ritual consists of inserting a small bundle of hog hairs into the mouth, along with certain magical powders, and then moving the bundle in a highly formalized series of gestures.

In addition to the private mouth-rite, the people seek out a holy-mouth-man once or twice a year. These practitioners have an impressive set of paraphernalia, consisting of a variety of augers, awls, probes, and prods. The use of these objects in the exorcism of the evils of the mouth involves almost unbelievable ritual torture of the client. The holy-mouth-man opens the client's mouth and, using the above mentioned tools, enlarges any holes which decay may have created in the teeth. Magical materials are put into these holes. If there are no naturally occurring holes in the teeth, large sections of one or more teeth are gouged out so that the supernatural substance can be applied. In the client's view, the purpose of these ministrations is to arrest decay and to draw friends. The extremely sacred and traditional character of the rite is evident in the fact that the natives return to the holy-mouth-men year after year, despite the fact that their teeth continue to decay. . . .

The medicine men have an imposing temple, or *latipso*, in every community of any size. The more elaborate ceremonies required to treat very sick patients can only be performed in this temple. These ceremonies involve not only the thaumaturge but a permanent group of vestal maidens who move sedately about the temple chambers in distinctive costume and headdress.

The *latipso* ceremonies are so harsh that it is phenomenal that a fair proportion of the really sick natives who enter the temple ever recover. Small children whose indoctrination is still incomplete have been known to resist attempts to take them to the temple because "that is where you go to die." Despite this fact, sick adults are not only willing but eager to undergo the protracted ritual purification, if they can afford to do so. No matter how ill the supplicant or how grave the emergency, the guardians of many temples will not admit a client if he cannot give a rich gift to the custodian. Even after one has gained admission and survived the ceremonies, the guardians will not permit the neophyte to leave until he makes still another gift.

The supplicant entering the temple is first stripped of all his or her clothes. In every-day life the Nacirema avoids exposure of his body and its natural functions. Bathing and excretory acts are performed only in the secrecy of the household shrine, where they are ritualized as part of the body-rites. Psychological shock results from the fact that body secrecy is suddenly lost upon entry into the *latipso*. A man, whose own wife has never seen him in an excretory act, suddenly finds himself naked and assisted by a vestal maiden while he performs his natural functions into a sacred vessel. This sort of ceremonial treatment is necessitated by the fact that the excreta are used by a diviner to ascertain the course and nature of the client's sickness. Female clients, on the other hand, find their naked bodies are subjected to the scrutiny, manipulation and prodding of the medicine men.

Few supplicants in the temple are well enough to do anything but lie on their hard beds. The daily ceremonies, like the rites of the holy-mouth-men, involve discomfort and torture. With ritual precision, the vestals awaken their miserable charges each dawn and roll them about on their beds of pain while performing ablutions, in the formal movements of which the maidens are highly trained. At other times they insert magic wands in the supplicant's mouth or force him to eat substances which are supposed to be healing. From time to time the medicine men come to their clients and jab magically treated needles into their flesh. The fact that these temple ceremonies may not cure, and may even kill the neophyte, in no way decreases the people's faith in the medicine men.

There remains one other kind of practitioner, known as a "listener." This witch-doctor has the power to exorcise the devils that lodge in the heads of people who have been bewitched. The Nacirema believe that parents bewitch their own children. Mothers are particularly suspected of putting a curse on children while teaching them the secret body rituals. The counter-magic of the witch-doctor is unusual in its lack of ritual. The patient simply tells the "listener" all his troubles and fears, beginning with the earliest difficulties he can remember. The memory displayed by the Nacirema in these exorcism sessions is truly remarkable. It is not uncommon for the patient to bemoan the rejection he felt being weaned as a babe, and a few individuals even see their troubles going back to the traumatic effects of their own birth. . . .

Our review of the ritual life of the Nacirema has certainly shown them to be a magic-ridden people. It is hard to understand how they have managed to exist so long under the burdens which they have imposed upon themselves. But even such exotic customs as these take on real meaning when they are viewed with the insight provided by Malinowski when he wrote (1948:70):

> Looking from far and above, from our high places of safety in the developed civilization, it is easy to see all the crudity and irrelevance of magic. But without its power and guidance early man could not have mastered his practical difficulties as he has done, nor could man have advanced to the higher stages of civilization.

---

not instinctive. Proper dress varies widely from culture to culture. Central Australian men wear a tassel hung from a belt made of human hair, as well as fur armbands. Their wives wear only necklaces. Botocudo women of the Amazon wear cheek plugs and feel undressed without them, even when their bodies are fully clothed.

We may judge these people to be indecent, but we in turn are judged indecent by others, perhaps by the women in Indian villages who keep their legs covered or by the women of some Arab countries who do not show their faces in public. Despite these variations, the sense of modesty serves an important social function in many countries—that of regulating the potentially explosive relationships between the sexes.

Another manifest function of clothes in many countries is that of adornment. People around the world like to be beautiful and to be noticed. A walk through any Western clothing store would convince you that modern people are not content with a few drab wraparounds, which would meet their needs for protection and modesty. But tribesmen and peasants also expend a great deal of effort and wealth on the color, pattern, texture, style, and decoration of their dress. Add to this an array of hairdos, mustaches and beards, tattooing, jewelry,

Moro girl from Jolo Island, Philippines.
Photo courtesy of Burke Museum, University of Washington,
Seattle.

cosmetics, and perfumes, and the variety of human adornment is
staggering.

Latent functions In contrast to manifest functions, which are the
expressed goals for which human activities are organized, latent functions are the unintended and generally unrecognized consequences of
these activities. For example, the wealthy may not build expensive
houses with the intention of reinforcing a system of social classes, but

this, in fact, is one of the consequences of their action. Merton pointed out that these latent functions may be either functional or dysfunctional, and he made it clear that functionalists are often more interested in latent than in manifest functions.

Thus, in addition to protection, modesty, and adornment, dress serves a number of less obvious functions. One is as a visible indicator of sex. Distinctions are made in all societies between the behavior and social positions of men and women. It is important, therefore, to be able to identify the sex of other people on sight, so that a person may act appropriately towards them. In most cultures, differences in dress are a highly visible way of marking the sexes. Men in south Indian villages in the past wore mustaches, and clean-shaven foreign males were often mistaken for women. In the West, men wore pants, and the first women to do so were often the brunt of ridicule.

But differences in clothing not only identify the sexes, they help maintain the social distinction between them. The current trend towards unisexual clothing is more than the whim of fashion. It reflects and advances the growing equality of the sexes and the decline of a specialized treatment, sometimes called chivalry, that was accorded to women.

In many societies, clothes speak of status. Royalty and nobility need ways to show their superiority from the common people, and clothes are a convenient and public way of doing so. Prior to the French Revolution, French noblemen wore long square-tailed coats, embroidered waistcoats, tight knee breeches, three-cornered hats, and wigs which they powdered to give them a touch of artificiality. These set them apart from the common rabble, who wore trousers and shirts. Sometimes, however, even commoners have their day. Following the French Revolution, the everyday garb of the common man gained respectability and widespread acceptance at all levels of French society.

While Americans do not use clothes to distinguish a noble class, we do use them to reinforce differences in social rank. Formal attire for men at rites such as weddings range from business suits to tuxedos, pin-stripes, and swallow tails. And while women's haute couture may be threatened by instant ready-to-wear imitations, furs and jewelry remain.

Clothes often indicate and reinforce a person's vocation and role in a society. Doctors' coats, military dress, priestly garbs, nuns' habits, and a variety of uniforms for postmen, clerks, waitresses, and "bunnies" indicate and reinforce a person's place in the society.

Clothes may also serve as symbols of identity for subcultural groups in a society. For the Amish and the Pennsylvania Dutch, dress is an expression of theology, but socially it also serves an important function in preserving their identity. For others, like the Black Muslims, distinctive dress instills a new sense of identity.

Clothes reinforce differences in social occasions. A professor would not appear in class in a bathing suit, nor would a student arrive at a banquet in pyjamas. Dress also varies with the time of day and night, with the nature of the event (wedding or bowling), and with the kind of people attending (mixed company or sexes alone). By dressing appropriately for various occasions, we reinforce their social significance.

Finally, clothes reflect—and in a measure create—personality. They express our self-image, what we think of ourselves. American individualism is reinforced by the fact that we normally do not want to be seen wearing clothes identical to someone else. Even when we choose to drop out of society, we say it largely by dress.

Summary

One of the major interests of early anthropologists was the variety in material culture: houses, tools, dress, and so on. Human artifacts from around the world were collected in museums and detailed descriptions published on how they were made and used. In the process, important concepts had to be defined, and classification systems devised that would be useful in organizing the data in meaningful ways.

Contemporary anthropologists are seeking to go beyond simply collecting and classifying cultural data, to constructing theoretical models that somehow explain human behavior. The endless collection of descriptive information may be interesting, but it leads us nowhere. Good theories, on the other hand, may enable us to predict and control social events.

Cultural evolutionism and social functionalism are two of several models that have played an important part in the development of anthropological theory. Both have been severely criticized; both have been modified; and both have left a lasting imprint on anthropological thought.

Suggested readings

Fortes, M.
1949 The Web of Kinship Among the Tallensi. London: Oxford University Press. (Chapter 3 is an excellent case study of the relationship of residence patterns and family life.)

Hambly, W.D.
    1927   The History of Tattooing and Its Significance. New York: Macmillan
           Co. (A general survey of tattooing around the world.)
Hoebel, E.A.
    1972   Anthropology: The Study of Man. 4th ed. New York: McGraw-Hill.
           (Chapter 16 provides a good survey of clothes and ornaments.)
Jarvie, I.C.
    1973   Functionalism. Minneapolis: Burgess Publishing Co. (A brief but ex-
           cellent discussion of the nature of functionalism, its strengths and its
           weaknesses.)
McLuhan, M.
    1964   Understanding Media: The Extensions of Man. New York: McGraw-
           Hill. (An interesting discussion of how cultural forms mold
           meanings.)
Morgan, L.H.
    1965   Houses and House-Life of the American Aborigines. (A classic re-
           printed by the University of Chicago Press, 1965.)
Roach, M.E. and J.B. Eicher eds.
    1965   Dress, Adornment and the Social Order. New York: Wiley. (An excel-
           lent collection of readings on the cultural significance of clothing.)

 **Types of adaptation**
Levels of subsistence
The current revolution

Cultural ecology

Ecology is the study of the interactions among organisms and their physical and biotic habitats. Like all other animals, humans are closely linked to nature, and they depend on it for all the basic requirements of life. Nature, however, also produces what humans regard as dangers, such as predators, diseases, storms, droughts, and fires that destroy people.

But people are not passive receptors of the forces and fortunes of nature. They clear forests, cultivate the soil, carve roads through mountains, produce medicines to counter disease, heat their homes in winter, and air condition them in summer. In short, they create artificial environments, which are the products of their interaction with nature. A great deal of the history of humankind records people's continuing efforts to surmount the restrictions of biological makeup and physical habitat by means of technologies that enable them to exploit the products of nature and thus guard themselves from its dangers.

As technologies have developed in complexity, humanity has become increasingly dependent on metals, plastics, fuels, and nuclear energy to maintain the culture it has developed. Try to imagine, for a moment, what American life would be like if it were suddenly deprived of electricity or the automobile. It is not difficult to see that the former tyranny of nature could be replaced by an equally dangerous tyranny of technology.

Man's actions have changed the fundamental balances in nature. Cutting down forests can change patterns of rainfall and cause serious erosion; the use of chemicals and firearms can kill off species of animals and birds that have survived for millions of years. The full effects of human actions on nature often take decades or centuries to develop; thus, many side effects of human activity can never be fully predicted.

As nature changes under people's influence, people must change their ways of adapting, resulting in a chain reaction of change and response. Often before a balance is reached between nature and a particular form of human culture, new technological innovations are introduced which again radically change the picture. Human adaptation is thus a dynamic process of maintaining a viable relationship to nature, often culminating in changing environments and cultures. Whether humankind can maintain its successful adaptation to nature is not certain.

The study of this interaction between people and the environment, sometimes referred to as cultural ecology, has become an important topic in contemporary anthropology.

Types of adaptation

People, like other animals, depend on nature to satisfy their biological needs and drives, but, unlike other animals, which rely solely on biological changes to adapt to nature, people also create cultures that enable them to mold nature to serve their needs. The rise of human beings as the dominant form of life on earth is evidence of their successful adaptation and control of their natural habitat.

Biological adaptation

The human being's ability to survive depends, in part, on the ability of the human body to adapt itself biologically to specific environments and, in part, on the person's ability to create cultures that modify the environment.

An example of the first, biological adaptation, may be seen in the natives of the Andes Mountains in South America. While most people at elevations over 17,000 feet suffer from dizziness, shortness of breath, and light-headedness because of a lack of oxygen, these mountain dwellers live what would be considered normal lives anywhere. Their bodies have developed 1.5 times the hemoglobin content of the blood and the lung capacity of people who live at or near sea level, and this enables them to survive in the rarified air (Cohen 1971:176). On the other hand, when these highland Peruvians descend to sea level, they suffer from high red blood cell counts and from an excess of several important body acids. A successful adaptation in one environment thus becomes a weakness in another.

The Eskimos provide another case of biological adaptation to an extreme environment. Studies have shown (Brown and Page in Cohen 1971:172) that the flow of blood in their hands is double that of most white men; therefore, they can survive in extremely cold climates with minimal danger of frostbite to their hands.

While the human body may, within limits, adapt to specific environments, it is not highly specialized, with the exception of the brain. That is, the human body is not restricted to a particular environment; it can adjust to a wide range of alternative climates and types of social organization.

It is significant that humans possess the biological characteristics necessary to build cultures and that some of these are shared with other primates. Humans are able to communicate through voice and gesture, to learn by experience, and to transmit their learned behavior to their offspring. Like other primates, the human being is gregarious and builds systems that foster social interaction. Like other animals, the human being has senses of territoriality and possessiveness of space and material objects. Without such biological characteristics, human cultures would be impossible, but these traits alone do not accomplish the job. The marvelous human brain must be added to provide the platform on which people build their cultures.

Cultural adaptation

By building cultures, people can push back the limits of their environment. Clothes and houses enable them to live in regions where they could not otherwise survive, from the rock huts and igloos of the far North to the modern scientific settlements in Antarctica. Medicines, likewise, alter the natural patterns of disease and death. Modern cities could not survive without the advanced agricultural technology that enables the farmer to extract more food from the soil than it would produce untended.

As technologies develop and improve, the influence of many natural occurrences on human life-styles decreases. People in preindustrial societies are dependent on the sun for light, and the timing of their activities is governed largely by the cycle of day and night. Moreover, their nighttime activities are widely influenced by the cycles of the moon. At full moon, there is often enough light to visit other villages, fish, or do other outdoor activities, but the darkness of the new moon often compels retreat to poorly lit houses at an early hour. The development of artificial light permits human beings to extend many of their daylight activities well into the night.

Seasons of the year also influence human behavior, particularly among people closely tied to the soil. Those who live by hunting game and gathering wild foods are bound by the seasonal movements of animals and supplies of water. Agriculturalists are freed from the daily search for food by their systematic production and storage of grains, but the seasons still govern their patterns of planting and harvesting.

In peasant societies, agricultural cycles influence other cultural activities. For example, South Indian farmers work hard from June, when the first rains fall and crops are planted, to January, when the harvest is gathered. Marriages, festivals, and evening entertainments are reserved for the nights of February through May, when the hot dry days make field work impossible but the nights are pleasant. Because there are few ways they may be stored or preserved, vegetables are available only a few months each year. Grain prices rise when the crops are growing and supplies are low and then drop sharply after harvest, when the new crop is in. Thus, all aspects of villagers' lives are affected by the cycle of the seasons. (See Figure 5.1.)

In modern industrial societies, with their artificial climates and food reserves, the seasonal changes have less effect on people. People do choose their outdoor clothing and arrange their vacations with a view to the weather. But while they may complain of icy streets and hot days, most urban dwellers continue their normal activities throughout the year without regard to changes in the weather.

While people modify their natural habitats through their cultures, these habitats, themselves, exert forces and set limits on the development of particular cultures. The Bushmen of South Africa, for instance,

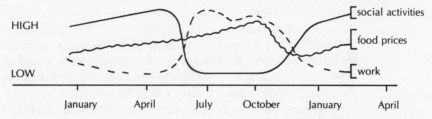

Figure 5.1   All aspects of the people's life-style in a south India village are affected by the cycle of seasons.

must adapt their culture to the dry Kalahari Desert in which they live, and the Eskimos must contend with the cold deserts of the North.

However, geography does not completely determine the particular form a culture will take, as some scientists believed at the turn of the last century. Different cultures often develop in the same geographical settings, as may be seen by comparing the sheepherding Navajos and the agricultural Hopi Indians of the southwest United States. The range of alternative cultures people can devise may be more restricted in the tundra, desert, and heavy rain forest regions of the earth, but even in these regions, an astonishing variety of cultures can be found.

Levels of subsistence

Food is one of the basic requirements for the existence of people and societies; it is, therefore, not surprising that the acquisition of food plays a key role in the formation of any culture. On the other hand, methods for procuring and processing food are closely linked to technological development, social organization, and religious beliefs. Muslims do not eat pork, and Hindus refuse to eat beef, even though these may be in plentiful supply, just as Americans of the last century rejected horse meat.

Throughout the course of history, humankind has risen through several levels of subsistence technology, and the introduction of a major new technology has led, in each case, to a cultural revolution and an expansion of the limits that food supplies set on population size. Broadly, there has been a movement from simple gathering of wild edibles to highly systematized production of food by natural and synthetic means. The amount of nutrition extracted from an acre of land has increased a thousand fold, permitting the formation of ever larger and more complex societies. Nevertheless, simpler levels of subsistence continue to operate in those regions where the newer technologies have not reached or cannot be employed.

Here we must reject a common myth—cultures with simple subsistence technologies do not necessarily have simple social organizations, art forms, and value systems. On the contrary, cultures often elaborate on certain themes which they value highly. Our factories and department stores, our research investments and stock markets indicate that our society places a premium on material goods. We measure the development of other societies by their levels of technology and assume that cars are superior to oxcarts, that material possessions reflect a man's status, and that everyone would like to own a refrigerator.

In sharp contrast, other cultures place high values on human relationships and social organization or on religious beliefs and values. They may not have adequately solved the environmental problems of famine and disease, but they may provide more satisfactory answers to the human questions of old age, orphans and widows, or the very meaning of life itself. Extensive development in one area of a culture thus does not imply development in all areas of that culture.

Subsistence levels are only one criterion for the study of cultural development, but a comparison of contemporary cultures at various subsistence levels, such as what follows, can give us an idea of the impact that this aspect of technology has on the whole of culture.

Food-gathering societies

Early human beings survived by hunting and gathering their food. They were omnivorous, eating not only wild roots and berries but also the animals and fish which they hunted. They learned to expand their abilities to get food, first by developing simple tools (digging sticks, stone hand axes, scrapers, clubs and throwing sticks) and later by creating composite tools, made by joining several pieces together (spears, harpoons, nets, traps, blowguns with poisonous darts, and various types of bows and arrows).

As environments varied, so the game and plants available to early humans varied. American Indians of California depended on wild seeds and berries, as well as on small game, such as rabbits. Indians of the northwest coast caught salmon and trapped beaver, while those on the plains, at a later date, hunted bison. The Eskimos of the north Alaskan coast depended on sea mammals, which they harpooned from their kayaks.

Despite the wide variety of food-gathering practices found around the world, there are some basic cultural similarities in most societies at this low level of subsistence. Dependence on hunting and gathering for

Northwest Coast American Indian trapping fish.
Photo courtesy of Photography Collection, Suzzallo Library, University of Washington, Seattle.

food sets limits on the development of other areas of culture; at least, this is what we find when we compare food-gathering societies that exist today. Hunting, fishing, and gathering normally provide enough food to support only small populations. Rarely is there more than one person for each square mile of land, and commonly the ratio may be one person in fifty to 100 square miles. People are usually grouped into small bands of twenty to fifty persons, moving throughout the year to take advantage of seasonal food plants, roving game, and water supplies. Larger concentrations of people are possible only during those periods of the year when food may be plentiful.

Small bands are often linked by marriage and interaction into tribes numbering from 200 to 500 people. In comparison, American college students relate to about 1,000 people on a first-name basis (Murdock in Pfeiffer 1969:354) and to a great many more in casual relationships.

The combination of small populations and nomadism tends to restrict the types of cultures that can be developed. Most able-bodied adults in hunting and gathering societies are involved daily with getting food; men generally hunt and fish, while women dig roots and pick wild berries and fruit. The children, the aged, and the sick remain in camps which are often temporary shelters constructed near springs, water holes, rivers, or other water supplies.

As in any society, individuals differ in their personal characteristics. Some are high achievers and pride themselves on their hunting, house-building, tool-making, and religious abilities, while others are content to expend as little energy as possible and to live in unkempt huts. Hunting and gathering societies probably offer more free time for their members than any type of society yet evolved (Pfeiffer 1969:345), but most have only the simplest means for storing food and are heavily dependent on nature's seasonal variations for daily meals.

The quality and type of leadership in these bands varies considerably. Some have a headman, who leads by common consent over generally egalitarian bands. He is often the head of a family but has few powers to enforce his decisions on the people, and those who wish to may leave the band. Other bands have chiefs who exercise greater power over simple social hierarchies based on kinship and inheritance.

In hunting and gathering societies, there are few "specialists" or people who live by performing nonfood-producing tasks. Someone may serve as a medicine man in his spare time, and others may earn reputations for making tools that are essential to life. Potters, weavers, businessmen, traders, priests, professors, students, and other specialists who depend on food produced by others are characteristic only of societies with higher subsistence technologies.

All of humanity lived by hunting and gathering until about 10,000 B.C. At that time, there were an estimated 10,000,000 people on the earth (Pfeiffer 1969:311). During the last 12,000 years, the spread of pastoralism and agriculture has displaced the hunting and gathering subsistence pattern, until today there remain only about 30,000 people in food-gathering societies, scattered in the marginal regions of the earth.

Food-producing societies

The domestication of plants and animals turned man into a producer of food, generating the cultural revolution that ushered in the Neolithic era of human history. No longer were people passively dependent on what nature offered in the way of food.

The earliest evidence of food production appears at about 10,000 B.C. For a time, people practiced a crude kind of farming, harvesting wild plants where they were found in large quantities and allowing seed to fall in order to assure a harvest the following year. Systematic cultivation of the soil and the selection and breeding of plants began shortly thereafter.

Farming seems to have originated in several places: in southwest Asia, with the domestication of wheat, rye, flax, peas, apples, pears, and plums; in southeast Asia, with the cultivation of rice, sugar cane, coconuts, bananas, citrus fruits, breadfruit, yams, and cotton; and later along the Gold Coast in Africa, where millets and sorghum were raised.

Three fifths of our current world agricultural production presently comes from crops, first grown in Central and South America, which were unknown in Europe and Asia before the time of Columbus. These crops include varieties of beans and squash, maize or corn, pumpkins, potatoes, sweet potatoes, tomatoes, manioc, chili peppers, artichokes, avocados, guavas, passion fruit, pineapples, and tobacco.

The effects of agriculture on other areas of culture were revolutionary. New technologies were developed for the production and storage of food, and pottery, woven baskets, loom-woven cloth, and refined tools made of polished stone appeared. Land became valued as a commodity that could be owned by groups and individuals, and methods were devised to survey it.

Food surpluses made it possible for some people to specialize in the production of tools, while others chose religion or trade. Groups settled in permanent villages, built houses, and made more and more products not essential for life, such as mirrors, combs, chairs, and plates. Social and political organizations increased in complexity as the number of people living together became greater.

A second major cultural change that occurred at about this time was the domestication of animals. Dogs as pets and scavengers were early companions to people, but raising of animals for food and harnessing their energy for work were later developments. Cattle, sheep, goats, and cats were domesticated in southwest Asia; chickens, pigs, and water buffalo in southeast Asia; and horses and reindeer in central Asia. The New World is notable for its small array of domesticated animals: llamas, alpacas, ducks, guinea pigs, and dogs.

A later phase of the Neolithic era is sometimes treated as a separate cultural revolution and called the Urban Revolution. During this period, bronze, gold, silver, copper, and, later, iron were discovered. The most significant development was the rise of complex social and political organizations that permitted the maintenance and mobilization of large numbers of people in cities and states. This resulted in the rapid development of temples, palaces, and roads; of religions, with priests and philosophers; of governments, with kings and nobles; and of trade by merchants and manufacturers. The development of organized warfare, including the construction of armies and massive fortifications, was an unproductive side effect of these great changes.

In time, food-producing cultures displaced food-gathering societies in the fertile regions of the earth, leaving the latter to marginal lands, such as tundras, deserts, swamps, and steep mountain slopes. Even now, people cultivate only an estimated 7.6 percent of the surface of the earth, for the remainder is too dry, too cold, too hot, too salty, or too steep to farm. The survival of food-gathering societies today rests in part on their ability to adapt to and thus live in a wider range of environments than food-producing societies are able to inhabit.

Food-producing cultures of our day may be divided broadly into four types. While there is no sharp distinction between them, these types are useful in general discussions of subsistence patterns.

HORTICULTURE OR GARDENING   Horticulture or gardening is an early type of agriculture still found in some areas of limited agricultural development. Seeds are planted by hand with the aid of a simple digging stick or hoe, and specific tasks, such as planting, weeding, and harvesting, are often assigned to either men or women. In many instances, a particular society may depend mainly on food raised by women, supplemented by game hunted by men.

In dense forests, where the land must be cleared, a specialized type of horticulture has developed known as "slash-and-burn," or "swidden" agriculture. Men girdle the trees to kill them, burn the dead branches, and plant their seed between the stumps, which offer no hindrance to hand-planted crops. In the tropics, however, exposure of the earth to the hot sun and heavy rains depletes the soil of plant nutrients within a few years, forcing the farmer to move on to a new piece of forest and repeat the process, while allowing the old land to revert to jungle. Years later, he may return to the old plots and repeat the cycle.

A work party hoeing an old man's fields in Uhehe, Tanzania.
Photo courtesy of E.V. Winans.

Slash-and-burn agriculture provides a steady supply of food, but it requires large tracts of land to maintain relatively small populations.

ANIMAL HUSBANDRY   Pastoral people depend on the animals they raise for food, although they often trade with agriculturalists for grain and many of their tools and artifacts. There is a great deal of variation among pastoral cultures, both in the animals that are kept and in the products that are consumed. In some societies, people drink milk and make cheese; in others, they eat the animals' meat and blood. Animal hair is often woven into cloth or matted into felt for clothing and tents.

Most pastoralists are nomadic, moving from one grazing land to another, often in a regular yearly cycle that is referred to as "transhumance." In such cases, semipermanent residences may be set up to permit people to winter with their flocks or herds.

Domesticated animals are also kept by agriculturalists, as supplementary sources of food, raw materials, and fertilizers, as well as for power. Their care is assigned variously to men, women, or children.

PLOW AGRICULTURE   The combination of plow and animal traction enables man to greatly increase the amount of food he can produce. But plow agriculture requires specific kinds of soil and a technology that allows for farming the land over long periods of time without significantly depleting soil nutrients. Prior to the sixteenth century, it was unknown in the New World and Oceania and rare in southeast Asia and Africa south of the Sahara.

People learned early to improve their crops and animals by selective breeding, to control the supply of water by irrigation, and to market surpluses. The result was a rapid expansion of trade and social interaction over an increasingly wide area.

When human beings became food producers they moved from a balanced, nonexploitive economy to one in which they manipulated nature and used nonrenewable resources. Clearing the forests and grazing the lands caused the destruction of fertile soils by erosion and the drying up of springs, while irrigation occasionally produced waterlogged or alkaline soils no longer fit for agriculture. Through bitter experience, humans learned they had to conserve and replace the resources on which they depend for their very existence.

INDUSTRIAL SOCIETY   The industrial revolution began over two centuries ago, but its full impact is only now being felt in many parts of the world. The basis of the revolution was the harnessing of new forms of power, particularly those derived from burning fuels. Human and animal power became less significant, as steam, gasoline, electricity, and, today, atomic fission and fusion increased tremendously the power available for human consumption.

New sources of power made new machines possible. Pumps, drills, railroads, and steamships enabled people to extract natural resources, such as coal, oil, and metal ores, from the earth around the world. Blast furnaces, rollers, and automatic hammers permitted them to convert these resources into products, and mass production in factories led to standardization of products and low prices, which made them increasingly available to the ordinary person. Technical innovations generated new information, from which new innovations, machines, and products sprang, causing an extraordinary growth in technical knowledge.

The mass production of goods called for new systems of marketing, based on transportation and credit. Advertising created new needs in the minds of people; and successful sales stimulated production. Production and marketing both required supporting services, such as banking, financing, insuring, and accounting. When these services fail to emerge, as in the case of some developing countries, the growth of production and marketing is hampered.

Industrialization leads to a high degree of specialization in tasks and the development of complex administrative bureaucracies. Individuals are recruited according to their ability, rather than status, and make careers of rising through the institutional hierarchy. As industrialization progresses, the tasks of gathering resources and producing goods are increasingly taken over by machines, through the process of automation, causing service and administrative jobs to dominate. In the United States, for example, more than one half the labor force is now found in nonmanual occupations.

Industrial principles have been applied to agriculture with far-reaching effects. The use of machines, fertilizers, and modern management techniques have greatly increased the food production and transformed the farm into a food factory or "agrobusiness." Modern farmers sell their products on the world market and purchase their preprocessed foods in supermarkets, like their urban cousins.

While industrial societies are largely insulated from the natural habitat by their sophisticated technologies and knowledge, they remain dependent on nature for the basic resources to support life and industry. This reality, long ignored or forgotten, is now being painfully relearned.

Food-synthesizing societies?

The tremendous increase in knowledge and recent technological breakthroughs are revolutionizing the relationship between nature and humans. New chemical and biological technologies, atomic energy, and the computer could have an impact on cultures equal to that of the industrial revolution. While machines have multiplied people's physical powers and extended their senses of perception, computers extend their brains. The end result of this development is not yet in sight.

But people are still dependent on nature for the creation of food. People may supply raw materials, such as water and nutrients, and destroy pests that ravage crops, but plants remain the factories for food on which all life ultimately depends. Chemical factories have not replaced photosynthesis—at least, not yet. However, the next level of subsistence adaptation may well be synthetic foods produced from inorganic materials.

While it appears that in future societies, humanity will increasingly be in the driver's seat, it is not at all clear that it will steer a safe course for itself.

The current revolution

The introduction of new technology over the past century has initiated a revolution, with consequences that cannot be fully predicted. The old balances between people and nature are gone, and no new stable, balanced relationship has developed, so far. The vast scope of the imbalance and the tensions rising from it are only now becoming apparent.

The population explosion

There are, right now, 148 more people on the earth than a minute ago; 213,700 more than yesterday; 78,000,000 more than last year. The increase in world population over the last three years equals the total current population of the United States! (See Table 5.1.)

Obviously, humankind has not always grown at this rate. Through the long stretches of prehistory, the human population grew only to an estimated 10,000,000 people. With the coming of the Neolithic Age and the resulting increase in food, there was a growth in population, but

Table 5.1   World Population Increase in 1973

	Babies Born	People Dying	Population Increase
Per minute	256	108	148
Per day	369,900	139,560	213,700
Per year	135,000,000	57,000,000	78,000,000

Source: Compiled from United Nations, *Monthly Bulletin of Statistics*, April 1975 (29:1) and from U.S. Bureau of the Census, *World Population 1973: Recent Demographic Estimates for the Countries and Regions of the World*.

plagues, famines, and wars restricted it, as people began to live in large numbers in villages and cities.

As late as 1348 A.D., the plague, aptly called the "Black Death," eliminated from a quarter to a third of Europe's population in a single year. By 1650 A.D., the population of the earth had grown to only about 500,000,000 people, and many societies were weak because of under-population.

The present explosive growth in population which began in the middle of the eighteenth century and is continuing to accelerate can be seen in Figure 5.2. It was not until 1800 A.D. that the world population reached 1,000,000,000 people; 130 years more added the second billion; 30 more years added the third; and 15 more years added the fourth. The fifth billion will appear in about 12 years, the sixth in 9; and by the end of the twentieth century, the total may well be over 7,000,000,000 people!

The population explosion is due largely to modern health measures.

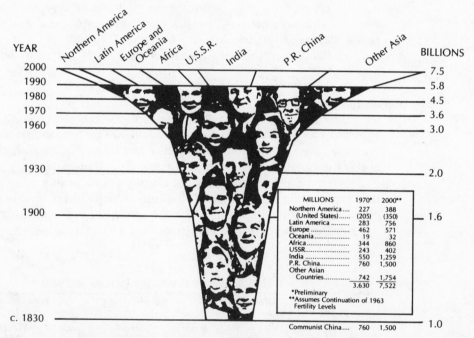

MILLIONS	1970*	2000**
Northern America....	227	388
(United States)......	(205)	(350)
Latin America	283	756
Europe	462	571
Oceania..................	19	32
Africa.....................	344	860
USSR......................	243	402
India	550	1,259
P.R. China..............	760	1,500
Other Asian Countries.............	742	1,754
	3,630	7,522

*Preliminary
**Assumes Continuation of 1963 Fertility Levels

Communist China....	760	1,500

Figure 5.2 A projection of the world's population to the year 2000. The effects of the population explosion will be greatest in Africa, Asia, and Latin America.
Source: Adapted from Department of State publication 8749.

Vaccines, sanitation, and modern medicines have cut death rates in half (from about 40 to less than 20 deaths per 1,000 people per year), while birth rates have remained high. The greatest reductions have been in infant and child deaths, so that more girls are living to become mothers. Obviously, this increase cannot go on indefinitely. Unless people are able to slow their rate of reproduction, the limitations of food, space, and other vital resources will stop population growth in a tragic competition for survival.

Population growth hinges ultimately on two factors: births and deaths. The "population equation" is: Present population + Births − Deaths = Future population. Death rates have been drastically reduced; to increase them in order to stabilize the population is clearly unacceptable. This only leaves the alternative of controlling births if the explosion is to be stopped.

Birth rates have recently dropped significantly in some parts of the world, particularly in the developed countries—those in which industrialization and urbanization have reached a high level. There appears to be a correlation between low birth rates and socioeconomic conditions such as education, desire for higher standards of living, social mobility, nuclear families, and higher levels of health and nourishment. Where these have been achieved, population growth has slowed down.

However, populations continue to grow rapidly in the poorer countries, which account for two thirds of the world's population. Their death rates have dropped sharply since the second world war, and their birth rates are only now beginning to show some decline. These countries, trying desperately to raise the standards of living for their people, can least afford this rapid increase in population.

The past decade has seen an increase in worldwide concern over the control of populations. New techniques for birth control have been developed, and governmental programs have been introduced to make them available to all citizens. But most of these programs have stressed contraceptive methods, rejecting abortion, which was a major factor in reducing population growth in Japan, the Soviet Union, and eastern Europe. The critical question remains: Even if adequate technology and education put family planning within reach of all people, will they voluntarily limit family size, or will governmental controls eventually become necessary? Family planning programs, for the most part, are still too new to provide an answer to this question.

Even if birth rates dropped sharply, populations in many countries would continue to grow for some time. Approximately one half of all people in developing countries are below sixteen years of age and have

Peace corps backlash

Washington, D.C. Thailand has just announced that she will send Peace Corps volunteers to the United States as a reciprocal gesture for American Peace Corps volunteers dispatched to Thailand.

The announcement said that several projects, including the teaching of the Thai language to Americans, would be worked out.

No one in his wildest dreams ever thought that there would be this kind of blacklash to the Peace Corps. While the United States has been very eager to send Peace Corps volunteers abroad, we're not too certain it's such a great idea to have other countries send Peace Corps volunteers to the United States.

I can just see the first Thai Peace Corps volunteer, after spending two years in the United States, returning to Thailand and being interviewed by a newscaster on Bangkok television.

"We have in our studio Mr. Yok Bin Lin, who has just returned after serving two years in the United States as a Peace Corps volunteer. Mr. Lin, how was it over there?"

"I had a wonderful time and I think I taught them a lot. The village where I worked in New Jersey was called Hoboken. By our standards it was very primitive, but the people were simple and friendly and willing to learn."

"Was it dangerous, Mr. Lin?"

"Well, you couldn't go out at night, but in the daytime it was perfectly safe to wander in most areas."

"Where did you live?"

"As you know, Thai Peace Corps volunteers are trained to live with the natives, so I moved into an urban housing development. It was hard at first, because the plumbing kept me awake at night, but after awhile I got used to it."

"Did you eat the native food?"

"I tried to, but it wasn't easy. The Hoboken people refuse to raise any food themselves and they must buy it at supermarkets frozen and wrapped in cellophane."

"You must be joking?"

"No, I'm not. One of my first projects was to try to teach the natives how to grow their own vegetables so they wouldn't have to spend money, but they were too set in their ways."

"What did you find was the Americans' biggest problem?"

"They're full of fears. It's very hard to work with the people because, in the world they live in, they've lived with fear for so long."

"What do you think the origin of the fear is?"

"It starts with their young, who are told at a very early age that they have bad breath, that they perspire too much, that they will probably get cavities, that they are susceptible to headaches, neuralgia, and stomach acids. By the time the young grow up, they are afraid of everything.". . .

"Looking back over the two years, Mr. Lin, what do you consider was the greatest contribution you made?"

"I got everyone in Hoboken to practice birth control."

---

not yet established their families. Thus, the mothers of the next two decades are already alive and outnumber present mothers.

Long-term predictions range from pessimistic views that nothing can be done to avoid worldwide catastrophe and famine to cautious optimism that predicts reduced birth rates before the end of this century and a stable population before the twenty-first century if adequate efforts are made. The unanswered question is: How will the quality of life be affected?

Resources

What is the "carrying capacity" of the earth—the optimum population possible, taking into account people's concept of the "good life"? What level of material affluence can be supported worldwide for an indefinite time without destroying the earth's resources? No doubt the answer to these questions dictates smaller populations than today or lower levels of affluence than Americans are accustomed to.

People in the United States consume almost one half the resources used in the world each year, yet they comprise less than one fifteenth of the world's population. It is estimated that more than 100,000,000,000 gallons of gasoline were used to power 87,000,000 cars 1,000,000,000,000 miles in the United States in 1970, producing 100,000,000 tons of carbon monoxide and more than 2,000,000 tons of other pollutants.

Also in 1970, Americans threw away 2,360,000,000 tons of refuse, or an average of ten tons per person. This includes 7,000,000 junked cars, 8,000,000,000 pounds of plastics, and 74,000,000,000 bottles and cans. Even if agricultural and industrial wastes are omitted, individuals dispose of an average of six pounds of waste each day.

A man from the
Palm-tapper caste
(India) extracting
sap for use in
making palm beer.
Photo courtesy of
J.N.C. Hiebert.

How long can we continue to use the world's resources, many of them irreplaceable, at this rate? What will be the result if the rest of the world reaches a similarly high standard of living, and demands on natural resources increase ten or twenty fold?

Available food is the indicator most often used to project the population that the earth can support. The average American purchases 3,300 calories of energy a day, of which he consumes about 2,600. One third of this comes from meat, milk, eggs, and other animal products. But animals are inefficient factories for converting vegetable foods to animal foods, and much of the food they eat is used to support their own life processes. The amount of vegetable food needed to support one person with American-style eating habits is six times what it would be on the normal vegetarian diet in other parts of the world.

Table 5.2   Per Capita Food Consumption in Selected Countries (1968–1970)

Country	Calorie Intake per Day		Total Protein Intake per Day in Grams
	Total Calories	% Animal Origin	
U.S.A.	3,290	39	97
U.K.	3,180	40	88
Denmark	3,140	44	89
Mexico	2,620	11	67
Japan	2,450	14	75
India	1,940	6	48

Source: Adapted from United Nations, *Statistical Yearbook, 1971*, pp. 504–509.

At the current rates of production, the world could support only 1,200,000,000 people if all enjoyed American food standards. The current population of 3,600,000,000 is maintained only because most people lack meat diets and because an estimated two thirds of the total population are undernourished. (See Table 5.2.)

People depend on photosynthesis not only for food but also for wood and its by-products. The United States uses one sixth of the lumber cut each year, as well as 20,000,000,000,000 pounds of paper, much of which is thrown away as waste. The present rate of world production of paper would meet the needs of slightly more than 1,000,000,000 people at the American level of consumption.

Water is yet another vital resource. An estimated 15,000 gallons of water are used per person per day in the United States. Of that total, 300 gallons are needed to raise and process the grain for 2.5 pounds of bread, and 2,300 gallons are used to produce a pound of beef (Bradley 1968:99). Baths, laundry, and cooking account for 30,000 gallons per person each year. All of this makes a substantial contribution to the yearly production of 18,000,000,000,000 gallons of sewage, filled with organic wastes and chemical poisons. It is estimated that if we were to use all the rainwater that now flows out to the sea, we could accommodate a population of 230,000,000 in the United States without affecting our present standard of living, a population we will undoubtedly reach before the year 2000 (Bradley 1968:102).

The problems are just as serious, if not more so, when we turn to nonrenewable resources. The world production of energy in 1970 was equivalent to 7,000,000,000 tons of coal, most of it produced by burning fossil fuels, such as coal, gas, and oil. Of this total, Americans used almost 2,300,000,000 tons (United Nations 1972:337). At today's level of energy production, this rate of consumption would support fewer than 600,000,000 people. Even if all the energy now converted into organic materials by photosynthesis were burned for fuel, it would supply less than 4,000,000,000 people at the American level of consumption, leaving nothing for food or other organic products. Our civilization is thus maintained by a limited supply of energy that has been stored over millions of years, a hard fact we are only beginning to comprehend.

When we look at fertilizers, steel, aluminum, and practically all other mineral resources, the world's present industrial complex is capable of providing for less than 1,000,000,000 people at our own standards of affluence. But the population is already 3,700,000,000 and continuing to rise rapidly.

Finally, the problem is not only that of finding renewable resources but also of facilitating an equitable distribution of these resources throughout the world. The extent of the imbalance can be illustrated by means of a simple economic comparison. If we divide the total value of goods produced and services rendered within a country by the number of people living in that country, we get the gross domestic product per

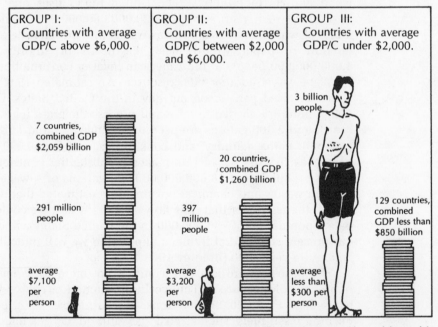

Figure 5.3 This figure dramatizes the unequal distribution of world wealth (1974).
Sources: Statistics from Union Bank of Switzerland, *Business Facts and Figures*, May 1975; and U.N. Statistical Office, *Statistical Yearbook, 1972*. Chart adapted from a U.S. government publication.

A Karaja woman preparing a meal in Santa Isabel, Brazil.
Photo courtesy of Burke Museum, University of Washington, Seattle.

capita (GDP/C). Only six countries—Kuwait, Switzerland, Sweden, Denmark, United States, Canada and Germany—had a GDP/C greater that $6,000 in 1974 (Union Bank of Switzerland 1975:18-19). Twenty countries had a figure between $2,000 and $6,000. One hundred and twenty-nine countries, with 8.6 percent of the world's population, had a GDP/C of less than $2,000—96 of them with 63.1 percent of the world's population were under $500! (See Figure 5.3.)

Summary

Like other forms of life, human beings are dependent on nature for their livelihood. But unlike the others, which depend on purely biological adaptations to survive, people can and do modify their environments by means of their cultures.

The degree to which people control their environments has increased as technologies have become more complex. Hunting and gathering societies depend on food found in nature; pastoral societies raise their food by tending herds and flocks; agricultural societies develop food by sowing and tending crops; and industrial societies create food by converting their farms into mass production factories.

But the technological revolutions of the past have upset the delicate balances between humans and their environments, producing population explosions, shortages of resources, and pollution of the environments. It is clear that the current human adaptation to nature is an unstable one that cannot continue indefinitely and that some major changes will be necessary if wide-scale disasters are to be avoided. It is not clear, however, just what changes are needed and how they will be brought about.

Suggested readings

Barth, F.
    1961   Nomads of South Persia. New York: Humanities Press. (A good case study of Middle East pastoralism based on sheep.)
Goldschmidt, W.
    1965   Theory and Strategy in the Study of Cultural Adaptability. American Anthropologist 67:402–408. (An important work in developing an ecological approach to the study of anthropology.)
Murphy, R.F. and J.H. Steward
    1956   Tappers and Trappers: Parallel Process in Acculturation. Economic Development and Cultural Change. Vol. 4. (A case study of cultural adaptation.)

Steward, Julian H. et al.
   1968   Cultural Ecology. *In* International Encyclopedia of the Social Sciences. Vol. 4. New York: Macmillan. (A survey of the field and the key issues involved.)
White, Leslie
   1959   The Evolution of Culture. New York: McGraw-Hill. (An important synthesis of an adaptive approach to the study of culture over a long range of time.)

The symbolic process
Communication

Symbolism and communication

Humanity's basic achievements—its technology, social organization, knowledge, and beliefs—as well as its ability to communicate depend on people's ability to think in symbolic terms. All animals have receptor or sensory systems to receive external stimuli and effector systems to react to them, but people are unique in possessing a symbolic system, by which they assign meanings and values to sensory experiences. People's ability to substitute signs and symbols for ideas, actions, and other phenomena, thereby giving them cultural significance, sets them apart from other animals and enables them to create complex cultures.

Symbolism among people, to use Whitehead's phrase, "has a tendency to run wild, like vegetation in a tropical forest." This is graphically described by Hayakawa:

> Everywhere we turn, we see the symbolic process at work. Feathers worn on the head or stripes on the sleeve can be made to stand for military rank; cowrie shells or rings of brass or pieces of paper can stand for wealth; crossed sticks can stand for a set of religious beliefs; buttons, elks' teeth, ribbons, special styles of ornamental haircutting or tattooing, can stand for social affiliations. The symbolic process permeates human life at the most primitive and the most civilized levels alike. Warriors, medicine men, policemen, doormen, nurses, cardinals, and kings wear costumes that symbolize their occupations. Vikings collected their victims' armor and college students collect membership keys in honorary societies, to symbolize victories in their respective fields. There are few things that men do or want to do, possess or want to possess, that have not, in addition to their mechanical or biological value, a symbolic value. (Hayakawa 1972:22)

The symbolic process

Symbols may be objects, colors, sounds, odors, acts, and events—in short, anything that can be experienced—to which people have assigned meaning or value. On the one hand, symbols have an observable physical form, by which they enter our experience; on the other hand, symbols are mental concepts. The word "tree," for example, is a particular combination of sounds and a set of marks on a piece of paper, but it is also a category in the mind of the speaker or writer. It is this link between physical things and abstract ideas (the symbolic process) which makes human thought and communication possible. (See Figure 6.1.)

Symbols as human creations

People are uniquely free to create symbols and to manipulate them to form new and complex ideas. We can agree to let "X" stand for dollars and "Y" for hours. We can change the symbols and let "X" stand for gallons of gasoline and "Y" for miles. If we wish, we can create a new symbol, "Z," to stand for both X and Y and then combine these letters with numerical and procedural symbols in complex math-

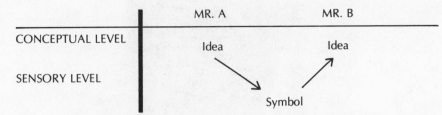

	MR. A	MR. B
CONCEPTUAL LEVEL	Idea	Idea
SENSORY LEVEL		
	Symbol	

Figure 6.1 Symbols make communication possible, for they put ideas into sensory forms.

ematical equations. We develop numerous other symbol systems—money, rituals, dress, drama, dance, painting, music, academic degrees, and, above all, language—to convey our ideas.

The ability to create and manipulate symbols is one of the characteristics that sets people apart from lower animals. Both a child and a dog can be taught to obey the command, "roll over." The difference between them is that, to the child, these words may be either a sign or a symbol, but to the dog, they are only a sign. The distinction, as Leslie White points out, is an important one (White 1940:451–463).

Signs are direct representations of other things. Snow is a sign that it is cold outside; smoke is a sign of fire. In addition to such natural signs, people are bombarded with countless cultural signs: street lights, highway markers, arrows, barber poles, trademarks, flowers at funerals, and rice at weddings.

Symbols, on the other hand, link physical things with mental concepts, and these concepts can be distinguished from the form and immediate context of the symbols and can be combined in new contexts to create new ideas. Words can be used as symbols, because they enable us to talk about snow even though the weather is not cold and there is no snow in sight. Symbols thus become labels for abstract concepts.

Difficulty and confusion may arise from the paradox that one thing may be a sign in one context and a symbol in another. The words "roll over" are a sign to a dog trained to turn over at this command, but the child can use them as symbols to create a variety of new ideas and responses, such as "No, you roll over," or "Dolly, roll over." Students can learn to read Latin aloud without understanding the words, because to them, the printed words are signs instructing them to utter particular sounds. To Latin speakers, however, the words are symbols, conveying meanings which can be abstracted from the printed and spoken form and rearranged into new sentences.

Trophy head of the
Jivaro Indians,
Ecuador.
Photo courtesy of
Burke Museum,
University of Wash-
ington, Seattle.

The arbitrary nature of symbols

Because people arbitrarily assign meanings to things, meanings are
in the mind, rather than in the symbols themselves. There is no necessary connection between a symbol and the ideas and things it symbol-
izes. A woman may say, "I am hungry," or "J'ai faim," or "Akaligon-
nanu" and mean the same thing. No one set of sounds more naturally
conveys the idea of hunger than any other set, nor need the speaker be
hungry when she emits the appropriate sounds.

We are all tempted at times to confuse symbols with the ideas and things they symbolize. Some movie audiences in Africa jeered when John Wayne acted the part of a bumbling cowhand, because they knew from a previous film that he was an expert gunslinger. They did not comprehend that movies are symbolic representations rather than factual enactments. Likewise, many Englishmen felt that the government deprived them of twelve days of their lives when a calendar change was made in 1752 and September 2 became September 14. We in America are encouraged to go deeply into debt to buy big cars and expensive homes to show our prosperity, and students cheat to get high grades, which supposedly stand for a high level of achievement.

People are also tempted to use abstract terms, which have been cut loose from the concrete space/time events to which they refer. Words are generalized categories, and it is easy to overlook the individual differences between the objects in the groups to which they refer. We often make statements like, "Hippies are troublemakers," or "Americans are racist," or "Polynesians have more than one wife,"—statements which we support with only a few specific instances. We rarely trouble to survey data to test whether our generalizations actually fit all or most of the cases involved. The result is oversimplification and prejudices that have little connection to reality.

A similar danger is using words like "democracy," "socialism," and "Christianity" without defining them clearly, causing them to mean different things to different people. Words are slippery abstractions, playthings of our minds; yet, without them, thought would be impossible.

Symbols may also change their meaning over time. Hayakawa points out that at the end of the nineteenth century, deeply tanned skin was associated with outdoor labor, and women shielded themselves from the sun with wide hats, long sleeves, and parasols, to preserve their pale color. Today, a tanned skin indicates a life of leisure on the beach, particularly in northern areas in winter, so people who cannot afford an expensive vacation turn to sun lamps and tanning lotions to darken their skins.

Symbols based on convention

For the most part, symbols have a degree of conventional acceptance in the community that uses them. Individuals may develop their own personal symbols. A child pretends her doll is grandpa, and an adult devises ways of reminding himself of things he must do. But communication and the building of elaborate cultures depend on sets of symbols shared by groups of people. Benjamin Whorf, an anthropologist interested in language, wrote:

We cut nature up, organize it into concepts, and ascribe significance as we do largely because we are parties to an agreement to organize it in this way—an agreement that holds throughout our speech community and is codified in the patterns of our language. (Whorf, in Postman and Weingartner 1969:126)

We learn the meanings of words and other symbols from the way they are used in everyday life, though the meaning of any symbol varies slightly from person to person. For example, a dog lover and a postman may agree as to what a "dog" is but have quite different feelings toward the animal, itself.

Despite these individual differences, people do reach a general consensus on the meanings of symbols, in part because they share similar experiences. Most people in our society have seen trees, hills, stop signs, cars, and clocks and have learned to associate specific symbols with these experiences by listening to and observing the behaviors of others. They learn to associate the word "red" with the color of ripe tomatoes, stop signs, some lipsticks, and certain roses.

However, people are at a loss when new words are defined in terms outside their experience. In a poor dictionary, the word "badinage" is defined as "persiflage," and "persiflage" is defined as "badinage." Unless the reader knows one or the other of these words, he has no clue as to their meaning. To make sense, the meanings of symbols must relate at least indirectly to a person's past or present experiences.

The world of our experiences, however, is an extremely limited world: the things we ourselves have seen, heard, tasted, felt, and smelled. George Washington, Shakespeare, and Galileo never existed for us if we have not met them in books, plays, or movies, nor do Africa, Europe, and China if we have never been there or seen films of them on television. This world of personal experience, sometimes called our "extensional world," is very limited.

Symbolic systems enable us to communicate and learn about the extensional worlds of other people. Most of our knowledge is acquired through the words, spoken and printed, of parents, friends, teachers, and strangers, and from these we create a "verbal world." The only proof we have that the Civil War took place is the reports we have of its battles. Moreover, these reports are most often not from those who saw the battles, but reports based on other reports, which originally derived from the first-hand accounts of those who were present when the battles took place.

The fact that symbol systems can be held in common with other people makes cultures possible. Ideas and knowledge can be passed from one generation to the next, accumulating and changing as people have and create new experiences and reinterpret old ones. Thus, people learn the symbol systems of their particular culture—to call this thing a "tree" and not a "chettu" and to drive on the right rather than on the left side of the road.

Symbols and perception

Thought categories and their associated symbols begin as rooms to house our experiences and end as jails confining them. We cannot perceive nature or think or communicate about it without language, but language, to a great extent, also molds what we see and how we see it. As Dorothy Lee points out:

> Symbols are a part of the process whereby the experienced world, the world of perception and conception, is created out of the world of physical reality, the so-called given, the undifferentiated mass, or energy or set of relations. (Lee, in Bryson *et al.* 1954:73–74)

Benjamin Whorf was one of the first to explore how languages influence our perceptions of reality. He noted that underlying each language there are basic assumptions about the nature of things. For example, the English language divides time into three segments, past, present, and future, which are expressed in the verb tenses. Time is perceived, in a sense, as one dimensional, flowing perpetually and uniformly from the future through the present into the past. The English language treats the future as if it were just as "real" as the past. One is not forced to qualify statements of the future, like, "I expect to go to town tomorrow," but can state the future as a fact, "I will go to town tomorrow." It took Einstein and modern physics to challenge these assumptions about time, which most of us still firmly hold.

In contrast to English, Hopi language and culture make a basic distinction between objective things (things which can or have been experienced by human senses) and subjective things (expectations, desires, thoughts, and other potential experiences). In Hopi, past and present events are objective experiences, accessible to the senses without distinction of time. The future, however, belongs to the category of subjective anticipation, a category which is different from but no less real than that of objective experience.

There is another basic difference between English and Hopi. English stresses things, and Hopi stresses events or happenings. Like other Indo-European languages, English has a subject/predicate form of sentence, in which things act or receive action. Each verb must have a noun to make it work. We say, "lightning flashes" and "death occurs," even though lightning and death are processes. Modern physics, in fact, has had a great deal of trouble with this tendency to treat events and processes as things. A Hopi speaker says "Reh-pi," meaning "flashing," to indicate an event or happening such as lightning, and comes closer to the way modern physics perceives the world of experience.

The ambiguity of symbols

It is obvious that no two people mean precisely the same thing by the same word and that no two words in any one language are identical. It is less obvious that two apparently similar symbols or words in any two languages do not have exactly the same meaning. Swastikas, which may evoke nationalistic feelings in parts of Europe, are symbols with religious significance in India. The English words "father" and "uncle" are not found in many other languages; more often, fathers are lumped together with certain uncles to form a different category and word. Even in languages with words equivalent to "father," the feelings and expectations associated with the words vary greatly.

As a result of these differences in the meanings of symbols, absolutely accurate communication among human beings is impossible. Nevertheless, as Eugene Nida points out, effective cross-cultural communication is possible, for several reasons (1960:90). First, the processes of human reasoning are essentially the same around the world. Clyde Kluckhohn, a noted American anthropologist, writes:

> In a certain deep sense the logic (which means the modes of interpreting relationships between phenomena) of all members of the human species is the same. The differences in thinking and reacting arise from the value premises and existential conceptions about the nature of the external world and of human nature. (Kluckhohn, in Learner 1959:278)

Second, all people share a common range of human experiences: they must make provision for physical needs, such as food and protection, and they face disease and death and interact with their fellow humans and with nature. Communication *is* possible in those areas where similar experiences are shared.

Finally, people can adjust their symbolic frameworks to take differences into account. For example, we can learn to listen to someone who speaks English with a strong accent, by adjusting to his broken sentences. So, also, we can understand a message, even though there are minor differences in the meanings of the words.

A work party shares some welcome refreshment after tilling fields in Tanzania. Photo courtesy of E.V. Winans.

Communication

Early anthropologists developed an interest in communication, particularly in language, because they were often faced with learning exotic languages in order to study other cultures. For the most part, these languages lacked written forms, grammars, dictionaries, and teachers to give instruction. Anthropologists, such as Franz Boas, Edward Sapir, and Leonard Bloomfield, developed techniques which enabled them to learn languages quickly and accurately by using local informants. They also aided in analyzing the language structure and reducing the spoken language to a written form.

At first, languages were treated as autonomous structures, independent of the rest of culture. "Linguistics" developed as a separate field of study in its own right, concerned with the nature, history, and variety of human languages. Anthropological linguists, however, became increasingly interested in the problem of the relationship of language to culture, and it became obvious to them that culture would be impossible without language. On the other hand, they found that language is molded by the culture of which it is a part.

Linguistic anthropologists are now focusing on the broader context of communication, which includes not only language but all symbol systems, such as use of time, space, gestures, and rituals.

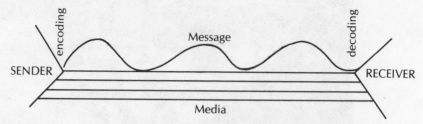

Figure 6.2 Communication involves encoding and decoding messages in the media of symbolic systems.

Communication, in general, is the transmission of information from a "sender" to a "receiver." It may occur between animal and animal, animal and machine, or machine and machine. Bees communicate to each other the direction in which honey can be found. Men turn keys to start their cars and feed information and directions to computers, which solve complex problems. Time clocks ring school bells; signal lights regulate traffic; and computers control precise machinery in factories. In all of these cases, information is transmitted to cause change in or be changed in some way by the environment. This is the purpose of all communication.

Machines, lower animals, and human beings can communicate by means of signs, but humans are unique in that they also communicate abstract ideas by means of symbols. Symbols relate ideas to concrete things, a form which can be experienced by other people.

Theoretical models of human communication generally have four basic components: senders, receivers, messages, and media. (See Figure 6.2.) A brief look at each may help sharpen our awareness of the complex nature of what appears to be the *simple* process of communication, in which we all engage so naturally and continuously.

The sender

The sender initiates communication by transmitting a "message." To do so, he must select a symbol system, or "medium," and encode his ideas into the symbol forms, which can be experienced by the receiver. This process of encoding is so nearly automatic when we are in our own culture and are speaking our native tongue, that we rarely give it conscious thought. Most of our attention is given to formulating the message. Only when we try to learn a new language and culture are we made aware of the processes of communication rather than its content.

Encoding is dependent on a great many factors. (See Figure 6.3.) First, the sender puts his message into the language and symbol system of his culture. Though it is obvious that Frenchmen use French gestures and language and Italians use their own, it is less obvious to us that in the process of encoding, the message is also molded to fit the differing thought categories and assumptions of the language and culture in question.

The sender also encodes his message in terms of his own experiences. His choice of words, the way he pronounces and arranges them, the feelings they carry, and even the message he communicates are determined by such personal factors as his position in the society, geographic location, past experiences, and present attitudes.

Encoding varies according to sex and age, as well. Among the Carayaki Indians of Brazil, men and women actually speak different languages. In our own society, at least until very recently, the style of speech and topics of discussion of men and women were presumed to differ. Furthermore, speech patterns of children can readily be distinguished from the idiomatic jargons of adolescent and adult life.

Finally, encoding takes the occasion into account. Each of us shifts smoothly in the course of a single day from one type of speech and set of vocabulary words to another, from one system of communication to another, depending on where we are and whom we are addressing. We communicate one way with our friends, another with our spouses, and still another with teachers, preachers, policemen, and presidents. Like many other cultures, we have special languages for courts, politics, trade, and religious ceremonies.

The process of encoding is complex. The speaker must select words, modify them according to the tense, gender, and number, using the rules of the language, and then arrange them in the proper sequence.

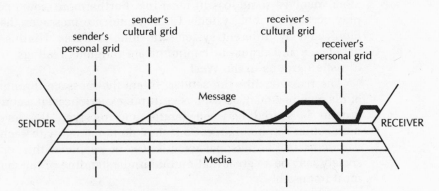

Figure 6.3 Senders and receivers filter messages through the grids of their own cultural and personal experiences.

He must also reproduce sounds with sufficient accuracy to permit the listener to understand him. Each individual also adds inflections of voice, such as anger, scorn, or fear, as well as dialectic variations, speech styles, facial expressions, gestures, postures, and mannerisms, to help convey his meaning. Often a speaker is unconscious of the many levels and systems of symbols by which he is communicating the message.

The receiver

The receiver receives, decodes, interprets, and responds to messages. Obviously, he is limited to receiving messages transmitted in languages and symbol systems with which he is familiar. There is no communication if someone speaks Arabic to a person who knows only English. Often there is also considerable loss between dialectic variations of the same language based on subcultural or regional differences. Imagine, for example, the response of an American service station attendant to an Englishman who asks him to fill the tank with petrol, check under the bonnet, and clean the windscreen while the Englishman rearranges the luggage in the boot! At this level, the impairment of communication is caused by differences in pronunciation and vocabulary.

An even greater problem is faced in communicating between different languages and cultures. Messages must be put into symbolic languages, but as we have seen, languages reflect the cognitive categories and assumptions of their particular cultures. No two languages or cultures divide their conceptual worlds in exactly the same way, just as no two words convey precisely the same ideas and feelings, so that even the most painstaking translation of a message from one language to another involves some loss in meaning. Furthermore, some cultures employ certain symbol systems to communicate messages that are communicated by different systems in other cultures. Hindus commonly use dance and drama to communicate religious feelings, unlike most Christian groups in the West.

The receiver, like the sender, filters the message through the grids of his own personal, as well as cultural, experiences. If a common background is shared between sender and receiver, the level of communication can be high, even if they do not agree with each other. But variations in the personal experiences of people within one complex society may be so great that mutual understanding of the message is almost impossible.

Loss or distortion of communication may arise when the receiver blocks out part or all of the message. To test this fact, students in a large college class were once asked to record whatever they were thinking about whenever a cap gun was fired. The results showed that, on the average, only twenty percent of the students were listening to the lecture at any one time the shot was heard.*

A more subtle form of screening occurs when people expose themselves only to messages that confirm their own opinions, or when they limit their attentions to those parts of a message that reinforce their present attitudes. A politically conservative person will often select books, magazines, newspapers, and even friends that support his views, and when confronted with information that contradicts these views, he may distort it by interpreting it in ways that allow him to keep his own ideas intact. He may, for instance, blame the failures of his political party on peculiar circumstances or on the opposition rather than on the party itself. The liberal person will, of course, do likewise.

Yet, as we know, people do change their ideas and behaviors. New ideas may be found acceptable when the rewards outweigh the losses by change. Rewards are, for the most part, changes that lead to a more stable organization of personal information and experience, as defined by the receiver rather than by the sender.

The medium

The medium is not the message but the symbolic system by which a message is conveyed. Just as there are various ways to transport goods to their destinations, so are there different ways to communicate ideas. But, unlike transportation vehicles and their contents, the relationship between the media and the message is close, as we shall see later on.

In their studies of other cultures, anthropologists make detailed observations of the everyday activities of the people and have learned that the meanings of these activities and the ways people view them can only be learned through language. Occasionally, an anthropologist must rely on an interpreter, but this raises the problem of the interpreter's personal bias in the translations. Only as he begins to master the language personally is the ethnographer able not only to communicate effectively with the people he studies and learn to know their thoughts and feelings, but also to discover the fundamental concepts which mold their language and their world.

Broadly, there are two approaches to the study of language. The first is known as a "synchronic" approach, and it is concerned with the structure of a language at any given moment in history and how it operates.

* This test, which was made at Wayne State University in Detroit, was reported by U.P.I. on August 31, 1968.

The second is called a "diachronic" approach; it analyzes the historical origins of languages and how languages change over time.

SYNCHRONIC STUDIES OF LANGUAGE Languages are highly structured—that is, they show a great deal of predictability. For example, study the following sentence:

Yesterday Jane _____ the car to her friend ___ house.

It is not difficult to fill in the blanks. The first blank indicates a need for a word that is a verb in the past tense, such as "drove" or "took." The second blank requires an "s," pronounced as /z/, indicating possession. As this example shows, any complete description of how a language works must analyze two levels of structure, the system for organizing sounds and the system for organizing meaning, called, respectively, "phonetics" and "grammar."

Phonetics The mobility of lips and tongue working in combination with the throat and nasal cavity enables the speaker to make a surprisingly wide variety of sounds. The sounds employed by particular languages, however, are limited, ranging from thirteen for Hawaiian to thirty-five or forty for English and close to sixty for a few other languages. These basic sounds, in their various permutations and combinations, are quite sufficient to express all human thought.

The first step, then, in the analysis of a language is defining what sounds are used and how they are made. This is determined by a careful study of speech and by mimicking the informant until he is satisfied with the way the learner makes the sounds. Precise descriptions of the positions and actions of the various parts of the speech apparatus, together with phonetic alphabets, enable linguists to reproduce sounds accurately and record them in written form.

Children learn early the basic phonetic structures of their native languages and develop speech habits that make it increasingly difficult for them in later life to make sounds found in other languages. Often, in the effort to use a new language, students give too little attention to making sounds accurately. Thus, a foreigner is most commonly betrayed by his accent.

Most people can learn to speak a new language with minimal accent if, at the outset, careful attention is given to the ways sounds are made. Phonetic habits are formed quickly, and unless learned correctly, a heavy accent will result. For example, the English sound /t/, as in "ten," is made by placing the tip of the tongue on the alveolar ridge located just behind the upper teeth. Telugu, a south Indian language, has two types of /t/. One is formed by placing the tip of the tongue against the edge of the top teeth, the other by rolling the tongue back, placing the underside against the roof of the mouth, and then snapping the tongue forward. Native English speakers speaking Telugu, however, frequently use only the English /t/ for both.

Study of the phonetic structure of a language alone will not tell us what the people who speak the language consider to be its basic units of sound. There are often slight variations in the ways a sound is made, depending on its context within a word. For example, by holding a strip of paper in front of the lips and saying "pill" and "lip," it is easy to see that in English the sound /p/ is accompanied by a puff of air if it occurs at the beginning of a word but not if at the end. English speakers do not treat these as two distinct sounds and are usually unaware of the fact that they change the sound according to the phonetic context.

The minimal units of sound that the speakers of a language themselves distinguish are called "phonemes." They are discovered by testing different sounds in order to determine what are called "minimal pairs." Take, for example, the English words "bat" and "pat," which are identical except for the initial sound. A change from /b/ to /p/ is significant in English, for it changes the meaning of the word. Other examples contrasting these same sounds are "bill" and "pill" or "lib" and "lip." The English speaker invariably detects the difference whenever they are interchanged.

A closer look at /p/ and /b/ shows that these sounds share a great many similarities. The position of the mouth and tongue is the same for both. The only difference is that the vocal cords are used for /b/ and not for /p/. In other words, one is voiced, and the other is unvoiced. Many languages, in fact, do not make a distinction between these sounds but, depending on the context, treat them as phonetic variations of a single sound.

Examples of other minimal pairs in English are /p/ and /s/, as in "pat" and "sat," and /p/ and /f/, as in "pat" and "fat." By testing minimal pairs and noting structural similarities and dissimilarities between sounds, the total range of phonemes in a language can be mapped.

No language permits a random arrangement of sounds in the formation of words. Thus, the sound /ng/ in English is normally permitted only in the middle or at the end of a word. Most Americans find it difficult to pronounce names borrowed from other languages, like "Ngoro," or nonsense words like "ngis." The latter can be pronounced correctly with a little self-deception by going through the paradigm "singing," "inging," "nginging," and "ngis." Obviously, each language has complex rules regulating its particular arrangement of sounds, and these must be discovered in order to describe its phonetic structure completely.

But languages use more than basic sounds to convey meaning. Variations in tone, loudness, stress, inflection, and speed can make subtle alterations in the meaning of a sentence or change it completely. The English sentence "He went to jail" can be a question, a matter of fact statement, or an expression of surprise or foreboding, depending on inflection and stress.

Grammar Linguists are interested not only in systems of sound, but also in how these sounds relate to meaning. Such study, called grammar, divides broadly in two parts: "morphology," the study of words and how they are formed, and "syntax," the study of rules by which words are combined into meaningful sentences and groups of sentences.

"Morphemes" are the smallest units of meaning in a language and may be words or parts of words. "Touch," for example, can be used as a "free morpheme," a word by itself. It can also be used as a "root," to which "bound morphemes" (morphemes which cannot stand alone) are attached in the form of prefixes and suffixes, as in "untouchable." Finally, it can be combined with other root morphemes to form complex words, such as "touchdown," "touchtype" or "touch-me-not."

Morphological changes in words are often associated with phonetic shifts. This may be seen in the rule that permits many nouns to change to plural in English by the addition of an "s." The different phonetic consequences for different words is shown by contrasting what happens to the "s" in the plurals of "bat," "hand," and "house." In "bats," the "s" is pronounced /s/; in "hands," it becomes /z/; and in "houses," not only is the last "s" pronounced /z/, but also the middle "s" changes from an /s/ to a /z/.

"Syntax" refers to the structural rules by which morphemes are grouped into meaningful phrases and sentences. In the sentence, "The lady is going to town tomorrow," we can see the pattern that is typical of most English sentences: subject + verb + qualifiers. If the order is changed (verb + subject + qualifiers), the statement becomes a question: "Is the lady going to town tomorrow?" Sense can be made of an arrangement such as, "The lady to town is going tomorrow," but the listener is aware that something is wrong. He may assume the speaker is a foreigner. However, an arrangement such as, "Town tomorrow lady going to is the," is meaningless.

Syntax deals not only with the order of words but also with their relationships to each other. In English, as in many languages, there must be agreement in number between the subject and verb and in time between verbs and other morphemes indicating time. One does not say, "The lady am going to town now," nor "The lady went to town tomorrow."

In all languages, there is much redundancy or repetition of information in the matrix or framework within which the message is cast. In the sentence we have been considering, the number of actors is communicated by both a singular noun, "lady," and a singular verb, "is." Time orientation is repeated in the verb and in the adverb, "tomorrow." Such redundancy serves a purpose in reducing the possibility of error or misunderstanding in communication.

Phonetics and grammar provide us with the rules of sound and the structure of a language, but alone they are still not sufficient to teach us how to speak a language properly. The sentence "The town is going to lady tomorrow," is phonetically and grammatically correct, because "town" and "lady" are both nouns and theoretically interchangeable, but the sentence is meaningless, nonetheless.

Problems like this led the linguist Noam Chomsky and others to develop a transformational model of language (Chomsky 1968). By means of this model, they hope to explain not only the basic patterns of sound and grammar which lie at the surface of a language but also the deeper, more subtle structures which relate structure to meaning.

How can people, with a limited number of sounds and structural forms, create an infinite variety of sentences, which they may never have heard or said before? How do listeners decode complicated sentences and understand the fine shades of meaning in them? Only recently are anthropologists becoming aware of the complexities of language; yet by the age of four or five, the average person has learned to master them to a surprising degree.

Language and culture Languages are cultural phenomena and are not biologically determined. While people of one race may in general speak a language different from those of another, this is due to geographic and cultural isolation rather than to genetic factors. There is no inherent relationship between particular languages and specific races.

However, there is a close relationship between the language and other aspects of a culture, and for this reason, anthropological linguists have been interested in the connections between dialects and subcultural groups, based on social, class, and ethnic differences and on geographic distribution. Linguistic differences can be found, for example, between professors, politicians, and laborers. The natures of linguistic boundaries and multilingualism, together with the influence of social contexts on languages, have also attracted much study.

Recently, some anthropologists have begun to analyze the meanings of words in an attempt to explore the cognitive domains of other languages and cultures. The objective of this new disciplinary focus, known as "ethnoscience," is to arrive at an emic view of cultures, that is, to see the world as other people see it.

The method of ethnoscience consists primarily in mapping the boundaries of word meanings and their relationships to each other. For example, the English words "rain," "hail," and "snow" are distinct concepts within the broader category "precipitation." "Showers," "downpours," and "drizzles," on the other hand, are subdivisions of "rain." By applying this process to various areas of language, cognitive taxonomies can be developed which show how people divide their mental worlds. Moreover, these taxonomies can be compared with similar studies of cultural behavior. One of the important contributions of ethnoscience has been to provide anthropologists with a precise method for studying the semantic and cognitive structures of a language.

DIACHRONIC STUDIES OF LANGUAGE Languages continually change, and studies of their change have given anthropologists additional insights into the nature and history of language. These studies have taken two forms: the comparative method and glottochronology.

The comparative method It is possible to study linguistic changes by comparing languages and noting identical words, although it cannot be inferred from a few words resembling each other in meaning and sound that particular languages are related. Under the law of limited possibilities, there is always a statistical probability that some words in any two languages will be similar. If, however, more than eight percent of the basic words, such as "I," "you," "are," and "is," are similar in two languages, the probability that there is some historical relationship between them is exceedingly high.

Since languages do borrow from each other, some linguistic similarities can be explained by this practice. For the most part, however, borrowing is restricted to cultural items, such as the borrowed words in English, "pyjama," "kayak," and "taboo." Basic words, such as "he," "she," and "I," and names for parts of the body are less likely to cross linguistic boundaries.

A second explanation is genetic descent. If a speech community is split into regional groups by migration and geographic separation, each group will develop its own dialect. In time, and especially if communication between them ceases, the differences between the dialects become so great that they are no longer mutually intelligible. The result is a genetic derivation of two languages from a common ancestral one.

Early in the nineteenth century, Jacob and Wilhelm Grimm collected and compared fairy tales from a number of Indo-European languages and formulated what became known as Grimm's Law of phonetic change. This law described the manner in which sound changes within a language tend to follow definite patterns. For example, the Latin sound /p/ regularly became /f/ in German and English words

Three English versions of the Lord's Prayer

The Lord's Prayer in Pidgin English (with a literal translation)

Papa blong mipela i stop on top
Narim blong yu i tambu
Lotu blong yu i hom long mipela
Mipela doon alasaem ol ontop
I harim tok boy blong yu
Yu bringum kai kai teden long mipela
Yu larim mipela alasaem mipela larumol
Yu no bringum mipela kloster long rot i nogut
Yu lusim altogeta somting i nogut
I rousa long mipela. Amen.

Father belongs myself he lives on top,
Name belong you he holy.
Spirit belong you he comes to me.
Myself down (below) all the same on top.
He hears me talking to you.
You bring me food today for myself.
You teach (learn) me, likewise me learn all.
You don't bring me close to the road that is no good.
You take away everything that is bad.
He looks after me. Amen.

The Lord's Prayer in 1350 (after the Norman Conquest, when English had a tang of French to it)

Oure Fadir that art in heuenes, halwid be thi name; thi kyngdom cumme to; be thi wille done as in heuen and in earth; gif to vs this day oure breed oure other substaunce; and forgeve to vs oure dettis, as we forgeve to oure dettours; and leede vs nat in to temptacioun, but delyuere vs fro yuel. Amen.

The Lord's Prayer in 1000 A.D. (when English was in its Teutonic infancy)

Faeder ure thu the eart on heofonum; si thin name gahalgod. To-becume thin rice. Gewurthe thin wille on eorthan swa swa on heofonum. Urne gedaeghwamlican hlaf syle us to daeg. And forgyf us ure gyltas swa swa we forgyfath urum gyltendum. And ne gelaed thu us on costnunge ac alys us of yfele. Sothlice.

derived from Latin: pater–father; pro–for; piscis–fish. Similarly, Latin /t/ sounds regularly became /th/ in English: tres–three; tu–thou.

By applying this method of comparing vocabularies and phonetic structures, it has been possible to group the languages of the world into a limited number of family trees. Most of the languages of the Old World, from English, French, German, and Spanish to Persian, Pashto, and Hindi, can be traced back to a single proto–Indo–European stock. Similarly, the languages of Africa and North and South America, as well as other parts of the world, can be grouped into families, according to the degree of relationship between them.

Glottochronology A second way to study linguistic change is to compare written forms of the same language over different periods of time. The spoken word could not be preserved for the archaeologist before the recording came into use, but written records go back several millenia in some instances.

By comparing written records over long periods of time, M. Swadesh, an early linguist, found that only about nineteen percent of a language's basic vocabulary changed every 1,000 years. By drawing up and testing lists of basic words, such as pronouns, names for parts of the body, and general verbs, and by statistical methods, linguists have developed a method known as "glottochronology" for measuring linguistic change. Applying this method to the present-day vocabularies of related languages, they are able to determine the approximate date the languages split from a common parent language. (See Figure 6.4.)

Underlying glottochronology is the assumption that the basic vocabularies of all languages change at the same uniform rate, but recently this has been called into question. Nevertheless, the approach can give us some clues to the broad historical movements of peoples where no other historical information is available.

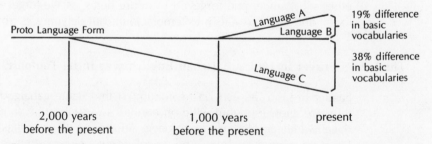

Figure 6.4 Glottochronology attempts to trace common historical origins of languages by comparing lists of basic vocabularies.

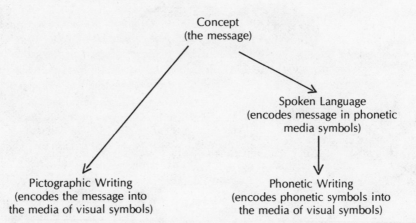

Concept
(the message)

Spoken Language
(encodes message in phonetic
media symbols)

Pictographic Writing
(encodes the message into
the media of visual symbols)

Phonetic Writing
(encodes phonetic symbols into
the media of visual symbols)

Figure 6.5 Pictographic and phonetic systems of writing encode different concepts.

WRITING One of the earliest and most universal means of human communication is speech, but until the modern era of voice recordings, speech had two significant limitations: it was restricted in time to the present, and it could be heard only by those within listening distance of the speaker. These limitations were historically overcome by the use of signs and written language.

Throughout the world, people use objects to communicate ideas. Sticks, rocks, knots on string, and beads are widely employed to keep count of things, like cattle and sheep. Shells, feathers, palm nuts, large stone doughnuts, pieces of metal or paper, and even human skulls have served as indicators of economic value. But the use of objects to develop a system similar to language for communicating ideas appears to have been impractical, for none has been created by man.

True writing is basically speech encoded in visual symbolic forms, although not all visual symbols are writing. Pictures communicate ideas, but although they often follow cultural conventions, they are not considered writing; nor are stylized decorations, such as pottery, that may express meanings.

In the first writing systems, such as the Egyptian, Sumerian, and Chinese, visual signs represented words rather than sounds, and each character conveyed an idea. One result of such a system today is that two Chinese people may speak mutually unintelligible dialects but read the same newspapers. A similar phenomenon can be seen in mathematical equations, which are understood around the world by people who speak many different languages. (See Figure 6.5.)

The creation of phonetic signs, in which alphabetic letters repre-

Children of different ages in Uhehe, Tanzania communicate with the ease and directness common to children everywhere.
Photo courtesy of E.V. Winans.

sented language sounds rather than ideas, had certain advantages and disadvantages. Because the number of phonemes in a language is limited to a few dozen at most, the number of signs needed to represent them also is limited. Instead of a sign for every word in the vocabulary, only one sign for each sound is needed.

The efficiency of this close tie between writing and speech is obvious, and the rapid spread of alphabetic writing around the world testifies to its advantages. On the other hand, the close tie between writing and language means that written communications can be understood only by those who know the language.

OTHER MEDIA People have created media other than language and writing to convey their messages. Kinesics is communication by means of gestures and body actions. Americans point to things with their index fingers, a gesture considered obscene in some societies, where the hand, head, or lower lip is used to point. Facial expressions convey a great many subtle messages in ordinary conversation, with the result that an inexpressive or deadpan face is cause for unease.

People communicate with sounds other than language, such as car horns, church bells, clapping, and hisses. They use artifacts, like dress, beards, crosses, stars, and crescents; touch, like holding hands, kissing, and pulling ears; smells, like perfumes, incense, and tracers in gas lines; and tastes, like ethnic foods and birthday cakes.

And, as we have already seen in Chapter 2, humans use time and space to communicate important information. There appear to be few avenues humans have left unexplored as potential media for communicating their ideas.

The message

We have already noted that meanings reside in people, not in symbols or media, and for this reason, we cannot speak of a message, only of the message as understood by various individuals. For example, the usual definition of meaning in communication is that the sender wishes the receiver to understand certain things by means of his message. On the other hand, the receiver has his own understanding of the message, which may differ considerably from that of the sender. Later, students of history will have their own ideas of what the sender and the receiver understood by a particular message. Thus, if we consider the U.S. Constitution to be a message from the founding fathers, the Supreme Court becomes the interpreter of the message.

Communication is a cyclic process, as information is passed from the sender to the receiver, who in turn feeds his responses back to the sender by various channels. During a lecture, students transmit their feelings by facial expressions, such as smiles or yawns, and by means of body movements. The teacher, in turn, adjusts his message, taking into account the students' feedback, and they in turn react to the new message with increased attention or boredom. Communication is comprised of a great many such cycles. (See Figure 6.6.)

The importance of feedback can be seen by noting what happens when it is withheld. Anyone talking on the phone depends on a frequent grunt from his listener for assurance that he is still listening, just as in conversation, speakers depend on facial gestures to convey the same information. If the listener does not provide this feedback on the phone, the speaker demands a response with the question, "Are you still there?" Effective communicators are sensitive to the feedback from their audience and continually adjust their message to make sure of good reception.

In every communication, there is a certain amount of noise or static—anything that interferes with the reception of the message. A blinding headache, a noisy neighbor, or a cold room can distract the listener at a concert, as can outlandish dress, bad manners, or bad

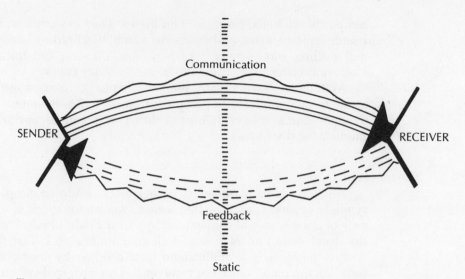

Figure 6.6 Interpersonal communication is a series of ongoing cycles of sending messages and responding to feedback from the receiver.

breath at a party. Like the message, static is related to the receiver. What distracts one person may convey meaning to another, as young people who enjoy modern rock music know very well.

Finally, the message is closely related to the general context within which the communication occurs. One normally does not propose marriage in a classroom, in the style of a lecture, nor does one crack a joke at a funeral.

Summary

All people create symbols by linking ideas to forms of expression, and all people arrange symbols into elaborate systems, whereby they store and communicate these ideas. Languages, in their spoken and written forms, have been the most important media for communication in human societies. People devise these systems to express their thoughts, but in turn the systems become the molds in which thought takes place.

The transmission of culture involves communication, in which senders encode their messages into the media of one or more of these symbol systems for transmission to receivers, who, in turn, decode them. In this process, a number of biases are introduced, including the sender's and the receiver's respective cultural and personal biases. The result, particularly in cross-cultural communication, is often a loss or misinterpretation of the message.

Because they were often faced with languages having no written form, anthropologists were forced to develop new techniques for learning languages. In doing so, they discovered the complex phonetic and morphological structures within language and applied this knowledge to the study of cultural history. More recently, anthropologists have begun the study of other, more subtle media of communication, such as the use of time and space.

Symbolic systems are important, because they form the core of any culture, linking thought to behavior and objects, and thereby bringing a measure of order and meaning to life, itself.

Suggested readings

Bollinger, D.
  1968   Aspects of Language. New York: Harcourt Brace Jovanovich. (A technical discussion of linguistics and some methods of learning a second language.)
Burling, R.
  1970   Man's Many Voices: Language in Its Cultural Context. New York: Holt, Rinehart and Winston. (A good discussion of the relationship of language to its sociocultural context.)
Gudschinsky, S.C.
  1964   The ABC's of Lexicostatistics (Glottochronology). In Language in Culture and Society: A Reader in Linguistics and Anthropology. D. Hymes, ed. New York: Harper and Row. (A very useful survey of the state of the art in glottochronology.)
Hymes, D. ed.
  1964   Language in Culture and Society: A Reader in Linguistics and Anthropology. New York: Harper and Row. (A comprehensive set of readings on all major areas of modern sociolinguistics.)
Kochman, Thomas
  1975   Toward an Ethnography of Black American Speech Behavior. In Cultural and Social Anthropology: Introductory Readings in Ethnology. P.B. Hammond, ed. New York: Macmillan Publishing Co. (An interesting analysis of black English in America and how it fits into the American society.)

Key concepts
Characteristics of statuses and roles

Statuses, roles, and relationships

The teacher entered the classroom, seated himself near the front, and began to read a novel. At first, the students were surprised and amused and then, as the minutes passed, confused and resentful. What was going on? Did they have to stay if there was going to be no class? Only when the teacher stood up and took his place at the front of the class did the students relax, letting their minds wander over plans for the evening or catching some much-needed rest. What had gone wrong? Why the confusion?

Social anthropology is the study of human interaction, of what makes relationships possible and what causes them to break down. It is the study of an important part of our lives, for much of human life centers around other people. Our greatest joys, our deepest sorrows, and our most difficult problems relate, for the most part, to our interactions with others.

Even a brief study of human interaction is enough to convince one that interpersonal behavior is largely patterned. Each culture has its own acceptable ways of conversing, gesturing, loving, and fighting. When a person's actions do not fit these expectations, as in the case of the teacher above, confusion results. The patterns of interpersonal behavior characteristic of a society are collectively referred to as its "social organization."

Social organizations can be studied on three levels: the organization of interpersonal relations, the organization of groups, and the organization of society. At the simplest level, all relationships can be seen as interactions between pairs of individuals. For example, in the instance above, an observer could watch the reaction of each student to the teacher's action and the interaction of each student with the other students around him for interpersonal relations. On another level, the observer could look at the interaction of groups of people: at the students, the teachers, the administrators, and the parents who want to know what is going on in school. On a still higher level, social organization can be analyzed in terms of the total society. How do colleges and universities fit into American society! How does the American educational system compare with that of the Chinese or the Nigerians?

In this chapter, we will look at the organization of interpersonal relationships. The broader organizations of groups and societies will be considered in Chapters 9–14.

Key concepts

Concepts and their symbolic forms, words, are the tools a social scientist uses to analyze his data. On the one hand, new concepts provide him with a more precise and shorthand way of expressing existing ideas. Take, for example, the following excerpts from a popular hi-fi magazine. The technical terms may be jargon to the general reader, but to the music enthusiast, they convey clear and often exciting information. Similar specialized vocabularies have been developed in photography, auto mechanics, tailoring, and many other popular fields.

On the other hand, new concepts also provide us with new ways of

Advertisement for a Quadraphonic Receiver

examining existing data and open up new areas for investigation. In this chapter, we shall use two concepts, "status" and "role," to show how carefully defined concepts can give us additional insights into human relationships.

Statuses

Like so many other terms, "status" has come to have a number of meanings. In ordinary conversation, we often use the word with reference to a person's general position in a society. For example, we say that a person has a "marginal" status or a "low" status. The former is a gross stereotyping of individuals into a general category within the society. The latter is a comment on what esteem or social approval people give to one of their fellows on the basis of some socially significant characteristic, such as the kinds of clothes he wears, the kind of house he lives in, or the job he has. Most social scientists use the word "rank" for such esteem.

Ralph Linton, an American anthropologist (1893–1953), gave a more precise definition to the word "status," one that has had wide acceptance in the social sciences. He defined "status" as a position in a social system occupied by designated individuals. Linton saw social organization at the level of interpersonal relationships as made up of a number of socially defined positions, such as teachers, priests, merchants, fathers, mothers, carpenters, and so on. The number and nature of statuses varies a great deal from society to society. But each society assigns all of its members to one or more social positions, for only then does a person have a social identity and a place in social interactions.

Roles

Every society has certain behavioral expectations of people who occupy a certain status. In the United States, for instance, we have an idea of how teachers should act, and we expect them to behave differently from employers, friends, parents, or bartenders. We refer to the behavioral expectations associated with a specific social status as its "role."

All people in a society have some idea of ideal role behavior, that is, the proper or exemplary ways people in any given status should behave. We, for instance, generally know how teachers and students *should* act. In practice, of course, a great deal of variation is permitted in the roles. Some teachers stand, some sit, and some wander around the room. The teacher may be a bad teacher but be considered a teacher, nonetheless.

There comes a point in role behavior when even the minimum role requirements are not met, and the person loses his status. A student may no longer be recognized as such by the society if he begins to riot or hires outsiders to write his tests and term papers. The term "role performance" is used for the way a person's behavior is assessed by his or her associates. (See Table 7.1.)

Role sets and status sets

The relationship between statuses and roles is a complex one. A little reflection should make it clear that a single status is often associated with a number of roles. For example, a teacher, because of his status, has certain role relationships to his students, his colleagues, the president or principal, and the alumni or P.T.A., to name a few. Each of these roles is different, yet all arise out of his particular status. The term "role set" is often used to designate the group of roles associated with any one status.

It is also obvious that the same individual occupies a number of different statuses at any one stage in his life. To return to our teacher, he may be a Democrat, a Presbyterian, a husband, a father, a member of the

Table 7.1   The Range of Role Behavior

Role Performance	Range of Behavior
Acceptable	ideal
	acceptable variations
	marginal
Unacceptable	deviant

Village barber in India attending to a customer.

bowling club, and have many other statuses in addition to his status as a teacher. Each of these statuses has its own role set and, taken together, all of the statuses constitute his "status set." Furthermore, some statuses in a status set form a natural "status cluster"—a group of statuses that commonly go together. For instance, the status of husband often leads to that of father and, later, grandfather. Likewise, a laborer may be expected to become a labor union member.

ROLE CONFLICT In everyday life, the individual moves freely from one status to the next and changes his behavior accordingly. At one moment, a person is a student, but at the bell, he turns into another type of social creature: a friend, a football player, or a waiter in a nearby café. To a stranger, the change in behavior can be dramatic.

The fact that the same individual occupies different statuses can lead to conflicts. The demands of his school for academic excellence may compete with those of his football team or job. To avoid the social and psychological tensions that arise from these conflicts, a person may use a number of different mechanisms. He may set certain priorities in his statuses (football comes before studies); he may ally himself with and seek the assistance of those in power (the coach can ask the teacher to excuse him from some assignments); he may make the conflicting demands known to other members in his role set (he can tell the teacher and the coach what the other is demanding); he can seek the support of others in similar difficulties (the team and student body can organize and put pressures on the administration); or he can break one of the role relationships (he can drop out of the team).

As we shall see later, this picture of interaction is complicated by the fact that individuals move through various role sequences in the course of a lifetime. The student becomes a teacher or businessperson and, finally, a retired member of the community. The child becomes a father or mother.

SOCIAL PROGRAMMING   Taken together, the statuses in a society provide it with a "social structure," a framework into which people are socially placed. Moreover, meanings and values are assigned to these statuses. The roles associated with them allow people in different statuses to interact smoothly and in predictable ways. People may seek to improve their situations and gain their goals by manuevering within the society, but they must generally do so within the role and status sets that are open to them. In one context, it is to a person's advantage to be known as a teacher or businessperson, in another, as a religious person, a Democrat, or a sportsperson.

To many people, it is upsetting to discover that much of human behavior is programmed by society, that relatively few of their own actions are based on rational and emotional decisions. The fact is, however, that without some mutually understood order, relationships end in chaos. Behavior, like language, is a symbolic way of communicating ideas, and to communicate, the symbols must be understood by all involved.

Furthermore, by structuring behavior and making it habit, we need not consciously make decisions about each act. To do so would take a great deal of energy, simply to maintain a relationship. Patterning of behavior helps us to relate to others efficiently and allows us to concentrate on the purposes for which the relationships are established—whether this is an economic transaction, social companionship, or something else.

Finally, order in relationships allows us to predict, to a degree, the actions of others and, therefore, to choose a course of action aimed at reaching our own personal goals. If no meaningful behavior patterns exist, relationships and planning break down completely.

Characteristics of statuses and roles

As we use concepts such as status and role to examine concrete social experiences, we are able to define their characteristics more precisely and to extend the range of their usefulness. It is this interaction between theoretical ideas and experiential data that leads to the growth of more general models.

Role pairs

All social relationships, for purposes of analysis, can be broken down into basic role pairs—into teacher and student, doctor and patient, employer and employee, and so forth. In any situation, the actors must select and agree upon a pair of socially defined statuses that are suitable for the interaction. So long as there is no agreement, smooth interaction is not possible. For example, when a student flirts with a professor, one or the other must change his or her role if a conflict in roles is to be avoided. Once a suitable status pair has been chosen, the associated roles of the actors will more or less complement one another, so long as each lives up to the social expectations of the role.

Role pairs provide us with a powerful tool for analyzing complex social relationships. For example, if we break the American family down into basic relationships, we end up with eight possible role pairs:

husband-wife	mother-daughter
father-son	brother-brother
father-daughter	brother-sister
mother-son	sister-sister

Each of these pairs has its own ideal role relationships. A man is expected to behave in one way towards a son, another way towards a daughter, and a third way towards his wife. When any family member deviates too far from these expectations, the organization of the family is threatened.

The study of the American family becomes more complex when we add the practices of adoption and remarriage or when we look at the broader ties of kinship. Children in one family are parents in another; moreover, they are linked by ties of marriage and kinship to still other families and individuals. Some of the secondary role pairs found in American families are as follows:

By remarriage and adoption:
stepmother-stepson
stepmother-stepdaughter

stepfather-stepson
stepfather-stepdaughter
father-adopted son
father-adopted daughter
mother-adopted son
mother-adopted daughter
By marriage alliances:
mother-in-law–daughter-in-law
mother-in-law–son-in-law
father-in-law–daughter-in-law
father-in-law–son-in-law
brother-in-law–brother-in-law
sister-in-law–sister-in-law
brother-in-law–sister-in-law
By descent:
grandmother-granddaughter
grandmother-grandson
grandfather-granddaughter
grandfather-grandson

The everyday behavior of actors in role pairs varies a great deal, according to a number of factors, such as the social context, the presence or absence of audiences, and the psychological attitudes of the actors at that moment. A husband treats his wife differently in church, at the store, in the home, or on the beach. He modifies his behavior when friends, children, parents-in-law, or strangers are around and according to how he feels that day towards his wife or the world in general.

Role expectations change over time. The ideal American father of a century ago was an authoritarian figure, a man of strength, and a breadwinner. Today, he is expected to be a companion to his son and a partner in marriage. When the change in roles is rapid, as in the case of the role of women in the modern Western world, a great deal of confusion and disagreement can arise.

Many of the tensions of early married life center around disagreements over the roles of the husband and wife in everyday situations. (See Figure 7.1.) Should a husband wash the dishes, do the laundry, or warm the baby's bottle? Should the wife handle the family accounts and help earn a living? The confusion stems not only from a question of the content of role behavior but also of where to look for new definitions or models of roles. Should people look to the past, to others in the society, or to mutual contracts to resolve the differences?

Role expectations also reflect cultural differences. Much of what we read or hear about the American family presents family roles from the white, middle-class perspective. Other American subcultural groups,

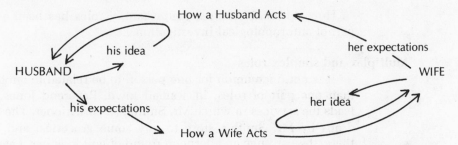

Figure 7.1 Role expectations in marriage involve both the self and the mate.

based on class and ethnic differences, define family roles in other ways. For this reason, marriages across subcultural boundaries are faced not only with working out personality adjustments to new and often changing roles but also with reconciling subcultural differences in role expectations.

Despite the variations in American family roles, there is a great deal of agreement on the fundamentals. This becomes obvious when we compare American families with those in other cultures. Some permit husbands to have more than one wife at one time, and others allow wives to have several husbands. Among the Trobriand Islanders of the South Seas, a man gives about half the yams he raises as food to his sister and her family, and he depends, in part, on the yams raised by his wife's brother. This is analogous to a man in the United States giving part of his paycheck to his sisters and receiving some of the earnings of his brothers-in-law.

Among the Kapauku of New Guinea, men marry as many wives as they can afford for an economic investment—the more wives a man has, the more fields he can cultivate. A husband can also "rent" one of his wives to a young man who cannot find one of his own.

The ideal wife in a south Indian village will avoid the proscribed behaviors described in the following folk poem.

> A wife who refuses the scraps from her husband's plate
>   will be reborn a buffalo,
> A wife who adorns herself with jewelry when her husband is away
>   will be reborn a pig,
> A wife who eats before her husband returns
>   will be reborn a dog,
> A wife who sleeps on the bed and gives her husband a mat
>   will be reborn a python,
> And a wife who murders her husband for another man
>   will be reborn a monkey.

How different cultures define family roles has been an important part of anthropological investigation.

Multiplex and simplex roles

It is not uncommon for one person to be related to another by more than one pair of roles. In a small town, Reverend Jones, the pastor, leads the services in which Mr. Smith is a parishioner. The next day, he drops by Mr. Smith's store to buy some groceries, and while he is there, they arrange an afternoon round of golf together. Later that week, they meet at the P.T.A., where Mr. Smith is the chairman and Reverend Jones is the treasurer.

Max Gluckman (1911–   ), a noted British anthropologist, has called the situation in which several role bonds exist between the same two persons "multiplex" relations. The opposite situation, in which an individual has only a single role relationship with another person, is called a "simplex" relationship. (See Figure 7.2.)

In multiplex relationships, we meet the same person in different social situations. Consequently, we become more aware of different facets of their lives, and in our conversations we are able to talk about a great many more areas of common interest. Discussions are no longer confined only to casual comments or to jobs, neighborhood, or beliefs. Because we interact with these people in many ways, we get the feeling we can see through the roles to the persons behind them. But the price of knowing others is to be known. When multiplex relations exist in a community, it is difficult to maintain personal privacy. Our acquaintances are not divided into groups of people between whom there is no communication. What we do in one area of life is soon known to the whole community.

Multiplex relations often lead to conflicts between different roles. In

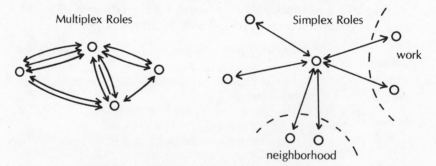

Figure 7.2 Multiplex and simplex role relationships are determined by the number of role relationships between any two people.

any given social context, people interact on the basis of a single role pair, but they cannot completely forget the other roles that relate them. In other words, there is "role feedback." Mr. Smith wonders if he should give his pastor a discount when he shops in the store. The professor feels uneasy about failing his friend's wife, who is in the class, and gives her the benefit of the doubt—an "A." It is the attempt to avoid such role conflicts that lies behind rules against nepotism.

Multiplex relations are particularly common in small societies, such as the small American town. The same people go to church together, meet at the P.T.A., do business with each other, and visit over the back fences. Their institutions, such as their schools, businesses, and churches, need to serve only single functions, because the people acquire a sense of community through interaction in many different social contexts.

By contrast, urban relationships are often simplex. We meet a great many people in the city but most in are single role relationships. You might exchange, in passing, a few remarks on the weather, sports, or some other general, nonthreatening topic with the checker in the supermarket where you shop. And, in time, all lines being equal in length, you may choose his line, because he will approve your check without

Student and teacher in India.
Photo courtesy of Margaret Adams.

identification. After all, he *knows* you. However, if you see him on the street the next day, you may be confused. The face is familiar, but you cannot place it. Only later, when you return to the store do you put face and place together. The checker is a part of the economic transaction and is not thought of in any other social situation.

Because urban relations are often simplex, cities are often charged with being impersonal. The fact is, people in cities meet a great many other people, too many to learn to know intimately, for intimacy requires time and effort. Moreover, city people are forced into groups, whose members have little in common. These people are associates at work, those are neighbors, and there is little or no overlap or communication between them. So city people often feel that their lives are fragmented.

But intimate, holistic relationships do develop in cities. People choose from among the circles of their associates and identify with one or another of the groups more closely. Within one group, they often develop multiplex relationships. For instance, people who work together may bowl together and later invite each other's families out to dinner. Faced with a great many social relationships, building intimacy in a city often takes more effort. There is less of the small-town group pressure to participate in community activities.

Personal and impersonal roles

Roles differ also in the degree of intimacy involved in the relationship. Some roles are masks worn only for specific occasions, as for instance, when the clerk smiles and thanks you for shopping at the store where he works or when a professor assumes an oratorical voice to lecture. Other roles involve closer relationships and a greater degree of personal exposure.

Tournier, a Swiss psychiatrist, speaks of the "personage" as the outer social mask or role a person wears, and of the "person" as the personal thoughts, feelings, and actions of the individual. In impersonal relationships, interaction takes place primarily on the basis of formally structured roles, or as "personage-to-personage." Loewen (1922-   ), an American linguist, has also called communication at this level "station-to-station" communication. In impersonal relationships, we are not particularly concerned with who occupies the role, only that someone does. For example, we do not particularly care who checks out our groceries, as long as someone is at the cash register.

In some impersonal relationships, interaction is at a minimum, and communication proceeds in one direction. A guide leads a tour through the museum or a teacher repeats the same lecture he has given for the past twenty years. Loewen labels this type of communication "this-is-a-recording."

On the other end of the continuum are deeply personal relationships, where the level of communication is "person-to-person." It does make a difference in these cases who the other person is. For example, we *are* particular about whom we marry.

Ascribed and achieved statuses

People are born to certain statuses. A woman may be born a princess, an heir to an industrial empire, or an outcaste. In fact, through birth, everyone acquires certain characteristics, such as sex, class, ethnicity, and geographic location, that affect his social position. These statuses are called "ascribed" statuses. "Achieved" statuses, on the other hand, are gained by effort or by circumstances. A person may acquire wealth, education, or a vocation by his own efforts.

Some societies, such as the American, stress achieved roles. We believe people should be able to rise to the highest level of their ability and efforts. Life does not usually work out this way, and there is, as a consequence, a great deal of competition and up-and-down mobility in the society. It is possible for some people to become rich or highly educated through hard work, and those of high birth are not guaranteed a high status for life. Close social relationships often break, as people

Nurse Bernice Johnson observing a trainee extract a tooth at the West Indies Mission Hospital dental clinic, Aux Cayes, Haiti.
Photo courtesy of Vaughn Chapman.

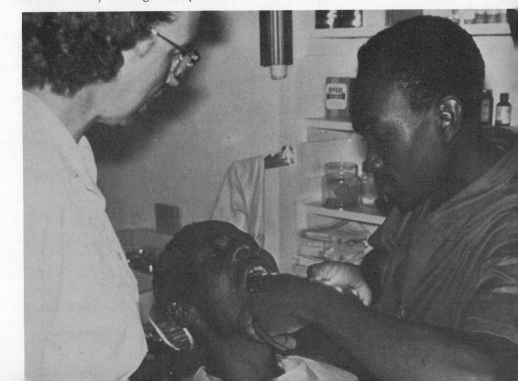

move from one social class to another or from one part of the country to another. Even family ties suffer when one son becomes a wealthy doctor or executive and the others, like the father, remain blue-collar workers. The high degree of social mobility and the lack of strong group ties often lead, in such societies, to a sense of insecurity.

Some societies, on the other hand, emphasize ascribed roles. An Indian villager, for example, is born into a caste which not only provides him with a general social position and clearly defined ways of life but also dictates whom he can marry, when and how he should bathe, what he should eat, where he should live, and the way he should be buried. In many cases, it also provides him with a job, clients, and servicepeople, whom he inherits from his father. Thus, a farmer inherits his carpenter, blacksmith, potter, barber, washerman, and many of his fieldworkers, who can claim the right to work for him. If he fires them, no one else in their caste will work for him, and those outside the caste do not do those jobs.

While there is a great deal of competition even within such a rigid social system for status, wealth, and power, the caste system does provide a person with a measure of security in his social position.

Vertical and horizontal roles

Human relationships also vary in the extent to which they are egalitarian or hierarchical. Master-slave, employer-employee, teacher-student, and parent-child are examples of hierarchical or "vertical" role pairs in American society, in which one person assumes a social position superior to the other. Friends, work associates, neighbors, and brothers and sisters are generally thought to be egalitarian or "horizontal." Husband-wife relations are becoming increasingly egalitarian.

In many societies around the world, hereditary vertical roles, called "patron-client" relationships, are common. The patron is a master who assumes full responsibility for the welfare of his clients, seeing to it that they have at least a minimum of food, shelter, and protection. In one sense, he is their father. Clients, in turn, must give their patron their full loyalty and labor. They not only work in his fields and household but also vote for him if he runs for office and wield sticks on his behalf if there is a fight. In exchange, they get security and the prestige of associating with an important man. In such systems, there is little or no calculation of whether the values and services exchanged are equal. The relationship is one of mutual interdependence.

Americans often misunderstand the fundamental nature of patron-client relationships. Taught to value their freedom and contractual relationships, in which the independence of each of the actors is preserved, they see such relationships as exploitive. Above all, they find it hard to be obliged to someone else. For example, one American administrator in a South Indian hospital fired the washermen when they staged a work slowdown for higher wages. He soon found out that no one else would do the work, because the original washermen's families had acquired the publicly recognized hereditary right to work in the hospital. In the end, he had no recourse but to hire them back to negotiate wages.

Similarly, an anthropologist living in a village in India developed hereditary relationships not only to a barber, washerman, and several other workers but also to two beggers, who had their self-appointed days to receive gifts. Moreover, whenever he returned from a prolonged absence, the beggars carefully calculated the number of times he had missed giving them gifts and expected him to pay them a suitably larger sum. He knew that if he refused them, they would sing of his miserliness on their door-to-door rounds of the village.

Cross-cultural role confusion

Roles, like other traits, vary from culture to culture. Much of the confusion of moving from one culture to another arises from a misunderstanding of the behavioral ideals and patterns of the new culture.

One type of confusion arises when the native culture and the new culture have similar statuses associated with different roles. American teachers are often surprised and uneasy when students in some foreign countries stand and salute them as they enter the classroom. And unaccustomed to bargaining over their purchases, they and their American colleagues may return from the marketplace with a sense of guilt at having driven too hard a bargain or resenting having been cheated or having wasted time. In other societies, Americans are frustrated by the fact that they must visit with a shopkeeper over a cup of tea before they can make their purchases, not realizing that in these societies building personal relationships is essential, even for purely economic transactions.

A second type of cross-cultural role confusion appears when an outsider tries to play a role that does not exist in the new culture. What, for example, do people in a nonliterate village think when a stranger announces he is an "anthropologist"? Having no idea of what such a creature is, they can only observe his behavior to see what role in their society he fits most closely and assume that this, in fact, is what he really is. They may end up classifying him as a government official, a rich patron, a teacher, or a spy. The problem is that if he does not live up to the expectations of the role they have assigned to him, they may charge him with hypocrisy. It is important, therefore, that an outsider choose a role understood by the people or, at least, be aware of the role in which they have cast him. To fail to do so can create continual misunderstandings and possible rejection.

Summary

Social organization can be studied at several levels: individual interaction, group dynamics, and the structure of a society.

The concepts of status and role are fundamental to the understandings of interpersonal relationships within a society. Statuses are socially defined positions within the social structure. A person who occupies a status is expected to behave in certain ways, and these behavioral expectations are referred to as a role. All the roles related to a specific status are referred to as its role set. People have more than one status in a society, and all the statuses they have at any one time constitute a status set.

All social interaction can be broken down into simple role relationships for purposes of analysis. The structure of a society consists of sets of statuses and roles linked together in networks, and, as we shall see in Chapter 9, into institutions. The picture is complicated by the facts that people can share more than one pair of role relationships, a situation we refer to as multiplex relationships, and that the characteristics of the roles themselves vary a great deal. Some are personal and others are impersonal; some are ascribed and others achieved; and some are vertical and others horizontal.

The study of how cultures define their statuses and roles, and the differences between them, has constituted an important part of social anthropology.

Suggested readings

Berne, Eric
   1964   Games People Play. New York: Grove Press. (This bestseller introduced the basic ideas of transactional analysis and is a useful introduction to the concept of social games.)
Goodenough, W.H.
   1965   Rethinking "Status" and "Role": Toward a General Model of the Cultural Organization of Social Relationships. In The Relevance of Models for Social Anthropology. M. Banton, ed. New York: F.A. Praeger. (A reevaluation of the concepts "status" and "role" based on the author's work in the Truk Islands.)

1970   Description and Comparison in Cultural Anthropology. Chicago: Aldine Publishing Co. (A careful analysis of factors related to systems of kinship terminology.)

Mead, Margaret

1940   Male and Female: A Study of the Sexes in the Changing World. New York: Morrow. (An early classic in the roles of sexes around the world.)

8 Life cycles
Rites of passage

The life cycle

Time is a dimension of experience that no social scientist can ignore. Change is a fact of life. That anthropologists must include this dimension in any explanatory model of human beings is clear, but how to do so is not so obvious. The problem, in part, lies in the application of conceptual models. When we describe cultures and societies as orderly patterns of thought and action, the cultures appear to be stable, unchanging systems. When we introduce the concepts of change and flux, this order seems to vanish. Even as we are describing the relationships between various parts of a culture, these relationships are changing and assuming new forms. Where, then, do we find any pattern or order? Clearly, our models must take into account both the order which persists over time and the change that threatens its existence.

One way to include time in anthropological models is to take events in their historical contexts—to arrange experiences along the dimension of time and assume that the more recent ones are related to those that preceded them. We might, for example, explain a culture or, for that matter, an individual in terms of historical past. And, in fact, cultural histories and personal biographies have played an important part in anthropological literature.

A second way to deal with time is to look for cyclical processes (things repeat themselves again and again in our experiences) and to examine the order that underlies this repetition. For instance, days and nights and summers and winters are nature's metronomes, affecting not only our biological systems but also our cultural activities. Every society has its own established routines: times to eat, work, relax, and sleep. In some societies, the number of days in a week may differ from our own seven-day weeks which include weekends. Other cultures have no weekly cycles at all. Longer cultural cycles include lunar fortnights, months, annual seasons, and groups of years—each of which may play an important part in accounting for order within a culture.

Life, itself, is a biological cycle of birth, childhood, maturity, and death, a cycle that every society must take into account. Since it is our concern in this chapter to examine cultural patterns at the level of the individual, let us look into how societies deal with this cycle of human life.

Life cycles

Several approaches to the study of life cycles are possible. Demographers are concerned with how such phenomena as late marriages, epidemic diseases, ecological constraints, and wars affect people's lives and the growth of populations. Anthropologists also record the life histories of individuals, in order to gain insights into their cultures and the changes that occur within a lifetime.

A third approach is to trace the various life patterns permitted within particular societies. For instance, in the United States, a person may become a farmer, doctor, businessperson or teacher or enter one of many other occupations. In hunting and gathering societies, the number of alternative life careers is limited and may even be restricted to the simple distinction between males and females that is found in all societies. With the possible exception of the religious shamans, all men follow the same general pattern of life in hunting and gathering societies; women do likewise. In peasant societies and increasingly more so in urban industrial societies, the number of alternative life careers and styles increases markedly. This becomes obvious if you attempt to catalogue the various life patterns open to the average American.

A fourth way to study the life cycle of an individual is to examine the sequence of statuses he occupies in the course of his lifetime. For example, an American adult may go through the following status series: child, adolescent, college student, teacher, administrator, retired person. At the same time, he or she is moving from single to married to parent to grandparent and, possibly, from one social class to another.

The life cycle of the American family

A simple way to begin thinking about life cycles is to look at American families. American families vary greatly in the life spans of members, the number and spacing of the children, and the occurrence of divorce. Nevertheless, a study of the American family in the mid-twentieth century by Glick and Parke (1965) based on census statistics throws considerable light on what a normal family may expect. The following picture is drawn from 1960 statistics.

The average American woman marries by age twenty, the man by twenty-two. The couple's exclusive companionship is often short-lived, for the first child generally arrives within the first two years of marriage. For the following twenty-five years, there are children in the home. The last child is usually born when the mother is about thirty, and family life-styles change as the children grow older and assume more responsibilities. During this period, family income rises, reaching a peak when the husband is between forty-five and fifty-five years of age. Later, income falls, gradually at first, more abruptly at retirement, until it reaches a point below that for young families.

When the parents' ages range between forty-five and fifty-five years, the children are all launched into the world on their own careers. The marriage of the last child reduces the family to the original couple, assuming, of course, that both are alive and still living together. On an average, husband and wife share sixteen years together before one dies. Two thirds of all brides become widows, surviving their husbands by about nineteen years. Husbands who outlive their wives can expect to be widowers for about fourteen years.

Rites of passage

Comparing life cycles in a number of societies, the anthropologist Arnold van Gennep (1873–1957) noted in his classical work *Les Rites de Passage* (1909) that most societies have rituals marking the transition of an individual or a group of individuals from one important status to another. Americans, for example, have a number of transitional rituals, or "rites of passage" as van Gennep termed them: weddings, funerals, graduation ceremonies, military promotions, ordination rites, and so on. Some of these, particularly those associated with the biological cycle of birth, maturation, procreation, and death, are found in most societies, although obviously they are celebrated differently.

This chapter presents a brief study of these rites, to illustrate the importance of rituals in the human life cycle.

Birth rites

All societies must admit new members in order to survive, and, with few exceptions, such addition is by birth. But simply bearing children is not enough; they must be assigned a place in the society and taught its ways if they are to survive. Rituals associated with birth are one of the ways a society admits and incorporates new members into its ranks and recognizes the changes that take place in the roles of others when this occurs.

According to van Gennep, birth rituals, like other rites of passage, generally have three phases. The first is that of "separation," in which those involved in the birth are removed from their past statuses. This applies primarily to the mother, especially in those societies where a pregnant woman must live away from other people, in a special maternity hut, and observe taboos on sexual relations and certain foods. In America, the separation of an expectant mother from her previous roles in preparation for her new role as mother is not so clearly defined, at least not until the time of delivery. Nonetheless, subtle changes do take place in the way a woman is treated when others become aware of her pregnancy.

The second phase is one of "transition," in which individuals undergo a change to the new status. During this time, there may be rituals to guard them from the dangers that confront those in transition, to assure their success in their new status, and to educate them in their new roles. For an American mother, this means dietary restrictions, baby showers, instructions from older women, and rites in the hospital, where specialists give careful attention to cultural strictures concerning cleanliness.

"The Hasanlu lovers" (left, female; right, male) still in the position they assumed while hiding in a feed bin during a siege of Hasanlu (present-day Iran) in 800 B.C. Photo courtesy of The University Museum, University of Pennsylvania, Philadelphia.

The third phase is the "incorporation" of the people involved into their new statuses. At birth, this includes both mother and child. While the former is reincorporated into the society, now in the role of mother, the latter must be given a new identity and status in the social order.

IDENTITY A person's social identity develops, in part, from a name; nameless people are categories, not persons. The Ainu of northern Japan believe a child receives its body from the mother and its soul from the father. Body and soul merge on the twelfth day following birth, and only then does the infant become a person and receive a name. Children in India are considered human persons at birth but are not given permanent names until later, indicating their religious and, often, caste affiliations. A name is determined by astrological calculations, based on the moment of birth, and is assigned on an auspicious day that may be months after delivery. Many an Indian mother in the United States has been frustrated on finding she could not take her child from an American hospital until it had been named.

Obviously, names are more than labels, often providing information as to the sex and character of an individual. Among some American Indian tribes, a male was given a temporary childhood name and later an adult name that fitted his character. Americans often follow this practice by means of nicknames and diminutives, such as "Tommy," that are dropped in later life. South Indian villagers who have lost several infant sons may try to deceive the evil spirits that kill baby boys by giving a girl's name to a newborn male. Only when the boy is four or five years old and able to resist these spirits are his name and dress changed to that of his own sex.

SOCIAL STATUS   A new child needs not only an identity but also a social status to link him to others in the society, particularly to his parents. The biological mother is established at birth. Generally, although not without exception, she is also the sociological mother— the woman in the social role of mother. In the case of adoption, another woman assumes the role of sociological mother.

The biological father is not so easily determined. Middle-class Americans generally assume that the husband of the mother is the father of the child, and a social stigma may be attached to a child sired by a man other than the woman's husband. However, this assumption is by no means universal. In some societies, it is commonly expected that someone other than the husband should father the first child. Even in Western cultures, a study of the roles of mistress and unwed mother would show that the equation of father and husband is not always assumed.

A father is often needed to provide the child with a legitimate status in the society. In India, a child gets his caste and family ties from his father. Without these, he has no inheritance and cannot marry, for no man would permit a marriage between his daughter and a man of unknown status, for fear that the marriage might be incestuous or out-of-caste. Consequently, in cases of adultery, considerable effort is made to find a sociological father, as we may see in the following case study.

> Balayya, the leader of the Weaver caste, was responsible for guarding his widowed daughter from immorality after she returned home because her husband had left her no inheritance.

When he found out that she was pregnant, he called the caste leaders together and explained the facts. They fined him for negligence and were investigating the case further when the frightened adulterer appeared, offering to pay to keep the matter quiet. The elders decided that there was no use in forcing another wife and child on a man who already had difficulty supporting his own family. On the other hand, the expected child needed a father to give it family and caste ties. In the end, the elders let the adulterer off with a fine and ordered Balayya to find his daughter a husband before the child was born.

After a long search, the parents found an old Weaver of seventy whose cantankerous wife had died previously. He was now content to live alone. When they first approached him, he was not interested. Even after they promised to pay the wedding costs and to support the woman and child, he was not interested. Only when Balayya sought the support of the elders who appealed to the old man to help the child did he consent and a simple marriage was arranged. The baby girl who was born shortly thereafter was given the family name of the old man and thereby became an accepted member of the caste.*

The question of a sociological father is often resolved by special rituals in those societies where several men marry the same woman. Among the Todas of south India, the wife of the oldest brother is automatically the wife of all his unmarried brothers. The oldest husband can claim to be the father of his wife's child by making a small bow and arrow and placing them in the fork of a tree. If he fails to do so, the other husbands can claim the offspring.

The "couvad," a peculiar rite that often serves the same purpose, has been found among such widely scattered peoples as the Ainu of northern Japan, the Caribs of South America, and in parts of China, India, and Spain. In this custom, the father goes to bed following the delivery of his child while the mother returns to her work. This not only helps him to recover from the ordeal but also enables him to lay claim to the child. At times, the rite is also performed in order to protect the weakened mother from evil spirits, who are tricked into attacking the husband in the delivery hut.

Birth rites may also be used to incorporate a child into additional social groups. For example, in the United States, the rites of baptism, christening, or circumcision may mark a child's entry into a religious community.

* P.G. Hiebert, *Konduru* (Minneapolis: University of Minnesota Press, 1971). Copyright 1971 by the University of Minnesota, pp. 111–112.

Initiation rites

Initiation rites, marking the transition from childhood to adulthood, are widespread around the world. While they are often closely associated with the biological processes of maturation, they primarily symbolize a change in social status. In fact, as we know from American society, entrance into a social adulthood does not necessarily coincide with puberty. In some societies, the transition is celebrated only for males, in some only for females, and in others, such rites are absent altogether.

Among the Banaro, a tribe in the interior of New Guinea, girls are initiated after they have chosen a husband and arranged their marriages. About the elaborate initiation rituals of the Banaro, Richard Thurnwald writes:

> Wild pigs are hunted, and domestic pigs slaughtered on different occasions, once by the fathers of the girls, once by their mothers' brothers. During a lapse of all together nine months, the girls are confined to a cell in the family house, getting sago soup instead of water throughout that time. For the whole period their fathers are obliged to sleep in the goblin-house. At last their cell is broken up by the women, the girls released and allowed to leave the house. The women get cocoanuts laid ready beforehand, and throw them at the girls, whom they finally push into the water, again pelting them with cocoanuts. The girls crawl out of the water on the bank, receive portions of sago and pork, and are now dressed, and adorned with earrings, nose sticks, necklaces, bracelets and aromatic herbs. After this a dance of the women takes place.
>
> That same evening . . . the men assemble on the streets of the village. The old men consult with each other, agreeing to distribute the girls according to their custom. This custom was explained to me in the following way. The father of the chosen bridegroom really ought to take possession of the girl, but he is "ashamed" and asks his sib friend, his *mundu,* to initiate her into the mysteries of married life in his place. This man agrees to do so. The mother of the girl hands her over to the bridegroom's father, telling her that he will lead her to meet the goblin. . . .
>
> The bridegroom is not allowed to touch her until she gives birth to a child. This child is called the goblin's child. When the goblin-child is born, the mother says "Where is thy father? Who had to do with me?" the bridegroom responds, "I am not his father; he is a goblin-child"; and she replys, "I did not see that I had intercourse with a goblin."*

* Richard Thurnwald, "Banaro Society: Social Organization and Kinship System of a Tribe in the Interior of New Guinea," pp. 258–260. Reproduced by permission of the American Anthropological Association, *Memoir 16,* 1916.

The Banaro bridegroom, for his part, is initiated into sexual activity by the wife of his grandfather's friend.

AMERICAN INITIATION RITES   In American society, there are explicit initiation rites for admission into specific adult groups. For example, basic training transforms the raw recruit into a soldier. He is isolated from society, and his past social and psychological identities are systematically removed by means of strict discipline. He is then given a new identity and loyalties and taught a new vocabulary and behavior appropriate to his new status. After these rites, he emerges a new kind of person, a soldier. Similar rites, with different degrees of intensity, are found for initiations into some religious orders, secret societies, fraternities, sororities, and other groups.

Americans have, however, no single set of ceremonies marking the transition from adolescence to adulthood, only a confusion of rites marking various stages of independence. Religious maturity is often recognized at an early age by rituals such as confirmation, baptism, and bar mitzvah. The right to drive a car is generally granted at age sixteen or seventeen, and legal maturity is reached between the ages of eighteen and twenty-one, depending on sex, state of residence, and the restrictions involved. In addition, most states have laws regulating ages

American children celebrate birthdays with lively ceremony.

for legally consuming alcoholic beverages, attending X-rated movies, and disregarding curfews. For large groups of young people, intellectual maturity is celebrated at annual graduation ceremonies, and economic independence may come last of all.

Although they are taught from an early age the value of personal independence, young people in fact remain dependent on their parents well beyond the age of puberty. Added to the uncertainty of their status and prolonged dependency is the sweeping nature of the change from dependence to independence in a relatively short span of time. Not only do many societies have clearly defined rituals marking entry into adult rights and obligations, but the change itself is not so great or so sudden. Children of other cultures often gradually begin to assume adult responsibilities early in life, but even after they become adults and marry, they remain members of a larger family, in which many important decisions are made by the elders. Only after the deaths of the members of the oldest generation does the next generation assume full responsibility for themselves, their children, and their grandchildren.

Do young people in societies with initiation rites have less stormy and awkward adolescent periods than do Americans? The American anthropologist Margaret Mead thinks so. In her study *Coming of Age in Samoa* (1928), she concluded that young girls in Samoa lived a carefree and peaceful life in contrast to their American peers, who seem to go through a period of psychological stress. However, these conclusions have been the center of considerable debate in anthropological circles.

Marriage rites

Birth and initiation customs illustrate one of the functions of rites of passage—that of moving people from one status to another. Another is shown by marriage ceremonies, where changes in roles require a reorganization of social relationships.

In many societies, marriage is the most elaborate transition rite. Ironsmith Narayana, an old south Indian villager, once explained why:

> There are three important days in a person's life: the day of birth, the day of marriage, and the day of death. We are not old enough to celebrate the first and not around for the last, so we make the most of our marriages. (Hiebert 1971: 94–95)

MATING AND MARRIAGE Marriage as a social institution is related to the biological processes of mating and procreation, but the two are not the same. Americans tend to equate marriage and mating and traditionally have placed strong emphasis on chastity before marriage. This attitude, however, is found largely in Judeo-Christian and Muslim cultures, whose cultural roots are in the Mediterranean region.

Premarital mating is common in many societies, particularly in the Pacific Islands. This should not be taken to mean that moral standards are lacking or that sexual behavior is unregulated. Rather, mating during adolescence is accepted as biologically natural and essentially a personal matter. Marriage, on the other hand, is seen as a social status that legitimizes sexual union between spouses and assigns them new roles in their relationships to each other, to their offspring, to their relatives and friends, and to society in general.

Marriage involves more than the couple; it functions as an alliance between family groups. This fact is recognized in many societies, where marriages are arranged by family heads in order to cement social relationships between different kinship groups, in much the same way that European kings once arranged the marriages of their offspring to seal international alliances. But even where marriages are not explicitly used in this way, they affect a great many more people than the bride and groom. The success or failure of a marriage is of concern not only to the couple involved, but to others as well; hence the fact that in many cultures, the wedding rituals are very elaborate and involve large segments of the society.

Marriages, like other rituals, serve several social functions. They provide entertainment and excitement, which break the monotony of everyday life, and they provide group support and recognition for the participants at the time of their achievement. The rites also act as public announcements, informing everyone about changes in the status of the bride and groom so they may make appropriate adjustments in their behavior towards the couple. Finally, weddings help the man and woman being married to learn and psychologically adjust to their new roles.

Some of these functions may be seen in the marriage ceremonies of the Andaman Islanders of the Indian Ocean. A.R. Radcliffe-Brown (1881–1955) writes:

> When a marriage has finally been arranged an evening is appointed for the ceremony . . . . The bride is seated on a mat at one end of the dancing ground, her relatives and friends sitting near her. Torches or heaps of resin are lighted near by, so that the ceremony may be seen by the onlookers. The bridegroom is seated with his friends at the other end of the dancing ground. One of the older and more respected men addresses the bride, telling her that she must make a good wife, must provide for her husband such things as it is the duty of a wife to obtain or make, must see that he does not run after other women, and must herself remain faithful to him. He then addresses the bridegroom to the same effect, and taking him by the hand or arm, leads him to

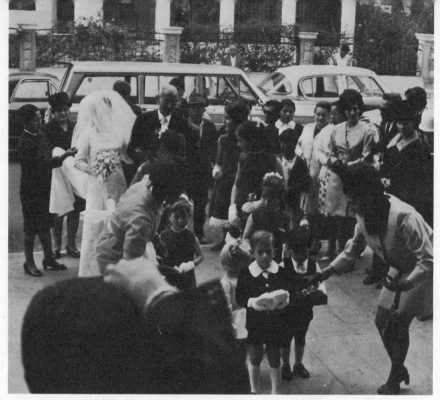

Upper-class wedding party forming outside church in Quito, Ecuador.
Photo courtesy of Vaughn Chapman.

where the bride is seated and makes him sit down beside her.
The relatives and friends weep loudly, and the young couple
look very self-conscious and uncomfortable. The shyness of the
young man is such that he often attempts to run away, but he is
caught by his friends, who are prepared for such an attempt.
After some minutes the officiating elder takes the arms of the
bride and bridegroom and places them around each others'
necks. After a further interval he again approaches and makes
the bridegroom sit on the bride's lap. [When a husband and wife
greet one another the man sits on the lap of his wife.] They sit so
for some minutes and the ceremony is over. The other members
of the community generally have a dance on such an occasion,
but in this the newly wedded pair do not join. A hut has already
been prepared for them, and . . . they retire shyly to their new
hut, while their friends continue dancing. (Radcliffe-Brown
1964:73–74)

AMERICAN MARRIAGE RITES   The American rituals of dating and
marriage reflect the growing individualism in our culture. For cen-

turies, courtship in Western countries was strictly regulated, and marriage required parental consent and, often, arrangement. Dating, as we know it today, had its beginnings only decades ago, around the turn of the century.

Modern American dating practices develop through several ritual stages, including casual dating, going steady, and serious dating—each with its own symbols, such as the wearing of pins or rings, as well as its own degree of permitted sexual intimacy. Formal engagement marks the public announcement of the couple's intentions to marry. During this period, there may be bachelor parties, marking the end of the single life for the groom, and bridal showers, preparing the bride for her new role.

The wedding, itself, is an assortment of legal contracts, religious vows, and social feasts, replete with symbols, such as the bridal gown, veil, and train, flowers, candles, blue garters, pennies, wedding cakes, and rings. Some of these have lost their significance over the years. Bridesmaids were once used by Germanic tribes to confuse evil spirits which would come to the wedding to carry off the bride, and wheat was thrown on the couple to guarantee prosperity, just as rice assured fertility.

Finally, there is the honeymoon, which encourages the couple to practice their new roles, and possibly a reincorporation rite or two: a house warming, shivaree, or welcoming ceremonies, as the young couple joins other couples in informal social groups and clubs.

Funeral rites

Death is the last crisis every individual must face. Many people believe in the immortality of the soul, and some believe in the social interaction between the living and the dead, but for everyone, death brings normal social relationships to an end. Therefore, it is not surprising that death rites are universal.

FUNCTIONS OF DEATH RITES Rites associated with death serve a number of important functions, including disposal of the body and preparation of the spirit for its new existence. The latter may include providing food and transportation for the journey to a spiritual land, as in the burials of the Egyptian pharaohs. Or, as in the case of many African tribesmen who believe that spirits of the deceased continue to be more or less active participants in everday affairs, it may mean reintegrating the "living dead" into their new roles in the society. For these tribesmen, ancestors are as much a part of the present society as the living and the yet unborn. Other people fear the return of the dead in the form of ghosts, and rites to placate them and assure their quick departure may be performed.

A second function of funerals is to channel the expression of grief and provide comfort and support to the living relatives and friends. Death is a time of psychological crisis, when the will of survivors to live may be lost, and even simple decisions become difficult. Thus, rituals structure the lives of those in mourning and provide for continuity of activity until the shock is past and they can adjust to the loss and again begin to function normally.

A third function of funeral rites is to restore balance in the social relations of the living that the death has disrupted. The death of an adult, particularly one with major roles in the society or group, often entails elaborate rites, in which these roles are redistributed so as to permit the society to continue to operate. An example is the funeral arrangements for the assassinated President John F. Kennedy. The nation watched the processions and ceremonies on television, numbly trying to fully comprehend what had occurred and what the results would be. In the case of infants and children, whose roles are not crucial, the rites are often simple. Property owned by the deceased must also be redistributed—a task governed by the rules of inheritance, which vary greatly from culture to culture.

Finally, each culture must provide an explanation for the major events and crises of life, and particularly for death, which seems to challenge all the meaning of life. It is thus reasonable that ceremonies associated with death frequently provide important occasions for reaffirmation of the beliefs and meaning attached by a culture to life. For example, among the Tiv of West Africa death is believed to be caused by curses, and ways are sought to detect the witch responsible for the affliction. (See "The Death of Amara," an accompanying extract.) As people enact rituals, they reaffirm and strengthen their faith in the explanations these rituals support. In the same way, funerals are significant events in the religions of most societies.

AMERICAN FUNERAL RITES The Egyptians embalmed their elite, in the belief that the departing spirits would one day return to the earth if their bodies were preserved. The lavish Egyptian funeral was not practiced in Western civilization, as the Greek practice of cremation spread and as Jews and early Christians condemned the Egyptian practices as pagan. Embalming was reserved for royalty in most Western cultures.

Early American burials were generally simple affairs, with members of the family preparing the body by washing it and wrapping it in a sheet, then holding a last vigil as it lay in the family parlor. After services in the house or church, the body was buried with a brief prayer of committal. Widow's weeds and a black veil, black crepe arm bands and ties for men, drawn blinds, still clocks, and dampened hearths were some of the symbols of mourning.

The death of Amara
Laura Bohannan

[The impact of death in terms of sorrow and social dislocation is common to all societies, whether or not they have beliefs that give it meaning and rituals to express their grief. Laura Bohannan vividly describes her own experience among the Tiv of West Africa when a young woman, Amara, returned to the house of her uncle Yabo, a medicine man, for the delivery of her child.]

The sun sank lower, thrusting yellow fingers of light through the dilapidated thatch of Yabo's reception hut. Amara still lived, her hand held in her husband's. . . .

Yabo's senior wife held her pipe from her mouth. "She dies." Amara's husband still clasped her hand. "Bring me a feather!" he snarled at the old woman. Then to me, "Is she dead? She cannot be dead." I could find no pulse. The feather below her nostrils did not stir. . . .

[The] women broke into a terrible wailing, a banshee lament tore from soul and body. Standing, hands clasped behind the head, body arched and shaking with the cry that began in a high scream and sobbed itself slowly down the scale into silence. . . .

Yabo's senior wife . . . knelt by Amara, lifted her head and tied the torn cloth about her face, masking it completely. . . .

The women washed the body and smeared it heavily with cam-wood. . . . I helped them lift the body—it was very heavy—so we might wrap it in the white cloth that had covered Amara during her last hours of life.

This task done, they called her husband. "Watch, while we go wash death from us," they told him. "Come," they said to me, "take your lamp, and we will go wash in the stream." . . .

[The next day the] women of Yabo's homestead sat closely about Amara's body, with leafy branches in their hands to wave away the flies. The hut was packed. All the senior women of the neighborhood, all the young women who had known and liked Amara, were crouched close together, covering the floor and even under the eaves. . . .

[Outside] Yabo rose. Slowly, without evident emotion, he told us of Amara's death and manner of dying. . . .

Someone had killed Amara. The guilt must be fixed. . . . Amara was past help, and the judgement was a foregone conclusion. It would be Yabo.

Source: From *Return to Laughter: An Anthropological Novel* by Elenore Smith Bowen, copyright 1954 by Laura Bohannan. Reprinted by permission of Doubleday & Co., Inc.

His guilt had been in their eyes yesterday. Who else among them was so ruthless? Who else so selfish? . . . Yesterday Yabo had defended himself with powerful conviction. He wanted to prove his innocence because he wanted to find the guilty one. Today, this motive gone, he was slowly entrapped in his own character and by his own reputation. . . .

As the hours wore on, Yabo's protestations of innocence became formal, set phrases. His repetition of the indictments leveled against him—"I, a witch?" "I wish her death?"—lost their first shuddering denial, became empty, then gradually were tinged with an evil, mocking pride that attested their truth. . . . A witch's reputation grows like a philanderer's: every new conquest is attributed to the same man; and his denials are called discretion. . . .

At the end, he stood alone and upright, contemptuous of the accusers snarling about him, laughing at their horror of the crime, until they gave way before him in fear and loathing. . . .

The elders sat immobile and withdrawn. Some of the women came out of the reception hut and began to move about in their own huts. It seemed hardly the right atmosphere for a funeral feast, yet I could not imagine what else they might be doing. No one paid any attention. . . .

The men all rose to follow the body to the grave. Yabo drew me along, and Kako nodded approval. There are many sights forbidden to women, but only to protect the women from powers they are not strong enough to withstand. As a European, I was considered probably immune to many of these influences· my continued survival confirmed their opinion. Only some of the women . . . thought I might possibly be a witch. But today even the men looked curiously at me as I stood by the side of the open grave and watched them lower Amara's body into it. They covered her with branches, so the soil might not touch her. Soon only a raw mound of red earth marked her grave. There had been no ritual, no ceremony of any kind. . . . Everything that had been in contact with the corpse must be destroyed or washed. The women might come out; they too must bathe, and the gravediggers.

[When] the women had returned from the stream, I saw the reason for their former activity. They were leaving. The young men with their wives and possessions were leaving. . . . Yabo sat, intent, but making no sign, as one after the other of his wives and children walked away and out of his homestead, without saying a word. . . . Yabo's senior wife came out. . . . She alone was not afraid to remain with Yabo. . . .

By the time I got home, the boys all knew. "The evil at heart are left alone, sitting in a silent homestead. Yabo is a witch. He could not refute it. And it is thus that witches are punished."

Embalming and the use of metal coffins regained popularity among the general populace following the Civil War. Burial services moved to the commercial funeral parlors, and signs of public mourning decreased after the first world war.

Current American rituals are largely borrowed from the last century but reflect changing cultural values, with emphasis on comfort and affluence. Today, the deceased may be viewed by friends and relatives in a Colonial Classic Beauty Casket, made of 18-gauge lead-coated steel with seamless top and lap and joint-welded body construction which rests on a Classic Beauty Ultra Metal Casket Bier. The body, restored with Nature-Glo cosmetics, is dressed in handmade original fashions, and wearing Ko-Zee shoes, with "soft cushioned soles and warm luxurious slipper comfort, but true shoe smartness" (Mitford 1963:46). The well-dressed corpse rests on a Beautyrama Adjustable Soft-Foam Bed. Following the service, it is transferred by hydraulically operated Porto-Life onto a Glide Easy casket carriage and taken to the Cadillac Funeral Coach.

At the graveside, where the Lifetime Green artificial turf covers the ground, the mourners, surrounded by stands of preserved flowers and shaded by a Steril Chapel Tent which "resists the intense heat and humidity of summer and the terrific storms of winter," watch as the casket is lowered into a vault decorated with pictures of the Tree of Life. The final earth is scattered with a Gordon Leak-Proof Earth Dispenser, to prevent the discomfort of soiled fingers (Mitford 1963:48–63). Such a ceremony was purchased in 1960 at an average price of about $1,450 per funeral, which comes to more than $1,600,000,000 dollars for the nation in one year—a worthy tribute to affluence.

One can be quite satirical about American death rites, but American funerals do reflect more than our sense of cleanliness and status based on material affluence. Our concern with the psychological well-being derived from beautiful memories of the departed are presumed to justify the expenditures. Americans also have rites that reflect religious and ethnic differences and employ grave markers, sympathy cards, flowers, obituaries, and legal notices to inform the society; probation of wills to redistribute the decedent's economic goods; and often family reunions that reinforce kinship ties and redefine roles.

Summary

Rites are often associated with major changes in roles in the course of a lifetime, and they serve important functions in adjustment, for

A mother and child from south India spend almost all their time together.

both societies and individuals. For society, rites announce changes in status and provide for reorganization of the society and its goods if affected. Rites are also important occasions for society to reaffirm its values and beliefs.

Rites of passage also assist the individual undergoing role change to adjust psychologically to his new status, by giving him an opportunity to learn and practice his new role and by providing him with the support of the community. Whether in celebration or in mourning, this interaction of individual and community strengthens the individual's place within the community.

Suggested readings

Bowen, Elenore Smith
    1964 Return to Laughter. Garden City, N.Y.: Doubleday and Co. (An anthropological novel, providing deep insights into both the indigenous culture of west Africa and the changes experienced by an American anthropologist living in a bush tribe.)

Cohen, Y.A.
    1964 The Transition from Childhood to Adolescence: Cross-Cultural Studies of Initiation Ceremonies, Legal Systems and Incest Tabus. Chicago: Aldine Publishing Co. (A comparative study of pre- and post-puberty rites in various types of social organizations.)

Mitford, Jessica
    1963 The American Way of Death. Greenwich, Conn.: Fawcett Publications. (A documented study of the commercialization and extravagance of the American funeral industry.)

van Gennep, Arnold
    1960 The Rites of Passage. Chicago: University of Chicago Press. (Published first in French in 1909, this is a classic study of transitional rites, from a theoretical and comparative point of view.)

9

Types of groups
Group dynamics
Institutions

Social groups and institutions

People are social beings, born, raised, married, and usually buried in the company of their fellow humans. In their relationships, people form groups and societies, and these, too, with the exception of a few hunting and gathering tribes, do not exist in complete isolation. Most tribes have trade, social, and ritual networks that link them to their neighbors, while complex societies (composed of great numbers of groups) increasingly grow to be parts of a worldwide community of societies.

The difficulty in describing human groups is not only that there are many kinds of people that constitute different groups but also that there are different ways of defining "kind," so that the same people may belong to a number of groups. One might speak, for example, of Christians, Muslims, Jews, Buddhists, and Hindus; of plumbers, physicians, policemen, and physicists; of tribals, peasants, and city folk; of the literate and the illiterate; of the rich and the poor. Moreover, there are Chinese, Nigerians, Samoans, and Englishmen. People come in a variety of sizes, shapes, and colors, and to these differences they have added a great many more social distinctions.

Types of groups

The problem of classifying human groups is a difficult one. As we have seen, there are a great many ways of dividing people into kinds or sets. One approach would be simply to list all of these groups alphabetically, but this overlooks the fact that there is a marked difference in the ways in which they are formed. Moreover, the list would be so large, it would be unmanageable.

A second approach to classifying groups is to construct a set of all possible combinations of human beings. For example, one might talk of all people who are five feet and four inches tall, blond, blue-eyed, and wearing size eight shoes or of all men under thirty who have hunted crocodiles. But this leads us to an infinite number of sets, most of which are useless to the anthropologist and do not exist in the minds of the people involved.

Anthropology, like other social sciences, is interested in forming generalizations, which requires the reduction of unique experiential forms into broader categories.*

Statistical groups

Anthropologists frequently define groups of people on the basis of certain characteristics they have in common. One can speak of all those in a society who are over twenty-one, marry their cross-cousins, are rich, or live along the Amazon river. These are statistical groups created by anthropologists for the sake of analysis, and the people in the groups are generally unaware of their existence.

We have already seen that a great many of the statistical groups that can be formed by logical thought have no scientific significance what-

* One particularly useful taxonomy of groups and the one used here is based on the ways in which groups are formed, provided by Robert Bierstedt, a sociologist (Bierstedt 1970:272–284).

ever. There is little use in talking of the group of people in the world born on March twelfth between one and two P.M., or of those who have read both Shakespeare's Hamlet and the Koran.

Statistical groups, however, can be extremely useful for analyzing a society, even though the people involved are not conscious of them. For example, shoe manufacturers must know what percent of a population has a given foot size. (When they export their product, it is all too easy to assume that the same distribution holds unchanged for people in other countries.) Health officials need to know the incidence of various diseases. For anthropologists, there are significant differences between a society that is nonliterate and less than ten percent urban and one that is fifty percent urban and ninety percent literate. Likewise, societies with less than 10,000 people are different from those with a population of more than 500,000,000.

The critical test of statistical groups is not whether they exist in the minds of the people but whether they help the analyst to answer the questions he is asking about the society. Most modern ethnographies include some statistical information about a society and its members.

Societal groups

Unlike statistical groups, which are essentially etic in nature, societal groups are emic—they exist in the minds of the people. Franklin Giddings, a sociologist, has called the recognition that we belong to a group of people who are like ourselves in some ways "consciousness of kind." Why people like to live and associate with others similar to themselves is not clear. Appeal to some social instinct or attraction does not explain it. But it is clear that consciousness of kind is a powerful stimulus to social interaction and group formation.

People who are conscious of their common identity usually share certain visible signs, by which they recognize one another. These may be biological characteristics, such as age, sex, skin color, or body shape, or they may be cultural traits, like general styles of clothing, distinct accents, and specific customs. Christians revere the Bible, Muslims the Koran, and Hindus the Vedas. American blacks have their soul food and Americans, in general, their hamburgers and milk shakes. Such markers come to symbolize the identity of the group and reinforce the members' consciousness of the uniqueness of their kind.

Societal groups are the mental categories by which people sort out themselves and other human beings on the basis of similarity of kind. For example, Americans classify themselves politically as Republicans, Democrats, and Independents. Or they can be divided into Protestants, Catholics, Jews, and so on. It is important to note that people need not necessarily interact to share a consciousness of kind. No Republican has met all his fellow Republicans, nor a Presbyterian all who share his faith.

Taken together, societal groups provide people with a model of the organization of their society. By placing everyone into broad categories, it is possible to reduce the bewildering array of human relationships to a manageable number of kinds of interaction. You, therefore, do not need to work out a personal role relationship with every stranger you meet. The result is a mental map, in which each person has a place. It is this consciousness of kind that sets societal groups apart from statistical ones.

Social groups

The word "social" implies interaction, and social groups are groups of people who *associate* and *interact* with one another. There are social groups of many kinds. For example, people riding a bus or cheering at a football game form a loose type of social group. Colleges, neighborhood communities, and businesses are more institutionalized and have continuity over time, but the relationships between the participants are largely impersonal. Families and clubs are primary groups, in which members interact in personal, face-to-face relationships.

Both societal and social groups have a consciousness of kind or of identity. The difference between them is that members of social groups interact with one another, but not all members of societal groups do. For example, the Democratic party is a societal group, a mental category made up of a great many people who have never met and, in fact, do not know that each other exists. A local Democratic chapter, on the other hand, is a social group. The members meet in common sessions and work together for the advancement of their party. Many social groups in the United States, such as churches, clubs, and unions, are parts of larger societal organizations.

Both social and societal groups vary considerably in the extent to which they are formally organized. A group of Americans touring Europe together (a social group) may develop a sense of identity in the course of a month. So also might the doctors (societal group) in a country that is trying to introduce socialized medicine. In both cases, there may be no organization beyond simple interaction and a consciousness of kind. On the other hand, social and societal groups may develop highly structured organizations. A local church, a large corporation such as United States Steel, and the American Marine Corps are examples of groups that have formally defined memberships, leaders, and rules of operation.

Fishermen casting
their nets in
Uhehe, Tanzania.
Photo courtesy of
E.V. Winans.

Group dynamics

Emic groups, both societal and social, share many similar characteristics. A look at a few of these characteristics can help us understand
how groups in general operate.

Identity and consciousness of kind

To a great extent, groups provide people with their sense of individual identity, with an awareness of who they are and how they fit into
the world. A Californian in New York is happy to meet a fellow Californian, who, though a stranger, is somehow closer to him than all those
"foreigners" surrounding him. They are even happier to discover that
both come from San Francisco and are Rotarians. Abroad, of course, the
same Californian is delighted to see a fellow American, even though he
comes from New York.

The nature of groups can change as a sense of identity is created
and interaction begins. Statistical groups faced with a common cause
or crisis may develop a consciousness of kind. If, for example, a government passed a law barring left-handed people from government
jobs, left-handed people would soon develop an awareness of one another, based not only on their similarity but also on their common
plight. They would begin to talk to one another, and in time hold meetings and form associations of left-handers opposed to suppression. In
the same way, people living in a town, when faced with a possible

disaster, often develop a strong sense of identity and organize to meet the challenge.

The extent to which people identify with their groups varies greatly. To a few groups, people commit a great deal of time, effort, and themselves. In many, they are content to be general participants without any great personal involvement. Even in complex urban societies, with their many diverse groups, most people participate in a few primary groups, such as families and friendships, in which they develop intimate personal relationships and a sense of belonging.

Stable groups often develop cultural symbols that set them apart from other groups. In other words, they have their own ways of doing things. Each family has its own family traditions and behavioral patterns, its own name and place of residence. So does each school, club, business, and society. These symbols are informally taught to the members within the group, and outsiders who try to pass as members can usually be detected, because they are not aware of these cultural shibboleths.

Membership

Groups are made up of people, and in all but the most casual gatherings, each member assumes certain statuses and roles, defined by the group. A stable group is made up of sets of roles, and its continuity over time depends on its ability to maintain these roles apart from the individuals who temporarily occupy them. When a college president resigns, a faculty member dies, and students graduate, new people must be found to fill their roles if the college is to continue to function. Stable groups, in fact, are seen by their members as spanning more than one generation, even though they often undergo a great deal of change in that time.

Recruitment procedures vary a great deal from group to group. Students are admitted, often casually, into many clubs on a campus but are usually chosen with a great deal of care and ceremony by sororities and fraternities. Ethnic groups and castes generally admit members by birth, but there are exceptions. The commune founded by the Shakers of Mt. Lebanon, New York, in 1787 prohibited mating. New members were gained by adoption of children and conversion of adults.

Some groups we join voluntarily, and we become members of others without choice. We are members of ascribed groups, based on age, sex, and other biological properties, but we join street crowds and parades. Most groups, however, combine ascribed and achieved characteristics in complex ways to determine their memberships. In our society, people are born into social classes, religious communities, and linguistic groups, but in later life, these can be changed, at least to some extent, by individual effort and choice. As we shall see later, this pattern is not true of many other societies.

Admission into a group means that a person is admitted to the roles, knowledge, values, and customs of the group. This often involves a period of training, in which the newcomer is taught its ways. The initiation may be an informal slap on the shoulder or formal training, as in boot camp.

Admission also means that a person is accepted by the members of the in-group as one of their kind. This acceptance is often expressed by subtle social cues. For example, Max Gluckman has pointed out the importance of gossip as an indicator of admission to a group. Outsiders generally do not know the personal information and secrets about members of the group, which are the proper topics for gossip. Even if they do, members will not allow them, as outsiders, to criticize a fellow member without rising to his defense. To be accepted into the gossip circles of a group is one sign that a person has been admitted.

Boundaries

Groups include some people as participants or members, and by the same token, they exclude others. This leads to a distinction between in-groups, or the "we-group," and out-groups, or the "they-group." "We" may mean members of a family, town, or tribe. The rest of the people are "they."

H.G. Wells, in an amusing description, captures some of the feelings between in-groups and out-groups.

> [The botanist] has a strong feeling for systematic botanists as against plant physiologists, whom he regards as lewd and evil scoundrels in this relation; but he has a strong feeling for all botanists and indeed all biologists, as against physicists, and those who profess the exact sciences, all of whom he regards as dull, mechanical, ugly-minded scoundrels in this relation; but he has a strong feeling for all who profess what he calls Science, as against psychologists, sociologists, philosophers, and literary men, whom he regards as wild, foolish, immoral scoundrels in this relation; but he has a strong feeling for all educated men as against the working man, whom he regards as a cheating, lying, loafing, drunken, thievish, dirty scoundrel in this relation; but so soon as the working man is comprehended together with these others, as *Englishmen,* he holds them superior to all sorts of Europeans, whom he regards. . . .*

* H.G. Wells, *A Modern Utopia* (London: Chapman & Hall, Ltd., 1905), p. 322. Reprinted with permission of The Estate of H.G. Wells.

Members in stable groups tend to look at one another as individuals and notice personal differences but stereotype those in other groups on the basis of some, generally derogatory, similarities. To many Americans of European origin, all Africans "look alike." To many blacks, all South African whites are racists, even though many have taken a stand against the discriminatory policies of their government. To most Communists, all Americans are imperialists and warmongers. Stereotyping discourages personal interaction with outsiders and thus maintains the boundaries and identity of a group.

Pride is based, in part, on differences, and without these differences, life might be monotonous. Imagine a society composed only of Swiss bankers or, for that matter, American anthropologists! But the pride that gives rise to group consciousness can also lead to discrimination and conflict. Ours is a world of blacks and whites, Americans and Russians, Arabs and Israelis, farmers and city folk, and aristocrats and commoners. Moreover, conflict is greatest between groups geographically close to each other, who compete for the same resources and status. The Miami Dolphins football team, for example, has little conflict with the Los Angeles Lakers basketball team or the Methodist churches in New York, except when the groups' events are scheduled in the same place at the same time.

Discrimination must be distinguished from simple exclusion. Colleges do not admit students who fail to qualify, nor do churches ordain unbelievers to positions of leadership. Admission to groups is for the benefit of the members, and the exclusion of those who do not choose or qualify to join does not mean that the members are against them or want to deny them privileges for which they qualify. Discrimination, on the other hand, is *against* some individual or group and denys some privilege or pleasure that is reserved for the in-groups. Often, the privilege denied is membership in the group, itself, not on the basis of some qualification that is essential to the nature of the group, but simply to keep certain people out, on the basis of personal likes and dislikes.

If we agree that discrimination in contemporary societies is wrong, the solution is not to deny that differences exist between people or that groups based on these differences should be formed. There are obvious differences among groups of people, in roles, wealth, religions, skin colors, and cultures, and without some types of groups, no society can exist.

Nor is the answer to deny that group differences are important. As we already know, what is important is what people think to be so, no matter what the outside observer says. The problem lies with those who are discriminating, not those discriminated against.

As Gunnar Myrdal has pointed out, the "black problem" in the United States is really a problem of the whites. The solution lies not only in creating laws that prohibit discrimination but in changing cultural values and practices to allow different kinds of people and groups to live together in a multicultural society.

As we have seen, groups can be divided into those that are social and those that are societal. They can also be divided according to the types of bonds that hold the members together. Roughly speaking, three important types of groups can be distinguished by mode of recruitment: 1) groups based on birth and kinship or an extension of these by social fiction; 2) groups based on geography, such as neighborhoods, towns, and nations; and 3) groups based on an association of people who share a common interest or characteristic, such as clubs, churches, and social classes. Each type will be explored further in discussions of specific groups.

Social stratification

Relationships between members within a group and between groups of the same kind are frequently characterized by "stratification." Imagine for a moment that you and a few friends are organizing a company baseball team in a small town. Not only would you have to decide what sorts of people you would want to admit but also how the team should operate. It would need a place to practice and some basic equipment. It would need players for each position in the team and probably a manager and treasurer to run it. In time, each person would acquire a status, high or low, in the team, and the team would gain a general standing in the league and in the total world of baseball.

Social stratification is based on the division of labor into different roles within a group or society, and on the fact that these roles generally receive different rewards. These rewards take the form of 1) material goods or wealth, 2) authority or power, and 3) prestige. For example, in your baseball team, the best players gain prestige by leading the league in home runs or games won. If it is a professional team, this can be translated into higher salaries. The manager gains a high status but on another basis. As an administrator, his role is not to play the game, the purpose for which the team is organized, but to maintain the operation of the group. His reward is in terms of power, which can also be converted into prestige and wealth.

The value of power and wealth are obvious. The problem of defining prestige, which is a group's value of an individual's social standing, is more elusive. It may be expressed by such symbols as titles, awards, deferential behavior, and standings in baseball ratings. It

Men gathering to
fish for dinner.
Photo courtesy of
UNESCO Courier,
United Nations.

covers the abilities to collect scalps, wives, or high grades. It includes
associating with those who also have a high status, being invited to the
"right" parties and mentioned in the society pages. This was vividly
described by Sinclair Lewis for a fictional American city, in which a
realtor named George Babbitt was trying to climb to the social level of
Charles McKelvey, a powerful businessman and politician. (See the
passage from *Babbitt* in the accompanying extract.)

Social rewards, such as wealth, power, and prestige, can be sought
as ends in themselves. Wealth can be consumed to provide a better life-
style, as is common in America, or given away in extravagant rituals
that display the status of the givers, as in the potlatch ceremonies, in
which certain northwest coast American Indians gave away wealth to
gain titles or shame their rivals. This custom in some respects is not
unlike the practice whereby American industrial tycoons set up
humanitarian foundations in their names and thus gained a reputation
of generosity.

Social rewards can also be used as resources for getting something
else that the individual or group desires. Power can be used to gain
wealth and prestige, and these, in turn, help one to get power. But
there are right ways and wrong ways of converting resources. It is considered improper, for instance, in the West to use money to buy politi-

Babbitt

Sinclair Lewis

The Babbitts invited the McKelveys to dinner, in early December, and the McKelveys not only accepted but, after changing the date once or twice, actually came. . . . Babbitt hoped that the Doppelbraus [his neighbors] would see the McKelveys' limousine, and their uniformed chauffeur, waiting in front.

The dinner was well cooked and incredibly plentiful, and Mrs. Babbitt had brought out her grandmother's silver candlesticks. Babbitt worked hard. He was good. He told none of the jokes he wanted to tell. He listened to the others. He started Maxwell off with a resounding, "Let's hear about your trip to the Yellowstone." . . .

But he could not stir them. It was a dinner without soul. For no reason that was clear to Babbit, heaviness was over them and they spoke laboriously and unwillingly.

He concentrated on Lucille McKelvey. . . "I suppose you'll be going to Europe pretty soon again won't you?" he invited.

"I'd like awfully to run over to Rome for a few weeks."

"I suppose you see a lot of pictures and music and curios and everything there."

"No, what I really go for is: there's a little *trattoria* on the Via della Scrofa where you get the best *fettuccine* in the world."

"Oh, I—Yes. That must be nice to try that. Yes."

At a quarter to ten McKelvey discovered with profound regret that his wife had a headache. He said blithely, as Babbitt helped him with his coat, "We must lunch together some time, and talk over the old days." . . .

When the others had labored out, at half-past ten, Babbitt turned to his wife, pleading, "Charley said he had a corking time and we must lunch—said they wanted to have us up to the house for dinner before long." . . .

For a month they watched the social columns, and waited for a return dinner-invitation.

[The invitation never came, of course, but that is only part of the story.]

Ed Overbrook was a classmate of Babbitt who had been a failure. . . . At the class-dinner [Babbitt] had seen poor Overbrook, in a shiny

Source: Abridged from pp. 194–197 of *Babbitt* by Sinclair Lewis. Copyright 1922 by Harcourt Brace Jovanovich, Inc.; renewed 1950 by Sinclair Lewis. Reprinted by permission of the publishers.

blue serge business-suit, being diffident in a corner with three other failures. He had gone over and been cordial. "Why, hello, young Ed! I hear you're writing all the insurance in Dorchester now. Bully work!"

They recalled the good old days when Overbrook used to write poetry. Overbrook embarrassed him by blurting, "Say, Georgie, I hate to think of how we been drifting apart. I wish you and Mrs. Babbitt would come to dinner some night."

Babbitt boomed, "Fine! Sure! Just let me know. And the wife and I want to have you at the house." He forgot it, but unfortunately Ed Overbrook did not. Repeatedly he telephoned to Babbitt, inviting him to dinner. "Might as well go and get it over," Babbitt groaned to his wife. . . .

It was miserable from the beginning. . . . Babbitt tried to be jovial; he worked at it; but he could find nothing to interest him in Overbrook's timorousness, the blankness of the other guests, or the drained stupidity of Mrs. Overbrook, with her spectacles, drab skin, and tight-drawn hair. He told his best Irish story, but it sank like a soggy cake. Most bleary moment of all was when Mrs. Overbrook, peering out of her fog of nursing eight children and cooking and scrubbing, tried to be conversational.

"I suppose you go to Chicago and New York right along, Mr. Babbitt," she prodded.

"Well, I get to Chicago fairly often."

"It must be awfully interesting. I suppose you take in all the theaters."

"Well, to tell the truth, Mrs. Overbrook, thing that hits me best is a great big beefsteak at a Dutch restaurant in the Loop!"

They had nothing to say. Babbitt was sorry, but there was no hope: the dinner was a failure. At ten, rousing out of the stupor of meaningless talk, he said as cheerfully as he could, " 'Fraid we got to be starting, Ed. I've got a fellow coming to see me early to-morrow." As Overbrook helped him with his coat, Babbitt said, "Nice to rub up on the old days! We must have lunch together, P.D.Q." . . .

For a week they worried, "We really ought to invite Ed and his wife, poor devils!" But as they never saw the Overbrooks, they forgot them, and after a month or two they said, "That really was the best way, just to let it slide. It wouldn't be kind to them to have them here. They'd feel so out of place and hard-up in our home."

---

cal influence or admission to heaven. And it is not clear if politicians should appoint priests or the church should speak out in condemnation of actions of the state.

The result of unequal distribution of social rewards is a social hierarchy, in which people and groups are ranked according to their social statuses. Rank, in turn, determines to a great extent access to future rewards, which reinforces the system.

Social mobility

A fourth term used in analyzing social groups and processes is that of "mobility"—the movement of people from one status to another. This mobility may be individual; for example, in our baseball team, a player may win the batting title of the league. On the other hand, mobility may involve a whole group; the team may win the championship, even though they do not have all of the best players in the league.

Horizontal social mobility occurs when people move from one status to another of essentially the same rank. A teacher may resign to start a small industry of his own, or a successful businessman may enter politics. Vertical mobility takes place when people move up or down the social hierarchy.

Mobility varies greatly, depending on the kinds of boundaries, that surround groups. Almost anyone who can afford a ticket can attend a public concert, but admission into the American Medical Association, United States citizenship, or membership in an ethnic group is another matter. Exclusiveness, itself, may be the primary reason for the existence of an elite group and its symbol of high status.

Institutions

The concept of institutions is an important one in the social sciences. Unfortunately, however, it has been used in a great many different ways, and its meaning has become ambiguous.

Some writers use the term "institutions" when referring to large social groups, reserving the term "associations" for small groups. The distinction is then only one of size. But no one knows how large a group must be to become an institution; furthermore, used in this way, the term adds little to our understanding of social structures.

Others use "institution" for any consetllation of cultural traits, collected around some function or set of functions. Thus, for example, we might refer to all customs associated with teaching the young as the institution of education, to those related to worship as the institution of religion, and to those related to ruling in all of its forms as government. To do this is to equate institutions with different areas of culture, the only difference among them being one of scope. This usage, too, adds little to our ability to analyze societies.

People perform thousands of cultural activities, some thought of as institutionalized, some not. What is the difference? Robert MacIver (1949:11–18) suggested a distinction that is both clear and useful. According to him, an institution is a set of formal, regular, and established procedures, characteristic of a group or number of groups that perform a similar function within a society. In short, an institution is an *organized way of doing something.*

Institutionalization

The nature of institutions can be made clear by contrasting them with groups and by looking at "institutionalization" as a process. Almost any autumn day, improvised football games can be observed on campuses and parks across the United States. Almost anyone around can join, and there are few or no boundaries, uniforms, or penalties. Moreover, there is no continuity of teams from one day to the next. High school and college football, on the other hand, are more institutionalized. They have clearly defined teams, stadiums, prearranged schedules, uniforms, programs, parades, and formal rules enforced by umpires. In other words, they have a set of formally organized procedures. Professional football, with its highly paid players and coaches, its national television coverage, and its league championships and Super Bowls, is even more highly institutionalized.

The same distinction can be made in other areas of cultural activity. As Bierstedt points out in an excellent discussion of institutions (1970:320–321), almost everyone at some time or another teaches someone else how to do something. A child teaches his younger brother how to play a game; a mother shows her daughter how to sew her own clothes; an employer instructs a worker about the job; and a grandfather tells his grandchildren about the old days.

In some societies, however, certain types of instruction are formally organized, creating groups whose members have clearly defined roles. The institution of education thus includes teachers, a body of information to be taught, suitable rituals of instruction, places for meeting, and material equipment and supplies. Other areas of culture may be institutionalized within a society. In the United States, we can speak of the institutions of religion, business, industry, government, medicine, art, music, drama, movies, transportation, television, journalism, and even war.

From the above discussion, it should be clear that institutions are distinct from but closely linked to at least one and usually many more social groups. Organized activities cannot exist apart from actors. For instance, religion as an institution in America is related to specific congregations of believers, such as Presbyterians, Catholics, and Jews, which are located in different towns and cities. But religion, as such, has no specific location. Government as a process is carried out by legislative bodies, courts, and police, but it cannot be equated with these groups. In other words, we must make a distinction between government (an institution) and *a* government (a set of groups).

It should be noted, in passing, that just as several groups may serve the same institutional function, so also a single group may perform a number of institutionalized activities. For instance, though a university may be primarily an educational institution, its football team is part of the institution of sports and its drama club a part of the institution of entertainment.

Institutions are also linked to the material culture produced and used by groups. Education in the West is commonly associated with buildings, blackboards, movie projectors, and books; war with guns, planes, rockets, and submarines; and journalism with presses, newspapers, and broadcasting stations.

Institutions and cultures

How do institutions relate to the broader concept of culture? Both are accepted ways of doing things. The answer is that institutions are cultural *procedures* that have become formally organized and enforced by the groups serving the institutional function. In any society, a great many acts are repeated again and again, and in time, they become accepted patterns of behavior enforced by public opinion or by entire communities. One example of cultural behavior is handshaking. In contrast, saluting is an institutionalized activity, because it is prescribed and enforced by formally organized groups within a society. Formal procedures are often much the same for all groups associated with a particular institution. There is, for instance, a general similarity among schools and classrooms throughout America.

Obviously, there is no sharp line between institutionalized and un-institutionalized cultural traits; they are poles on a continuum. A society turns events into precedents. In time, some may be formally organized and enforced by groups within the society. Thus, the process of institutionalization is a continuous one. Informal instruction is carried on in homes and communities, and eventually, some of it is formally incorporated into schools. Even so, many of the informal practices of teaching continue alongside institutionalized education.

Different societies institutionalize different activities. Religious behavior is highly organized in some societies, as are political processes and warfare in others. Moreover, people in one society may give higher priority to one institution than another. For instance, in medieval

A royal funeral in Sangli, India attracts a large crowd of onlookers.

Europe, religion was given prominence, while modern Europe stresses industry and business. Generally speaking, the extent to which a society institutionalizes an activity can be taken as a rough measure of its importance in that society.

It appears that as societies become more complex, the number of institutions within them increases. Complexity apparently demands a more formal organization of groups and their activities in order to maintain the integration of the society. The United States, as we have seen, has a great many highly organized institutions. In contrast, simple societies may have only a few, such as religion and the family, which are found in all cultures.

Summary

All societies are made up of a variety of groups, ranging from families and friendship circles to kinship groups, religious orders, and the society, itself. It is important to distinguish between statistical groups that are created by the anthropologists for purposes of analysis and groups that are perceived by the people themselves. The latter can be divided into societal groups, which provide people with a mental model of the broader organization of their society, and social groups, in which the people interact. The differences are not always sharp, and groups of one type can be transformed into another.

Members in ongoing societal and social groups create their own sense of identity by developing symbols that express their consciousness of kind and boundaries that set them apart from other people. In doing so, groups often become parts of larger social hierarchies, based on the control of wealth, power, and prestige. The extent to which people can move up and down in this hierarchy varies greatly, depending on the ways groups are formed and the nature and values of the society.

Equally important in social analysis is the concept of institutions—the formally organized procedures associated with groups that serve a particular function in a society. In simpler societies, fewer activities are institutionalized, and even in complex ones, different emphases are placed on different institutions. The concept is useful not only in studying social structures and dynamics but also in comparative studies of social organization.

Suggested readings

Bierstedt, Robert
    1970   The Social Order. 3rd ed. New York: McGraw-Hill Book Co. (See, particularly, Chapter 10, for a good analysis of groups.)
Bock, Philip
    1969   Modern Cultural Anthropology. New York: Alfred A. Knopf. (See Chapter 5.)
Homans, G.C.
    1950   The Human Group. New York: Harcourt, Brace and World. (An important earlier work on the topic of groups.)
Murdock, G.P.
    1949   Social Structure. New York: Macmillan. (A classic analysis of the broad range of social organization.)
Service, E.R.
    1962   Primitive Social Organization: An Evolutionary Perspective. New York: Random House. (A perspective different from that taken in this chapter.)

Bonds of kinship
The marriage dyad
The conjugal-natal family
Extended families
Households

Marriage and the family

One of the few cultural universals is that of groups based on the principles of kinship: mother and child, husband and wife. This does not mean that all societies have the same kind of families or even see kinship ties in the same ways; in fact, humans have developed a surprising variety of simple kinship groups. But in some form or other, kinship groups are found in all societies.

Beginning with the building blocks of families, an extremely varied set of kin groups can be constructed, because kinship ties can be traced out indefinitely from each individual. The only limits to such extensions are human interest and memory. Add to this the possibilities of extending kinship by social fiction, such as adoption, and kinship indeed becomes a versatile principle on which to organize social groups and activities.

Bonds of kinship

There must be arrangements for encouraging human reproduction and for the nuturing and training of offspring during their prolonged dependency on adults if a society is to be viable. These needs are met in all societies by means of kinship systems.

As we have seen earlier, all role relationships can be broken down into simple pairs. Kinship groups are built on two basic types of paired or dyadic relationships: "marriage" between husband and wife and "biological descent" of child from parent. To these must be added "adoption," which is the social extension of the principle of descent beyond the biological sphere. Anthropologists have devised a set of symbols for these relationships to assist them in their analyses of even the most complex kinship systems (see Figure 10.1).

Marriage establishes a socially recognized set of relationships among a mated pair, their offspring, and society. At the core is the dyadic relationship between husband and wife, which serves three im-

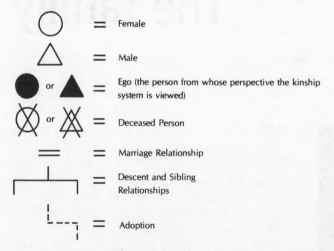

Figure 10.1 Shorthand symbols for kinship analysis help in diagramming relationships.

Marriage   Mother and children

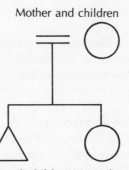

Figure 10.2 "Marriage" and "mother and children" are the principal dyadic relationships, from which all kinship groups are constructed.

portant functions: 1) it sanctions and regulates sexual mating; 2) it makes possible the reproduction of offspring; and 3) it provides for a complementary division of roles, labor, and goods between the couple.

The second important dyad in kinship groups is that between mother and child, by means of which the child is "enculturated," or taught the ways of its culture. While most societies place some responsibility on the father for rearing the child, this is not universal. But the biological and social dependency of an infant on its mother is recognized in all social societies. (See Figure 10.2.)

The "family" is a combination, in one form or another, of these two kinds of relationships within the same social group. In most societies, families meet the important needs of reproduction and enculturation, although there are some notable exceptions, where these functions are separate.

Among the Nayar, a high-ranked agricultural and military caste of south India, the household responsible for raising the children consisted of a woman, her brothers, and her children. Women often married according to Hindu customs, but this was followed in a few days by a divorce, without physical consummation of the union. Thereafter, she was free to choose her mates, and, in fact, she often set up a permanent relationship with one or more high-caste men, who fathered her children. These men, however, never joined the household nor supported their offspring. The males of the household (the brothers and sons) provided for the household and helped to rear the children. In this society, the sexual bond was separate from child rearing, and instead of the conjugal family as we know it, a household composed of a group of related women and their brothers and sons provided for enculturation and continuation of the society.

The marriage dyad

Marriage institutionalizes the relationships between a couple and serves as the basis for the establishment of a family. Different societies, however, give different answers to the questions of who, when, how, and how many one may marry.

Restrictions on marriage

All societies practice some form of "exogamy," the rule that a person must marry outside of the culturally defined kinship group of which he is a member. Mating between parent and child and between brother and sister are considered incestuous in almost all societies. The most striking exceptions are the brother-sister marriages which were required of the royal families of Egypt, Hawaii, Persia, Siam, and the Incas of Peru, to preserve the sacred nature of the royal lineages. A few societies require the marriage of boy and girl twins, on the basis that they have been together in the mother's womb.

Beyond the circle of immediate family members, the line of exogamy varies greatly from society to society, depending in part on how relatives are determined and defined. The Chinese prohibit marriage between people sharing the same surname, while high-caste Indians often prohibit marriages between seventh or ninth cousins. Even in the United States, there are differences from state to state in laws regarding marriage between first and second cousins.

Several explanations have been advanced for the universal presence of incest and exogamy. Early anthropologists, such as Morgan (1877) and Westermarck (1925), argued that inbreeding led to biological degeneration and that societies prevented this by imposing rules of exogamy. The fact is, inbreeding only intensifies the traits already present in the population. "Good" genetic traits, such as those related to high intelligence and resistance to certain diseases, found in a group of people are reinforced and spread by inbreeding. The same, of course, is true of undesirable traits, like low intelligence and susceptibility to specific diseases. However, in balance, given the slow rate of human reproduction and the small populations of human tribes throughout much of history, it appears that the effects of exogamy have been genetically beneficial. The intermingling of genes in new combinations gives rise to an increased variety of biological forms, and new possibilities emerge.

Malinowski (1931) argued that the family would disintegrate as a viable social unit if there were no sanctions against sexual unions of members within the family. These sanctions serve to reduce conflicts in both emotions and roles between family members.

Tylor (1888) and Fortune (1932) advanced other structural arguments to account for exogamy; exogamy, they said, reduces the development of hostile factions within a society. One of the primary threats to any society is the potential for conflict between groups. Marriage alliances between groups help prevent these hostilities from erupting into feuds and wars. In this sense, the exchange of brides, like the trading of economic goods and giving of gifts, helps to integrate the society. Some have questioned the validity of this argument, for while marriage may be useful in forming social alliances, as we see in the history of European royalty, there is no proof that such alliances are crucial to the survival of the society.

A second principle regulating marriages in many societies is that of "endogamy," the rule that people must marry others of their own kind. While exogamy excludes marriage to kinsmen, endogamy excludes those who are culturally defined as "outsiders." (See Figure 10.3.) Tribes and village communities are frequently endogamous groups. So, too, are some tightly knit ethnic groups in the United States, like the Pennsylvania Dutch and the Hutterites.

Classic examples of endogamy are caste systems, such as that in India. Marriages in rural Indian society, with rare exception, take place only within one of thousands of subcastes, many of which number no more than 3,000 people. The selection of a spouse is often limited, and

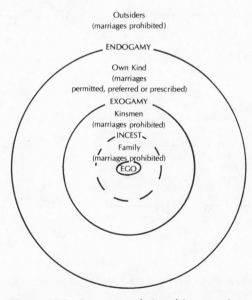

Figure 10.3   In some relationships marriage is permitted; in others, it is prohibited.

parents frequently make marriage arrangements for their children when they are still young. Similar patterns of endogamy may be found in the United States within particular racial groups.

Prescribed and preferential marriages

Societies not only forbid certain types of marriages, they may also encourage or require others. A common social preference is marriage to one's cross-cousin. Kinship systems, such as our own, do not distinguish between descent through the male line and descent through the female line and, therefore, make no distinction between different types of cousins. Many societies, however, trace kinship ties through either the male or the female line. In such societies, a person belongs to the kinship group of his father or to that of his mother but not to both. Thus, distinctions between types of cousins assume importance.

In such societies, "parallel cousins," who are the children of two brothers or two sisters, may belong to the same kin group; but cross-cousins, who are children of a brother and a sister, are not related to each other and therefore can be married. (See Figure 10.4.) In some societies, as in south India, people prefer cross-cousin marriages so that parents do not have to marry their children to strangers, about whom they know little and over whom they can exercise little influence.

Some societies practice asymmetrical cross-cousin marriages, which

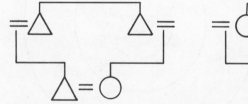
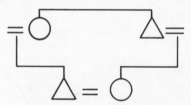
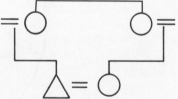
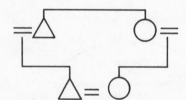

Patrilateral Cross-Cousin Marriage

Matrilateral Cross-Cousin Marriage

Parallel Cousin Marriages

Figure 10.4 Cross- and parallel cousin marriages are of three types: patrilateral, matrilateral, and parallel.

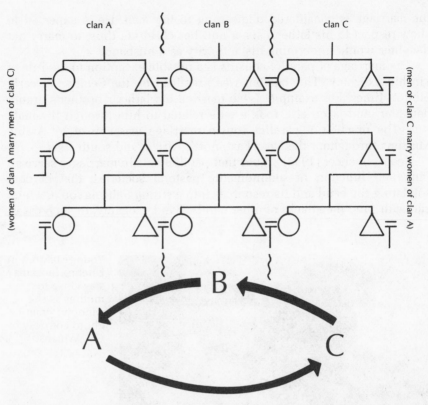

clan A   clan B   clan C

(women of clan A marry men of clan C)

(men of clan C marry women of clan A)

Figure 10.5 Matrilateral cross-cousin marriages ideally lead to a circulation of women among kinship groups and to greater interdependence among the kinship groups.

permit men to marry their fathers' sisters' daughters but not their mothers' brothers' daughters or vice versa. As Levi-Strauss (1969) has pointed out, this leads to a pattern of marriage exchange, in which one kinship group takes brides from a second group and gives brides to a third. In other words, a man takes a bride from the group from which his mother came. (See Figure 10.5.)

Cross-cousin marriage may not only be preferred; it may be required, if a suitable bride is available. Among the high-ranked Komati caste in south India, for example, a man can demand the hand of his mother's brother's daughter (matrilateral cross-cousin) in marriage, and many a father has had to bribe an undesirable nephew to keep him from pressing this claim. Marriage to a father's sister's daughter (patrilateral cross-cousin) is permitted, but there is no right of demand, and the marriage is considered demeaning to the man. He is expected to show respect to his father's sister and her children; thus, to marry her daughter would undermine his authority as a husband.

The marriage of parallel cousins is a notable exception to the rule of kinship exogamy. This custom was practiced by the Semites in early biblical times. For example, Isaac married his father's brother's granddaughter, and Jacob also took a wife related to him through the male line. The practice of parallel cousin marriage was spread by Arabic Muslims throughout the Near East, north Africa, and south Asia.

Robert Spencer (1952) argues that parallel cousin marriages serve an important function in seminomadic pastoral societies, that of consolidating the band and its resources into a strong fighting force, which can withstand the attacks of other bands. Band exogamy, in such cases,

Young children in Uhehe, Tanzania stay close to mother as she winnows grain. Photo courtesy of E.V. Winans.

would undermine group solidarity in a highly mobile and competitive society.

Marriage payments and gifts

Marriages are frequently associated with some type of economic exchange. Most common is that of the "bride price," in which the groom and his family make a payment to the bride's family at the time of marriage. This does not necessarily mean that women are bought and sold as property or that they rank low in status and power within the society. Rather, the payment serves several important functions, which strengthen the marriage and family.

Among the Baganda of east Africa, for example, a man may inherit a wife by means of the levirate,* be given a wife as a gift, or capture one in a raid, but it is preferable that his first wife be obtained by negotiations and the payment of a bride price. The final price agreed on reflects the social prestige of the families of both the bride and the groom.

The groom is particularly careful in selecting a suitable bride, because accumulating the amount needed is often a long and difficult task. Later, he will think twice before divorcing her, because his kinsmen, who contributed towards his first marriage, may be unwilling to finance a second.

Bride price is, in part, a compensation to the bride's family for their investment in her and their loss of her future labor. It also serves, in a sense, as a prepaid alimony, since it is generally not returned if the husband later initiates a divorce. In many cases, the payment represents claim of the husband to his wife's children and the compensation he pays to her family for the loss of their daughter's offspring. For this reason it has sometimes been called a "progeny price." In some societies, children born before the full price is paid belong to the bride's family. Furthermore, the relatives of a barren wife must often provide another bride or return the payment. The Vezo Sakalva of Madagascar go so far as to require that women who divorce and remarry must give one or more of their children by their second husbands to the first husbands, who paid their bride prices. Refunds or substitutions are forbidden.

"Suitor service" fulfills many of the same functions as the bride price. The groom meets his obligations to his in-laws by serving them in specific ways. Sometimes this service may be in lieu of a bride price, but often it is required. Moreover, a man may have life-long obligations to his parents-in-law.

* See the discussion "Marriage Substitutions," following.

Sun Chief: The Autobiography of a Hopi Indian

Leo W. Simmons

One evening . . . my old pal Louis came from Moenkopi. . . . He was as eager to go out among the girls as ever and asked me to suggest one. I told him that I was not familiar with any girls in Oraibi and did not like it so well for that reason. Louis said, "I have made love with Iola of the Fire Clan before, but now she does not like me very well." I knew that she was staying with her clan sister, Irene, whose parents had gone to the field house at Loloma Spring. Since we could think of no other available lovers, Louis said, "Let's take these girls by force." I discouraged it and told him that I had never used force on any girl. . . . But Louis urged until I finally agreed.

We found the girls grinding corn and decided to sneak into Irene's house and wait in the dark. Finally, as the two entered, Louis grabbed Iola and blew out the light. I caught hold of Irene and quickly assured her that she had nothing to fear. . . . I put my arms around Irene, drew her to me, and said, "What is in your mind?" "Have you asked your parents about this?" she inquired. "No, but I will shortly," I answered. . . . I begged Irene urgently with words of love and promises of marriage. Finally she said, "It's up to you." . . .

The next day . . . I asked for the hand of Irene. He replied: "My daughter is not a good-looking girl. If your relatives are willing, you may have her." I told him that I had my parents' consent and that they were well pleased. This was a lie, but a necessary one in order to spend the night with Irene. They agreed and arranged for us to have the next room. . . .

At [home the next morning] I raised the subject of marriage. "I spent the night at Huminquima's," I said. "And now I want to marry his daughter, Irene." "What did they say?" asked my mother. I assured her that Irene's parents had already agreed. . . . My father spoke: "Well, I won't object, for then you would think I am against you. You are not a good-looking man, and she is not a beautiful woman, so I think you will stay together and treat each other fairly. A good-looking woman neglects her husband, because it is so easy to get another." . . .

The wedding costumes were completed in January. For each bride* there were two blankets whitened with kaolin, a finely woven belt, and an expensive pair of white buckskin moccasins. Soft prayer feathers were attached to

---

* [Sun chief and Louis arranged a joint wedding.]

Source: Leo W. Simmons, *Sun Chief: The Autobiography of a Hopi Indian*. (New Haven: Yale University Press, 1942), pp. 212–214, 216–217, 220–223, with omissions.

the corners of the blankets. Each bride was to wear the large blanket and carry the small one rolled in a reed case when she returned to her house. The small blanket was to be carefully preserved and draped about her at death—as wings to speed her to dear ones in the House of the Dead. The beautiful belt was to serve as tail to a bird, guiding the bride in her spiritual flight.

There was a feast for our close relatives on the day that the men completed the wedding outfits. The brides made puddings, and we butchered and cooked the two sheep that Kalnimptewa had given to us. We gathered at sunset, and the brides took special pains to be good hostesses and to see that everyone was happy and well fed. After the meal they cleared the food away, and our great-uncles, Talasquaptewa and Kayayeptewa, made speeches to them: "We Sun Clan people are very thankful that you brides have come to our household and have taken such good care of us. You have proven yourselves to be good housewives by feeding us all. The wedding outfits are completed, and tomorrow you will return to your homes. We are now the same people, sisters, brothers, uncles, and aunts to each other. Look on the bright side of each day, treat your husbands right, and enjoy your lives. . . ."

[At a later feast, Talasquaptewa addressed his nephews.] "Thank you, my nephews. You are not very good-looking, and I thought you were never going to marry. I am glad that you have chosen such fine wives. You know every woman hates a lazy man, so you must work hard and assist your new fathers in the field and with the herding. When they find that you are good helpers, they will be pleased and treat you like real sons. When you kill game, or find spinach or other food plants in the field, bring them to your wives. They will receive them gladly. Make believe that your wife is your real mother. Take good care of her, treat her fairly, and never scold her. If you love your wife, she will love you, give you joy, and feed you well. Even when you are worried and unhappy, it will pay you to show a shining face to her. If your married life is a failure, it will be your own fault. Please prove yourselves to be men worthy of your clan. . . ."

It is customary for the groom to decide when he will move into his wife's house. . . . As I returned from hobbling the horses, Irene came to our house calling, "Come and eat." She invited all my family—according to custom—but they properly declined. I meekly followed my wife to her home and sat down with the family to a dish of hot tamales wrapped in cornhusks and ties with yucca stems. But I ate so slowly that Irene's mother unwrapped the tamales and placed them in a row before me. I thought, "This old lady is very kindhearted, perhaps she will do this for me always." But I was mistaken; at breakfast I had to unwrap my own tamales, and was put to work for my wife's people.

Mother and child
at market, Ambato,
Eucador.
Photo courtesy of
Vaughn Chapman.

"Dowry," or payments by the bride's family to the groom, are less common. Among the higher classes in Europe and higher castes in south Asia, where the custom was once widespread, the dowry was a means of assisting the couple in the expensive task of establishing a household. Much the same function is served in our own society by the practice of giving gifts to the couple at the time of marriage.

Marriage dissolution

No society approves of divorce, but very few (less than four percent) forbid it completely. Most societies make constant efforts to strengthen the marriage relationship by means of rewards and threats. Nevertheless, there are people in every society caught in intolerable binds of social relationships and cultural expectations, for whom the only solution appears to be dissolution of the marriage.

Murdock (1949) studied forty non-European societies and found that more than seventy-five percent permitted divorce on the basis of repeated infidelity, sexual impotence or unwillingness, and laziness or nonsupport. More than half permitted divorce for reasons of incompatibility, infidelity, childlessness, and nagging. Less than a third permitted divorce on any grounds, however trivial.

Twenty-four of the same forty societies had an incidence of divorce which was greater than our own, but sixteen gave evidence of more stable marriages than in our society. In three quarters of these societies, it is as easy for a woman to obtain a divorce as for a man. Six make it easier for the man, but four make it easier for the woman.

Divorce in societies with strong extended kinship groups appears to be less disruptive than in American society, where the nuclear family remains the basis for most social activities and responsibilities. Women in these societies return, with their children, to live with their relatives or remarry without delay, because often there are no acceptable roles for unmarried adult women.

Wife stealing is another cause for marriage dissolution which is found in a number of societies. Eskimo men used to steal a neighbor's wife, but the neighbor in turn was expected to kill the thief and get back his wife. The wife-stealer, therefore, often found it prudent to kill the husband before taking his wife. Murders associated in one way or another with wife stealing were once common in Eskimo society and a source of considerable social tension.

The conjugal-natal family

In many societies, marriages give rise to "conjugal-natal families," consisting of a husband and wife and their children. In the course of a lifetime, most people twice belong to such a family, once as a child and again as a parent. Consequently, a person faces conflicts of loyalties, to parents and siblings on the one hand and to spouse and offspring on the other. (See Figure 10.6.)

Types of conjugal-natal families

As with other cultural traits, patterns of marriage and family life vary from society to society. The Judeo-Christian practice of "monogamy," or taking only one wife in a lifetime, is found in a relatively small number of societies around the world. Even in Western countries influenced by Christian thought, strict monogamy is not always enforced. Often, men and women may have as many spouses as they choose, so long as they are married to only one at a time, a practice known as "serial monogamy." Many high Indian castes enforce strict monogamy, at least for the female, by prohibiting divorce and forbidding the remarriage of widows.

Middle-class Americans stress the importance of the husband-wife relationship within the role pairs of the family, while also stressing the individual's loyalty to his spouse and to the family in which he is a parent. Consequently, young people move from the home of their

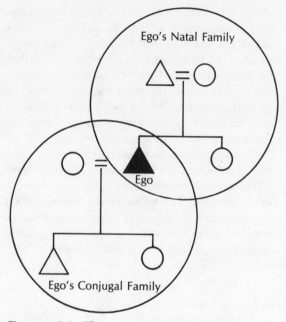

Ego's Natal Family

Ego

Ego's Conjugal Family

Figure 10.6 The generational nature of the conjugal-natal family shows the potential for a conflict of loyalties.

parents to live with a new spouse, whom they may have known for only a few months. If the wife should quarrel with her mother-in-law, the husband is expected to side with his wife against his mother.

Independent nuclear families, such as we have in the United States, are the smallest type of kinship group that can be formed by combining both the marriage and descent dyads. (See Figure 10.7.) The small size and relative independence of such families is an adaptation to the rapid change and status mobility that modern achievement-oriented societies such as ours demand. Nevertheless, a price must be paid for independence and social flexibility, in that conjugal families are relatively unstable groups, with little continuity over time. Children form their own families, leaving parents alone in their old age. Divorce or death may break the marriage relationship, leaving the children with no parents or with parental substitutes to care for them.

Moreover, the constant change in families, as old ones die out and new ones are formed, keeps the family from becoming the basis for organized, long-term social or economic activities, such as providing for the social security of its members, organizing an industry, or main-

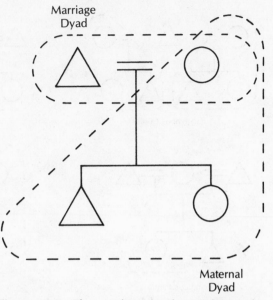

Marriage
Dyad

Maternal
Dyad

Figure 10.7 The nuclear family combines the
marriage and maternal dyads into a single social
unit.

taining an estate. In a few generations, the separation of heirs into different families makes joint action increasingly difficult.

As we shall see later, larger kinship groups have nuclear families as subgroups within them, but the interests of these families in many areas are subordinated to those of the larger kin body.

"Polygamous" marriage, in which a person is married to more than one spouse at a time, can be divided into "polygyny," the marriage of a man to several wives, and "polyandry," the marriage of a woman to several husbands. (See Figure 10.8.) The former is practiced in almost one half of the world's societies, but the latter is rare.

In polygynous families, several mother-child dyads are linked to the same husband. Each of the wives may be housed in a separate hut with her children, or all the wives may share the same house. Jealousy and quarreling between co-wives is common, and many societies encourage "sororal polygyny," or the marriage of a man to several sisters, in the belief that this will help to prevent discord in the household. On the other hand, it is not uncommon for a wife to ask her husband to take another wife to help with the family duties, to produce offspring, or to add to her prestige as the dominant wife in a polygynous family.

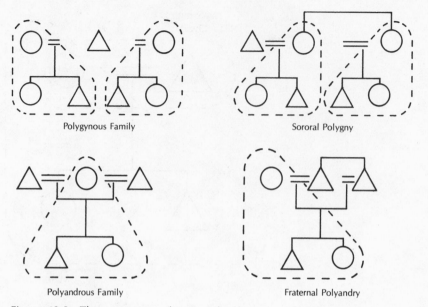

Polygynous Family	Sororal Polygny
Polyandrous Family	Fraternal Polyandry

Figure 10.8   There are several types of polygamous families.

Polygyny serves different purposes in different societies. Additional wives may add labor and income to the family, as well as prestige. It is common in west Africa, among tribes which prohibit sexual intercourse between a couple after the birth of a child until the child is more than a year old. This postpartum (after birth) taboo on sexual relationships enables a child to nurse longer and therefore have a better chance of surviving kwashiorkor, a disease caused by protein deficiency. During this period, husbands with more than one wife are able to satisfy their sexual drives legitimately. As we shall see later, polygyny may also serve as the solution to major social crises.

Polyandry is found primarily in Tibet and among the Eskimos and some tribes in south India. A common form is that of fraternal polyandry, in which a woman becomes the wife of her husband's younger brothers. In some cases, a man may be unable alone to pay the price of obtaining and supporting a wife, so he seeks the assistance of his brothers. In others, as Leach points out (1961:104–113), the custom is associated with the inheritance of land through the male line.

While many societies permit polygamy of one type or another, the number of multiple marriages in any particular society usually is low. The relatively equal balance between men and women and the

Mothers in Tanzania are obliged to carry their infants as they work at essential tasks. Photo courtesy of E.V. Winans.

problems of organizing and maintaining a large family dictate monogamous marriage, except for those with wealth and power.

"Group marriages" are very rare, and apart from experimental attempts at communal life in America, have only been reported mainly in the Himalayan region, where a group of brothers sometimes marries a group of sisters. In these cases, there is a fairly clear distinction of the rights and responsibilities among the members and between them and their offspring. There is little evidence that group marriages were ever normative for early humans, as suggested by anthropologists at the turn of the century, in their attempts to formulate a theory of the evolution of the family.

Marriage substitutions

Marriage not only serves the primary purpose of establishing families; it also may be used by a society to solve some difficult problems arising from social crises. The sudden deaths of men and women in their prime years, when they bear major responsibilities for reproducing and maintaining life, are common to all societies, and the problems which result from such losses must be dealt with.

In American society, we are primarily concerned with meeting the economic needs of the surviving family. Thus, parents are expected to make adequate arrangements by means of savings, insurance, and social security. However, the society does a poor job of fulfilling the other primary functions of the family. There is little provision for parent substitutes to raise the children and to produce more offspring.

Many other societies solve the crises caused by death by arranging for a substitute spouse to assume the roles and responsibilities of the deceased, in much the same way that we make provision for a new President when one dies. Among these, the most common form of substitute marriage is the "levirate," in which the dead man's brother or a close male relative assumes the roles of husband and father when death occurs. In such cases, the sexual rights of marriage are incidental to the responsibilities of supporting the family and rearing the children.

The "sororate" serves a parallel function on the death of a wife—the kin group which provided the husband with a wife is expected to provide him with an unmarried sister or female relative of the first bride as a substitute wife and mother. (See Figure 10.9.)

Among people who practice the levirate, it is common for a man's younger brothers to discipline his children and to assume other parental prerogatives, even during his life. Although death of a parent is psychologically traumatic for young children everywhere, it is apparently less so where a substitute parent is arranged, particularly if this person is one who has already served in a parental role. These same principles hold true in the sororate.

The levirate and sororate also serve social functions. By arranging a substitute marriage to a man within the male kin group by means of the levirate, the group retains its hold on the children who are essential to its perpetuation. The sororate, on the other hand, reaffirms the alliances between the kin groups.

Levirate   Sororate

Figure 10.9 Marriage extensions are either levirate or sororate in type.

In cases where there is neither sibling nor relative of the same generation in a kin group to substitute for a deceased husband or wife, a few societies arrange for a replacement from an older or younger generation within the kin group. Where kinship is reckoned through the male line, a widower may marry his former wife's brother's daughter. If the kinship group is formed on the basis of female ties, a woman may marry her deceased husband's sister's son. Such arrangements reinforce the identity of the kin groups and the ties between them.

Marriage extensions

Not all societies restrict the rights and responsibilities of marriage to the immediate pair. Many allow the partners to extend these privileges to others by socially recognized means. For example, some societies which practice the levirate allow a man to share his sexual rights to his wife with his younger unmarried brothers, reasoning that they will replace him as husband if he dies. This custom, sometimes referred to as "anticipatory levirate," is a form of de facto polyandry, but in many cases, the privileges are withdrawn when the younger brothers marry.

The parallel practice of "anticipatory sororate" permits a man to have sexual intercourse with the unmarried sister of his wife, on the assumption that she is potentially his wife, on the death of his present wife.

Marriage extensions are carried one step further in some societies by allowing men to extend marriage rights to other men, whom they consider to be sociological or blood brothers, or even to close friends and partners, whether or not they are already married. This practice of wife hospitality generally serves several important functions other than sexual gratification.

An example may be seen in the Eskimos of northern Alaska, who inhabit small villages along the seacoast and trade with nomadic bands of Eskimos, who live in the interior near the mountains. A coastal male forms partnerships with men in other villages and in the interior bands, who provide him with protection and assistance whenever he is away from his home village. Partners will also offer him their wives to dry and chew his clothes, in order to keep them soft, and to seal the bond of friendship. The hospitality is reciprocated when the partners visit his village. A man also needs a partner or partners in his own village to care for his wife and children during his absence.

In tribal societies, there is danger and possible death in traveling beyond one's own territory and tribe. Thus, male partnerships, affirmed by wife hospitality, become a means of guaranteeing a measure of security and making trade and travel possible.

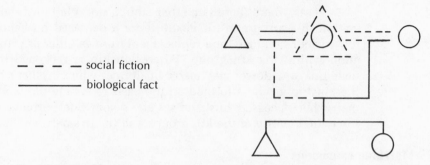

— — — — social fiction
——————— biological fact

Figure 10.10 The Nuer "woman marriage" is a combination of social fiction and biological fact.

Fictive marriages

A few societies have developed special forms of marriage to meet specific needs. One of these is "adoptive marriages," which are found in Indonesia, Japan, and south India. In some Indian castes, a prosperous family having only daughters is faced with the problem of maintaining the family name and inheritance. The legal fiction of an adoptive marriage (*illitum*), in which the husband of one of their daughters becomes a "son" in his wife's family and carries on the family name, solves a critical problem. In giving up his own name, a man loses some prestige, but the economic gains may outweigh the social losses.

Among some west African tribes, a barren woman may arrange for a second wife for her husband, in order to provide him with children. The children of the second wife call the first wife "father," because she filled the male role of negotiating the marriage.

The Nuer of east Africa practice a "woman marriage" for wives who are barren. The childless woman marries another woman, with whom her husband has sexual relationships. The children, however, are considered to be the offspring of the first rather than the second wife. (See Figure 10.10.) In some cases, a woman may be married to the "ghost" of a man, and children she has by another man are attributed to the deceased and perpetuate his name.

Fictive marriages such as these serve important social functions, even though the biological processes may not fit the normal patterns of the society.

Extended families

While Americans place a high priority on the marriage relationship, which results in the constant fragmentation of kin groups into nuclear families, a majority of the world's societies emphasize parent-child relationships. In some, a man's first loyalty is to his father, and when he marries, his wife joins him in his father's household. In other societies, the mother-daughter relationship is considered dominant, and a husband joins the family of his mother-in-law. The result in both cases is the "extended family," which links two or more nuclear families into a single household. (See Figures 10.11 and 10.12.)

In many societies, the ideal is that siblings remain together following the death of the patriarch or matriarch (this is sometimes referred to as the "joint family"), but in fact, few seem to survive the passing of the older generation. The social bonds between brothers and particularly half-brothers in polygynous families appear unable to bear the economic stresses of limited resources.

The extended family provides a greater measure of security than do nuclear families. In event of sudden illness or death of a husband or wife, there are others who can take over the responsibilities. The extended family also provides parents with assistance and guidance in child rearing. Usually, there are several women who care for the children and a number of men who can perform essential family tasks. The extended family also provides a check on maltreatment of children by

Boundaries of the Patrilineal Extended Family

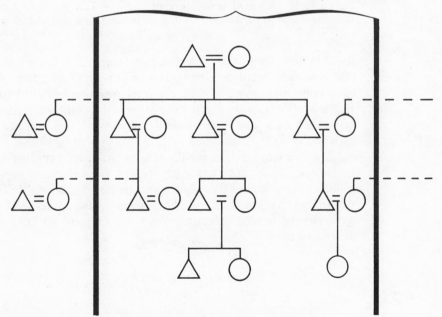

Figure 10.11 A patrilineal extended family is composed of a patriarch, his sons and grandsons, and their wives and offspring.

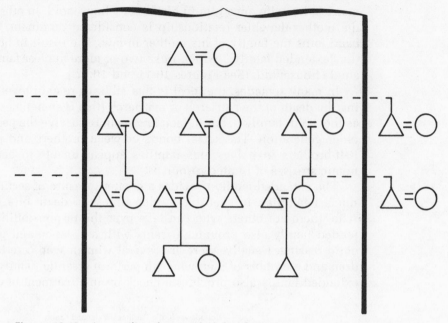

Figure 10.12 A matrilineal extended family is composed of a matriarch, her daughters and granddaughters, and their husbands and offspring.

incompetent parents, a danger not uncommon in nuclear families. Marriages are not accompanied by the setting up of new households, and a new couple may build their sleeping quarters adjacent to the central house, but frequently it joins the others in a common kitchen. The husband and wife join in the overall responsibilities and tasks of the extended family.

Another explanation for the rise of extended families appears to be economic. They are frequently found in sedentary agricultural societies, where large labor forces and consolidated land holdings are an advantage. As we shall see later, some types of kinship systems can give rise to larger kinship groups, which can act in a corporate or united fashion.

Households

People tend to cluster together into "households," or domestic groups which share a common residence. We have already seen, in the case of the Nayar, that households do not always include a marriage dyad, but such cases are the exception rather than the rule. Technically, households, like other residential groups, are based on the principle of geographic proximity, but because of their close ties to the family, they will be discussed here.

Anthropologists use a number of terms for different patterns of residence for the newly married couple. One must keep in mind that these terms describe residential rules or the expectations of a society, and that in practice there may be many exceptions. Furthermore, the terms are imprecise. When it is said that the couple lives "near the groom's father," it is not clear whether they live in the same house with him, an adjacent house, or even in the same community. Nor is it clear to what extent they join in the affairs of the household. Nevertheless, the terms are commonly used in ethnographic descriptions.

"Neolocal residence" means that the newly married couple is expected to establish a new residence apart from either parent and other relatives. This practice, which is so familiar to middle-class American society with its stress on independence, is, in fact, found in only about five percent of the world's societies. Far more common is the idea that young couples should live near and likely join the household of one of their relatives.

In "patrilocal residence," the wife comes to live with or near her husband's parents. This pattern, found in about two thirds of the societies around the world, is commonly associated with the patrilineal extended family. "Matrilocal residence," in which the couple lives near the bride's relatives, is not so common. "Bilocal" is the term used when the couple is expected to live with the parents of either the bride or the groom.

In some societies, the couple is expected to live with the husband's mother's brother. This pattern, known as "avunculocal residence," is commonly associated with kinship groups in which a man has a close relationship with and often responsibility for his sister's son.

"Duolocal residence" refers to the relatively rare cases where the husband and wife live apart, each with his kin. In such cases, as among the Ashanti of west Africa, marriages do not mean common residence, and husbands periodically visit their wives in their wives' homes.

The reasons why one residence pattern arises in particular situations rather than another is not always clear. As Ember (1973) points out, there is some evidence that neolocal residence is associated with commercial economies in which money is a medium of exchange. Unlike food and other material goods, money can be preserved indefinitely, and stored by the nuclear family to guard against future crises. Societies based on the trade of goods and services apparently depend on extended residential groups for security.

Summary

All kinship systems are built on two types of relationships: marriage and descent. With these two, an astonishing variety of groups can be constructed, from various types of families to complex networks involving hundreds, even thousands of people.

Every society has cultural rules prohibiting marriage to certain people, generally close kinsmen and those who are considered outsiders, as well as rules giving preference to other people. Each also has norms regulating divorce.

Marriages serve a great many different functions. In most societies, these include the granting of sexual rights, a division of labor, and the responsibilities of caring for the offspring, but this need not always be the case. An exception is the Nayars, among whom the residential economic family consisted of a woman, her brother, and her children, and where sexual rights were dealt with outside of the family context. In many societies, substitute marriages are also used to solve social crises created by the death of a spouse by prescribing a substitute. And in a few societies, marriages are used to reinforce bonds of friendship to insure safety in potentially hostile territories.

The marriage dyad is combined with the descent dyad of mother and child to form the nuclear family, which is found in almost every culture. In addition, many societies extend the kinship network to form larger groups, such as the extended family. While these larger groups may take precedence over loyalties to the nuclear families that exist within them, the fact is that all societies have some type of family group which constitutes the primary form of social organization on which all other forms are raised.

Suggested readings

Bohannan, Paul, and John Middleton, eds.
   1968   Marriage, Family and Residence. Garden City, N.Y.: The Natural History Press. (A very useful collection of readings, covering both theoretical and ethnographic articles.)
Goody, J.R., ed.
   1958   The Developmental Cycle in Domestic Groups. Cambridge: Cambridge University Press. (A dynamic view of family organization.)
Homans, G.C., and D.M. Schneider
   1955   Marriage, Authority, and Final Causes: A Study of Unilateral Cross-Cousin Marriage. New York: Free Press. (A critical analysis of the concept that marriage is a form of exchange.)

Radcliffe-Brown, A.R., and D. Forde, eds.
   1950   African Systems of Kinship and Marriage. Oxford: Oxford University Press. (Brief studies of marriage in nine African tribes.)
Schneider, D.M.
   1968   American Kinship: A Cultural Account. Englewood Cliffs, N.J.: Prentice-Hall. (An interesting application of anthropological methods to American life.)
Winch, R.F., and L.W. Goodman, eds.
   1968   Selected Studies in Marriage and the Family. 3rd ed. New York: Holt, Rinehart and Winston. (Readings in contemporary sociology of the family; an excellent collection of articles on Western families.)

Kinship systems and groups

Many Americans grow up with few important kinship ties other than those of their immediate family and are surprised to learn of the elaborate and varied kinship systems found in many parts of the world. Relationships to kinsmen take precedence over other social bonds in much of the world, and large kinship groups serve a variety of important functions in many societies. An old Pomo Indian of California expressed the importance of relatives in his tribe:

What is a man? A man is nothing. Without his family he is of less importance than that bug crossing the trail, of less importance than the sputum or exuviae. At least *they* can be used to help poison a man. A man must be with his family to amount to anything with us. If he had nobody else to help him, the first trouble he got into he would be killed by his enemies, because there would be no relatives to help him fight the poison of the other group. No woman would marry him. . . . He would be poorer than a new-born child, he would be poorer than a worm. . . . The family is important. If a man has a large family, . . . and upbringing by a family that is known to produce good children, then he is somebody and every family is willing to have him marry a woman of their group. In the White way of doing things the family is not so important. The police and soldiers take care of protecting you, the courts give you justice, the post office carries messages for you, the school teaches you. Everything is taken care of, even your children, if you die; but with us the family must do all of that.

Without the family we are nothing, and in the old days before the White people came, the family was given first consideration by anyone who was about to do anything at all. That is why we got along. . . .

With us the family was everything. Now it is nothing. We are getting like the White people and it is bad for the old people. We had no old people's home like you. The old people were important. They were wise. Your old people must be fools.*

Who *are* one's relatives, and how does one relate to them? The answers vary greatly from culture to culture, and there is not always agreement within a culture. Americans, for example, often disagree on who is a second cousin. Some hold that a person is a second cousin to the children of his first cousins. Others refer to this relationship as "first cousin, once removed" and speak of children of first cousins as second cousins. How one relates to cousins also varies, as those who discover the meaning of "kissing cousins" well know!

Principles of descent

Marriage and descent are the two bonds by which all kinship systems are held together. As we have seen, the social relationship of marriage is distinct from, although associated with, the biological

* B. W. Aginsky, "An Indian's Soliloquy," *American Journal of Sociology*, 46 (1940): 43–44. Copyright 1940 by University of Chicago, publisher.

process of mating. Likewise, cultural beliefs about birth and descent must be distinguished from the biological process of procreation. These beliefs also vary enormously from society to society.

Kinship systems can roughly be divided into those which consider the contribution of both parents to the life of the child to be equal and those which assert that one parent contributes more or less than the other. The former are referred to as "bilateral" kinship systems. In Western folk traditions, for example, father and mother were thought to contribute equally to the blood on which the life of the child depended, hence the term "blood relatives" was used for one's biological kinsmen on both the mother's and father's sides. More recently, we have been taught that each parent provides one half of the infant's genes.

Many societies differentiate between the contribution of the male and that of the female to the reproductive process. The Ashanti of west Africa, for instance, believe that a child gets its blood from its mother and its spiritual nature from its father. It is important, therefore, to keep track of both the blood and the spirit relatives and to distinguish between them. The Murngin of Australia believe that spirit children inhabit certain sacred water holes in their desert-like land. If a child wishes to be born, it appears in a dream to a married man and asks which woman is to become its mother. When the mother-to-be passes by the water hole, the spirit child enters her womb as a fish. In later life, people retain a special attachment to the sacred water hole from which they came and to the territory around it.

Differentiation between descent from a male and descent from a female is the basis for lineal kinship systems. In its simplest form, the "unilineal" system is that which grants membership into kinship groups only on the basis of descent from a male or a female, but not from both. Other lineal systems differentiate between these two types of descent but combine them in complex ways.

In discussing kinship, it is important to distinguish between "kinship systems" and "kinship groups." A kinship system consists of the rules in a society which determine who is related to whom and in what way. These rules give rise to kinship categories—the sets of people who share the same relationship to ego. For instance, we have rules about who is an uncle, an aunt, and a cousin and consider all those who fit these categories to be our relatives, even if we have never seen or heard them.

Kinship groups, on the other hand, are the sets of relatives of which we are a part, who know each other as individuals and who interact in some fashion as a corporate group. The difference is similar to that we observed earlier between societal groups and social groups. There may be a close relationship between them, but they are not identical.

Bilateral kinship systems

Each individual has a circle of relatives to whom he or she can trace definite genealogical and marriage ties: parents, grandparents, children, grandchildren, and a great many relatives descended from some common ancestor, as well as spouses. There are two ways to approach the study of these networks of kinship. The first is to study the overall structure and operation of the system, much as an outsider viewing the total picture. The second is to look at the system from the perspective of one's self or ego, when ego is a person living within the system.

Boundaries and groups

If we examine bilateral kinship systems from a structural perspective, each person's relationships are reckoned equally through male and female lines. Since there are no principles limiting the extension of a person's relationship, the networks of kinship multiply rapidly and become more vague as genealogical ties become more distant. The number of relatives tends to increase geometrically, forming a loose and ill-defined network. For example, few Americans today know most of their third, fourth, or fifth cousins, in part because no obligations exist between them. The Anglo-Saxons, on the other hand, required that a man contribute to the progeny price and avenge the death of his third cousins, so it was important for him to keep track of relationships at least to that distance.

The lines of bilateral kinship networks form the endogamous boundaries of a society. This means that all people within a society are potentially related in some manner. Consequently, rules of exogamy in bilateral systems do not exclude marriage to all kinsmen, but only to those within a culturally defined genealogical distance.

Bilateral systems have no kinship boundaries dividing the society into a set of nonoverlapping kinship groups. Each individual is the center of a "kindred," a circle of people to whom he can trace a blood relationship, and few people share the same kindred. Even brothers and sisters, after they marry, do not have the same kindreds, since each acquires the relatives of the spouse. A person's kindred changes throughout his life cycle, with the discovery of previously unknown relatives and with the addition or subtraction of relatives through birth and marriage, death and divorce.

Individuals are not only the centers of their own kindreds; they are also members of the kindreds of all their kinsmen. From a structural perspective, the result is a series of overlapping kindreds within the domain of the endogamous society.

Technically speaking, a kindred is not a kinship *group*, because its members often do not know each other, nor do they unite in joint activities. Rather, as Hoebel has pointed out (1972:443), a kindred forms a pool of personnel, from which different groups of kinsmen as well as individuals are drawn for specific occasions and specific purposes. The circle of relatives with whom an American has speaking acquaintance is almost always greater than that with which he exchanges Christmas cards, and this in turn is greater than the circle of relatives with whom he exchanges gifts or gathers in reunions. An individual may expect many relatives to attend a wedding, but those to whom he can turn for financial aid are likely to number only a few. Moreover, in America, most activities associated with kinsmen, such as weddings, are also open to friends (nonrelatives).

Kinship interactions

From the perspective of the ego, bilateral kindreds can be viewed as a series of concentric circles with ego at the center surrounded by relatives with varying degrees of kinship. Interaction among relatives depends on a number of factors: 1) biological factors—respective sex and age, 2) geographic factors—how close they live to each other, 3) sociological factors—cultural expectations of the relationship, and 4) personal factors—how they feel towards each other. No two sets of relationships are exactly alike.

The flexibility of bilateral kinship systems and the transitory nature of the kinship groups to which they give rise allow the systems and groups to adapt readily to change and permit the individual a great deal of freedom. This probably accounts for the fact that bilateral kindreds are commonly found in seminomadic hunting and gathering tribes and in urban industrial societies. In both cases, there is a great deal of mobility and dependence on individual initiative.

On the other hand, because kindreds are not clearly defined groups with stability over time, they cannot serve many of the important functions of a society. People in bilateral kinship systems generally turn to groups and institutions based on other principles to meet many of the needs of society. For example, many religious and educational functions in America are performed by nonkinship organizations.

The overlapping nature of bilateral kindreds often leads to conflicts of loyalty, as individuals must set priorities in the kindreds of which they are members. This further undermines the solidarity of kindreds. One need only consider the celebration of Christmas in this country to see how difficult it can be to organize so simple an activity as a family gathering. Young couples must decide which reunions they will attend and when, and older parents try to arrange their celebrations so that they will conflict least with the plans of their married children, who may have obligations elsewhere. The result is often a rush on Christmas day, as young couples frantically go from one family gathering to another. You can readily see that extensive, long-term activities by large bilateral kin groups are virtually impossible in our society.

Unlike American society, with its temporary ego-centered groups, some bilateral societies have nonoverlapping groups, with clearly defined memberships and stability over time. These groups are called "ramages" or "cognatic lineages" and consist of people who can trace a known genealogical relationship to the founder of the ramage through the male and female descent. Founders are important men who command wealth and prestige, which attracts followers seeking security and aid. Members of a ramage have the right to use any lands it may own and to speak in its governing councils. The corporate nature of ramages helps overcome the weaknesses of the more nebulous kindreds of bilateral systems.

Individuals may affiliate with the ramage of their father or mother, and a married couple may join the ramage of either spouse, depending on which is more advantageous. Admission, however, depends on the consent of a group, and the ramage may reject or ostracize anyone who does not fulfill his obligations to the group. When a person joins one group, he ceases to be an active member of other ramages to which he can lay claim but may maintain some relationships with them.

Unilineal kinship systems

Unilineal kinship systems trace descent ties through the male or the female line, but not through both. In "patrilineal" systems, descent is traced only through the male line, with the result that patrilineal groups have at their core a set of men linked by male descent to a common ancestor. (See Figure 11.1.) This does not mean that a person has no interaction with his mother's relatives, but these relationships are distinct from and subordinate to his ties to his patrilineal kinsmen.

Unmarried women belong to their father's kinship group in a patrilineal system, but the status of wives varies from society to society. Sometimes they retain membership in the kin groups of their fathers, and sometimes they join their husbands' groups.

"Matrilineal" systems reckon kinship through the female line; thus, the core of these groups is a line of females descending from a common ancestress. Males generally belong to the lineage of the mother, as do all females.

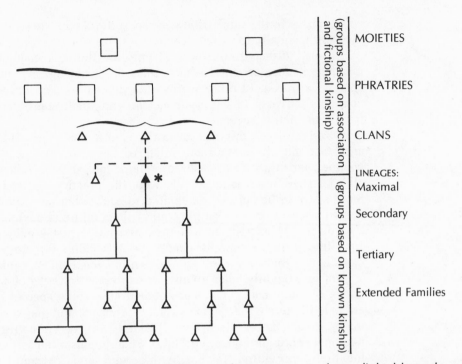

Figure 11.1 Patrilineal units have at their core a set of men linked by male descent from a common ancestor (*). Lineages are based on known descent and clans on fictive descent. Phratries and moieties are further groupings of clans into larger units. The same pattern is true for matrilineal units except, of course, the core is composed of females.

Unilineal categories and groups

The basic social unit larger than the family in unilineal systems is the "lineage." (See again Figure 11.1.) These are sets of kinsmen who can trace their genealogical relationship to one another through a common *known* ancestor. "Patrilineages" do so through the male line and "matrilineages" through the female line.

Patrilineal lines of descent split whenever a family has more than one son. Consequently, over several generations, lineages divide into sublineages and those, in turn, into smaller lineal groups. There is no sharp distinction between a maximum lineage, which is the largest set of males who can trace their kinship to a common ancestor and which may extend over six or more generations, and the secondary and tertiary lineages within them. Lineages continually divide as offspring are added and ancestors are forgotten. Some increase in size and strength, while others in the same tribe weaken and die out. These same principles apply equally to matrilineages.

"Clans" differ from lineages only in the fact that while clan members consider themselves related, genealogical relationships cannot be traced. In other words, "patriclans" reckon descent from a common fictive, or imaginary, ancestor, and "matriclans" trace descent from some fictive ancestress.

Clan identity is thus based on the fiction of kinship. While remote ancestors may be lost in the mists of the past, the awareness of a common kinship remains. Chinese clans, for example, consider as kin all who share a surname. If this were the practice in our country all Smiths would be considered related to each other, as would all those named Jones or Brown. People could expect minimal hospitalities from their fellow clansmen, even if they had never met previously. When traveling, a person might check the telephone directory to locate clansmen in the area, who might give him a meal and a night's lodging.

Not infrequently, clan identity is expressed in terms of a symbol or name. In many tribes, clans are named after some species of plant or animal, in much the same way that stickers and flags, names and mascots, such as "Wildcats" or "Huskies," are used in college and professional sports in the United States. Such totems often serve important functions, providing people with social and psychological links between the worlds of man and nature. Members of a clan may trace their origin to a totemic ancestor and feel a special attachment to that species. Frequently, they are forbidden to eat of the species or are required to do so in special ceremonies. Or they may perform rites to ensure the plentiful supply of the species as a food for the rest of the tribe. A classic example of totemism is found among the American Indians of the northwest coast. There the identification between unilineal kin groups and animals was expressed in the construction and rituals associated with the totem poles.

Clans are grouped at times into larger sets, "phratries," whose members, while not considering themselves related, share a sense of common identity and cooperate in specific ways. If all clans are grouped into two such sets, related on the basis of reciprocity, such as the exchange of wives, the sets are called "moieties." Both phratries and moieties are forms of large-scale social organization and, as such, serve many of the functional needs of the society as a whole.

A unilineal kinship system, like its bilateral equivalent, provides the ego with a pool of kinsmen from which his kinship networks and groups are drawn. This pool, however, is not symmetrical, because it includes only the kinsmen of one's father or of one's mother. In some cases, it may include both, but expectations from each are different. For example, in patrilineal societies, it is not uncommon for a man to live and work with his patrilineal kinsmen but to turn to his mother's brother for counsel and friendship.

Nature and function

Unilineal systems overcome some of the difficulties inherent in bilateral systems. For one, they section the society into clearly defined, nonoverlapping kinship categories and groups. Each person belongs only to one clan or lineage and therefore does not face the conflicting loyalties common to bilateral systems. Consequently, it is easier to build large, stable groups on the principle of kinship, which can unite in long-range activities. The kinship group thus takes on a corporate nature of its own, and the individual is subordinate to the activities and decisions of the group.

The corporate nature of many unilineal groups accounts for their functional importance in many societies. Members share economic aid and support each other in their quarrels and legal disputes with outsiders. The lineage or clan may own land and assign it to members for use. It may also regulate the behavior of its members and represent them in the tribal government.

Unilineal groups often serve important religious functions, as we may see among the Ashanti of west Africa (see Figure 11.2). Each lineage is protected by its own ancestors, who are believed to watch over their living relatives, punishing, by misfortune, illness and death, those who break the customs or fail to fulfill their obligations to kinsmen. On the other hand, those who obey the customs and fulfill their obligations may be blessed by ancestors with plentiful crops and many children.

Each Ashanti lineage possesses a blackened stool, the shrine and symbol of its ancestors, on which the chief of the lineage offers food and drinks to the ancestors, while praying for prosperity and long life. The land belongs to ancestors, and the living inherit only the right to use it and to hand it down, in turn, to their children.

Dead Ashanti rulers, the ancestors of the royal lineage, guard the tribe as a whole. The stool of these royal ancestors is the symbolic soul of the nation, and the chief who occupies it forms a link between the living and the dead. The welfare of each lineage and of the tribe is preserved by rituals which maintain the relationships among the spirits of the ancestors, the living, and the yet unborn (Forde 1954:201–205).

A fundamental weakness of unilineal systems is their vulnerability to social splits and feuds, as the division of the society into clans, lineages, and sublineages leads to opposition between individuals and

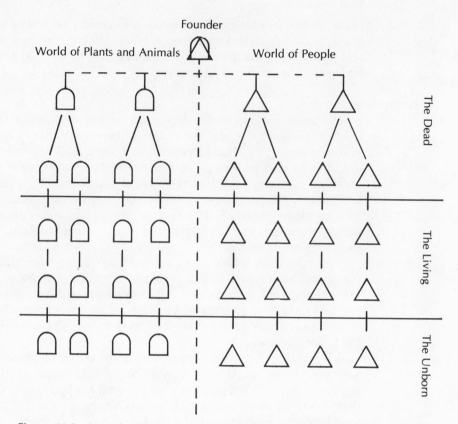

Figure 11.2 An Ashanti clan is made up of ancestors, the living, and the unborn, both animal and human, descended from a single founder.

groups. Brothers support one another in quarrels with other men of their own sublineage; members of a sublineage support their man in a fight with someone from another sublineage; men of a lineage or clan may join their members in conflicts with other lineages or clans. The danger is that these disputes will remain unresolved and, like the legendary Hatfields and McCoys in American culture, generate feuds and bloodshed. Clans and lineages are frequently exogamous, so that marriage ties often help to prevent potential rifts, but, as in the case of Romeo and Juliet, open hostilities between familial groups may be unavoidable.

Sikh men in India enjoy an impromptu celebration.

Double-descent

Complex kinship systems, with both patrilineal and matrilineal principles, are found in parts of Africa and Oceania. Unlike bilateral systems, these "double-descent" systems differentiate between descent through the male and female lines.

The first description of double-descent was given by R.S. Rattray in 1927 in connection with the Ashanti. As we have seen, the Ashanti believe that people are both biological and spiritual beings and that a human being is formed from the blood of the mother and the spirit of the father. The mother-child bond makes one a member of the mother's clan and of her lineage, which forms the basis for residence and political groups. The father-child bond is a spiritual one, in which the father transmits his spirit to the child, molding its personality and disposition. Each person therefore belongs to a biological matrilineage and a spiritual patrilineage.

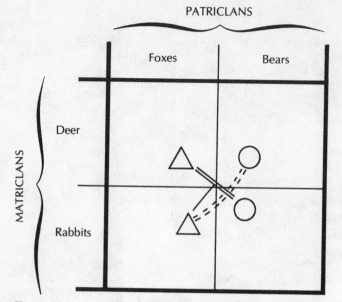

Figure 11.3   A simple double-descent system.

The simplest form of double-descent is the four-section system. For purposes of analysis, imagine a tribe with two exogamous patriclans, the Foxes and the Bears, and two exogamous matriclans, the Deer and the Rabbits. From the former, one receives spirit, and from the latter, blood. (See Figure 11.3.)

A man whose father belongs to the Fox patriclan and whose mother belongs to the Deer matriclan is a Fox-Deer. Since both sets of clans are exogamous, he must marry a woman who is a Bear-Rabbit. Their children will be Fox-Rabbits, because they receive their spirit (Fox) from their father and their blood (Rabbit) from their mother. These children in turn must take spouses who are Bear-Deer.

There are several interesting characteristics in four-section systems. First, both patriclans and matriclans remain distinct. Deer women are related to their mothers, daughters, and matrilineal grandmothers and granddaughters, who are all, also, Deers. On the other hand, Fox men belong to the same patriclans as their fathers, sons, and son's sons.

Second, unilineal descendents of alternate generations belong not only to the same clans but also to the same sections. In other words, the son of a Fox-Deer man is a Fox-Rabbit, but the son's son is a Fox-Deer, like the grandfather. Likewise, a woman belongs to the same section as her matrilineal grandmother. The result, in practice, is a close relationship between grandparents and grandchildren in the same section. Also, fathers and sons cannot compete for wives from the same section.

Third, although a person is restricted in marriage to roughly one-fourth of all potential mates, cross-cousin marriage is possible and often desirable, for cross-cousins share neither patriclans nor matriclans.

Finally, the double-descent rules set up a system of marriage exchanges, in which a patriclan gives its women to the other patriclan but in the next generation receives their daughters as brides for its sons. Every family of husband, wife, son, and daughter-in-law has within it members from all four sections. The result is that all of the sections are tightly knit by ties of marriage and kinship, which reduces the tendency of division and feud found in other unilineal systems. Examples of such four-section systems are the aboriginal Arunta and Tiwi of Australia.

Double-descent systems may have more than two exogamous patriclans and matriclans. In such cases, a person may marry anyone who is not unilaterally related. (See Figure 11.4.) An exception is one eight-section system which has rules requiring that marriage take place only between certain sections. For example, in a system with four patriclans (A, B, C, and D) and two matriclans (1 and 2), the rules for marriage among sections are: A-2 = B-1; B-2 = C-1; C-2 = D-1; and D-2 = A-1.

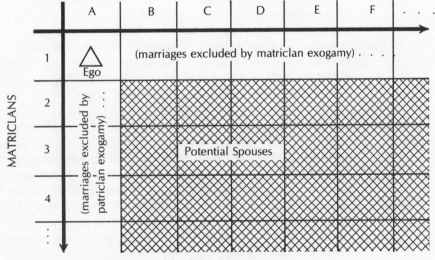

Figure 11.4   A multiclan double-descent system.

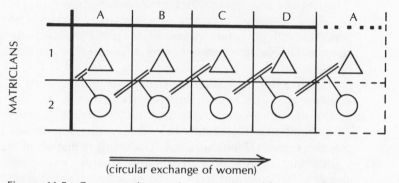

PATRICLANS

Figure 11.5 Cross-cousin marriages are possible in double-descent systems and ideally lead to a circular exchange of women among patriclans.

This leads to a circular exchange of women among patriclans. It also means that men belong to the same sections as their patrilineal grandfathers and grandsons. (See Figure 11.5.)

Kinship terminologies

Lewis H. Morgan, an American lawyer and ethnologist, was the first man to point out the importance of kinship terminologies as a means of understanding kinship systems. He found that the terms a culture uses to describe different types of relationships, such as "father" and "mother," follow certain systematic patterns. Moreover, a system of kinship terminology gives us some insight into the organization of the kinship structure associated with it, and all systems of kinship terminology can be classified into a few basic types.

Kinship terms are symbols for the role relationships existing between two individuals. The great number of potential genealogical relationships makes it virtually impossible for a system to provide a unique term for each one. In all systems, there are some terms, called "classificatory terms," which lump several types of genealogical relationships into a single category. An example of this is the English term "uncle," which includes ego's mother's brother, ego's father's brother, and all men married to ego's "aunts." "Descriptive terms," on the other hand, refer to particular types of genealogical relationships, such as the English terms "father" and "mother."

Organizational criteria

In 1909, A.L. Kroeber (1909:77–84) identified eight basic criteria which are used to organize terminologies in kinship systems. Forty years later, G.P. Murdock (1949:102–106) elaborated on these and added a ninth. Not all of these criteria will be found in any one system of terminology. In fact, the Anglo-American kinship system uses only five. A study of them, however, can help us understand criteria not used in the Anglo-American system.

GENERATION   English kinship terms make clear distinctions as to generations. In other words, people from different generations are identified by different kinship terms. The words "father," "mother," "uncle," and "aunt" carry the connotation of a relative one generation above ego, just as the term "great grandfather" implies a relative three generations above ego. The one exception to generational differentiation is the term "cousin." Some Americans distinguish among cousins, cousins once removed, cousin uncles, and cousin aunts. Others merge relatives from several generations into the general category of cousin.

LINEALITY AND COLLATERALITY   English, like many other kinship terminologies, distinguishes consistently between "lineal" kinsmen, who are related to ego by direct genetic descent (father, mother, grandfather, grandmother, sons, daughters) and "collateral" kinsmen, who are not (uncle, aunt, sister, brother). (See Figure 11.6.) In other words, ego does not receive from or contribute to the genetic makeup of a collateral relative.

This differentiation between lineal and collateral relatives is consistent with the American equation of sociological parents and biological progenitors. The terms "stepfather" and "stepmother" are used when this is not the case. Furthermore, the distinction fits with our patterns of monogamy. There is no term children might use to address a wife of their father other than their biological mother. For many Americans, the parent-child dyad is the dominant relationship next to that of husband and wife. Brothers and sisters are close relatives, but rarely are one's obligations to them felt to be as great as to one's children.

SEX   The term cousin, which is used for more distant relatives, is also an exception to the fact that English terminology differentiates between the sexes. (See Figure 11.7.) When necessary, the speaker may add a qualifying adjective, such as "my female cousin," but the term itself has no connotation of sex of the relative in the manner of terms like "uncle" or "aunt." There are general kinship terms ("grandparents"), but there are also specific terms to indicate the sex of the relative without requiring a qualifying adjective ("grandmother" and "grandfather").

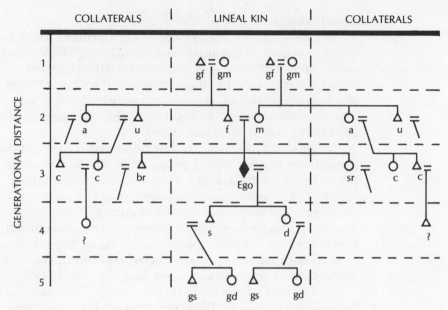

Figure 11.6   Kinship terms in the English language distinguish between lineal and collateral kinsmen and between kin of different generations. (The exception is the term "cousin" for those who do not use such terms as "first cousin once removed" to indicate generational differences.)

Key: gf = grandfather, gm = grandmother, f = father, m = mother, a = aunt, u = uncle, c = cousin, s = son, d = daughter, gs = grandson, gd = grand-daughter, sr = sister, br = brother.

AFFINITY   To some extent, English differentiates between "consanguinial" relatives, who are related to ego through ties of descent or blood whether lineal or collateral, and "affinal" relatives, who are related to ego by marriage. The distinction is made only for a small circle of close relatives, such as mother and mother-in-law or brother and brother-in-law. There are no such terms as "uncle-in-law" or "cousin-in-law." (See Figure 11.7.)

POLARITY   A fifth distinction found in the Anglo-American kinship terminology is that of "polarity." Terms show polarity when two kinsmen refer to each other by different terms, for example father and son or uncle and nephew. Nonpolar terms, such as cousin and cousin, are interchangeable.

In English, polarity coincides with generational differentiation. In many societies, kinsmen from alternate generations, as with ego and a grandparent, refer to each other by the same term, with little danger of confusion. This fits with the close ties that develop between alternate generations in some kinship systems, as examined above.

BIFURCATION   Four of the Kroeber-Murdock criteria are absent in English. One of these is "bifurcation," a distinction based on the sex of the person through whom the relationship is established. Unlike our own system, bifurcated terminologies use different words for those related through the female line (mother's brother) and those related through the male line (father's brother).

Occasionally, Americans use a phrase such as "on my mother's side" to convey the same information. However, in our bilateral kin-

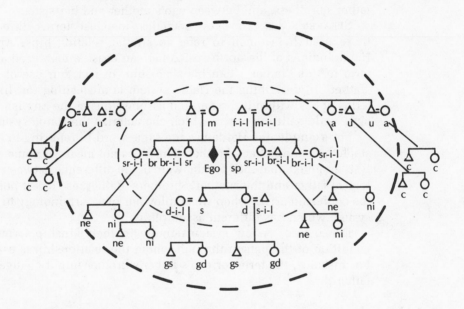

— — — — border within which terms differentiate between consanguineous and affinal

▬ ▬ ▬ ▬ border within which terms are differentiated on the basis of sex

Figure 11.7   At certain distances from the ego, kinship terms in English differentiate between the sexes and between consanguineous and affinal kinship.
Key: sp = spouse,   sr = sister,   sr-i-l = sister-in-law,   br = brother,   br-i-l = brother-in-law,   f = father,   f-i-l = father-in-law,   m = mother,   m-i-l = mother-in-law,   a = aunt,   u = uncle,   c = cousin,   ne = nephew, ni = niece,   d = daughter,   d-i-l = daughter-in-law,   s = son,   s-i-l = son-in-law,   gs = grandson,   gd = granddaughter.

ship system, we normally make no role distinction between collateral relatives on both sides, a difference which is important in unilineal systems.

RELATIVE AGE Some terms indicate the relative ages of kinsmen in the same generation. In south India, for example, the concept of social hierarchy is important in daily life, not only for caste distinctions but also for individual status. Respect should be shown for kinsmen who are older than ego but of the same generation. Different terms are used to distinguish an older brother, to whom ego should show respect, from a younger brother, who is expected to show respect to ego. Similar distinctions are made between ego's sisters, between ego's father and father's brothers, and between ego's mother and her sisters.

SPEAKER'S SEX In a few societies, men use terms different from those used by women to refer to similar relationships. Among the Haida Indians of the northwest American coast, a man used a different term for his "father" than his sister did. In fact, our use of the word "father" in describing the Haida system is misleading for, like all our terms, it has within it the implicit assumptions of the English terminology, while omitting others which characterize the Haida system.

For example, the Haida use the same word in referring to a father, a stepfather, and father's brother. This does not mean, as some early analysts assumed, that they are unaware of the difference between their biological father and their father's brothers. Rather, as Hocart pointed out, the confusion arises when we employ our own terminology to discuss a system which has different assumptions.

DECEDENCE A few systems imply in their kinship terms the life condition of the person through whom the relationship is established. For instance, the term for ego's father's brother might change after the father dies.

Additional criteria

All systems of kinship terminologies use one or more of the Kroeber-Murdock criteria in organizing relationships, but the ways in which they are combined vary greatly. In his study of social systems, Murdock classified six types of terminologies with respect to the way cousins were defined. Even within these types, there is a great degree of variation in how specific relationships are treated.

The study of kinship terminologies is complicated by the fact that people may use one term when *referring* to a relative and another when *addressing* the same person. The terms may also vary from person to person and from age to age. A young middle-class American male, when talking to his peers, may refer to his "old man" or "father," de-

A priest reading scriptures to lineage leaders in India.

pending on the circumstances. He may, however, *address* his father as "Dad" or "Pop," until he grows up. Girls frequently use informal terms for their fathers, even in later life.

Another common practice is "teknonymy"—referring to or addressing a relative as if from the perspective of another person. Thus, when talking to his child, a father may refer to "Mommy" when speaking of his wife. In doing so, he is identifying with the child who sees this woman as "Mommy." In time, the husband may address his wife as "Mom," at least in the presence of their children. In a similar fashion, he may address his mother-in-law by the less formal term "mother."

Kinship terms are extended to other types of relationships in order to convey the affect or feeling associated with the kinship bond. A priest is often addressed as "Father" and a nun as "Sister." Various ethnic groups in our society make wide use of such extensions to convey feelings of kinship beyond immediate genealogical circles.

We must not confuse kinship terms with behavioral practices between kinsmen, even though kin terms, like other role labels, may give us some clue as to the behavior society expects in the relationship.

For example, in societies which practice matrilateral cross-cousin marriage, a man may address his mother's brother's daughters by the same term he used for his wife, because they are potential spouses. But not all societies practicing matrilateral cross-cousin marriage have this kind of terminology, and the practice of matrilateral cross-cousin marriage may be absent from some groups that do.

Summary

In all societies, networks of kinship are greater than the family. The degree to which broader circles of kinsmen join in concerted action and the specific functions they serve, however, vary greatly in different societies.

Bilateral systems, with their flexibility and proliferation of kinship ties that can be activated on necessity, appear to be most suitable for simple hunting and gathering bands. Unilineal systems, with their ability to give rise to large corporate groups that have stability over time, are most closely associated with peasant agricultural societies, with their greater needs for mobilizing human activities.

The picture for highly mobile industrial/urban societies is more complex. The autonomy of the nuclear family and the bilateral kinship system provide obvious advantages, but there are many specific functions which must be met. It appears that in complex societies, such functions are increasingly satisfied by specialized groups and institutions not based on the kinship principle.

Suggested readings

Befu, H. and L. Plotnicov.
  1962 Types of Corporate Unilineal Descent Groups. American Anthropologist, 64:313–327. (A useful discussion on unilineal descent groups.)
Bohannan, P. and J. Middleton, eds.
  1968 Kinship and Social Organization. Garden City, N.Y.: The Natural History Press. (A collection of readings on a wide range of kinship systems by some of the best authors in the field.)
Mitchell, W.E.
  1963 Theoretical Problems in the Concept of Kindred. American Anthropologist, 65:343–354. (Deals with bilateral descent groups.)

Ottenberg, S.
   1968   Double Descent in an African Society: The Afikbo Village Group.
          Seattle: University of Washington Press. (An ethnography and analysis
          of a double-descent system.)
Schusky, E.L.
   1965   Manual for Kinship Analysis. N.Y.: Holt. (A useful manual for working
          out problems in anthropological analyses of kinship systems.)

The nature of associations
Types of associations
Institutionalization

Associations

Kinship groups serve important functions in all societies, particularly in less complex ones. But they are everywhere complemented by groups based on nonkinship distinctions, such as mutual interest, age, sex, and other shared characteristics. American students, for example, enroll in a college, attend classes, patronize local restaurants, use books published by a publishing firm, play games in teams, and go to local hospitals when ill, forming a group in each instance. They may also join clubs to share a variety of mutual interests, such as chess, hiking, or skiing. Groups in which kinship and geography are of little importance in the recruitment of members are called "associations," "clubs," or, sometimes, "sodalities."

In complex societies, such as the United States, associations proliferate almost endlessly, but they are widespread even in simpler societies. However, unlike modern Western societies, where both men and women participate in associations, in primitive societies, men are more devoted to club life. Household duties and male dominance make women's associations relatively rare.

Without the organization provided by associations, many human activities would be difficult or even impossible. Try to imagine what society would be like if people had only themselves and their kin groups for association. Theoretically, this might be possible in the simplest societies, but in complex ones, ordinary living requires a great deal more organization.

Associations provide organization, but the extent to which they do so varies greatly. Car pools are formed by individuals with informal arrangements among themselves. If one individual discontinues his role in the car pool, it is not unlikely that the association, itself, will end. The U.S. Army, on the other hand, has a great many formally defined statuses and rules, and it can exist for a long period of time despite high personnel turnover. Formal organizations, such as armies, with clearly defined roles and leadership, are less dependent on specific individuals for their maintenance than are smaller, informal groups.

The nature of associations

All associations have certain common characteristics by which they can be analyzed and classified. We shall examine them in some detail here.

Function

An association is a group of people who have one or more interests in common. These interests are the group's functions, the purposes for which it was formed; and the range of such interests is as broad as culture, itself. This can readily be seen by tabulating the clubs, committees, businesses, churches, and political parties found in an American town or city or the variety of associations in which a typical college student may participate.

Commonly, an association has one or two principal functions and several subsidiary ones. Colleges exist primarily to provide education, but all have secondary functions, such as football games, social life, and entertainment, that some students consider major attractions. However, things are not always what they appear to be. A motel may be a front for a brothel, and political parties organized to contest elections often operate at the local level to find jobs, fix traffic tickets, and generally influence the political machinery for the benefit of their members.

Other than their primary functions, most associations also serve the important functions of reenforcing an individual's sense of personal identity, of validating his status in the community, and of exercising social control. Associations, in turn, develop public reputations that must be maintained through members' behaviors. A rogue discredits not only himself but his associates, as well. The motives of members of an association, however, are often mixed, as human motives usually are. One may join a church for religious purposes, another to make acquaintances with the hope of selling insurance, a third to meet some attractive person.

Norms

Like other groups, associations develop their own norms of appropriate conduct for their members. Many norms are common to the society as a whole or to broader classes within it, but some are unique to each association. Grades, credits, transcripts, student identification cards, and commencements are characteristic of colleges but would be inappropriate for factories, social clubs, or an army. Moreover, these practices tend to vary in different colleges.

Statuses

Norms are closely related to the statuses developed within associations. Roles, such as student, teacher, secretary, general, foreman, nurse, and quarterback, are linked to particular types of associations and are significant primarily within the activities of those specific groups. The role of quarterback, for example, is important to the football team but is supposed to carry no weight in the classroom.

Significant status differences are often made within an organization that are ignored by outsiders. The public may divide a college into staff and students, but students consider themselves as graduates or undergraduates and as freshmen, sophomores, juniors, and seniors, while the staff distinguishes between faculty, administration, and staff and between instructors, assistant professors, and professors.

Division of labor and status differentiation are the basis of organization. No baseball team is composed only of catchers, nor a university solely of deans. Complex associations enable a great many people with specialized skills to work together to achieve a common goal which no one or few could reach alone.

The structure of associations also permits newcomers to enter with remarkable ease into the activities of associations with which they are somewhat familiar. Surgeons can perform emergency operations in a hospital in which everyone is a stranger, and students quickly enter into the complex activities of college life.

Authority

Even the simplest association has some type of leadership or recognized authority. This may be only informal and based on the charismatic personality of the leader, as in the case of a neighborhood club, or it may be a formal office, such as the chairmanship of the American Medical Association, that exists apart from the person who occupies it. Some form of authority is essential to an association.

Symbols

Associations have names or other identifying symbols to express their uniqueness, such as songs, emblems, slogans, colors, flags, letterheads, secret languages, or rituals. Symbols serve to distinguish one association from another. An association's identification with its symbols can be very intense, as in the instances of the Christian cross and the flags of nations.

Property

Associations mobilize people, and in most cases they also mobilize property. The latter may include a place of meeting and simple artifacts

Labor in rice fields is hard, but a good crop is essential to everyone's well-being in India.

used in gatherings; or it may include a large amount of property in various forms.

Membership qualifications

Most associations demand certain qualifications for membership. They may be minimal, for the purpose of making admission easy, or they may be restrictive, in order to maintain closed associations. Admission requirements may be based on ascribed statuses or on achieved ones; but the recognized memberships of associations set them apart from statistical or societal groups and from crowds and other random aggregates of people.

Types of associations

There are a number of ways of developing taxonomies of associations. One could categorize them on the basis of their property, their types of leadership, or the complexity of their status structures. A common taxonomy, the one used here, is based on the natures of the relationships within associations and on the restrictions placed on membership.

Friendships

Probably the most widespread human association, friendship, has received little attention from anthropologists. This should not be surprising, for unlike most other types of social organization, friendships show little formal structure and duration across generations. It is not at all clear, for instance, whether friendship should be considered a true role in the structure of a society (Nadel 1957:27–33).

While formal reports on this kind of association are few, it appears that friendships are universal, though their nature and extent vary from society to society. Among the Bangwa of the Cameroons, west Africa, friendships form between men and women just as they form between two women or between two men—these relationships have no sexual implications (Brain 1969). Friendships between women are often close and may serve to prevent jealousy between wives married to the same man.

When a young Didinga of east Africa becomes a member of the association of Junior Warriors, he forms a close friendship with a man in the Senior Warriors, who becomes his teacher. The young man tries to live up to the expectations of his older friend, and the bond between them is considered to be stronger than blood or marriage. Such friendships cut across the men's different associations and weld the society into a closely knit whole (Druberg 1935:101–102).

Americans feel that friendships should not be mixed with economic and other obligations. While friends are expected to help one another on occasion, too many requests by one party may threaten the relationship. This is confusing to people who come from cultures where friendships often develop into closely knit relationships, involving economic, social, and ritual exchanges. It is not uncommon for friends in such societies to be trade partners, political associates, and allies, who guarantee the hospitality and safe conduct of one another, particularly when a friend comes from a different, often hostile, tribe.

Among formalized friendships, the extreme is that of blood brotherhood, in which friends ritually affirm their friendship so that it takes on the permanence of a kinship bond. In some cases, this relationship is thought to be stronger than family ties.

Friendships are most often relationships between pairs of individuals, but they may lead to the formation of groups and networks of friends. The former may develop interests and goals other than socializing, and the latter are important to the flow of communication within a community.

Associations based on sex

All societies differentiate social roles on the basis of sex, and in many, sex is one of several criteria used for admission into certain associations. For example, the Boy Scouts, the Catholic priesthood, the Masonic Order, and the Rotary Club are restricted to males, and the Girl Scouts, the Eastern Star, and the Daughters of the American Revolution consist only of females. In fact, many, if not most associations in the U.S., have sex as a rigid criterion of membership, and many actively discriminate against the other sex.

In many societies, sex alone determines admission to certain associations, especially for men. Nowhere is this more highly developed than among the people of New Guinea and the surrounding islands, where men's clubs provide a place for male entertainment and solidarity and a refuge from females, whose sexuality is considered spiritually dangerous. Young boys are admonished to avoid their mothers and sisters and to join in male activities, and formal puberty rites mark their initiation into the fraternity of men. These rites symbolically portray the death of the childhood personality and the resurrection of the novice into a new life, in which he is given a new name and new male privileges and told the secrets that set men apart from women and make them superior.

Women are rigidly excluded from many rituals connected with the men's associations and often from the clubhouses, where men may choose to live permanently (Read 1965).

Men's associations are numerous in tribal societies, but women's associations are not uncommon. The most famous is the "bondu," the female equivalent to the male "porro." Both are found in Liberia and Sierra Leone, in such tribes as the Mendi, the Temne, and the Kpelle (where the bondu is known as the "sande"). Initiation into the bondu involves seclusion and special training in the female roles. Leaders in the association discipline those who are a discredit to womanhood and join with the leaders of the porro in making decisions involving the whole tribe. No important event can be conducted without the cooperation of the "bondu" or the women members who dance at all significant ceremonies.

Like male counterparts, women's associations offer an alternative to life in nuclear families and kin groups, a refuge from people of the opposite sex, and an opportunity to associate with others of one's own kind.

Age grades

Age, like sex, is a basis for social categorization in all societies, and it influences admission to most associations. Even associations that include all men or women of a society do not admit children until they are initiated into adulthood. Societies simply cannot ignore the biological differences between childhood, with its dependency on adults; adulthood, with its maturity; and old age, with its declining powers.

In American society, for instance, people generally find their friends and spouses among their age-mates. New suburban communities are often made up of young couples with their small children, while older communities may consist primarily of middle-aged or senior citizens.

Age dictates an explicit system of social hierarchy for men in many tribes of North and South America and sub-Saharan Africa. In the course of a lifetime, men move according to their age from one age group or grade to another, with changes in responsibilities corresponding to the level they occupy.

A classic example of such age-grading is the Karimojong of Uganda, east Africa, a tribe of cattle herdsmen. All males are members or potential members of one of four major age grades that are seen as generations: the new generation forming, the junior generation, the seniors, and the retired old men. Every five or six years, rites are held in which young boys are initiated into a single "age set"—the group of peers with whom they will proceed through life in the various age grades. After such sets are fully formed, about every twenty-five years, the generation is considered closed, and a new one is begun.

When men in the senior generation, who have served as judges, administrators, and priests of the tribe, grow old, junior generation men, who have been warriors and policemen, become impatient with their elders' senility and incompetence and apply pressure for their retirement. The old men finally agree, and a ceremony is held in which the seniors are retired, the junior men are promoted to the senior grade, and the newly completed generation is raised to the status of juniors. (See Figure 12.1.) Only then can initiation rites for a new generation begin (Dyson-Hudson 1963:353–401).

Karimojong age grades provide each man with secure knowledge of his status in the society and link him to the past, as well as to the future. All men in the generation immediately older than he are treated as

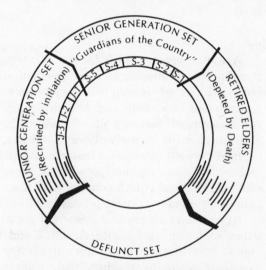

Figure 12.1 All Karimojong males initiated into manhood over a period of five or six years form an age set. Five such sets comprise a generation set. Every 25 to 30 years, all generations move up a generation grade. Age grades provide each man with a clear place within the society.
Source: Modified from N. Dyson-Hudson, *Karimojong Politics* (Oxford, Eng.: The Clarendon Press, 1966), p. 157.

fathers, and those two generations removed are considered grandfathers. Males in younger generations are thought of as sons and grandsons. Also, each man belongs to the same grade his forefathers did four generations before him and as his descendants will four generations after him. As we shall see later, age grade systems, such as this one, also serve important governmental functions in the society.

Formal age grading in the United States is found largely in the childhood years, when children are introduced into schools. With their set of peers, they move up through the grades, and classes often develop an *esprit de corps*, symbolized by class rings and/or identification, such as "The Class of '75." Throughout adult years, admission to other associations, such as the United States Senate, is limited by age, though age is only one of many qualifications for membership for the Senate and most other associations.

Secret societies

In anthropological literature, certain types of associations are called "secret societies" or "fraternities." The word "secret" in such usage can be misleading. In some instances, such as the Ku Klux Klan, members wear masks to hide their identity. But in tribal societies, where everyone is known, masked individuals can be recognized by their absence from the onlooking crowd or by exposed familiar features, such as their feet. The secret aspect of such societies lies in the esoteric knowledge that the association claims to possess, rather than in the membership of the group.

Secret societies are widespread, and their functions are varied. In west Africa, they provide for mutual aid among members and mutual support in conflicts with outsiders. Among the North American Indians, the curing of illnesses was a common activity. Secret doctors' associations had various ranks of shamen who acquired their magical prowess by learning new rites, paying special fees, and getting new titles. In some cases, women were also admitted, but usually only to the lower grades.

The Ku Klux Klan in the United States, the Leopards of west Africa, and the Mau Mau of Kenya exercised political power outside the law. Secrecy of membership and rituals calculated to inspire terror in the public and brutal revenge on outsiders contributed to the power of such organizations to undermine the control of existing governments, and to assume quasi-governmental functions.

Many chiefs of west African kingdoms maintained their power by cooperating with the leaders of secret societies. Modern states have found it very useful to create their own secret agencies (F.B.I., C.I.A.,

K.G.B.), which strengthen their hand in dealing with other nations and help to control crime and dissension within their own populations.

Prestige associations

Membership in age grades and sex-based associations often is compulsory for all who meet the basic qualifications. Every man in the tribe may be initiated into its men's society and move up through the ranks with his peers. But not all tribal associations are so egalitarian. Many are exclusive and admit members only on the basis of wealth, heredity, status, individual achievement, or selection by members of the association. Even among the plains Indians of North America, known for their egalitarianism, admission to a military society involved a costly initiation rite. Many warriors were invited to join on the basis of their brave deeds, but only the wealthy could afford to accept. In west African age grades, the junior grades were open to all men, but higher grades were often restricted to the old leaders of the tribe.

Prestige associations are common in tribal societies and contradict the widely held notion that primitive societies are egalitarian and democratic. Their presence provides for a ranking of people even in the absence of social classes, with power and prestige awarded to the elites, who control, directly or indirectly, much of the everyday life of the tribe.

Exclusive associations are also common in complex societies, where they reinforce the hierarchy of social classes. In the United States, for example, many associations have a general social ranking, and an individual's place in the social hierarchy is determined in part by his membership in more or less exclusive groups. Membership in the Masons, Elks, Daughters of the American Revolution, American Medical Association, and other restricted clubs are based on wealth, birth, or individual achievement, and these criteria are rarely independent of each other. Members of a community's political, economic, and religious elite often meet in such prestige associations.

Special interests

A great many associations, particularly in modern societies, are based on the common interests of their members. In American society, many associations are based on economic interests: unions, cooperatives, trade associations, businesses, corporations. Others are religious in character: churches, parochial schools, seminaries, and mission societies. Some may be political or educational: parties, lobbies, parent-teacher associations, and schools. Even a small American town boasts a list of associations long enough to convince the most skeptical observer of their importance in Western society.

Ironsmiths re-
treading an oxcart
wheel in a south
Indian village.

Special interest associations, however, are not confined to complex
societies. Because they often have short life spans, they may be overlooked in studies of tribal societies. Work groups are a common example. Men or women toil together to clear fields, plant crops, harvest
grain, build houses, and undertake public works, such as roads. Other
associations may deal with markets, trade, crafts, religion, entertainment, and defense.

Institutionalization

Associations may be short-lived groups of people drawn together by
a single task or interest, or they may be formal organizations that endure over time. Moreover, informal associations may evolve into formal
ones: casual entertainment groups into elite country clubs, corner
markets into supermarket chains, political revolutions into governments, religious revivals into sects and denominations, and the ideas of

a few into universities. The patterns of organizational change that transform casual, loosely structured groups of people into stable, organized, and socially integrated ones are known collectively as "institutionalization." They are present to some extent in all human groups but are most easily seen in the development of associations.

Formalization

New associations are generally characterized by informal patterns of organization, leadership, values, and beliefs. So long as the group remains relatively small or the tasks it performs are not crucial to its members, its loose structure may persist.

Associations are parts of a broader social environment, and at times there are benefits to be gained for members if the group is more stable and has its own distinctive competence, reputation, and network of alliances. The American Medical Association, for example, not only provides doctors with opportunities for visiting and exchanging ideas, but also protects their interests by lobbying in federal and state governments. The growth in size of an association may also require a greater degree of organization. In any case, each association is a creature of its own history. The degree to which it develops a formal organization rests in part on its own nature and size and in part on its place in the broader social context.

Formalization results when the informal customs and beliefs of the founders are transformed into the accepted practices and explicit dogmas of their followers. For instance, leadership in informal groups is often vested in charismatic spokesmen, who inspire others to action. As the need for organization grows, there is increasing specialization of

Wai-Wai's of Guyana preparing to carry the "good news" to neighboring tribes.
Photo courtesy of Missionary Dentist.

labor and the formation of specific leadership roles. Ways must be developed to insure continuity of leadership and to invest in it the authority to enforce decisions. Thus, leadership becomes identified with formal offices.

The shift of leadership from individuals to offices is particularly difficult when the founding fathers are strong charismatic leaders, whose decisions are accepted with little question. Their successors are often caught in the thankless task of creating formal leadership roles that are stable and efficient, even though they lack the charisma and popular appeal of the founders. Ralph Abernathy faced this problem when he assumed leadership of the Southern Christian Leadership Conference (SCLC) after the assassination of Martin Luther King.

Obviously, as associations grow larger, it is not possible for all members to participate in day-to-day decisions. Even in democratic forms of association, power and leadership tend to become concentrated in the hands of a few. As a German political sociologist, Robert Michels, noted (1949), leadership in large groups tends to be in the hands of a few, who form self-perpetuating oligarchies that are careful to look out for their own interests.

Patterns of behavior also undergo formalization, as informal practices become traditions, and some in time may develop into enforceable rules or laws. Names, symbols, and paraphernalia of the group acquire sacred value, and the structure of social relationships becomes more defined and rigid. Roles become formal offices, and the relationships between them are rigidly defined. (See Figure 12.2.)

As relationships become more impersonal under the influence of formal roles, informal social relationships develop, which permit people to relate to one another as persons again. Students, for example, cultivate friendships with their teachers to obtain help in planning their careers or to gain personal favors. Teachers, in turn, develop informal channels of communication with administrators at events such as cocktail parties to help them in their work or to make a personal request.

Since formal systems usually deal only with normal affairs and may lag behind changes taking place in the actual operations of the group, ways must be found to deal with special cases and problems, for which there are no solutions within the formal structure. Informal structures serve this important function. In time, informal structures may undergo formalization and be absorbed into the system as new informal relationships develop. Consequently, there is no sharp line between formal and informal structures, and any analysis of how associations and other human groups operate must take both into account.

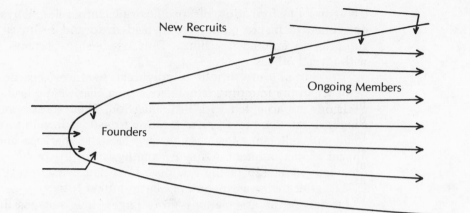

New Recruits

Ongoing Members

Founders

PROCESSES OF INSTITUTIONALIZATION

Informal Roles and Camaraderie ⟶ Formally Defined Roles and Etiquette
Charismatic Leadership ⟶ Official Leadership
Informal Goals and Beliefs ⟶ Explicit Goals and Creeds
Ad Hoc Processes ⟶ Rationalized Rules and Laws
Task-Oriented ⟶ Self-Maintenance as a Main Goal

Figure 12.2 The processes of institutionalization may transform a new association, marginal to the social order, into an integral part of the traditional structure.

The values and beliefs of an association comprise a third area in which formalization takes place. At the outset, these may be expressed simply as a set of commonly shared ideas and interests; but as time passes, the group may develop myths to explain and justify its existence and importance and creeds to make its beliefs explicit. Thus, formalization of leadership, structure, beliefs, and values contributes to the continued existence of associations over long periods of time.

Self-maintenance

At its inception, an association may be formed to express common interests or achieve certain tasks, but many of its members, especially its leaders, soon see personal advantage in its continued existence. As they become habituated to its activities, participation becomes, for them, a valued source of personal satisfaction and identity, and concern arises over maintaining the organization.

Self-maintenance often becomes a high priority in formal associations and consumes a great deal of the leaders' efforts and resources.

Ultimately, self-preservation may take precedence over the goals for which the group was formed, and new goals may be defined to justify its existence after the original ones have been met.

Traditionalization

As associations persist over time, they generally become established in the social order and are infused with social value. On the other hand, they may disappear when their reason for being erodes. However, many become part of the society's traditional way of doing things, successfully establishing themselves in the community's identity.

Anthropologists have noted the force of tradition in tribal societies, but it is also common in modern urban societies. For example, rivalries among the Army, Navy, Air Force, and the Marine Corps of the United States have continued despite government attempts to merge them under a single command. Another example is the delay of the United States in shifting to the metric system of weights and measures, even after most of the world has done so. Vested interests are a powerful force of conservatism in any society.

Summary

Associations play an important part in all societies. By organizing roles, setting norms, allocating authority, and mobilizing resources, they provide the organization necessary to achieve certain tasks. They also help to integrate a society and to provide the people within it with a sense of identity and belonging.

Associations are organized on a great many bases; friendship, sex, age, power, prestige, and common interest are a few. The flexibility that accompanies such variety accounts, in part, for the prevalence of associations in complex societies. The increased specialization of roles and differentiation among groups in urban industrial societies means more organization is needed to maintain the social system. Moreover, in urban societies, kinship groups often play a decreasing part in organization above the level of the family. The result is rapid growth in the numbers and types of associations. As Chapple and Coon point out (1942), the number of associations in a society is one indicator of its relative complexity.

Clubs, churches, age sets, secret societies, companies, and other types of associations frequently begin as informal groups that arise in response to a need. In time, many are transformed by the processes of

Men of south India join together to accomplish tasks, such as treading sesame seeds.
Photo courtesy of Margaret Adams.

institutionalization into stable associations with formal organizations that endure over time.

Structures, however, tend to become rigid and impersonal, and new informal relationships arise to restore a personal touch to communication. These, in turn, are frequently absorbed into the formal structure of the association. In a sense, people and societies are caught between the need for pattern and structure, on the one hand, and freedom to act, relate, and find expression, on the other.

Suggested readings

Banton, M.
    1968   Voluntary Associations: Anthropological Aspects. *In* International Encyclopedia of the Social Sciences, 16:357–362. (A very useful summary on voluntary associations.)

Chalmers, D.M.
    1965   Hooded Americanism: The First Century of the Ku Klux Klan, 1865–1965. Garden City, N.Y.: Doubleday. (An account of a secret society in the United States.)

Eisenstadt, S.N.
    1956   From Generation to Generation. New York: Free Press. (An analysis of age-based associations and the impact of age on social organization.)

Little, K.B.
    1965   West African Urbanization: A Study of Voluntary Associations in Social Change. Cambridge: Cambridge University Press. (A detailed ethnography of voluntary associations in west Africa.)

**Crowds
Communities
Tribes and nations**

Geographic groups

Geography ranks with kinship and association as one of the important principles by which human groups are organized. As we have already noted, kinship and associational groups are influenced in large measure by the geographic distribution of their members. For instance, family members and relatives who live in the same town generally have more to do with one another than with kinsmen who live in a distant city. Other groups in which geography is the principal means of organization vary widely from casual gatherings of people to national and international organizations.

Crowds

One of the most elementary forms of collective behavior may be seen in crowds. These short-lived gatherings of people in one place take many different and often spectacular forms. Mobs, riots, fans at a concert or ball game, evangelistic meetings—these and more are the many faces of the crowd.

Whatever their shape, all crowds have certain characteristics in common. For one, they are transitory and, therefore, lack the stable social organization that is characteristic of groups that persist over time. For another, they have a potential for developing a sense of common identity and purpose. The situation is often unstructured, and the people tend to look to others around them for cues to behavior. Such readiness to follow the group is further stimulated by the emotional excitement and tension that often develop in large crowds. It is this emotional contagion that causes people to lower their critical responses and to accept the norms of the group. Lost in a crowd, people do things they would not do if alone.

As people in crowds develop a sense of solidarity, they also create a kind of morality. Group conformity becomes an important form of identification, and heavy pressure may be brought to bear on individuals who do not conform. Norms emerge as a general consensus develops concerning appropriate or unacceptable actions, and these norms may be related to goals that give expression to the feelings of the crowd. Crowds may lynch a man or rise up in his defense. They are capable of savage, destructive behavior and of the most lofty acts of devotion and sacrifice.

Finally, crowds have some form of social organization. It may range from gatherings like those at a market or fair to socially organized and controlled assemblies, such as political conventions.

Casual crowds

Casual crowds arise spontaneously, without systematic preparation, for example, "sidewalk superintendents" at a construction site and visitors at a zoo. If no great emotional cause attracts everyone's attention, drawing the people together, crowds disperse as soon as the cause of the gathering is gone.

Large gatherings provide the conditions for emotional contagion.

Excitement mounts as people stimulate and are in turn stimulated by one another. As collective emotions intensify, normal judgments are suspended in favor of collective action. At this point, a crowd is readily swayed by a charismatic, authoritarian leader and can be turned into a destructive mob or a mass of screaming fans.

Organized crowds

Not all crowds are spontaneous and unguided. Organized gatherings, in which emotional contagion is controlled, serve many useful functions. Examples are religious rituals, dances, parties, and football games. Such crowds allow people to express their feelings in constructive ways, and the heightened suggestibility of group behavior stimulates response.

Like casual crowds, organized crowds may be passive, displaying little emotional unity, as in people attending a symphony or students at a lecture. Or organized crowds may be emotionally charged, as in some religious mass meetings, political conventions, and rock concerts. But, unlike casual crowds, organized crowds can be controlled. They therefore play an important part in the orderly operation of societies.

There is always the possibility, however, that emotional contagion may turn an organized crowd into an angry mob or a nearly spontaneous riot or revolt. This is a principle well-known to leaders of unstable governments, who frequently ban public gatherings in an effort to prevent revolts against their power and control.

Communities

The basic stable geographic group is the "community," a territorially localized group of people, in which the members satisfy most of their daily needs and deal with most of their common problems. Communities are found in all societies, from the simplest bands to the most complex cities. The character of communities, however, changes as their geographically defined units become larger and more complex.

Earliest communities

We have seen that hunting and gathering societies are generally organized into subsistence bands that migrate in search of game and plant food. Because food supplies are usually limited, the bands are small and may even break up into family camps during seasons when the food is scarce, in order to forage over a larger territory.

AGRICULTURAL VILLAGES With the beginnings of agriculture came

American Indian camp on the waterfront, Seattle, Washington, circa 1890.
Photo courtesy of Photography Collection, Suzzallo Library, University of Washington, Seattle.

sedentary village communities. By 7000 B.C., small villages of about 500 people appeared in parts of southwest Asia. They seem to have been little more than bands that settled down near their fields at first, but in time, such villages developed into complex, agriculturally oriented communities, growing more numerous as farming expanded. The isolated farmer living on his fields, as we know him in the West, is a relatively rare phenomenon throughout the world.

In contrast to cities, which appeared later, with their kaleidescoping change at every passing block, the countryside offered little variety of life-styles to those who inhabited it. The farmer and his village associates were tied to the land and to the natural forces that determined the crops: the hours of daylight and darkness, the progression of the seasons, the weather, and the wind. Farmers thus built a common culture in responding to the environment.

Agriculture was the dominant occupation in the village, and there were often few specialists other than those required for agricultural activities—potters, basketweavers, ironsmiths, carpenters, and the like.

The skills required in an agricultural community were of a more general nature, and each person performed a great many different tasks.

Life in a village was also public; everyone and almost everything was known by all. This led, on occasion, to mutual assistance and to a sense of mutual responsibility in times of need. It also led to gossip and criticism and to envy of others' good fortunes. The fact that the village was (and is) a small, closed system often leads to a feeling that George Foster has called the "image of the limited good."

> By "Image of Limited Good" I mean that broad areas of peasant behavior are patterned in such fashion as to suggest that peasants view their social, economic, and natural universes—their total environment—as one in which all of the desired things in life such as land, wealth, health, friendship and love, manliness and honor, respect and status, power and influence, security and safety, *exist in finite quantity* and *are always in short supply,* as far as the peasant is concerned. Not only do these and all other "good things" exist in finite and limited quantities, but in addition *there is no way directly within peasant power to increase the available quantities. . . .* If "Good" exists in limited amounts which cannot be expanded, and if the system is closed, it follows that an *individual or a family can improve a position only at the expense of others.* (Foster 1965:296–297)

Given this perspective, a person could improve his social or economic position only at the expense of others. Thus, individual ambition was perceived as a direct threat to other members of the community, and there may have been constraints which functioned to encourage the individual to be content with what he had and to discourage him from seeking more.

Social control in a village was generally characterized by a moral order that appealed to tradition. There was a set of commonly accepted values and norms which dictated appropriate behavior in various roles and situations, and conformity to these norms and values was enforced by social sanctions, such as gossip, rebuke, and community action.

NOMADIC COMMUNITIES About the time agricultural villages emerged, another type of highly developed community appeared—nomadic encampments based on animal husbandry. A classic example is the nomadic empires on the steppes of inner Asia, where pastoral peoples developed great oral traditions, abstract art styles, sophisticated crafts, and self-sustaining cultures. Led by warrior chiefs, these migratory people were often at war with the settled agricultural communities around their borders (Bacon 1958).

The basic unit of social organization was the patrilineal extended family, made up of a father, his sons and grandsons, and their families. It was considered good for a father and his sons to live together indefinitely; however, it was not uncommon for them to divide their households before the death of the patriarch. The chief reasons for leaving the parental home were grazing needs and family dissensions.

The family property might be divided anytime after a son reached maturity, depending on the decision of the father. One son was expected to remain permanently with his father and to assume the parental rights when the latter died, but the others could choose to remain in the parental camp or, after marriage, to take their share of the property and move off to set up a new camp or join one already established.

Several patrilineal extended families formed a tribal section, and these were grouped into subtribes and tribes. Tribes and tribal subdivisions were thought of as kin groups, but the factor of common descent was not emphasized. Men generally married women to whom they could trace a genealogical tie, often beginning with their father's brother's daughter and working through more and more distant relatives until a suitable bride was found. Outsiders could be absorbed into tribal sections by marriage or adoption.

The segmentary kinship units of these nomads were also territorial units. Each large segment occupied, by customary right, a certain territory within the territory of the next larger segment, and there was strong identification of a patrilineal group with the territory it occu-

The village well is a community meeting place in India.

pied. Furthermore, small segments or bands often had established rights to certain camp sites for winter quarters and, in some cases, to wells.

The basic territorial group was the camp, which centered around an extended patrilineal family. In addition, a few families that were affiliated with the dominant family through females or friendship or as hired laborers might be allowed to join. The size of a camp was determined by economic factors, certain minimum amount of manpower being needed for herding and other activities. On the other hand, the requirements of pasturing the flocks set the maximum size. Consequently, a father with few sons might find it necessary to join forces with some unrelated families. These bands had a right to migrate in search of pastures within the territory of the tribal section to which they belonged.

The camp was also the basic political unit, and its leadership was in the hands of the patriarch of the dominant extended family. The ability of these camps to mobilize into larger tribal armies, their mobility, and their flexibility in absorbing outsiders conquered in battle account in part for the great kingdoms that developed in central Asia in the Middle Ages.

Towns and early cities

The earliest towns and cities developed between the sixth and first millenia B.C., in widely separated areas of Asia. While we cannot reconstruct their history nor answer all questions concerning their social origins, there is archaeological evidence of several important developments.

First, cities depended, as they still do, on a steady supply of food grown on the land. Early cities were small and scarce, since agriculture was still primitive and demanded a great deal of human labor. It took many farmers to support one man in the city. Ox-drawn wooden plows and stone hoes and sickles were inefficient. But with the discovery of iron, agriculture became more productive. Cities are thus a product of the neolithic revolution, which ushered in agriculture and domesticated animals, and of technological innovations, such as the ox-drawn plow, the wheeled cart, metal tools, irrigation, and boats, that made agriculture efficient.

But food supplies alone did not account for cities. In addition, there had to be a social organization based on specialists who controlled certain types of power: religous and governing officials, military leaders, traders, artisans. The power of city dwellers did not depend on the land. In fact, their concentration in towns reinforced their domination over the cultivators, who worked and often lived outside the walled fortresses of cities.

Transportation and storage were additional key factors limiting the growth of cities. In the absence of roads and, in some cases, wheeled vehicles, the movement of foods and goods to and from the city was difficult. To this was added the danger of bandits, particularly in cases of long distance transportation from city to city. Because of these hazards, regional famines, in which one area suffered drought and food shortages while another had an abundance of grain, were not uncommon. Oxcarts and pack animals provided transportation to and from towns, though only for short distances. Long distance trade was generally reserved for small, high-value commodities used by the elite, such as spices, silks, and gold ornaments.

Tribal loyalties, the absence of new sources of power, and primitive sanitation facilities also limited the growth of the cities. The difficulties of storage further limited the supply of food. Drying was the principal method used to preserve food, probably supplemented by fermentation and pickling. But rot and decay, rodents and insects undoubtedly took a heavy toll, from harvest to harvest.

Despite their difficulties, these small early cities marked the beginning of an urban revolution that is still sweeping the world. In contrast to the localized worlds of the peasant communities, city markets attracted products from ever more distant places, creating a growing demand for new goods and services. Their communication routes brought information and new ideas that helped erode the parochialism of the villages.

The early cities of India, Egypt, Persia, and Greece probably numbered no more than 200,000 people and accounted for only a small percentage of the total population in those regions. Estimates of the population of Rome, with its strong administration, high level of engineering, and good roads, range from 250,000 to almost 1,000,000 people. But by A.D. 800, Rome's population had declined to some 20,000 persons, as the medieval period began in Europe, characterized by feudal estates, tribal invasions, and small city-states. The feudal castle and the monestary gradually replaced the city as centers of cultural activity.

Modern cities

The recent growth of cities has been phenomenal. In 1800, no city in the world had a population of 1,000,000, and fewer than twenty-five had more than 100,000 inhabitants. By 1950, forty-six had more than 1,000,000 people, and thirty-one more than 2,000,000. The New York metropolitan area, which had over 15,000,000 people in 1970, may reach 22,000,000 by 1985. About 16,000,000 people lived in cities over 100,000 in 1800, but by 1950, the number had risen twenty-fold to more than 313,000,000 (Bierstedt 1970:414—415).

What *is* the modern city? It is crowded streets of nameless people rushing to work, shop, and play; and it is stores with neon signs advertising a thousand wares from around the world. Today's city is a trade center and home of stock markets, international banks and corporations, as well as a center of culture, with government buildings, cathedrals, universities, libraries, museums, and sports arenas. There are private clubs, expensive restaurants, corner bars, hamburger stands and pizza shops, movies, ballets, symphonies and rock bands, beaches and parks, pinball machines, and prostitutes.

In other words, the city is paradoxic, an attraction of opposites. In it are creative vitality and decay, crowds and loneliness, hope and despair. It attracts people of all types with its opportunities and offerings, and it often drives them back to the country in quest of peace and quiet!

The study of most modern cultures would be incomplete without some reference to cities. It is in cities that much culture is defined and where change begins, and it is there that power in most of its forms is exercised. Through systems of rapid transportation and electronic communication, rural areas have increasingly become extensions of nearby urban areas, both geographically and culturally.

The suburbs

Unhappy with urban problems and blights and increasingly mobile, by automobile, bus, and train, many people who can afford it have moved out of the city to a new utopia, the suburbs. Suburbs are smaller communities around the borders of cities, which share the "best of both worlds," city and country. It is common in the suburban phenomenon for young married couples to contract heavy morgages for attractive homes in middle-class neighborhoods, where a characteristic lifestyle has emerged.

The working residents of suburbia, mainly men, commute to the city to work, stoically riding the local train or fighting traffic on the freeway. Their reward is to return in the evening to a comfortable home in a town where they are individuals, each with an identity. A man knows his neighbors, the policemen, and local officials in his town, and he votes on local school issues and joins in community activities.

During the day, the suburbs belong mainly to the nonworking women and the children. A few males—firemen, doctors, ministers, teachers—remain to maintain essential services. The children attend schools, which they usually share only with others of their own social kind. The wives and mothers are busy, also, chauffeuring children to school, music lessons, and movies; attending community meetings of the League of Women Voters, Parent-Teacher's Association, and the local church; and managing a household.

This is the suburban dream, and it is the actual experience of a few, particularly the relatively affluent middle-class. As such, it is more characteristic of wealth than social place. But, there are other suburbs, the settlements of the poor that increasingly encircle many of the major cities of the world. Here people live in ghettos, sometimes of tin and cardboard shelters, without proper sanitation facilities, hospitals, schools, or even adequate food. Often the people left rural poverty in search of riches in the city, only to lose what little they had.

The suburb is changing, even for the affluent. As suburbs grow, they demand more local goods and services, and open space becomes filled with shopping centers, factories, and the inevitable invasion of apartment buildings. As the suburb becomes part of the city, people move farther out, but there are limits to commuting, and soon the expanding suburbs of cities meet and merge.

Suburbs today are being absorbed into "strip cities" that stretch for hundreds of miles, with no clear distinction between city and country. Already, the urban strip of Boston to Washington, D.C. (Bos-Wash) contains over 30,000,000 people. Similar megalopolises are developing between Dallas and Fort Worth, between San Francisco and Sacramento, from Chicago to Milwaukee, and along the southern California coast around Los Angeles. Each year, 1,000,000 acres of crop land disappear to feed this urban growth in the United States alone—a total equal to one twentieth of all cropland in the United States in the last fifteen years.

Cities of the future

What will be the shape of future cities? There is a great deal of speculation about this by sociologists, urban planners, and futurologists. All agree that the cities of tomorrow will be radically different from those of today. The networks of computers and electronic communications, the era of nuclear and solar power, the sheer masses and concentrations of people, the threat of global conflicts and famines—all will affect the future growth of cities everywhere.

Technological advances and ecological adaptations will influence social, economic, political, and religious institutions, as well. Disease control, selective abortions, and genetic engineering will give people both the opportunity and the responsibility of controlling the number

Ethiopians drawing
water from a new
bore well.
Photo courtesy of
Sudan Interior Mis-
sion.

and nature of their offspring. Bisexual reproduction carried out in
population-replenishment laboratories or the reproduction of biologically identical individuals from a single cell could radically affect the
organization of society and its institutions.

Technology has brought about a tremendous increase in material
goods and services, and it will be increasingly called on to solve the
problems it has created: overpopulation, pollution of the environment,
power shortages, and, for some, the boredom that accompanies abun-
dant leisure. New legal and political institutions will be needed to
maintain order in an increasingly complex society, and new understandings of the world and the role of people in it will be required to

provide meaning and purpose to life. The potentials for creativity and destruction appear tremendous, but with new technological and social powers come new responsibilities.

Tribes and nations

Most modern societies are larger units, geographically defined, than the community and its extension, the city. These societies may be "tribes," made up of people of a single ethnic identity occupying the same area, or they may be "kingdoms" and "nations," divided into administrative units, such as states and counties; or they may be "international associations," such as the European Common Market or the United Nations.

As societies become more complex geographically, their separately defined units become increasingly important in overall organization. Since this organizational shift is closely related to the development of political power, it will be dealt with in Chapter 17.

Summary

Geography is an important dimension of all social organizations, from the simplest kinship groups to the most complex international organizations. In some social units, geography is subordinate to other principles of organization, such as kinship or associations; in others, it is the dominant defining principle of the unit.

The crowd is the simplest form of collective behavior. Because crowds are easily swayed by emotion, they are often destructive. But *organized* crowds play an important role in the everyday life of most societies.

Communities are the stable, geographically defined groups in which individuals live most of their lives and satisfy most of their needs. The nature of communities varies according to the subsistence base, from bands to villages and cities. In modern times, we have seen the rapid growth of megalopolises composed of a great many communities. But in the urban setting, the tightly integrated community life characteristic of bands and villages often breaks down in the face of a variety of opportunities outside and the rapid change inherent in city life, as diverse cultures are assimilated and new life-styles are created.

On the other hand, cities increasingly become the centers of cultural activity, whether this be economic, political, social, or religious. It is in cities that change often begins. Rural areas tend to become hinterlands of urban influence.

Finally, larger geographically defined units, like kingdoms and nations, have replaced tribes built on kinship principles as the dominant form of social and political organization at the highest levels in modern complex societies.

Suggested readings

Achebe, Chinua.
  1969 No Longer at Ease. Greenwich: Fawcett Publications. (An outstanding and empathic novel, written by one of Africa's leading writers, about a young man in Lagos torn between the old ways and the new.)
Boulding, K.E.
  1965 The Meaning of the 20th Century: The Great Transition. New York: Harper and Row. (One of the best contemporary social thinkers projects the development of civilization into the next century.)
Mangin, William.
  1970 Peasants in Cities: Readings in the Anthropology of Urbanization. Boston: Houghton Mifflin Company. (A collection of case studies from around the world dealing with contemporary problems of urbanization.)
Plotnicov, Leonard.
  1967 Strangers to the City: Urban Man in Jos, Nigeria. Pittsburgh: University of Pittsburgh Press. (An excellent, in-depth case study of urbanization in a Nigerian city.)
Toffler, A.
  1970 Future Shock. New York: Random House. (Looks at the tensions and possible solutions that arise from the rapid cultural changes modern Western people face.)

14

Ethnic groups
Social classes

Societal groups

With the exception of a few isolated hunting and gathering tribes, contemporary societies are so large that individuals do not interact with all or even most of the members of their society. Large societies are generally divided into "societal groups" of people, who are conscious of their common similarities and identity but who do not form a single interactional group. Rather, societal groups provide individuals with mental categories of social organization, which serve as models for interacting with other people in their society.

All complex societies are composed of a number of societal groups, and an individual may belong to many different groups, each dealing with a different area or domain of his life. For example, an American may be a Republican or a Democrat; a Protestant, Roman Catholic, Jew, or member of another religious group; and an Irishman, Swede, Japanese-American, or Chicano.

So far in this text, we have looked primarily at various types of social groups in human societies. In this chapter, we will turn to consider the ways societies, as wholes, are organized. We are thus concerned here with the societal groups that are the most fundamental social categories in a society, with the groups that provide people with the basic consciousness of kind and sense of identity which take priority over other group loyalities.

There are two types of societal groupings to be considered. One is "ethnic groups," which are defined largely in terms of birth and ascribed status. The other is "social classes," which are based to a large extent on achievement.

Generally speaking, the simplest hunting and gathering tribes are single ethnic groups without social classes. Ethnic groups and social classes are not mutually exclusive, however. In more complex societies, one or both may be present. A comparison of the ways these two kinds of groups define their identities and their boundaries and a look at the ways they handle mobility and stratification can give us some idea of how they structure a society.

Ethnic groups

A great deal of anthropological reasoning rests on the assumption that cultures are separate entities that can be clearly distinguished from one another, in other words, that sharp boundaries separate them. Moreover, a particular culture is often associated with a particular group or race of people and a particular language. It is becoming obvious that this is not always nor even usually the case, particularly in complex societies. One cannot make lists of cultural traits and determine from them the social or racial divisions within a society. It is important, therefore, to clarify how ethnic groups are defined and how they relate to one another.

The nature of ethnic groups

Ethnic groups have several basic characteristics that define their nature and distinguish them from other societal groups. These include:

ascribed status, consciousness of kind, shared values and traits, and limited interaction among groups.

ASCRIBED STATUS People are members of ethnic groups primarily by birth; thus, members of ethnic groups share myths of a common ancestry or place of origin and an historical heritage. Such myths may have a factual basis, but often this is difficult to determine.

Because of this biological dimension of membership by birth, ethnic groups are often associated with the idea of "race," as it is socially defined by the people themselves rather than the anthropologist. A feeling of kinship is common among members of a particular ethnic group.

CONSCIOUSNESS OF KIND Ethnic groups are categories by which people both identify themselves and differentiate themselves from members of other ethnic groups. Together, various ethnic groups comprise a map of the society, which helps everyone to organize their interpersonal relationships.

All people have an ethnic identity, which they retain so long as they identify with their group. Membership is not based on achievement, although, as we shall see, it is possible to pass from one ethnic group to another. A man may be a good Japanese-American or a bad one, a success or a failure, but he remains a Japanese-American. If he is rejected by his group, he does not automatically become a member of another ethnic group; he becomes a social outcast.

People from one group can, however, be "assimilated" into other ethnic groups. As individuals, they may be adopted or may marry into a group and thereby gain admission on the basis of fictional kinship. In groups, people may adopt the values and customs of another group and in time be assimilated into it, a process that may take several generations. For instance, it has taken descendants of Dutch and Danish immigrants one to six generations to assimilate into white American society and those of Japanese and African descent much longer (Warner and Srole 1945:283–296).

SHARED VALUES AND TRAITS Ethnic groups are not always culturally homogeneous groups, but the individuals within a group generally share certain distinctive cultural values and traits that symbolize their identity. Several ethnic groups in a single society may share a great many traits. On the other hand, the cultural patterns of members of one ethnic group may differ greatly. In America, for example, middle-class urban Jews are culturally more similar to middle-class urban Irish than to poor Jews or Jews in Europe. Or, if we look at the continuity of ethnic groups over time, the culture of modern American Jews is closer to that of other contemporary Americans than to the culture of Jews of the seventeenth century.

Ethnic identity is thus not based as much on a common culture as on a common sense of identity, which is expressed in certain cultural values and symbols. Of the total range of cultural traits, only particular ones are used by people as symbols of ethnic differences. The remaining traits are not held as bases for ethnicity and can, therefore, be held in common with others. The result is that only rarely can cultures be divided into separate entities, between which there is little or nothing in common. Rather, cultural traits and whole cultural patterns may spread across several ethnic groups or societies in different patterns of distribution (see Figure 14.1). The culture of any given ethnic group or society consists of its unique collection and integration of these traits by people who consider themselves to comprise a single group.

Cultural traits that distinguish ethnic groups from one another are of two kinds. First, there are certain basic values to which the members are committed and certain standards by which their behavior is judged. These may include specific religious beliefs, standards of morality, or assumptions about the nature of reality. Second, there are cultural signs and symbols—features such as language, dress, house form, general life-style, and specific rites expressing their distinctive belief—which people show to establish their identity. The preservation of these fea-

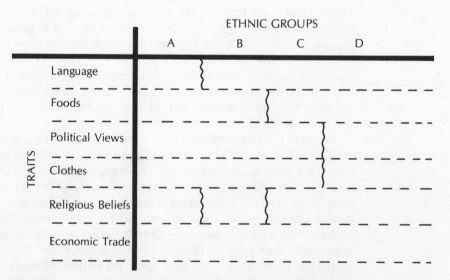

Figure 14.1 Ethnic boundaries are based on select cultural differences that become symbols of the identity of an ethnic group. Note that cultural traits may spread over several groups, forming patterns of distribution in the society.

tures is essential to the survival of the group as a distinct body and to symbolize its identity to others.

LIMITED INTERACTION AMONG GROUPS While members of one ethnic group may interact freely with people in other groups, these role relationships are colored by ethnicity. The others, in one sense, are always outsiders.

Interaction with outsiders generally occurs with the highest frequency in those areas of life not considered crucial to the identity of the group and not reserved only for its members. People of diverse ethnic backgrounds commonly meet in marketplaces or at political or religious centers, for example. On the other hand, interaction with outsiders that threatens to diminish the cultural distinctions of a group must be resisted. Intermarriage with outsiders is particularly threatening, making group endogamy—marriage within the group—mandatory. Attendance at the religious services of others is considered threatening by groups whose identity is centered in terms of religion, for it undermines the boundaries that help to keep groups separate and distinct.

Particular roles in an ethnic group may be reserved only for members of the in-group. Thus, outsiders may be permitted to attend ethnic ceremonies, but priestly offices and leadership are generally reserved for members of the group.

Ethnic boundaries persist despite a great deal of interaction between groups, including what Fredrik Barth, a Norwegian anthropologist, terms the "osmosis" of persons from one group to another (1969:21). It is becoming clear that this flow is more common than formerly believed and that it results from conquests, migrations, social interaction, trade, and the assimilation of ethnic groups by dominant societies.

Types of ethnic groups

From the viewpoint of cultural ecology, ethnic groups may be seen as occupying distinct niches in the social and natural environments to which they are adapted. In this view, the nature of ethnic groups varies according to their relationships to other ethnic groups in the exploitation of natural resources within a territorial region (Barth 1969:19).

TRIBES Tribes are ethnic groups that occupy a single territory and exploit its resources with little or no competition from other ethnic groups. Because each group monopolizes a separate territory, interaction between tribes is often minimal, chiefly involving trade, raiding, and warfare over territorial boundaries. With the rapid spread of worldwide communication networks, isolated tribes have become increasingly rare and are found largely in portions of South America, Southeast Asia, and Africa. (See Figure 14.2.)

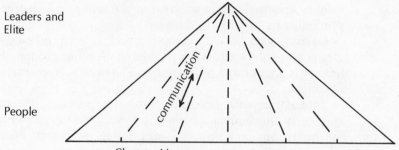

Leaders and
Elite

People

Clans or Lineages

Figure 14.2 Simple tribes are characterized by segmentation based on kinship principles, little social differentiation, and free communication between leaders and people.

More complex situations are found where different ethnic groups or tribes occupy adjacent territories and develop stable relationships with one another. An example of this is the northern Alaskan Eskimos described by Robert Spencer (1959). The Nuunamiut lived in bands inland, along the Brooks mountain range, hunting caribou and gathering plant foods. The Tareumiut lived in coastal villages and hunted sea mammals and fish. Each group spent winters in its respective community engaged in ceremonial and recreational activities and in spring turned to hunting game and whale, respectively. In summer, they gathered in large camps, forming ties of fictive kinship between friends and trading seal and whale hides used for boots and ropes, oil needed for light and fuel, and caribou skins for making clothes. Each was adapted to a particular ecological setting, but each also depended on the products of the other.

POLYETHNIC SOCIETIES It is not uncommon for different ethnic groups to occupy the same territory. To the extent that they compete for the same resources, there is potential for conflict and, in the long run, a breakdown of ethnic identities. Stable polyethnic societies evolve when groups develop symbiotic relationships, in which each depends on the others for certain goods or services.

The nature of the interdependence may vary a great deal. Two or more ethnic groups may occupy clearly distinct niches in the natural environment, with minimal competition for resources. The relationship may involve little exchange except trade of food and material goods. In other areas of life, there maybe little interaction, or the interaction may not be influenced by ethnicity.

One example of this type of relationship is found between the Mbuti Pygmies and the Bantu Negroes of Zaire. The hunting and gathering

Pygmies live in the forest on game, wild honey, and other forest products. They depend on their neighbors, the village Negroes, for metal arrow tips, spear blades, and cooking utensils, as well as for nonessential foods, such as plantains and manioc. The Negro villagers raise food by slash-and-burn agriculture and depend on the Pygmies for meat from the forest and labor in the fields. Whenever the Pygmies want to take a holiday from hunting to enjoy leisure in the village, they go to the village bearing meat and other small gifts from the forest. The Negro villagers try to assert control over the visiting Pygmies and put them to work, but the Pygmies use all their guile to avoid work. "When their welcome is outstayed, and the villagers refuse to give any more handouts, the Pygmies simply return to the forest" (Turnbull 1961:294–95).

Ethnic groups may also develop a close interdependence, providing important goods and services to each other. In this symbiotic relationship, they often draw on the same natural resources, but each occupies a different social niche, in which each has a monopoly on or responsibility for certain roles and means of production.

An example of a closely integrated polyethnic society is found in Rwanda, east Africa, where three groups, the Tutsi, the Hutu, and the Twa Pygmies, live, scattered across the same countryside. The Tutsi are tall Nilotic pastoralists, who, as patrons, political rulers, and military leaders, formerly controlled the labor and economic surpluses of the others. The Hutu are Negroid agriculturalists, who worked the fields of their Tutsi patrons, kept the Tutsi huts in repair, carried their patrons in litters when they traveled and attended them at night. In return, the Hutu clients counted on economic profit on the cattle loaned them by their patrons, help in times of distress, and protection in all spheres of their lives. The Twa Pygmies lived scattered amid the others in the mountain forests, dependent on hunting and gathering. Some were reported to be potters who traded their wares with the Hutu and Tutsi. Others gathered honey and brewed honey beer which was the favorite drink of the Tutsi. And still others served the king of central Rwanda as political spies, court buffoons, and executioners (d'Hertefelt 1965: 407–440).

In the past, relationships, particularly between the Tutsi and Hutu, were often close. Tutsi men occasionally took Hutu wives or concubines, and Hutus and Tutsis belonged to the same patriclans. Moreover, Tutsi men often made blood brotherhood pacts with Hutu men, who did not belong to their patriclan. Nevertheless, the groups remained distinct, for the Tutsi constituted the ruling aristocracy and the Hutu, the commoners. Tutsi chiefs ruled the countryside and commanded the army in which Hutu men were soldiers, so that differentiation in political roles tended to mark social boundaries between them. (See Figure 14.3.)

The political order represented in this sort of ethnically differentiated system was profoundly affected by European penetration into Zaire, which introduced a new ethnic element of great power. The old patron-client relationships were undermined by the German and Belgian systems of colonialism. This became violently evident in the crises of 1959–1963. On the eve of independence, a band of young Tutsi killed one of the Hutu subchiefs. In retaliation, the Hutu turned upon the Tutsi in a rampage of pillage and slaughter. In the end, thousands of Tutsi fled for their lives and between 10,000 and 15,000 of those who held positions of responsibility were executed (Mair 1974:180).

CASTE SYSTEMS   The close interdependence between the Tutsi, Hutu, and Twa also constitutes a simple form of a caste society. Castes are ethnic groups that are integrated into a larger society within which there is differential valuation of the several ethnic groups in a hierarchy. The classic case of such a system is the Indian, found in Asia, south of the Himlaya mountains.

Castes, or *jatis,* as they are often called in India, are integrated into a common social system on the basis of hierarchy. Each caste has a rank based on its ritual purity. At the top are the priestly castes, referred to

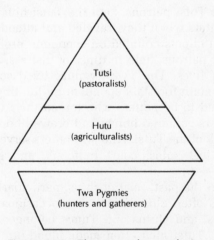

Figure 14.3   There are three ethnic groups of the polyethnic society in Rwanda, east Africa, based on occupations and social differentiation.

Priests leading worship in India.

in general as Brahmins. Beneath these are Kshatriya castes, once comprised of rulers and warriors; the Vaishya castes, which handle banking and trade; and a great many Shudra castes, comprising the farmers, craftsmen (Weavers, Winetappers, Potters, Tailors), and servicemen (Barbers and Washermen). At the bottom of the social scale are castes comprising workers such as the Sweepers and Leatherworkers, sometimes referred to as "untouchables." The number of castes in a village may range from a half dozen to more than forty, and in the country, as a whole, in the thousands.

Hierarchy is an integral part of the values and behavioral patterns of the rural society. The Hindu scriptures teach that all men are not born equal and that some are manifestly more spiritually advanced than others. Thus, priests and those who have spiritual insight deserve respect. The lower castes are responsible for maintaining the purity of the higher castes by performing ritually defiling tasks, such as washing clothes, cutting hair, and removing the refuse, and for handling the more mundane political and economic tasks of everyday life. Society is seen as a single whole, in which each caste has its prescribed duty, and each person who faithfully performs his or her part will be reborn in the next life at a higher level in the social order.

In everyday behavior, hierarchy is expressed symbolically in a great many ways. People in the higher castes abstain from such impure practices as eating meat and drinking liquor or eating food prepared by someone who ranks lower than themselves. Low caste men should not sit in the presence of their superiors, and, in the past, even their touch

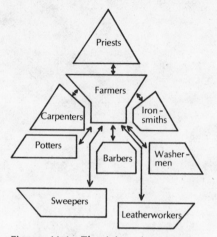

Figure 14.4 The *jajmani* system links families from different Indian castes into socioeconomic networks of interdependent relationships.

was defiling to those in higher castes. These practices not only reinforced the concept of hierarchy but also helped to maintain the boundaries between castes.

A second factor integrating castes into a single system is economic interdependence. Many castes have had monopolies on certain essential occupations, and specialization has been carried out to the extreme. There are blacksmith, carpenter, barber, and washerman castes, as well as castes of braceletmakers, winetappers, weavers of fine cloth, weavers of coarse cloth, fishermen, musicians, snake charmers, jugglers, and beggars of many kinds. The list is endless. Not all castes in India have occupational monopolies, however, and not all members of a caste can find work in their hereditary occupations. Certain jobs, such as day labor, farming, and general trade, are open to everyone.

An interesting variation on occupational monopoly occurred in some areas of India when a caste of thieves, the Thugees, threatened to rob village homes if the leaders did not pay them off. When the agreed upon sum was paid, the Thugees became policemen guarding the village from other thieves, making good their guarantee of security.

A third way castes are bound together is through hereditary networks linking patrons to clients. One type of network, called *jajmani*, links farmers to craft and service castemen, who work for them (Figure 14.4). Payments are made in portions of harvested grain, rather than in cash. The grain is heaped on the threshing floor for distribution. The first portions are sent to the family priest and the temple, as offerings to the gods for their blessings. Then the family blacksmith and carpenter take their shares of the harvest for maintaining the plows and other implements. The potter gets a share for providing pots, the washerman for washing the clothes, and the barber for shaving household males and serving as the family surgeon. The untouchable laborers then take their grain for their year's work. Even in times of drought, so long as the farmer has grain, his clients have a right to ask him for food.

For the most part, Indian castes are endogamous. It is as if in America, anthropologists, sociologists, economists, bankers, plumbers, and other occupational groups were endogamous ethnic castes. Anthropologists would arrange the marriages of their children to those of other anthropologists, and their sons would inherit the right to enter the profession. Other groups would do likewise.

MINORITIES AND PARIAHS In some polyethnic societies, there are ethnic groups that are rejected by the dominant population and thus live more or less apart from the rest of the people. Minority group members may be denied access to positions of high status. In a sense, they form relatively isolated social subsystems with their own values and culture. (Figure 14.5 depicts such a situation.) Their identity, imposed on them by the society as a whole, gives little possibility for interaction with and assimilation into the majority population.

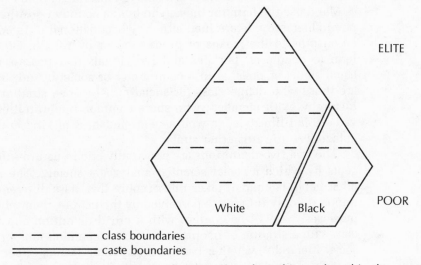

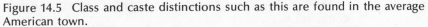
— — — — — class boundaries
═══════════ caste boundaries

Figure 14.5 Class and caste distinctions such as this are found in the average American town.

In extreme cases, minority groups become pariahs or social outcasts, condemned by the larger society as violators of its basic taboos. Examples are the gypsies in Europe of recent centuries, the hereditary butchers (*eta*) of Japan, and the lowest of untouchables in India.

Social classes

As we have seen, in all human societies, there is a differentiation of roles and a division of labor. In all except the simplest bands, this leads to hierarchies based on wealth, power, status, or a combination of these.

People who share essentially the same rank in a hierarchy belong to the same social "strata." They frequently have similar life-styles and may develop common values and form interactional communities. But the extent to which they develop a consciousness of kind based primarily on their social strata varies greatly from society to society.

Definition of social class

It is at this point we must introduce the slippery concept of "class." Unfortunately, "class" is one of those terms essential to a study of social organization, which is used in different ways by different writers. Generically, the term is synonymous with "category." But in the social sciences, class has taken several specific meanings. Some writers, such as Marx, use the term for those who hold a common position in an economic hierarchy determined either by occupational differences and relationships to the means of production or by wealth. Others use the term to denote all families and individuals that possess a relatively equal status or prestige in a community or society. And, finally, there are those who define class (or social class) as one stratum in a social hierarchy, with members who share common opportunities, attitudes, values, and life-style, as well as consciousness of kind and a sense of antagonism towards other strata.

The first two definitions are essentially etic in nature—they are concepts by which a social scientist analyzes a society. The last, on the other hand, is emic. It takes into account that class differences become important only if they are perceived by the people, themselves. For our purposes, we will be content with a broad definition and use "social class" for a stratum of people who share a common rank or status in a social hierarchy, whether based on economic factors or social prestige or both. This definition will be qualified when necessary in specific contexts.

From classless to class societies

Taking the world as a whole, George Murdock found (1967:57–58) that of 862 societies, the majority (sixty-eight percent) were classless. Two thirds of classless societies developed no hierarchy based on individual wealth, skill, piety, or wisdom. The rest recognized social ranks, but people of the same strata did not develop a consciousness of class. Their identities and loyalties lay in their clans, age groups, and other associations. The strata in actuality defined only statistical groups.

The Cheyenne American Indians were a classless society. People were ranked on the estimation in which their family was held by the rest of the tribe. A brave and wealthy man could raise his family to a high rank, and a lazy one would end up poor. But the prestige of the successful families rested in part on their generosity to the poor, particularly those of their own kinsmen, so that the social distance from the bottom to the top of the society was never very great. Moreover, the poor generally had influential and wealthy relatives to whom they could turn for support.

Most societies that have developed distinct classes are divided into two groups, the commoners and the elite, in which the latter control herediatry noble status or power and resources. Only one twelfth (eight percent) of the world's societies were found to have more complex class systems.

The relationship of class identities to other identities is complex. In polyethnic societies, people of different ethnic groups may share the same social rank but feel their primary identification with their ethnic group rather than their class. In many American towns, middle-class blacks are not accepted by middle-class whites into their clubs, churches, social circles, or marriages (see Figure 14.5). On the other hand, a strong class consciousness may provide people with their basic identity, as occurred during the French revolution.

The long-range historical trend appears to be a movement from classless societies based completely on ethnicity to societies in which role specialization, hierarchy, and classes play a significant role. This trend involves several social processes: stratification and the development of elites, class boundaries, interclass mobility, and slavery.

Stratification

Social hierarchies are not unique to classes. Ethnic groups in polyethnic societies are frequently ranked, as in caste systems. The difference between these caste hierarchies and class hierarchies lies in the ways they recruit members and the mobility of individuals within the system.

Unlike ethnic groups and castes, which are based on ascribed roles and recruit primarily by birth, classes depend to a great extent on achievement. It is true that people are born into a class and that the opportunities they have of achieving wealth, power, or status depend to a great extent on the class into which they are born. Nevertheless, in a class sytem, if a person does acquire the necessary resources and roles, it is possible for him to move into a higher class. It is also possible for him to drop into a lower class.

ECONOMIC RANKING   What is the basis on which classes are ranked? Karl Marx related it to economic factors: the control of wealth and the means of production. As an example, he used the post-Industrial Revolution society, in which an individual's standing in the traditionally noneconomic hierarchies did little to help him obtain economic wealth. People were more and more at the mercy of the economic markets.

Few can question the importance of wealth as a criterion for modern class structures, particularly Western ones. Money increases a person's opportunities and adds to his choices of life-styles. Money makes it possible for a person to live in the right part of town, in the right kind of house. It serves as a symbol of success in societies in which material goods are valued highly.

But wealth, in itself, is not sufficient as a criterion of social rank. A recluse may die in a slum with $1,000,000 in the bank. Money is important only because it provides access to many of the status symbols in a society. Furthermore, the manner in which it is acquired may be important. In the West, it makes a difference whether one's money is inherited; earned as professional fees, monthly salaries, or hourly wages; stolen; or welfare.

OCCUPATION   Economic standing is only one dimension of class status. A study by Pavalko (1971) of occupational ranking in the United States found that bankers, county judges, dentists, lawyers, ministers, physicians, and college professors ranked more or less equal, despite the fact that their incomes varied considerably. A bishop of the Episcopal Church may have a low salary, but his office gives him considerable prestige.

A study of six modern nations found that professionals, such as doctors, ministers, teachers, lawyers, and high government officials, ranked highest in all societies. Below them were white-collar workers and skilled labor; then came semiskilled workers, such as farmhands, barbers, and clerks; and unskilled labor was at the bottom (Inkeles and Rossi 1956:329–339).

EDUCATION   In all societies, learning and possession of knowledge,

Tibetan woman with high-class hairdo and jewelry. Photo courtesy of Burke Museum, University of Washington, Seattle.

whether sacred or secular, carries with it a measure of prestige. Chinese and Indian religious scholars were ranked at the top by their traditional societies. In the West, education has been one of the main roads of upward mobility for the middle and lower classes.

RURAL/URBAN LIFE Since their establishment, cities have attracted people with varied patterns of trade, work, recreation, education, political power, and religious activities. With this variety has often come a contempt for rural life, with its reputed sameness.

On the other hand, the peasant and villager has generally been suspicious, not without some reason, of his city cousin, who claims the superiority of urban life. Today, the rural/urban distinction has become one of the most widespread criteria for status ranking in countries around the world.

MULTIDIMENSIONAL APPROACH   One could point out a number of other criteria by which statuses are ranked in a society—sex, age, power, and the like—but it should be clear by now that social hierarchies are complex systems, with more than one dimension of ranking a person. Some writers, such as the sociologist Max Weber (1947), distinguish between three types of strata, based on the dimensions of wealth, power, and prestige. In tribal societies these frequently overlap, but in contemporary complex societies, there appears to be an increasing separation between them. In other words, there is a growing distinction between those who control power, those who control wealth, and those who control more traditional forms of prestige (Eisenstadt 1971: 132–133).

It is obvious that these criteria are related to each other, that people who rank high in one are able to associate freely with those who rank high in the others. Wealth, occupation, education, and other social symbols of success enable people in the same strata to live in the same area, join the same clubs and churches, send their children to the same schools, and develop common values. In other words, such symbols lead to a consciousness of kind. As we have seen, the degree to which this is achieved and the extent to which this class consciousness becomes the primary identity of a people differs markedly from society to society.

One almost universal symbol of a shared life-style is the exchange of food, sometimes referred to as "commensalism." We saw earlier (Chapter 7) that it was not difficult for the Babbitts to eat with someone ranked above them, but they resisted dining with those below them. It is a curious fact that people have sexual relations with and allow their children to be nursed by people with whom they never share a common meal.

Elites

Societies with social stratification have elites, those who hold the highest positions in the society. In some societies, the elite form a distinct class, very conscious of itself, its heritage and cultural distinctives, and the boundaries that separate it from the rest of the people. Membership usually follows along family lines. These "aristocracies" operate, in many ways, like ethnic groups.

In other societies, the elite are somewhat less dissociated from the rest of society. Their life-style may still be exclusive, but they are willing to admit outsiders who acquire the necessary requirements, whether these be in terms of wealth or power. In some cases, "oligarchies" develop, with more than one set of elites, each of which has separate, almost self-enclosed status groups which have a minimum of interaction with other elites.

Intellectual and religious leaders often have distinct places in a society. They may have little economic or political power, but they play a significant part in determining the values and beliefs of the society. Some groups of intelligentsia tend to uphold the cultural order and have a sort of *de facto* alliance with the political and economic elite. They consider their pursuits to be "purely intellectual." A second type is concerned with creating a new cultural order, by revolution, if need be.

Artists, writers, scholars, and other intellectuals in complex societies often remain unattached to the social hierarchy of the local community in which they live. For example, an anthropologist in a Western university may have little interest in joining a local country club but will certainly maintain membership in various scholarly associations. In this sense, intellectuals, like other elites, such as traders and military and political leaders, have commitments to a wider social order and interact with people on a broader scale.

Slavery

Systems of social hierarchy not only have elites at the top, they also have low classes, like slaves. Slaves are to class systems what pariahs and untouchables are to ethnic groups and castes. Both are outside the normal organization of the society, and both rank at the bottom.

Slavery existed in almost one half of the world's societies in the past century. It was most common in Asian (fifty-six percent), Mediterranean (sixty-one percent), and African (seventy-eight percent) societies and least common among the north and south American Indians (thirty and twenty-seven percent, respectively) and the Pacific Islanders (twenty-one percent) (Hoebel 1972:497).

Slavery takes a number of forms. In some societies, captives of wars and raids became slaves in the households of their captors and in time were adopted as members of the master's family and kin group. Slavery, thus, was a step in the assimilation of outsiders into the tribe. In other cases, slaves were considered subhuman and treated as chattels to be bought, sold, or killed at the whim of the master. But, in any case, the lot of a slave has rarely been a happy one.

Wars are not the only source of slaves. In more advanced societies, with practices of borrowing and lending, a poor man might pledge himself or his offspring as security on a loan or to pay back a debt. This form of slavery was common among the Israelites in Old Testament times. Their laws, however, distinguished sharply between slaves from within the ethnic group and those obtained by war or purchase from without. The former were to be respected as human beings and could not be sold or driven ruthlessly as could the others (Leviticus 25:39–46).

In a few societies, with strong legal systems, criminals were condemned to slavery. Other major devices used to punish offenders or to identify the criminal (so that other persons could protect themselves from him) included corporal punishment, disfigurement, exile, and execution. Imprisoning offenders in penal colonies and jails developed in England and Europe largely after the twelfth century.

Class boundaries

While boundaries in ethnic groups are often clearly defined and movement across them is marked by definite role transitions, class boundaries are more nebulous. There has been, in fact, a great deal of discussion as to whether or not they exist.

Studies of several American communities show that people divide their social world into classes in order to compare and evaluate their own behavior and that of others. The problem is that people do not always agree on what these classes are and who belongs to which one. This confusion is compounded by the fact that class structures are constantly changing. The extreme geographic mobility of Americans, the influence of mass communications, and vertical mobility from one class to another keep the classes from becoming closed groups and contribute to the fluidity of the society (see Lynd and Lynd 1929, 1937; West 1945; Warner and Lunt 1941; Warner and Bailey 1949).

There are two generalizations that must be avoided when considering social stratification in a larger society. The first is that the class structure of one community is similar to that of others. Because one town is made up of farmers and townfolk does not mean that this is true of all towns and cities in that society.

The second and more dangerous assumption is that the local class structure in complex societies accurately represents the class structure of the total society of which it is a part. For one reason, few, if any, communities contain a full range of the statuses found in that society. Not every American town has an atomic physicist, a major league umpire, an astronaut, and a representative to the U.S. Congress. There are also broader social networks that cut across the country and link people of one community to those of another. A complete description of social stratification in a society must take these networks into account.

Interclass mobility

Vertical mobility, in which a family or individual moves from one class to another, is characteristic of most class systems, but no society can permit everyone, or even a great number of people, into the upper levels. Middle-class offspring in the U.S. have almost double the chances of those whose fathers are skilled workers to reach the highest statuses in the society and six times the chances of sons of semiskilled laborers. Nevertheless, almost two thirds of the highest statuses are filled by sons of elite fathers (Miller and Fox 1965:6). It was even more difficult to enter the British aristocracy in the past.

In complex societies, with their multiple dimensions of hierarchy, there are many ways to rise in the social order. One can pursue wealth, political prestige, education, religious leadership, or other forms of prestige. Vertical mobility is often made easier by geographic mobility, particularly in moves to a city. A person of a low-class background does not have to carry the baggage of his heritage with him into a new community. But even more important, the society of a city is more fluid than that of the surrounding countryside. The social strata may be more apparent, and the range much greater, but the individual can often move more freely up—or down—the social scale.

The contrast between rural and urban life is particularly great in many Latin American and African countries and in Southeast Asia, where the rural communities are organized primarily by ethnic groups and the urban centers by classes. This, undoubtedly, is one reason why cities attract the ambitious from the countryside (see Lloyd 1966; van den Berghe 1965; and Odaka and Ikuta 1965).

Summary

As societies become increasingly complex, the number of statuses and roles multiplies, and societal groups develop. Societal groups are composed of people who share a consciousness of kind and provide those people with conceptual maps of how their society is ordered and how they should relate to one another.

Two types of societal groups provide the basic building blocks for most societies: ethnic groups and social classes. Simple tribes consist of single ethnic groups occupying their own territories. In polyethnic

The Bushmen of South Africa hunt game in small groups.
Photo courtesy of Burke Museum, University of Washington, Seattle.

societies, several ethnic groups occupy different ecological or social niches in the same region. They may have a minimum of interaction if they occupy different ecological positions. On the other hand, when the groups develop social specializations, a symbiotic relationship can develop, as in caste systems.

Classes develop as societies become more complex and stratify on the basis of social statuses and as people develop an awareness of status based on strata. Many contemporary complex societies have both ethnic groups and classes, and the extent to which ethnicity and class dominate the primary identity of the people varies from society to society.

Suggested readings

Barth, Fredrik.
　1969　Ethnic Groups and Boundaries. Boston: Little, Brown & Company. (An excellent and pioneering collection of studies on ethnic groups.)
Bendix, R. and S.M. Lipset.
　1966　Class, Status and Power: Social Stratification in Comparative Perspective, 2nd ed. New York: The Free Press. (A comprehensive reader approaching stratification principally from the perspective of modern complex societies.)
Bierstedt, Robert.
　1970　The Social Order, 2nd ed. New York: McGraw-Hill Book Company. (See, particularly, Chapter 17 for a discussion on class.)
Eisenstadt, S.N.
　1971　Social Differentiation and Stratification. Glenview, Ill.: Scott, Foresman. (A useful survey of the field and of processes of social differentiation.)
Hiebert, P.G.
　1971　Konduru: Structure and Integration in a South Indian Village. Minneapolis: University of Minnesota Press. (An ethnographic approach to a caste system.)

The nature of economic organization
Types of economic systems
Economic and social change

Economic organization

Social organizations arise for reasons other than gregariousness among people. They are needed to carry out a great many tasks within a society, such as acquiring food, producing material goods, settling disputes, and relating men to supernatural beings. One broad area of culture in which social organization plays an important role is that of "economics"—the creation, distribution, and use of property and labor.

The nature of economic organization

Economics deals with material goods and human property and with the labor associated with producing, distributing, and maintaining them. It is also concerned with how people exchange and utilize goods and services and with what strategies people develop to use goods and services for their own purposes.

Property and technology

All people use and consume material goods. They eat food, build shelters, make tools, and use the land. People themselves are material beings, who can be bought and sold and transported from place to place.

In their relationships to their natural environment and to their bodies, all people make rational observations of cause and effect and of the relationships between things. In short, all people have at least a rudimentary form of science and technology. By science we mean a body of knowledge, rules, and conceptions based on experience and derived from it by logical inference, and by technology we mean the application of this knowledge in dealing with the material world.

The Trobriand Islanders of the south seas have an easy and absolutely reliable method for catching fish in their lagoons—using poison. The Bushmen of the Kalahari desert can track a wounded giraffe for days through the scrub forest until they run it down. The Polynesians sail canoes across hundreds of miles of open ocean from one island to another, charting their course by the shapes and colors of the waves and the nature of the wind. These are all examples of people employing their scientific knowledge in useful ways, through technology.

But economics involves more than material objects and the technology necessary to produce and use them. It deals also with the social relationships that are associated with the production and use of material goods.

All societies have "property." That is, all societies have some things which certain individuals or groups of people have socially recognized rights to limit use of. For example, a stream that flows unused for years is not property. Even when a man builds a dam and uses the water, it is still not necessarily property, for it may be that others can use it at will. Only if the society recognizes that man's special *right* to limit the use of the water does it become his property.

Property includes nonmaterial as well as material things. Eskimo men own songs, and only others who have a man's permission may sing his songs. Ideas and words are important commodities in univer-

A village in Tanzania shows the effect of prolonged dry spells.
Photo courtesy of E.V. Winans.

sities, and people who quote a unique idea must give its author due credit. Property, therefore, consists of 1) things, material or nonmaterial, 2) the use of which is limited by a set of socially defined relationships.

In hunting and gathering and simple agricultural societies, tools and weapons are privately owned by the person who produces them. Moreover, in most societies, there is a distinction between goods owned by women and those owned by men. In more complex societies, where goods are more costly and critical to the success of the individual, the rights of possession tend to become more absolute. On the other hand, complex productive goods, such as irrigation and road systems, railroads, air and sea ports, and factories, are generally owned collectively by groups of individuals or governments in complex societies.

What constitutes property and what socially defined rights are associated with it differs markedly from society to society. As they saw it, many American Indian tribes sold the rights to use their lands, not its ultimate ownership, to the colonists. In American Indian cultures, this ultimate possession of land could never be sold. When they needed the land and asked for its return, they were only exercising this claim. The colonists, however, saw sale of land as a transfer of all rights, without reservations, to the purchaser. The results were misunderstandings and wars.

Labor

Economics deals also with "work"—the energy used in the production, distribution, and maintenance of property. In simple hunting and gathering societies, where this consists largely of human effort, the level of energy use is low. One adult can work at roughly the rate of one tenth of a horsepower. The average for society as a whole is, of course, less than this, because children, the sick, and the aged are largely nonproductive. In simple societies, the only other source of energy may be fire, used for heating and cooking. The total per capita energy output in a year for such societies is less than 200 kilowatt hours. In peasant societies, animal power is added, and in industrial centers, chemical and nuclear energy can raise the annual per capita consumption to over 90,000 kilowatt hours!

Physical labor is not the only economic commodity people have to offer; they may have special skills and knowledge. Particularly in complex societies, with their high division of labor and dependence on forms of energy other than human, knowledge and skills become increasingly important as economic services. Not only do they generally command more pay, they also carry a higher status than manual labor.

Types of economic systems

Societies vary greatly in the ways they organize economic activities. In the New Hebrides, men raise pigs. They trade them, lend them out at interest, and eat them in big ceremonial feasts. Melanesians grow yams. They have contests to see who can raise the largest and most perfect yams. They stack yams in piles until they rot in the sun, to the honor of their owners, who show by this that they have more wealth than they know what to do with. Affluent Americans accumulate money, which they throw away in big parties or use to set up foundations in their own honor.

There are two main dimensions by which these and other economic systems can be analyzed: technological and social differentiation, and systems and media of distribution.

Technological and social differentiation

Economic systems differ markedly in the complexity of their technologies and in the differentiation of their economic roles. At the beginning of this century, this variation was explained in terms of social evolution. Hunting and gathering societies were thought to have simple technologies and comprise the primitive base from which more sophisticated agricultural and industrial civilizations evolved. However, the situation is far more complex than this, and much of modern data, which does not fit a simple linear view of development, proves it.

Not all hunting and gathering tribes have simple technologies and economic systems. The northwest coast Indians had a technology, including fishtraps, whaling boats, and log houses, that was more advanced than that found in many agricultural societies. Nevertheless, a general correlation can be made between the complexity of economic systems and the size and complexity of societies.

TECHNOLOGICAL DEVELOPMENT Societies with simple technologies, limited to hand tools and human energy, are often small. In areas of the world where natural food supplies are limited, the absence of a technology for storing food, other than drying it, means that only limited amounts can be accumulated and that long-range planning is not easy. Furthermore, in many cases, the people lack the technology to use all the food sources available in their territory, or, as in the case of the Eskimos, there are few resources on which they can depend. Transportation is often limited, so that the people are largely at the mercy of the local seasonal variations and diseases that sweep their regions. There are, of course, many exceptions to the insecurity that marks many primitive economies. For example, food-gathering peoples, like the acorn-eating Yokuts of California and the Kwakiutl fishers of British Columbia, were blessed with an abundance of natural resources.

Small communities and simple technologies keep specialized economic roles to a minimum. Everyone of the appropriate age and sex learns the traditional skills, and fulltime specialists are rare. Such specialists as magicians, basket-weavers, boatbuilders, and smiths perform their work in their spare time. Production is rarely broken up into different tasks performed by different individuals, and when it is, the arrangement is often one of convenience, not of specialized skills. For instance, an older man may prepare the thread or raffia and a younger one handle the heavier task of weaving the cloth.

Roles are rarely purely economic, such as employer and employee. People work together because of complex relationships and obligations between them. Economic activities are part of multiplex relationships and inextricably mixed with politics, religion, and social interaction. Nor are institutions purely economic in nature. For example, when the Blackfoot Indians of the American plains gathered each summer for tribal buffalo hunts, the drives were followed by feasts and the Sun Dance, as the social and religious life of the tribe also reached its climax.

The development of complex economic systems is characterized by technological advance and structural differentiation. In technology, there is a shift from simple to complex tools and from human and animal power to machines driven by chemical and nuclear power. Conse-

Wood is the only available fuel in some areas, such as this village in Ecuador. Photo courtesy of Vaughn Chapman.

quently, with technology, people are able to exploit more of their natural resources.

SOCIAL DIFFERENTIATION AND INTEGRATION   As technologies become increasingly complex, structural differentiation begins to take place at several levels. There is an increase in the number of specialized jobs paralleling the complex technology: skilled craftsmen, technicians, engineers, managers, traders, transporters, and financiers. In the extreme case, each person performs one simple and repetitive task in an assembly line or in a system of producing and distributing economic goods.

Differentiation also occurs as multiplex roles give way to simplex roles, in which economic activities are separated from religious, political, and social ones (refer back to Figure 7.2). The family, for example, ceases to be the center of economic production, of religious worship, and of political activity. Work and apprenticeship move into industries, and one or more members leave the home to work in the labor market. Family activities become centered around emotional gratification and enculturation of the young. Even the latter is affected, since the children go to school and thus have little opportunity to learn the economic roles of their parents, by directly observing and imitating them.

Finally, differentiation takes place at the institutional level. There is an increasing specialization in and separation of economic, political, religious, and educational processes. Integration of the society is achieved by the rise of a great many new institutions bringing people together in new ways: factories, businesses, political parties, churches, and schools. Within the economic sphere, there arise specialized groups, such as labor unions, welfare agencies, cooperative societies, savings institutions, professional organizations, and business cartels. All specialize in integration.

Systems and media of distribution

There are three general ways people distribute economic goods and services: reciprocity, redistribution, and market exchange (Dalton 1968). While all three are found in most societies, one is usually the dominant form for economic activities. In general, reciprocity and redistribution are central in societies with simple economies, while various forms of market exchange are characteristic of societies based on advanced agriculture and industry.

RECIPROCITY OR GIFT EXCHANGE Gifts are occasionally given with no expectation of return and little gain, except in social prestige or feelings of moral satisfaction. But for the most part, gifts are part of stable networks of exchange between persons or groups of roughly equal status, in which each party expects to receive approximately as much as it gives. People who fail to reciprocate with gifts of approximately the same value are criticized, and relationships with them are broken.

To develop relationships Gift exchanges cement relationships between kinsmen and friends. This is true, for instance, of gifts given in the United States at birthdays, weddings, and Christmas. There is little room for bargaining, and generosity is praised. In India, separate records are kept of gifts given by the groom's kinsmen and the bride's kinsmen at the wedding. Later, the couple is expected to give comparable gifts at the weddings of the children of these kinsmen. A father arranging a marriage can calculate with some assurance what will be received, and this enters into the marriage negotiations.

In societies with simple technologies, gift exchanges play important economic functions and provide the basic mechanism for the distribution of goods and services vital to the survival of the people. An illustration of this is the Mossi farmers of west Africa. A Mossi farmer needs help to plant and cultivate his crops. He may need to borrow a knife to cut thatch for his roof, a bicycle to visit the market in a neighboring town, or some money for taxes. Even more critical is his need for help when he is too sick to hunt or farm or when his crops fail. At such times, he is able to turn to those whom he has aided in their times of need. It is to a person's advantage, therefore, to help others and build networks of reciprocal obligations.

Another illustration is that of the Pygmies of Zaire. The Pygmies are hunters and give their surplus meat to their agricultural Bantu neighbors, who fear the forest. The Bantu, in turn, give cassava, plaintains, and iron spear and arrow points to their Pygmy partners.

Gift exchanges often set the stage for other types of economic trade. The classic example of this is the Kula ring, described by Malinowski (1922) for the Trobriand Islands near New Guinea. There, an elaborate system of gift exchange was developed between tribes on different islands, in which red shell necklaces and white shell armbands were used. A man gave necklaces to his partner in one direction and received armbands in exchange. In the other direction, he gave armbands and received necklaces. (See Figure 15.1.) The largest and most valuable of these objects became well known throughout the region and

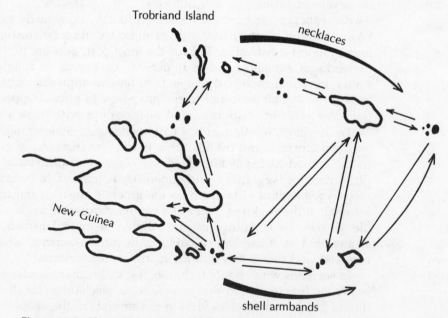

Figure 15.1 The ritual exchange of necklaces and armbands provided security in hostile territories, thereby facilitating economic trade.

were associated with stories of the high status and heroic deeds of their former owners, in much the same way that Lincoln and Washington memorabilia are valued in the United States today.

The economic importance of the Kula ring did not lie in the gifts of armbands and necklaces. Rather, these highly ritualized exchanges led to friendly trade relationships between men whose tribes were often hostile to one another. When men on one island accumulated enough goods, they set sail for a neighboring island on a gift-giving expedition, to a tribe that might normally be their enemy. After exchanging kula among partners, however, the men were free to barter goods in the community, their safety guaranteed by their hosts. This pattern of economic trade between hostile tribes based on partnerships is not uncommon in other parts of the world.

To distribute property Occasionally, reciprocal exchanges help level the uneven distribution of property among people. A case in point is the northwest Pacific coast Indians, who lived on the abundance of fish and forest produce and accumulated wealth in the form of goat and dog wool robes, copper nuggets and plates, canoes, and animal skins (Drucker and Heizer 1967). Periodically, a chief or prominent person would invite other leaders and rivals to a "potlatch" ceremony, to celebrate his claim to a new honorary title or to recognize the marriage or death of an important person. The success of a potlatch was measured by the feast that was given and by the great quantities of goods that were given away to the visitors and destroyed in a display of wealth. Money was thrown into the fire, canoes were destroyed and blankets torn to shreds to show the wealth of the host. The cost was high, and a man not only accumulated goods over a number of years for such a display but also borrowed them from his kinsmen, who shared in his glory. They could also expect a repayment of the loans with interest at some later date.

The potlatch was part of a system of competitive gift-giving. Leading guests at a potlatch were expected to reciprocate with an even more lavish potlatch in a claim to even greater status. The competition often continued intermittently for years until one or another could no longer gather the wealth necessary to challenge the victor. By means of potlatches, the rich gained prestige and the poor got food and other economic goods. In this sense, they are similar to the banquets and benevolent foundations sponsored by the wealthy in some Western countries today.

REDISTRIBUTION In systems of redistribution, goods and services are gathered by a central authority and parceled out among the people. For example, most modern nations levy taxes and use the money to

305

operate the government and to benefit the people. It is obvious that such systems are found in societies that have some degree of social stratification and a concentration of power in the hands of a few. Moreover, while there is some measure of reciprocity—the citizen can expect something in return for his taxes—the relationship is asymmetrical. The leaders have the power and prestige and can channel the wealth and labor to their own interests and benefits.

The jajmani system An illustration of redistribution is the "jajmani" system found in India, which we discussed in Chapter 14. In its classic form, the system centers around a high-caste landlord, or "jajman," and the raising of crops. To farm, the jajman needs the services of other specialist castes: priests to assure the favor of the gods; ironsmiths and carpenters to maintain the plows; potters, barbers, and washermen to serve his household; and untouchable laborers to work the fields. All of these are hereditary workers, who perform their services throughout the year and at harvest receive a portion of the grain in payment. The first measures of the crop heaped on the threshing floor are sent to the high-caste priests as offerings to the gods and to the village officials in respect of their authority. To the craftsmen, who share a rank roughly equal to himself, the landlord gives a payment and to his clients below him, a gift. (See Figure 15.2.)

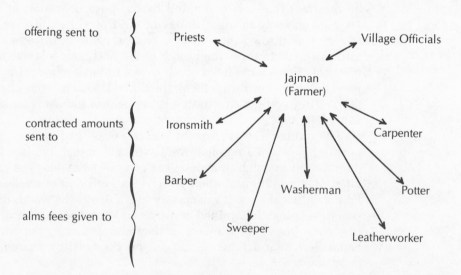

Figure 15.2 Hereditary relationships link the Indian jajman to his family priests and clients. They help him produce the crop and in turn share in its bounty or scarcity.

The relationship between a jajman and his workers is more complex than that between an employer and employees. As their patron, the jajman is responsible for providing the workers with their basic livelihood. They, in turn, have the hereditary right and responsibility to serve him as loyal clients. In a year of bad crops, the landlord gets little more than his own subsistence, because he must provide for his workers, whether there is work or not. For the workers, the system provides security in times of want. But in good years, the landlord makes a handsome profit, for he has to give the workers little more than a subsistence portion. For the landlord, the system provides power, prestige, and wealth.

Feudalism Similar patterns were found in European feudalism. After the ninth century, political and economic power lay in the lords who ruled relatively autonomous estates. Each estate provided for the basic livelihood of its lords and serfs. The serfs raised their own food, wove and tailored their own cloth, and made their own tools. The little trade that survived the collapse of the strong centralized Roman government brought in nonessential luxuries for the elite: spices, silks, jewels, and brocades.

Serfs and laborers tilled small farms and gave most of the crop to the lord of the manor. Smiths, tailors, weavers, cobblers, and ale makers worked in the manor shops and paid the lord their tribute. The lord, in turn, provided them with land and goods from those they had produced. He judged their disputes, organized them in defense of the territory, and provided for their religious worship. In the feudal estate, as in many redistributive systems, economic, political, and social status functions were closely intertwined.

MARKET EXCHANGE Gift exchanges and redistribution systems are increasingly displaced, as economies grow complex, by markets, in which goods and services are exchanged on the basis of negotiation. Negotiation, in turn, depends on a sense of the economic value of the goods being traded. The crucial difference between gifts and trade is that the primary object of gift exchange is to build a social relationship, while for trade, the social relationship is merely incidental to an economic transaction. In other words, market exchanges separate out the economic value of the transaction from the social and political values commonly found in the giving of gifts and the redistribution of goods.

In simple societies, this type of exchange takes the form of barter, which, with some exceptions, has two basic characteristics: 1) the products offered for exchange have not been produced primarily for trade but are surpluses from subsistence production, and 2) the exchange is one of economic things.

Money as a symbol The introduction of money into an economy has profound effects. Money is not an economic thing, as are coconuts, rice, canoes, and cars. It is an economic symbol, including bills, notes, bonds, coins, and the like, which represents the exchange value of the coconuts, rice, and canoes. Almost anything can be used as a standard for measuring relative values. The Polynesians used polished shells; the Melanesians used pig tusks; the east Africans used salt; the Aztecs used cocoa beans; and the Europeans used gold. At the end of the second world war, when much of the paper currency in Europe was worthless, packs of cigarettes became an important form of money. The value of money is its value as a symbol, not necessarily its value as a commodity. The dollar bill of the United States is worth more than the paper on which it is printed.

One of the effects of money is that it leads to an increasing separation between the production and consumption of goods. A person can produce goods he and his family do not need. By converting them into symbols that can be preserved and traded (money), he has an opportunity to save. Money he accepts now can be used at some future time to purchase something else. Or a person can accumulate large amounts of wealth and purchase expensive items he himself cannot produce. Money facilitates trade by providing a standard set of values for exchange and by providing value symbols that can be preserved and, with a few exceptions like the large Yap stone money, easily transported.

In some societies, the currency can be used to purchase only certain types of items. Among the Tiv of Nigeria, food can be exchanged for food or for brass rods. Brass rods can be used to purchase the most valued goods, women and slaves. Women and slaves cannot be exchanged for food, and anyone who attempts to do so would be considered illogical by the Tiv. The United States armed forces issued script money during the second world war, which could be used only in military stores. Americans buy postage stamps which are value symbols with a very limited use, and they collect bonus stamps that can be traded only for a narrow range of goods in certain stores. All such restricted currencies are called "special purpose money."

"General purpose money" is portable and divisible and can be used to purchase almost anything. This makes it easy for people to place an economic value on and trade in almost any goods and services, including those that have no subsistence value, such as antiques, used postage stamps, and professional sports.

The development of markets The introduction of money is associated with the rise of markets. In many tribal societies, markets are

Women attend a
weekly market in
Shambala, Tanzania
to sell produce and
buy manufactured
goods.
Photo courtesy of
E.V. Winans.

peripheral to the economy. People produce most of their own subsistence requirements and trade only their surpluses. An example is the markets of west Africa. There, women sell surplus crops and vegetables they have raised in kitchen gardens and buy cloth, shoes, and other commercial items. Some of the money they save, to pay taxes and to buy larger items, such as bicycles. Buyers and sellers have no social obligations to each other and are free to haggle over the terms of trade in order to maximize their own gains. The haggling, though sometimes heated, does not threaten to disrupt the social order. Prices are determined by the local supply and demand, not by a larger market economy, and land and labor are generally not sold in the market place.

In advanced agricultural and industrial societies, the market becomes central to the economic system. Production specialists arise who earn a living making pottery, cloth, baskets, or metal tools. As small industries arise, labor and money for investment become important commodities in the market.

The development of markets does not leave the farmer unaffected. Instead of subsistence farming, he finds it more profitable to produce cash crops and purchase his food. The farmer thus becomes increasingly dependent on market prices. Crop failures in other parts of the region or world may raise his income. On the other hand, a drop in world prices for one commodity may spell disaster and force him to raise some new crop. The development of national and international markets helps prevent local food crises due to crop failures, but it also increase people's dependence on the larger economic system.

The separation of economic activities   A second effect of money is to separate economic activities from social and political activities and to increase their importance in everyday life. In systems of gift exchange and redistribution, people work not only to survive but also out of social obligations to their kinsmen, the pleasure of working together, or common interest in the product of the work. They may be obligated to share their goods with their neighbors, or they may fear the jealousy of the community or the demands of the chief if they get rich. For a man to become wealthy, it is often necessary for him to leave his home and live alone in a strange village.

In market economies, the personal nature of relationships gives way to impersonal relations, and the individual is freer to pursue his individual gain. It is not that people in simpler societies are devoid of economic sense. They are as conscious of furthering their own advantage as people in market economies. The difference is that they must calculate gains in economic, social, political, and religious terms.

A third effect of money and markets is the development of social stratification based on the control of economic goods and power. Wealth becomes concentrated in the hands of a few, who use their money rather than their labor to produce an income. In cottage and small industries, the owners are also workers, but in factory systems, the separation between capital and labor is often complete. As markets become central to the economic system, wealth becomes an important factor in determining an individual's place in the social hierarchy. The distance between the rich and the poor tends to increase.

Economic and social change

What causes cultures to change? What determines the forms that they will take? Early anthropologists explained change in terms of natural law or man's rationality. Marx (1959), however, turned to an economic explanation of culture. He held that economic factors, such as the level of technology and the availability of resources, determine the type of social structure found in a society and that social structure, in turn, determines a culture's beliefs and values. Max Weber (1947), one of Marx's greatest critics, contended that changes in ideas lie at the base of cultural change.

It is obvious that economic systems place limitations on the social and political structures, as well as on the ideologies that can develop within a society. It is also clear that social, political, and belief systems influence and limit the types of economic systems that will arise. (See Figure 15.3.)

The extreme limitations that economics can place on life and the interplay of material goods, social relationships, power, beliefs, and val-

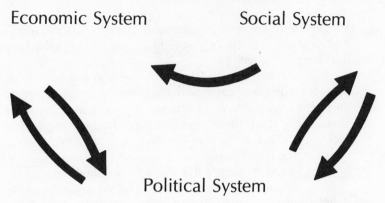

Economic System   Social System

Political System

Figure 15.3   Economic systems place limits on and influence the development of social and political systems, but these in turn limit and influence the development of economic systems.

ues have been poignantly described by Oscar Lewis in his study of the culture of poverty. The accompanying extract depicts poverty in Mexico City. The narrator, Manuel, finds that he must act on more than economic motives while trying to better himself and his family financially. Social ties, religious beliefs, and political influences are all interrelated with economics in the lives of the poor people.

But Marx and Weber saw economic factors, such as resources, labor, and products, as more than limiting factors within which cultures developed. They argued that *social* laws governed change in societies and, in the case of Marx, that material factors determined the general character of the social, political, and spiritual processes of life.

Marx argued further that the organization of material factors itself was in constant change, due to conflicts between two classes: the "haves," who control the means of production—the raw materials, land, buildings, on which technology operates—and the "have-nots," who labor in producing the goods and services. Marx saw human history as a series of economic stages evolving eventually into a classless society which would be harmonious. In his polemics on economic determinism and materialism as the prime mover in sociocultural change, Marx rejected the widespread idea that human reason and the "mind" dominated material factors and guided human history.

Marx makes an important point, but, as we shall see later, he does not take the whole of the cultural system into account.

The Children of Sanchez

Oscar Lewis

My mother-in-law and her husband lived in one room and a kitchen on Piedad Street, No. 30. At that time all four of her children, with their families, were living with her. . . .

The room had one bed, in which Faustino and his wife slept. The rest of us slept on pieces of cardboard and blankets or rags spread on the floor. The only other furniture was a broken-down wardrobe, without doors, and a table which had to be put into the kitchen at night to make more room. . . . That is the way the thirteen of us, five families, arranged ourselves in that little room.

When so many people live together in a single room, naturally there is a brake, a restraint, on one's liberty, right? As a boy in my father's house, I didn't notice it so much, except when I wanted to talk to my friends or look at dirty pictures. But as a married man, I had more bitter experiences. Living together like that, never, never can there be harmony. There are always difficulties, like the time my brother-in-law insisted on removing the light bulbs whenever he left the house, because he had paid the electricity bill. . . .

We really had it rough for a long time. Even when I found a temporary job, we were very poor, because I earned only a miserably low wage, and I had to wait a week to get paid.

My poor old woman never complained. She never asked me for anything or said, "Why do you treat me like this? Why should it be like this?" Because of the poverty in which we lived, I even went so far as to tell her, "Look, old girl, I feel like leaving you. You have a right to live a better life. I'm no good. I can't give you anything at all. I don't deserve you."

But Paula loved me—it was more than love—she worshiped me, all her life she worshiped me. And I loved her too. Every day, before going to look for work, I would say, "Here, take these three *pesos* and get yourself something to eat. That's all I have."

"And you, aren't you going to have breakfast?" she would say.

"No, old girl, the *señora* who has the stand in the market will give me credit." I told her this because I knew two people couldn't eat on three *pesos*. My thought was, at that time, to go to my friend Alberto and ask him to treat me to coffee and something. . . .

Well, so time passed. Paula and I had lived together for almost three years and we didn't have any children. I wasn't pleased and said, "Looks like I'm living with a man; you don't seem to be a woman. When are we going to have a child?" At that time I didn't know what it cost one to bring up children, or how bad one felt not to be able to provide for them. I didn't think of such things. . . .

Then, one day, my wife told me I was going to be a father. "Man alive!" I said, "Really? You're not fooling me, old girl?"

"No," she said, "It's true."

"Thank God!" I told her. Lets see if this doesn't change our luck. Come on, old girl, let's go to the movies." All I had was eight *pesos*. "It doesn't matter, we'll spend two *pesos* in the movies, but we have to celebrate this. Come on, *mama*, let's go." . . .

When Paula was five-months pregnant, Raúl Álvarez asked me to come to work in his lamp shop. . . . The first week I drew two hundred *pesos*, just like that. . . .

I worked there for about a month, when my brother-in-law Fuastino, the one who treated me like dirt when I wasn't working, became sick. He was paralyzed from the waist down. He said to me, "*Compadre*," (I'm the godfather of baptism of his two children) "be a good fellow, go and help out in the café, brother, won't you? If I don't go to work I'll lose my job. Take my job for two or three days, until I get better."

"Man alive, *compadre*," I said, "you can see I'm just barely getting on my feet. I've just gotten this job with *Señor* Raúl. How am I going to ask him to let me off for a couple of days?"

"Aw, come on, be a good fellow," and he looked at me so sadly that my conscience got the better of me.

"O.K., I'll go; but only for two days; here's hoping you get well soon!"

I went to work in the restaurant. But Faustino recovered slowly and the two days stretched out and became a week, then two weeks. I earned fifteen *pesos* a day and of this I gave my wife only five. The rest I turned over to my *compadre* to pay for the doctor, medicine, rent and food. I thought, "Well, I'm lending him the money; it's like a saving. He'll give me back the whole amount in a lump sum and I'll be able to pay my wife's hospital bill."

Well, it didn't turn out that way. One time, while my *compadre* was still sick, my godson Daniel became ill and at night I had to go every two hours to get a woman to give him penicillin injections. After that my *compadre* Eufemia got sick, and so there I was taking care of all three of them and paying for everything. But I would think, well, I'm actually saving money. I imagined I was saving. The situation dragged on like that for more than a month and a half. And so I lost the job with *Señor* Raúl. . . .

Santos, my daughter's godfather, suggested that I open up a shoe shop; I took to the idea. Santos said, "Get hold of two hundred *pesos*. You can make shoes and sell them at a profit of five *pesos* a pair." I thought, "Suppose I make five-dozen pairs of shoes a week. That makes sixty pairs . . . that makes three hundred pesos profit a week. Why that's wonderful!"

Santos loaned me the lasts and a stitching machine, and I borrowed the two hundred *pesos* from my father. . . .

So I went into business. Santos went with me to buy the leather, and we started making shoes. But I knew nothing about shoes or business then, I worked only by God's good will. . . .

I don't remember exactly what happened. . . one of my finishers, Chucho, went on a binge for two or three weeks, getting drunk every day. He later died in the street, abandoned and drunk, poor thing. But I took pity on him, thinking that the workers kill themselves to earn so little, so I raised the finishers twenty *centavos* for each shoe, and the machinist ten *centavos*. I wanted to show others how a boss should treat workers.

Instead of making a profit, without knowing it, I was actually losing on each pair of shoes. Then I sent someone, I don't remember who, to deliver twenty-five pairs of shoes, and he took off with the money. To make a long story short, my business went broke. . . .

After my business failed, I gave up trying to plan my life and get ahead. I lost the little confidence I had in myself and lived just from day to day, like an animal. I really was ashamed to make plans because I didn't have the will power to, well, to carry them out. . . .

To me, one's destiny is controlled by a mysterious hand that moves all things. Only for the select, do things turn out as planned; to those of us who are born to be *tamale* eaters, heaven sends only *tamales*. We plan and plan and some little thing happens to wash it all away.

Summary

One of the primary functions of social systems is to organize the way people relate to the natural world around them. This involves not only subsistence activities but also the development of economic systems that enable people to use natural resources for their own purposes. Material goods and human services acquire economic value only as they become part of social systems.

Societies with simple technologies have little differentiation in economic roles or institutions. Most of the people are concerned directly with gathering or producing food, and the groups to which they belong, such as the family, lineage, or band, have religious and political functions, as well as economic ones. As technologies become more complex, economic roles become more specialized, and institutions develop that are essentially economic in nature.

This shift towards differentiation can be seen in the ways people distribute goods and services. In hunting and gathering and simple agricultural societies, gift exchanges, which reinforce social relationships, are the chief means for exchanging property. In societies with centralized power structures, redistribution systems serve as important means for the circulation of economic goods in the society and occasionally as economic levelers that reduce the gap between the rich and the poor. Market exchanges and money are characteristic of complex economic systems, and their effect is to increase social differentiation and specialization in economic roles and institutions.

The relationship between economic, political, and social systems in a culture is complex. Each sets limits on and influences the development of the other; each, in turn, is influenced in its own development. And within their combined limits, individuals live out their lives, calculating their strategies, pursuing their goals, and, at times, choosing courses of action that will alter the limitations within which they live. For some, there are many options in life, a great deal of elbow room in which to move. But for many, the constraints are confining and oppressive.

Suggested readings

Belshaw, C.S.
   1965   Traditional Exchange and Modern Markets. Englewood Cliffs, N.J.: Prentice-Hall. (A good review of markets and their relationship to social organization.)
Dalton, G.
   1967   Tribal and Peasant Economies. New York: Natural History Press. (A reader dealing with much of contemporary research in the field.)
   1968   Primitive, Archaic, and Modern Economics: Essays of Karl Polanyi. New York: Doubleday. (Distinguishes between reciprocity, redistribution and market exchanges.)
Malinowski, B.
   1922   Argonauts of the Western Pacific. London: Routledge. (A classic ethnographic description of the Kula ring.)
Mauss, M.
   1954   The Gift: Forms and Functions of Exchange in Archaic Societies. New York: The Free Press. (An important but controversial work on gift exchange.)

16

Norms, customs, and laws
Classifications of laws
The case study method
Functions of law

Legal systems

While social groups and societies have organization, they also have internal conflicts and disputes which threaten their organization. There are always some individuals who deviate from the behavior expected of them and infringe on the rights of others. Disagreements arise as to what constitutes deviant behavior in familiar situations, and there are areas of organizational uncertainty as cultures change and new situations occur.

Most disputes simmer for a time and then die out, but some have a potential for violence and disruption of society. These must be resolved by the processes of feud, war, or law before normal societal activities may be resumed. But feuds and wars are the antitheses of law, and where they become the accepted ways of resolving conflicts, anarchy destroys social order. Obviously, all societies must have legal systems to regulate interpersonal relationships if they are to exist as functioning wholes.

We might take an emic approach to the study of human law, examining each folk law system in terms of its own cultural context and assumptions. A cross-cultural approach, however, requires an analytical model that is not derived from any one culture and that can be applied without an ethnocentric bias to all legal systems for comparative purposes. Such a model has been the goal of much anthropological study in recent years.

Norms, customs, and laws

All societies have "norms," the more or less covert rules that are intended to govern individual behavior. There are proper ways to eat, to sleep, to work, and to play—in short, norms for all thought and behavior. But societies also have accepted ways of deviating from these norms in actual practice. Students are expected to listen to lectures but may do something else, so long as they do not disrupt the class. The body of norms and the deviations and compromises that are regularly allowed in practice are referred to as "customs."

"Laws" are customs, but not all customs are laws. Individuals living in a suburb may leave their lawns unmowed or eat with their fingers in a restaurant despite their neighbors' disapproval. But if they are caught parked by a fire hydrant or shoplifting, they will be legally punished. Why the difference in social response? What are the characteristics that set laws apart from other kinds of norms and customs? (See Figure 16.1.)

In their book *The Cheyenne Way* (1941), Karl Llewellyn and E.A. Hoebel suggested three approaches to the anthropological study of law. The first was to define law as the explicit abstract rules, written or remembered, of a society. This was the way many early anthropologists defined law; it stemmed in part from the fact that Western concepts of law may be traced back to Mesopotamia, where rulers such as Hammurabi regarded laws as the absolute commands of the gods, to be applied uniformly to all mankind. From Mesopotamia this concept of law spread to Greece and Rome and then to Europe and North America.

This approach, however, leads to the ethnocentric conclusion that

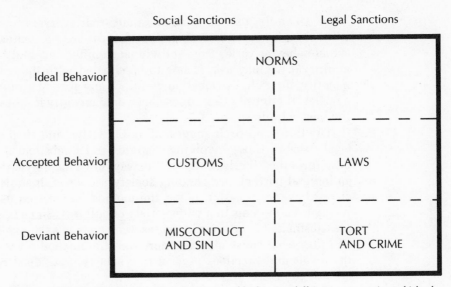

Figure 16.1 Social and legal definitions of behavior fall into categories of ideal, accepted, and deviant.

many societies have no law because their rules are neither written nor spoken. Yet, social disputes may be settled on the basis of concrete precedents or assumptions implicit in the culture, rather than by systematically arranged laws. This is true not only in tribal societies but also in complex civilizations, such as China. Even during the classic period in Rome, laws were not applied mechanically. A great deal of freedom was granted magistrates to formulate law on the basis of previous cases and on the advice of legal counselors. Studies of how conflicts are actually settled in societies with legal codes also show that many are not adjudicated in strict accordance with the law, but that laws are interpreted differently, bent, or even ignored to fit specific cases.

A second approach of Llewellyn and Hoebel is to define law as the patterns of *all* behavior characteristic of a society, rather than in terms of the philosophies of an elite few. Law is thus assumed to be simply what people do. As they point out, this approach is unacceptable for several reasons. First, it equates law with culture, rendering it useless as a term for analyzing specific portions of culture. It also confuses sociological laws derived by the anthropologist from scientific observations with jural laws defined by the people. Jural laws relate not only to actual behavior but also to the ideals of how people are expected to behave. Secondly, this approach assumes that everyone normally keeps within the law and that deviations from it are not patterned. Finally, actual behavior varies from individual to individual and from group to group. So we may ask, is law to be equated with the behavior of the majority, the rich, the most powerful, or any special group? Obviously, a powerful minority can impose laws on a majority if it has the will and the means to do so.

The third approach suggested by Llewellyn and Hoebel is to study legal cases or those involving disputes and to abstract the ideals and principles they imply. Seen in this way, law is merely a part, although an integral part, of any ongoing society. However, it shows that all societies have legal systems, and the method has proven useful for analyzing legal systems in a wide variety of cultures. Since laws are principles abstracted from concrete cases, they change as the culture changes and may even cause change. Moreover, the method takes into account the ideals and practices present in a society, not "dead rules," which are not enforced.

This approach has also been useful in developing analytical concepts that can be applied in cross-cultural comparisons of legal systems. Leopold Pospisil (1972) has derived from it four attributes characteristic of all legal systems—sanctions, authority, intention of universal application, and legal ties of rights and duties—which we will examine in some detail.

Sanctions

One attribute of law is that of "sanctions." Nonlegal customs are often maintained by social pressures, such as gossip, ridicule, and withholding wanted things, and by social rewards, such as commendations, recognition of higher status, and material gifts. So, too, are laws maintained, but laws are also backed by sanctions, which enforce compliance, since laws that are violated with impunity soon become dead rules that fail to exercise social control. While the threat of the law is often sufficient to prevent wrongdoing, in the last resort, the power of law lies in the enforcement of legal decisions. When those in a dispute reach agreement, law may not be needed; when agreement cannot be reached, law is essential.

The ultimate sanction of law in many societies is the legitimate use of physical force: the ability to destroy or confiscate property, to punish or imprison the wrongdoer, and, at times, to take his life. All societies have other, often more subtle, forms of coercion, such as ostracism and banishment, that may be very effective in forcing compliance. Some anthropologists, such as E.A. Hoebel, hold the view that all laws are based on the threat or use of physical coercion and that customs enforced by nonphysical sanctions are not law. Pospisil and others disagree, holding that what is important in determining law is not *how* the norm is enforced, but rather the fact of its enforcement. Psychological coercion, through the use of economic, social, or religious sanctions, is believed to be just as significant as physical coercion in enforcing law.

Authority

In order to be effective, laws must be acceptable to the parties in a dispute or must be enforced over their objection if resistance is encountered. However, to be law, they must be enforced by one or more persons who have the generally recognized power to do so.

The right to enforce the law is usually restricted or assigned. In many societies, wronged individuals or their associates have the publicly recognized right and responsibility of prosecuting their own cases and meting out punishments. This is termed "private law." But even in such cases, private prosecutors enjoy the support of public opinion only so long as they remain within accepted customs regarding sanctions.

A policeman stops to chat in Cuernavaca, Mexico.

All organized groups and societies have leaders—headmen, chiefs, fathers, councils of elders, priests, magistrates, or other individuals of greater or lesser status—who are granted, by common consent, the authority to initiate action and make decisions for the whole. Wherever two or more people act together, some member or members appear to take on the characteristics of leadership. If such officials are assigned specific responsibility for enforcing the law, it is termed "public law" or "criminal law."

The amount of authority a leader may exercise—his rights and his power to make decisions—varies greatly from society to society. Thus, some forms of leadership are quite informal, in that leaders may have no official status, no terms of office, no ceremonies or symbols of authority, no clearly defined rights, duties, or powers. Generally, they are charismatic figures, whose authority depends on an ability to earn the respect and the following of their fellows and not on the powers of office. At the other extreme are formal leaders, who derive their authority from the offices that define their roles, duties, and powers, as in the case of the President of the United States, who gets his power largely from the office he holds. A similar distinction is made in tribal organizations between tribal chiefs, who hold formal offices, and informal leaders, traditionally called "headmen."

Because offices persist over time and are made explicit by various rituals, symbols, and delegations of power, they are often easier to trace and study than the patterns of informal leadership that are more quickly forgotten. Thus, informal leadership is largely studied by observing actual situations.

Intention of universal application

Not all decisions made and enforced by authorities are laws; many are political acts. Laws are intended as general rules to effect social control. Political decisions are quick responses or solutions to immediate problems. In other words, laws reflect ideals that apply to a series of similar situations and are generally enforced over periods of time. However, a record of previous enforcement is not essential to the definition of a law. Law is distinguished from other decisions by *intention* to apply principles to similar cases in the future. New laws lack precedents, but they are models for later decisions—they become precedents, themselves.

Authorities may make this intention clear by reference in their judgments or opinions to the accepted rules of the society or to preceding cases; or it may be set down in a codified form that similar future cases will be judged in the same way. In many instances, however, the rule is implied in the manner in which the decision is made. However it may be expressed, law has an ideal component, pointing out how people ought to behave in all such circumstances, and it is this ideal which provides continuity to law.

Legal ties of rights and duties

Laws describe the sociolegal relationships existing between individuals and groups at the time the law is violated. The law defines the rights of those involved, with emphasis on the rights of the person who has suffered because of the illegal act of another, and it specifies the duties individuals have to each other.

Legal relationships can exist only between people who are living or who are represented by living persons. Obligations to the supernatural or to the dead who have no living representatives, are matters of religion rather than law. Religious rules, in which punishment is to come from a supernatural source, are "taboos," not laws, no matter how widely accepted they may be, while those in which punishment is inflicted by a priest or shaman are "religious laws."

Classifications of laws

Levels of laws

To traditional ethnologists, law was seen as operating throughout the entire society, rather than restricted to particular groups within the society. Consequently, law was dissociated from the social structure of a people and treated as an autonomous entity, apart from the rest of culture.

The idea that there are many legal systems related to the various discrete groups within a single society was stressed by the sociologist Max Weber and introduced to anthropology by Llewellyn, Hoebel, and Pospisil. According to this theory, groups within a society have leaders who enforce sets of norms within their groups—norms which may have all the attributes of laws. Since the sets of norms vary from group to group, there are as many legal systems as there are functioning groups. One may speak of laws at the level of the family, the lineage, the village, and the association, in addition to the law of the society as a whole. Thus, even decisions made by leaders of criminal groups, such as the Cosa Nostra, become law within the gang.

Since we tend to assume that all people within a society will behave alike, we also assume the existence of a single legal system within the society. A closer look shows that in every society there are many dif-

323

ferent leaders and groups and many different sets of norms operating at the same time. There is no single standard uniformly applied to everyone at all times.

Multiple levels of law imply differing levels of legal authority. At one level, families may have different laws, enforced by the family head, regulating the behavior of their own members. At higher levels, leaders of lineages and communities enforce laws over a number of families, though some areas of life may be left to regulation by the family. The highest level of law is often that of the society itself. Legal processes at this level may be formally structured as legal institutions, with authority to intervene in the malfunctions of other institutions in the society and in disputes between individuals and groups.

Types of law

Cases involving trouble between individuals or groups are the test of law, and their adjudication entails a number of legal questions. The first is the question of legal procedure: how are laws determined and enforced? All societies have, in one form or another, the notion of due process of law. That is, socially recognized ways of carrying out legal action are available when needed. These include not only recognition of those with jurisdiction and authority to handle the case but also how evidence is to be gathered and what kinds and to what extent sanctions should be applied. These rules governing the operation of law are termed "procedural laws." As Hoebel has noted (1954), people are protected from the terror of anarchy or tyranny only when the law itself is enforced in a legal manner.

The second question in a legal decision is one of substance: which acts are considered illegal? "Substantive laws" are those laws which regulate behavior and are enforced within the group or society. Obviously, behavior which may be objectionable but is not covered by law can not be subjected to legal action.

The third question is one of fact: did the accused actually break the law? In simpler societies, where little or no behavior is secret, the facts sooner or later become known. In complex societies, where the task of the law is greater and more difficult and evidence is easier to hide, more formal ways of gathering evidence are commonly found. Most often these include a court with judges, lawyers, juries, and witnesses.

Supernatural means for obtaining information or guaranteeing the truthfulness of a witness are widespread, in all parts of the world. One means is "divination." In Perak in the Malaysian Peninsula, contestants in a dispute would appear before the Sultan. There they were ordered to write down the truth of the matter and solemnly swear to it. The statements were sealed in identical bamboo tubes, mixed up, and given to two boys, who were led to stakes driven neck-deep in the river. At a given signal, both boys submerged, each trying to outlast the other. The tube of the one who came up first was flung into the river, and the tube of the victor was opened to discover the truth (Skeat 1966:543).

The case study method

The value of the case study method in providing us both with an actual view of how legal systems in a society operate and with the ideals behind the regulation of behavior may be seen in the following illustrations.

Cheyenne law

In the nineteenth and early twentieth centuries, the Cheyenne lived on the plains of North America, governed by a Council of Forty-Four and military societies. Theoretically, the Council was the ultimate tribal authority to which the military societies were subordinate. In practice, the military societies often took the law into their own hands, as we see in the following case.

> The tribe was moving in a body up the Rosebud River toward the Big Horn Mountain country in search of buffalo. The Shield Soldiers, who were in charge on that occasion, had their scouts out looking for the herds, and when the scouts came in with their report, the order was given that no one should leave the camp or attack the buffalo. Nobody was supposed to shoot a buffalo until the signal was given.
>
> All the hunters went out in a line with the Shield Soldiers in front to hold them back. Just as they were coming up over a long ridge down wind from where the scouts had reported the herd they saw two men down in the valley riding in among the buffalo. A Shield Soldier chief gave the signal to his men. They paid no attention to the buffalo, but charged in a long line on the two violators of the rules. Little Old Man shouted out for everyone to whip them: "Those who fail or hesitate shall get a good beating themselves."
>
> The first men to reach the spot shot and killed the horses from under the hunters. As each soldier reached the miscreants he slashed them with his riding whip. Then some seized the guns of the two and smashed them.
>
> When the punishment was done, the father of these two boys rode up. It was Two Forks. . . . He looked at his sons before talking. "Now you have done wrong. You failed to obey the law

of this tribe. You went out alone and you did not give the other people a chance. This is what has happened to you."

Then the Shield Soldier chiefs took up the talk. "Now you know what we do when anyone disobeys our orders," they declared. "Now you know we mean what we say." The boys did not say anything.

After that the chiefs relented. . . . They called their men to gather around. "Look how these two boys are in our midst. Now they have no horses and no weapons. What do you men want to do about it?"

One of the soldiers spoke up, "Well, I have some extra horses. I will give one of them to them." Then another soldier did the same thing.

Bear Standing On A Ridge was the third to speak out, "Well," he announced, "we broke those guns they had. I have two guns. I will give them one."

All the others said, "*Ipewa*, good."*

The Cheyenne military societies were responsible for buffalo hunting and war parties, activities that demanded a high degree of group cooperation. Individuals acting on their own could threaten the success and lives of others. Consequently, the military societies maintained a strong discipline within their own ranks, and the punishment of those who violated the rules could be harsh. Here the law and evidence were clear, and discipline was meted out without delay. However, rehabilitation of offenders was a widespread practice among the Plains Indians. Sanctions were necessary for the common good, but the guilty could not be left unaided, to suffer alone. Thus, the ultimate aim of law—to restore social order and harmony—was served.

Village law of India

Traditionally, laws in the villages of India have been enforced by "panchayats." Generally, there were several levels of kingdoms, ranging from rajas, who ruled a few villages, and maharajas, who ruled a larger territory including a number of lesser rajas, to maharajadhiraja-paramabhattarakas (Great King of Kings, Supreme Lord) and emperors, who ruled much of India. But apart from taxation, recruitment of soldiers and occasional interventions in village affairs, much of the governing of everyday life was left to the village headman and the local panchayats. In the eighteenth and nineteenth centuries, legal systems based on courts and police were introduced by the British colonial

---

* Karl N. Llewellyn and E. Adamson Hoebel, *The Cheyenne Way: Conflict and Case Law in Primitive Jurisprudence* (Norman: University of Oklahoma Press, 1967), pp. 112–113. Copyright 1941 by the University of Oklahoma Press.

rulers, but even now panchayats play a significant role in many villages.

Unlike modern Western style courts, which are formally organized institutions with clearly defined members, powers, and laws, panchayats are, for the most part, informal procedures for reaching consensus within the village. They consist of informal or formal groups organized to solve specific problems. Membership is not limited, and rules are unwritten.

THE CASE OF CHENDRAYYA   A case described by Lakshayya (the Washerman caste headman) of an unfaithful wife illustrates the ways in which panchayats work.

> One of our local bachelors got into trouble with the wife of another Washerman named Chendrayya. It was common knowledge, but no one, not even his friends, would tell Chendrayya; they did not want to get into trouble or make him feel bad. Chendrayya suspected something. He tried beating his wife; but she denied everything. Finally, one day Chendrayya left as though he were going to work but turned the corner and hid behind a mud wall. When he saw the bachelor sneak into his house, he crept up to the house and snapped a big lock on the door (like most houses this one had no windows or back door). Then he went to call the police. They were only too willing to arrest the culprits and lock them up in jail. When I heard about this affair, I said to myself that nothing good would come of it if the case went to court. I went to Krishna Chari (the village headman) and told him we should settle the matter within the village. He agreed and gave me a note for the patwari (village land officer). The patwari and I went to see the police. They agreed to release the couple to us for seventy rupees which I paid.
>
> Since the matter was serious, I locked the couple up in my house. I needed the support of my caste and the village so I called in more than forty men from many castes. Elders from the Barber, Muslim, and Harijan castes were also present. The problem was a difficult one. The guilty couple loved each other. On the other hand, the wife had several children including an infant boy two months old, and the bachelor was too poor to support a wife. If we granted a divorce, the husband would take the children, a solution that would be hard for the unweaned infant. We decided that for the children's sake the husband and wife should remain together. The husband was the key to the problem. He was proud and did not want his wife back. If we could first persuade him, the rest would be easy. I bought drinks around and we went to the husband's house. He said, "My wife slept with another man." "Did you have any proof?" we asked. "I

caught them both in my house and called the police," he replied. As soon as he admitted calling the police we found fault with him. He had insulted the caste by ignoring the elders and going directly to the police. Moreover, he had charged an innocent woman without witnesses. We knew the wife was guilty, but we did not dare admit it. We fined the man five hundred rupees for dishonoring the caste. By now he was quite humble and ready to take his wife back, and we agreed to drop the fine if he did so.

"Next we dealt with the woman. To make certain that the trouble would not be repeated, we made her sign a paper that if she were caught with the bachelor again she would have to pay the caste five hundred rupees. Finally we got to the bachelor who was the cause of the trouble. We fined him one hundred fifty rupees and made him sign a bond as well. I took seventy rupees to repay what I had given the police, and the rest we used for celebrations.*

A number of legal principles emerge from this case. First, individuals seeking redress must often resort to action or intrigue to bring the case to a crisis. So long as a dispute remains in the argument or name-calling stage, the defendants gain by maintaining the *status quo*. Some move must be made to force the issue to a crisis; in this instance, the husband caught the culprits red-handed.

Second, in panchayats, all parties involved in the conflict are considered guilty of disturbing the peace, and hence are under caste suspension until judgment is passed. They are seated apart from those gathered to discuss the case, and no one is permitted to socialize with them while the outcome is pending. After a successful settlement, however, all parties to the case are seated at the end of the row of elders, and a jug of palm beer is passed around, symbolizing the restoration of the offenders to caste fellowship. If there is no settlement, there are no drinks.

Third, disputes should remain under the jurisdiction of the caste and its panchayats or, if this fails, of the village headman and panchayat. In going to the police, Chendrayya violated the laws and authority of the caste and therefore was in trouble, himself.

Fourth, there are several levels of panchayat. Normally, a dispute is handled by several elders in an informal gathering. More serious cases, such as this one, and others which cannot be settled by an informal panchayat, are taken up by a formal caste panchayat, led by the hereditary caste headman or leader and including any number of elders from within and often from outside the caste. All who are interested or in-

* Paul G. Hiebert, *Konduru* (Minneapolis: University of Minnesota Press, 1971), pp. 110–111. Copyright 1971 by University of Minnesota.

volved in the case may join in the discussion, standing or squatting behind the leaders, who are seated in a half-circle in an open courtyard. Lesser members may express their feelings, but when the elders reach a consensus, their decision is rarely disputed.

Fifth, the judgment meted out by panchayats is not based on the narrow issues of a case. There is no inflexible standard of right and wrong that must be enforced at all costs. The elders have known the disputants for years and are aware of past relationships between them. They also realize that both parties must continue to live together in the same village in the future. A poor settlement only breeds more trouble; a good one repairs the seams of the social fabric.

Finally, headman and elders cannot enforce their decisions by the use of physical force. Authority to use force rested in the past with kings and more recently with the national and state governments, represented by judges and police. Panchayats can place fines and withhold favors; their ultimate sanction is to put the culprit out of caste or village life and deny him and his family fellowship, aid, jobs, economic goods, and religious services. Socially, he is dead. Few can withstand this ostracism for any length of time, but its effect is weakened if the ban is not enforced by everyone in a caste or village, hence the need for consensus in reaching decisions.

THE CASE OF THE LEATHERWORKER WEDDING PARTY   While panchayats are effective in maintaining social order at the local level, they are less effective on a regional level. The village often acts as a unit in relation to the external world of other villages. Villagers who compete with each other in everyday life usually present a common front when an external threat appears, if only because they must live together the next day. Sometimes their support may be limited to silence, when to speak up would endanger a fellow man. At other times, it may involve fighting castemen from a neighboring village. This is illustrated in the following case, which occurred before the establishment of the Republic of India.

> The trail from the hamlet of Chintalonpalli, home of the Leatherworkers, to Kumarlonpalli, where the Leatherworkers go for earthen pots, used to pass through the Weaver hamlet of Kalmulonpalli. One evening in 1946 members of a Leatherworker wedding party set out with drums and a band to fetch the ceremonial pots needed in the rites. Beyond Kalmulonpalli the trail passed close to an open well where a Weaver was drawing water with a pair of newly broken oxen. When the oxen bolted because of the noise, the farmer threatened loudly to break the wedding pots and bring bad luck upon the wedding should the party dis-

turb the oxen upon their return. On the way back, the Leather-workers, caught up in the spirit of festivity, and showing their disregard for the Weavers, beat their drums harder and shouted a little louder. The oxen bolted again. The infuriated Weaver grabbed his stick and shattered one of the pots. There were shouts of rage and loud accusations before the Leatherworkers finally moved on.

The next evening a wedding party left to fetch the bride. Again they had to pass through Kalmulonppali. Hearing of this, the Weavers decided to put the Leatherworkers in their place. All moved their beds and mats outside until the only street through the hamlet was clogged. At midnight the bridal party returned, only to find the road impassable. They shouted at the sleeping Weavers, but the Weavers refused to move. The Leather-workers were few so they withdrew to take counsel. A messenger was sent to the Konduru police station and soon three constables arrived. Beds and bedding were thrown aside as the wedding procession marched triumphantly through.

The Weavers outnumber the Leatherworkers on the plateau almost two to one, and they were ready for a fight. The next day the Leatherworkers found their road north blocked. They retaliated by barricading the road through their hamlet along which the Weavers drive their cattle to graze in the forests to the south. The Weavers called in the Weaver Mashti who are known for their skill in handling sticks and clubs. The Leatherworkers brought in Leatherworker Mashti. The boundary between the hamlets was an armed camp. Small fights flared, but neither side dared to make an all-out assault. The local police tried to break the impasse, but with little success. The hostilities continued as the Leatherworkers went to court. To raise money, they sent messengers to the Leatherworkers in the surrounding districts to obtain contributions. The case dragged on for several months while the elders of Konduru and of the Weaver and Leatherworker castes from the plains tried to mediate a settlement. They pointed out the needless expense and suffering, as well as the fact that both hamlets would have to live together peaceably in the end. Weary of the struggle, both groups finally agreed to restore free passage and the case was withdrawn from court.*

Obviously, not all physical force is legitimate. Feuds are the antithesis of law, the sign that law has failed to settle the dispute. But in this case, the violence put pressure on the elders of the two villages to negotiate a settlement with which all could live. In the past, disputes between villages that were not quickly settled were resolved by the ar-

* Paul G. Hiebert, *Konduru* (Minneapolis: University of Minnesota Press, 1971), pp. 75–76. Copyright 1971 by University of Minnesota.

bitrary action of kings. Today, the state government maintains peace. Hence, a central legal authority over the feuding groups will intervene if the crisis continues, comprising, in effect, a single system of law covering these villages. However, where separate communities do not come under a common authority, the relationships between them are based on political negotiations and power, rather than law.

PANCHAYATS AND COURTS   There is a deep-seated difference between panchayats and courts as we know them in the West—the difference, to use Landis' terms (1965:318–319), between therapeutic and punitive justice. While the aim of the court is to deter wrongdoing by punishment based on a single universal standard of justice, the panchayat seeks to restore harmony by acknowledging the uniqueness of each situation, the differences between men, and the necessity for saving face. Panchayat is the art of the socially possible in place of the dogma of the morally right, and its consequences have far-reaching effect. The arbiters of panchayat are those mutually involved with the outcome of the case, rather than detached, dispassionate judges. Both parties involved are on trial, and the case can swing against either, though usually a measure of compromise is involved.

In the court, based as it is on the adversary principle, one party is a plaintiff and the other a defendent, and the settlement is between the innocent or guilty. In panchayats, witnesses are intimately known and are expected to support their kin and castemen, while in courts witnesses are required to declare the impartial truth. Panchayats review the total social context, instead of a narrow point of law and frequently deal with some unnoticed problem beneath the facts of the case. Because decisions are enforced by social ostracism rather than active intervention, it is necessary that they be arrived at by community consensus rather than by a verdict reached by a few. The point is not that panchayats are more or less just than courts, only that they are different.

Functions of law

These and similar cases point out the fact that effective legal systems are essential to stable societies. As Hoebel has noted (1954), such systems serve four primary functions in maintaining social order.

First, they define the fundamental rights and duties of the members of the society in their relationship to one another. In doing so, they determine which activities are illegal and will not be permitted by the group or society. This is the "substantive" function of law.

Traffic moving on a modern city street.

Second, they determine who has the socially recognized right to enforce sanctions when laws are violated, as well as the extent and ways in which these sanctions will be applied. This is the "adjectival" function of law.

Third, they resolve trouble cases that threaten to disrupt the normal activities of the society and restore a measure of certainty and security to everyday living.

Fourth, they redefine relationships between individuals and groups as culture changes. Legal norms and procedures are constantly being extended to cover new situations that arise as a culture evolves. Without this continuity and flexibility of law, the stability of a society itself would be threatened by every change in technology, social organization, or values.

Societies maintain social order with varying effectiveness. Whether they do so with brutality and tyranny or with a minimum of force and injustice, the alternative to law is anarchy and social chaos.

Summary

No society can operate without *norms* or rules to regulate human behavior. Many of these are customary ways of doing things, but some, called *laws*, are enforced by the society on its people. All societies have laws, but not all laws are codified or written down, nor is their enforcement always formalized. The existence of these laws can best be discovered by studying cases of disputes that threaten to disrupt a society and how the society resolves these disputes.

Laws define the rights and duties of people in specific relationships. Moreover, all have sanctions; that is, they are enforced by some means, such as social pressures, ostracism, imprisonment, or the death penalty. And finally, to be law, they must be enforced by those who have the socially recognized authority to do so and who intend to apply them to the whole society.

Cases of legal disputes point out three questions that must be answered when laws are enforced. The first is: What behavior is required or forbidden in this case; this is the question of *substantive* law. The second is: Did someone violate this law; this is the question of fact. The third issue is: Who will enforce the law and how; this is the question of *procedural* law.

Without law and legal procedures, disputes caused by disagreements, and tensions created by social changes can lead to a disintegration of the society. Legal systems not only resolve the tensions that arise out of daily life but also help to direct the course of change within a culture.

Suggested readings

Bohannan, Paul.
  1967 Law and Warfare: Studies in the Anthropology of Conflict. Garden City, N.Y.: Natural History Press. (A comprehensive reader covering ethnographic and theoretical approaches to law.)
Hiebert, P.G.
  1971 Konduru: Structure and Integration in a South Indian Village. Minneapolis: University of Minnesota Press. (Has a more detailed analysis of panchayats and ethnographic conflict cases from an Indian village.)
Hoebel, E.A.
  1954 The Law of Primitive Man: A Study in Comparative Legal Dynamics. Cambridge, Mass.: Harvard University Press. (A classic work on comparative law.)
Llewellyn, K.N. and E.A. Hoebel.
  1941 The Cheyenne Way: Conflict and Case Law in Primitive Jurisprudence. Norman, Ok.: University of Oklahoma Press. (A pioneering ethnography in the use of the case study method with regard to the study of law.)
Pospisil, L.
  1972 The Ethnology of Law. Reading, Mass.: Addison-Wesley. (A short module presenting an excellent summary of current anthropological theories of law.)

17

The nature of political organization
Types of government
Political processes

Political organization

Leadership, power, control, and manipulation are aspects of all groups'and societies. In the broadest sense, the exercise of these within groups or societies is politics. It is obvious that politics has much in common with government and law, but they are not the same. Political anthropologists are interested in the relationships between the two and between them and other cultural processes.

The nature of political organization

Politics is the acquisition and use of power and leadership within a group or society, sometimes referred to as the "polity." As with other social institutions, we can look at political systems from both structural and functional perspectives.

Structural attributes of politics

There are two essential attributes in politics: the ability to make decisions and the power to enforce them.

LEADERSHIP AND DECISION-MAKING Decisions are the spice and the bane of life. No individual, group, or society can live without them. But decision-making involves choosing between alternatives, passing judgments, allocating power and resources, and initiating courses of action; and in most groups and societies, this means some form of leadership is in the hands of a few individuals. Even among simple societies, such as the Eskimo, which have informal leaders and group involvement in the making of decisions, temporary leaders usually emerge in times of crisis. In more complex societies, the roles of public leaders are more institutionalized and their powers are more explicit.

POWER The second attribute of politics is the use of power. Power is the ability of one person or group to exercise its will over the others, to cause the others to behave as one wishes even when they resist. It includes such things as the ability to control information and channels of communication, to persuade and exhort others to compliance, and to manipulate cultural symbols, such as beliefs, values, and goods. It is also the ability to mobilize and use physical force, if need be, although few societies can exist long on physical force alone.

As we have already seen, not all uses of power are considered legitimate by a society. In each society, some leaders are recognized by the people as having authority or the legitimate right to exercise power and make decisions governing the polity as a whole. Similarly, certain uses of power are considered legitimate. But in the political process, both legitimate and illegitimate uses of power, exercised by people with or without authority, come into play.

Functions of politics

Political systems serve a number of essential functions within a society. In general, these relate to processes by which the activities of the polity are organized on behalf of the whole.

ESTABLISHING GOALS Two of the functions served by political processes involve making legal decisions that define the law and making decisions that establish goals for the polity, the ends towards which its energies and resources are mobilized. The goals may be organizing hunting parties, moving camp to new grazing lands, or fighting wars to gain more territory. Or the goals may concern national prestige, territorial defense, economic development, social or religious reform, or world dominance. Since most groups and societies have multiple goals, decisions are also needed to determine relative priorities. Which goals are most important when there are conflicts between them or when there are not enough resources to achieve them all? For example, who in a society should receive the food, the land, or the gasoline, when these are in short supply?

MOBILIZATION AND ALLOCATION OF RESOURCES People within the political system mobilize and allocate the resources of the polity. These include its natural resources, such as land, water, game, and mineral wealth; its cultural resources, such as technology, material goods, and religious powers; and its human resources. Generally these must be mobilized by such provisions as taxation, recruitment, and requisitions before they can be used on behalf of the whole. Weapons and men must be prepared for defense and wars. Cattle, crops, trade, and production may be taxed to support the activities of the government. People can be organized to dig irrigation canals and build roads, palaces, and temples. As societies become more complex, the mobilization of resources by the political system increases.

Allocation involves setting priorities for the use of valued resources, which are always limited. One way to discover the goals and priorities of a group or society is to examine the ways its leaders allocate its resources. They may invest a great deal in material goods and economic welfare, in military systems, in the training of the young, or in religious activities. People in developing countries must often forgo consumer goods so that national investments can be made in basic industries, such as steel, coal, railroads, and heavy machinery, needed for developing the national economy. Those in developed countries may have to forgo many personal luxuries to avoid ecological disasters.

DISTRIBUTING RESOURCES TO MEMBERS   As part of the process of mobilizing resources, political systems are also involved in the distribution of valued resources (goods, money, prestige, services, power, and freedoms) to individuals and groups within the polity. This distribution in stratified societies is often unequal. Individuals, groups, classes, or castes that have more power generally benefit from the unequal distribution of resources and are in a position to maintain their advantage and leadership.

SOCIAL CONTROL Political systems exercise social control. This includes not only the enforcement of laws but also that of political deci-

A political gathering in Tanzania.
Photo courtesy of E.V. Winans.

sions which apply to immediate situations, such as the decision to go to war or a decision to cultivate communal lands. As in the case of law, social control may involve the use of physical force, but it is often restricted to the manipulation of ideologies by controlling communication, the use of economic rewards and sactions, and social ostracism.

Legal and political systems

It should be obvious by now that there are a great many similarities and a great deal of overlap between legal and political systems. They both deal with public matters that are the concern of the group as a whole. Their decisions are often made and enforced by the same authorities. These authorities, men and women who hold the statuses of public leadership and exercise public power, constitute the "government."

It is also obvious that just as there are levels of law, there are levels of political organization. Leadership and politics can be found in any organization, but their exercise at one level is often restricted by political systems at higher levels.

Types of government

Paul Bohannan has suggested (1967) a classification system for legal institutions that applies equally well to types of government at the level of a society. It is possible, in the first place, to divide governments into those in which power is centralized in a single system and those in which it is divided between two or more approximately equal power structures. An example of the first is the tribe rule by a single chief and his assistants, and the tribe in which social order is maintained by the segmentary opposition of lineages and clans is an example of the latter.

In the second place, a distinction can be made between governments that recognize a single legal culture and those that recognize more. A "legal culture" is defined as a system of law that reflects a single cultural perspective and is enforced on the members of a group or society. The Indian caste system is an example of a society in which there are many legal cultures. In the past, different castes often had different customs and laws, which were enforced only on their own members by the central government. Some permitted a man only one wife, others permitted him more. Whether or not having two wives was a crime depended on the legal culture of one's caste. In the United States, on the other hand, courts have tried, at least in theory, to enforce a single legal code on whites, blacks, Spanish Americans, Japanese Americans, Mormons, and people from many other cultures.

With these distinctions in mind, it is possible to construct a four-type classification for governments: stateless, state, colonial and international. Table 17.1 presents this system.

Table 17.1   Types of Government

	Unicentered Authority	Multicentered Authority
One Legal Culture	State Governments	Stateless Governments
Two or More Legal Cultures	Colonial Governments	International Governments

Source: Adapted from Paul Bohannan, "The Differing Realms of the Law," in *Law and Warfare*, Paul Bohannan, ed. (Garden City: American Museum of Natural History, 1967), p. 51. Copyright 1967 by Paul Bohannan. Reproduced by permission of Doubleday & Company, Inc.

Stateless societies

Many simple societies that are culturally homogeneous have no single person or group of persons with authority to govern. Public leadership is divided among a number of individuals and groups, each acting in specific situations. This lack of centralized government and the recognition of only one legal culture characterize stateless societies.

Governmental functions in stateless societies are often divided among different types of groups, no one of which is the central authority for the whole tribe. Some political matters may be handled by lineages, others by communities, age grades, mens' clubs, or other types of association. The political integration of the tribe as a whole, if it exists at all, is not permanent and fades when external threats disappear, leaving local groups to handle everyday affairs.

BANDS Bands, for the most part, are found in hunting and gathering societies. Most are small in size, raging from twenty to 500 persons. The majority are seminomadic, moving in regular seasonal patterns, following migratory game or fresh pasturage.

Band political organization is generally informal. The authority of family heads and band leaders rests not in any formal status or office, but in the ability to command respect on the basis of personal qualities. There is no obligation for others to follow their counsel. A good hunter or whaler who is generous and has good sense generally becomes a leader in subsistence activities; a band member experienced in healing and rituals becomes a religious leader; and so on. The same person may be a leader in more than one area of life, but there are usually several leaders in a band, whose powers lie in their ability to maintain influence and meet the needs of the band.

The !Kung bushmen of the Kalahari desert in south Africa form a band society. Headmen often inherit their positions but have no special honor or privileges that set them apart from the others. They normally make decisions on the distribution of food resources and admission of outsiders to the band, but these are usually made in line with long-standing customs. If they prove to be poor leaders, the band turns to other men for direction. As one headman said, "All you get is the blame if things go wrong" (Marshall 1967:41).

TRIBES Like bands, simple tribes lack centralized political power and hierarchies, but tribes are larger political entities, made up of a number of local groups or bands. Generally, they are sedentary food producers and thus have greater population densities. Governmental functions at the level of the tribe are performed by one or more groups or associations, which cut across local groups, integrating them into the larger tribe.

Kinship groups Kinship groups, such as clans and lineages, frequently perform important governmental activities. Clan elders settle disputes within their clans, which may be scattered through a number of villages. They also arrange for the cultivation of clan lands and the worship of clan deities and attempt to punish others who offend clan members.

A classic example of a tribal government organized on the principle of kinship is the Tiv of northern Nigeria. All of the nearly 1,000,000 Tivs are theoretically related to each other in a single geneology. In disputes between men who are closely related, each calls on his family members for support. The conflict is thus between minimal lineages. When the disputing men are distantly related, they draw on lineal kinsmen more closely related to themselves, and the conflict is then between larger lineal groups. Rivals in one context are united in support of a common group against more distant tribesmen (see Figure 17.1). This principle of "segmentary opposition" on the basis of kinship or territory is not uncommon in other societies. For example, the early American colonies were often bitter rivals, yet they managed to

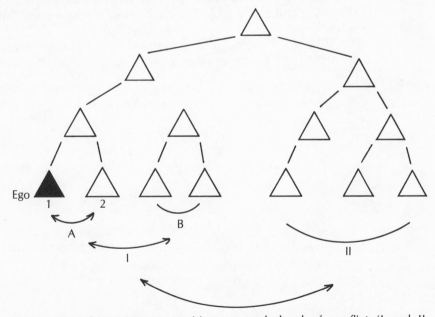

Figure 17.1 Segmentary opposition: at each level of conflict (I and II, above), the ego is allied with kinsmen closest to himself against kinsmen closest to his opponent.

unite long enough to successfully revolt against England. But this principle is frequently an explicit part of government in tribes with segmentary lineage systems.

Segmentary opposition is particularly effective in confrontations between the Tiv and outsiders. In such cases, the whole tribe is mobilized against neighboring villages, which are often unable to mobilize their tribes to resist Tiv encroachments on their territory. But tribal mobilization lasts only until the opposition is defeated; then the tribe breaks down again into rival factions.

Age sets Age sets serve governmental functions in many tribes, particularly in eastern Africa. Among the Bantu Tiriki of western Kenya, there formerly were four age grades responsible for the maintenance of social and religious order (see Figure 17.2). The Warriors were responsible for guarding the country and holding the land. The Elder Warriors organized community activities. The Judicial Elders settled local disputes by holding courts at the local meeting grounds to hear plaintiffs and defendants, question witnesses, and give judgments. The Ritual Elders presided over priestly functions at the ancestral shrines and expelled witches who threatened the well-being of the tribe. In this system, every grown male had some responsibilities in the governing of the tribe and could look forward to greater respect and authority as he grew older.

Village councils and headmen In stateless societies, village councils and headmen often handle local affairs. They settle quarrels,

Figure 17.2 Age grades among the Bantu Tiriki of western Kenya serve certain governmental functions.

allocate village lands, and organize community activities. They may also organize local defense and arrange joint activities with neighboring villages.

States

Political states are characterized by a centralized government and a territory. In a broad sense, the history of government has been an evolution from stateless governments, based on the principle of kinship and association, to states, based on the principle of territoriality, in which membership is defined in terms of the place of one's birth and residence.

CHIEFDOMS   In tribal states, authority lies in the office of a chief or council. Such governments characterize larger, more complex tribes, with social classes and hierarchies. The chief and his nobility have greater access to prestige and economic resources. They organize labor for public works, armies for defense, and rituals to assure good crops. They hold courts to settle trouble cases and see to the enforcement of the law. They are also responsible for the mobilization and redistribution of tribal resources, so that all receive at least a minimal share.

Authority may be divided to prevent a total concentration of power in the hands of a merciless tyrant. For example, many North American tribes had peace chiefs, who acted as civil governors, and war chiefs responsible for military activities.

A second separation of powers frequently made in chiefdoms is that between political and religious leaders, between the state and the power of the people on the one hand, and the religious order and the powers of the gods on the other. Sacerdotal chiefs and kings, who combine the powers of both in a single office, often command awesome powers.

In many African tribes, the chief was the priest who placated the ancestors and brought rain for the crops. Frequently, he represented the tribal soul. His well-being was symbolic of the well-being of the society. In fact, in a few tribes, when the chief became old or sick, he was killed by his counselors, and a new king was enthroned to preserve the prosperity of the tribe. Many kings, such as those in Egypt, Babylon, Rome, and Hawaii, were seen as gods on earth, and others, such as those of medieval Europe, were believed to be representatives of divine rule.

But power has its price—that of separation from the ordinary run of life. Samoan chiefs had Talking Chiefs, who acted for the rulers in public, in much the same way that the press secretary speaks for United

Woodcarving of a nineteenth century horseman, Afghanistan.
Photo courtesy of UNESCO/Cart.

States officials today. The reasoning is that a leader cannot become too
familiar with his subjects, lest he be caught up in political intrigues.

MONARCHIES Centralized governments are effective, since they
facilitate the mobilization of a great many people and resources, but
they face the problem of succession of power. Who becomes ruler when
a chief dies?

One way to avoid a struggle for succession is to make the office of
ruler hereditary, in other words, to establish a monarchy. But this solution raises other problems. What if the heir is unfit to rule or has the
egomanical pride of a tyrant? Hereditary succession does not guarantee
that the best or even a good man will ascend the throne.

To reduce these problems, kings in many Bantu African tribes were chosen from among the princes by a royal council, the queen mother, or the oldest son, who was prohibited from ascending to the throne himself. But even the flexibility of this system led to chronic palace feuds at the death of a monarch, as various power groups tried to place their candidate on the throne.

However, the advantages of centralized governments over stateless systems and of clear hereditary succession of authority over struggles for power account, in part, for the fact that monarchies were the most common form of tribal state governments until recent times. Some anthropologists believe that monarchies evolved from the tendency, found even in chiefdoms, for leadership to run in certain family lines. Sons of a ruler learned the qualities of leadership from their father, and people came to expect direction from certain families.

NATION-STATES Of all the political forces of recent times, none is more important than nationalism. Today, nation-states have become the dominant form of government around the world. On the one hand, they are able to mobilize people and change old ways of life, but on the other, the rivalries among them threaten world stability.

The emergence of nationalism from earlier forms of statehood was marked by two significant changes. First, there was a shift from political groups based on the principles of kinship, locality, or ethnicity to polities based on geographic territories with clearly defined boundaries. In many tribal societies and feudal monarchies, geographical boundaries were vaguely defined, and central governments exercise clear authority only over the territories immediately surrounding the centers of power. Rule over marginal areas is often partial and sporadic. On the other hand, land is vital to nation states, and they frequently fight over the boundaries. Land is important because people belong to nations on the basis of where they are born and live.

Second, there was a shift from loyalties to local, kin, and tribal groups to identification with the population within the boundaries of the nation-state. National consciousness broadens loyalties and gives them a new focus in the state. People become Colombians, Canadians, and Japanese. The ability of a nation to unify its people and mobilize its resources depends heavily on this national identity; therefore, governments frequently control educational structures and communication media in these societies in attempts to indoctrinate the population in a common ideology of national self-sufficiency and prestige.

Increase in size The growth of nationalism has been accompanied by several major political trends. One is the increase in size of polities. Nations tend to be larger than tribes. This is particularly true of nations recently formed in Africa, North and South America, Southeast Asia, Australia, and other previously colonial territories. In these areas, colonial governments from outside often simply drew lines on a map and gave names to the new "countries." The resulting nations cut across tribal boundaries and brought together numbers of different tribes. The political stability of some of these nations has been threatened by old tribal loyalties and rivalries that die hard. For thousands of villages, tribalism and isolation are still paramount facts of life, and nationhood has earned little meaning or place in the traditional mythologies.

Along with an increase in size has come larger bureaucracies and a shift in the ways people are recruited to the higher public offices. In tribal states and monarchies, political leaders are recruited largely on

Hand labor was the principal means of constructing this dam in Nagarjunasagar, India.

the basis of birth and kinship. Chiefs and kings are often first in the circle of nobles, who are set apart from the populace. Heads of nations, however, are generally chief administrators in bureaucratic institutions composed of judges, tax collectors, police, soldiers, and other officials scattered throughout the country. In time, these bureaucracies tend to become more rational, with recruitment and promotion increasingly based on the expertise, performance, and seniority of the individual, rather than on personal ties or influence. The result is some form of "civil service."

Recruitment to the higher national offices of a nation is often achieved through political parties, which may exercise a great deal of influence on the government. In one-party systems, the line between party and state is often fine, and the party is more or less an extension of the government. In multiple-party systems, the parties act more as mediators between the general population and various interest groups, on the one hand, and the government, on the other.

Rising aspirations A second political trend associated with nationalism has been a revolution of rising expectations among the people. As communication increases, people become aware of higher standards of living that provide alternatives to poverty. Aspirations are also raised by the dynamics of nationalism. Governments of new nations try to bind together their heterogeneous peoples by building roads, schools, hospitals, dams, and industries and by introducing new agricultural processes, community development, and electric power. Indirectly, these changes bring in new values and perspectives.

National governments, however, are rarely able to fulfill their promises for a better life and national glory. The result, at times, is a revolution or *coup*, as disillusioned segments of the society attempt to control the government. Such rebellions are produced not by poverty and hardship alone but by a new awareness of better alternatives. The new political elite faces the same dilemma, for they, too, must deal with the rising expectations of the people, and like their predecessors, they must often increase their control to guard against further revolutions. In one sense, however, the increase in the importance of the people and their aspirations and the fact that few modern governments can ignore them completely can be viewed as a process of increased democratization.

Centralization A third major trend is the greater centralization of national governments. As societies become increasingly complex, there is a growing need for administrative agencies with power to regulate and coordinate the specialized activities of people and institutions, as well as police and military organizations to maintain the law. But the leaders of expanding military forces often become independent from the rulers. The result is often a coup and some form of a military state. Military dictatorships, possibly even more than democracy or Communism, are becoming a common form of modern-day government. As de Tocqueville, a French lawyer and student of societies in the last century, noted (1966), even in democracies there is great danger in the tyranny of the majority over the minority.

Colonial governments

Colonial governments are marked by centralized authority but two or more legal cultures. For example, the British government in preindependent Kenya enforced "European" law on British subjects and African law in matters relating only to Africans. In British India, the colonial government had separate law codes for Hindu and Muslim communities, in addition to one for Europeans. A man from one community would be jailed for having two wives, while his neighbor from another was free to have three or four. The colonial power determined not only what legal systems it would recognize but also how and when each would be enforced.

Two main types of colonial rule have been practiced. Under "direct rule," the colonial power sets up its own centrally controlled administrative hierarchy and governs the people directly. For the most part, it introduces alien concepts of courts, police, and civil administrators to colonized areas and enforces these down to the level of the local villages and communities.

Under "indirect rule," colonial authority is administered through the existing governmental structures, through village leaders, tribal chiefs, and kings. This was practiced by the British in Nigeria, the Dutch in Indonesia, and the Muslims in India, to name only a few. The use of existing political institutions minimized the intruder's impact and often made social change more acceptable to the people.

Colonial governments have existed through much of history, for example, in cases where one tribe conquers and rules another. But the greatest expansion has taken place in the past four centuries, as European nations extended their control over tribal societies around the world in search of resources, markets, settlements, prestige, and power. As they did so, they exported the culture of the Western world in varying degrees of success but particularly to the elite of the tribal societies.

Modern colonialism also planted the seeds of its own destruction and the rise of nationalism in the colonies. The new borders drawn on the maps cut across old tribal lines and became the boundaries for nations. The establishment of centralized control over a colony created a more integrated social organization for the whole region. The rulers improved transportation and communications, and coined national currencies in order to pacify the territory, collect taxes, and rule the countryside. But these improvements also made the movement and interaction of people safer and easier.

The creation of schools and the training of national leaders, often in Europe, produced an educated elite committed to the establishment of an independent national state. Moreover, the existence of a foreign government generated new loyalties to the region and a sense of national identity. Rebellion against colonial rule and struggles for freedom often produced political leaders and institutions capable of assuming authority when independence was gained.

Paradoxically, direct rule, although generally more oppressive, fostered the development of an educated elite and strong nationalist movements that led to the formation of stable nations. Indirect rule, by maintaining the autonomy and identity of local tribes and by introducing as little change as possible, often left the colonies unprepared for nationhood.

International governments

The difficulties in forming international governments stem in part from the fact that they must recognize not only many different legal systems but also multiple centers of power. Autonomous governments are bound together not by a greater centralized power but by political negotiations and agreements precipitated by a growing interdependence between nations and a common fear of annihilation.

There are many who dispute that international law *is* law (Williams 1945–1946:61–62). Not only is there a problem of abstracting universal laws from the diverse legal codes of the various nations, but there is also the problem of enforcing them in the absence of a centralized world-state. Centralized governments can enforce their decisions, but multicentered governments must reach compromises that are acceptable to all authorities involved, for enforcement depends on their cooperation.

Political processes

As we have seen before, the structure of institutions provides the norms or guidelines for how things should operate. In everyday life, however, people and situations are infinitely varied, and actual events seldom follow the norms in every detail. No arena of life operates in complete isolation from others. This is as true of politics as of any other arena. Politicians, like other people, have economic, social, and religious needs and interests, other than political ones.

It is not always easy to separate the legitimate and illegitimate uses of governmental knowledge and authority. Can a politician use his office for personal gain? This raises the question of such practices as "honest graft," a term best defined by State Senator George Plunkett, who loyally served Tammany Hall in Chicago at the turn of the century.

> There's all the difference in the world between [honest and dishonest graft]. Yes many of our men have grown rich in politics. I have myself.
>
> I've made a big fortune out of the game, and I'm gettin' richer every day, but I've not gone in for dishonest graft—blackmailin' gamblers, saloonkeepers, disorderly people, etc.—and neither has any of the men who have made big fortunes in politics.
>
> There's an honest graft, and I'm an example of how it works. I might sum up the whole thing by sayin': "I seen my opportunities and I took 'em."
>
> Let me explain my examples. My party's in power in the city, and it's goin' to undertake a lot of public improvements. Well, I'm tipped off, say that they're going to lay out a new park at a certain place.
>
> I see my opportunity and I take it. I go to that place, and I buy up all the land I can in the neighborhood. Then the board of this or that makes its plan public, and there is a rush to get my land, which nobody cared particular for before.
>
> Ain't it perfectly honest to charge a good price and make a profit on my investment and foresight? Of course, it is. Well, that's honest graft.*

A closely related problem is the proper use of force. Government agents face violence and lawless use of force by criminals, but the improper use of legitimate power under any circumstances itself becomes a tyranny. A example is the experience of Carlos Alvarez, who had come from a small Puerto Rican village sixteen years before and worked as a night watchman at one of Chicago's museums.†

> It was about six o'clock in the morning when I was getting ready to go home. I walk out about five feet away from the back door out there, at Academy. A police was approaching to our parking

* From the book *Plunkett of Tammany Hall*, by William L. Riordan. Published by E.P. Dutton & Co., Inc. in a paperback edition and used with their permission.

† The following quote is from *Division Street: America*, by Studs Terkel. Copyright © 1967 by Studs Terkel. Reprinted by permission of Pantheon Books, a Division of Random House, Inc.

lot over there. The first question he asked me was what I was doing there? I told him I work here. He asked me if I have any identification. I said no, we don't have any right now. He asked me if I had the key. I said no, I just left it with the relief man. When he don't believe me, I ask him to come in and ask the relief man. He says in a kind of very rude manner, he pushed me against the car, he said he heard that before from other people, and he pushed me against the car again and called for help.

About six other cars answer his call. Another sergeant drop in, and this man grab me and put my hands in the back, cross my hands, throwed me into that holdup car. My cheek hit the glass, the hood. And my arm was hurt by the side of the car. And they were laughing about asking what my nationality I was. . . .

When I called the relief man and asked him to call Mr. Baird, who is the curator, Mr. Baird arrived about five minutes later. And he asked the police what happened. Nobody answered him any question. They asked him if he recognized me. He says, yeah, he worked for us for many years and we know him very good. What happened? Nobody happened to answer him. He went inside to call up the director. . . . They were talking there for a good half an hour before they decided to take me to the station. . . .

About nine o'clock the judge arrived. Everybody in line, like a pig, went to the courtroom. The courtroom where nobody is admitted. The public is not allowed to there. Behind bars. The lawyer was not allowed to go there. My cousin was not allowed to go there, even Mr. Baird was not allowed to go in there. . . . When I wait for my turn to come, the judge said. They talk all they want, they said I tried to punch the sergeant in the mouth or in his face. . . . And the judge, the only thing he asked me was if I have any family. And I say, yes, I have a family. He said, well, I'm gonna give you guilty with a suspended sentence. When I asked him guilty for what, he said, that's all, you're not allowed to talk any more. I say good-bye and I see you later. . . .

I took three weeks off. When I came back, the assistant director calls me and he says, I'm afraid we have to tell you right in your face that you have been fired. . . . And also one day, when the director mentioned the case to the board of directors, one of the women's board said, I should go back to Puerto Rico, what was I waiting for here in Chicago that I didn't go back to Puerto Rico, where I belong.

These and other areas of the political process need examination. What happens when those with political influence or office break the law? What takes place when governments collapse or revolutions occur? What are the dynamics of political leadership, and how do political elites relate to leaders in social, economic, and religious institutions? These and many more areas of political activity need to be explored if we want to understand the dynamics of power and the ways in which it affects other areas of culture. In order to do so, however, anthropologists will have to broaden the scope of their studies of stable tribe and peasant communities to include modern cities and states. They must also develop new concepts and methods of analysis which will permit them to investigate these complex societies. A great deal of work remains to be done in this area.

Summary

All social groups and societies have organization, and to the extent they do, there are political decisions to be made. What are the goals and resources? How will duties and rewards be distributed? Who will exercise authority and social control? The organization responsible for dealing with these issues constitutes a government.

Governments fall roughly into four types. Simple societies are characterized by *stateless governments,* in which political functions are carried out by different social groups as one of their many functions. Complex societies generally become *states,* in which the structure of the government is centralized, formal, and separated from other organizations within the society. Modern states are characterized by the spread of nationalism, the rising expections of the people for progress, and the centralization of power.

Colonial governments have two or more legal cultures but a centralized government to enforce them. The problems of *international government* stem, in part, from the fact that they have more than one legal culture but also many centers of power.

Governments provide the norms and structures for political activities but, as we have already seen, behavior does not always conform to the norms. The problem is that there is often little check to the misuse of political power, except for a government to govern itself or revolution.

Suggested readings

Apter, D.
1965   The Politics of Modernization. Chicago: University of Chicago Press.

(Deals with contemporary change in traditionally oriented political systems.)

Cohen, R. and J. Middleton, eds.
  1967   Comparative Political Systems. Garden City. N.Y.: Natural History Press. (A broad range of readings on the political structures of preindustrial societies.)
Fried, M.
  1967   The Evolution of Political Society. New York: Random. (A good source on general theoretical issues in political anthropology.)
Middleton, J.D. and D. Tait, eds.
  1958   Tribes Without Rulers. London: Routledge. (Deals with multicentric political systems, from both theoretical and ethnographic perspectives.)
Steward, J.H.
  1955   The Patrilineal Band. In J.H. Steward, Theory of Culture Change. Urbana, Ill.: University of Illinois Press. (An important analysis of political development on the level of the band.)

Two world views
Anthropology and other world views

World views

Faced with a bewildering variety of experiences, people continually seek to find meaning in existence and to impose order on the world. They cannot easily face the chaos of the external world, the senselessness of suffering and death, nor the gap between things as they are and as people think they ought to be without the conviction that these mysteries are somehow explainable. People may not know the explanation, but to lose the faith that there is meaning in life and in the universe is to lose part of what it means to be human. There are few fears so great as those which arise when our explanatory systems fail us.

As we have already seen, each person organizes his day-to-day interactions with his natural environment by means of technological systems, and his relationships with his fellows by means of social systems. Via religious systems, he explains the fundamental nature of the universe and his own place in it. Religion, in other words, is the model man uses to explain the reality of all things.

Explanatory models, as Clifford Geertz has pointed out (1972:169), have two sides. First, they are models *of* reality—they describe and explain the nature of things. Second, they are models *for* action—they provide us with the cognitive blueprints which guide our behavior.

Models *influence* human actions; the two are not the same. Our behavior is determined not only by our norms and ideals, but also by the conflicting forces and changing circumstances which pressure our everyday lives. Furthermore, mental blueprints do not account for the idiosyncratic variations in religious activities nor for deviant behavior. Therefore, an adequate description of a religion includes not only its assumptions and beliefs, but also its myths, rituals, sites, and objects. In this chapter we will look at religions as explanatory models, in the next at religions as patterns and products of human behavior.

Two world views

Behind the observable patterns of human cultures seem to lie certain assumptions about the way the world is put together. Some of these assumptions, called "existential postulates," deal with the nature of reality, the organization of the universe, and the ends and purposes of human life. Others, values and norms, differentiate between good and evil, right and wrong. Some of these assumptions are made explicit in the beliefs and myths of the people. Others appear to the anthropologist to be implicit in people's behavior. Taken together, the assumptions the anthropologist uses to explain a people's total response to their universe are sometimes called a "world view."

People in a society may not always be consciously aware of the assumptions the anthropologist ascribes to them. This is due, in part, to the fact that the anthropologist, no matter how hard he tries, can never see the world through their eyes. On the other hand, he is often aware of assumptions which seem to underlie their actions, of which the people themselves are not conscious. This is not surprising, for it is difficult to become aware of the basic ideas we take for granted,

Temple car in a procession celebrating the marriage of gods Rama and Sita in a south Indian village.

which determine the very processes of perception and thought, themselves.

Following are two examples of world views, one of middle-class Americans, the other of Indians of south Asia. The former has been influenced by Greek and Judeo-Christian ideas, the latter by Hindu thought. Beginning with much the same types of human needs and experiences, the two groups have constructed two very different and contrasting perceptual worlds. For the sake of comparison, point by point, these assumptions have been simplified and forced into the same mold. Nevertheless, they do point out the basic differences that can exist between different world views.

THE AMERICAN WORLD VIEW

1. Empiricism Most Americans believe that the physical or natural world around them is real and orderly and that they can experience it with a measure of accuracy by means of their senses. They therefore take the material world seriously. This natural life is seen as important and comfort and material possessions as worthy goals for human striving. To a great extent, material goods provide a measure of a person's status and success.

1.1 Absolutes In a real world, there are absolutes. There is a categorical difference between the reality of the natural world and the fantasies created by our minds and between history and myth, fact and fiction, truth and error, right and wrong. A person experiences reality most accurately when he is awake. Dreams and inner visions are illusions, and those who lose touch with the realities of the external world are considered mentally ill.

1.2 Naturalism There is a sharp distinction between the natural and supernatural worlds. The natural world is experienced directly through the senses and can be studied by means of the sciences and humanities. Supernatural experiences, on the other hand, are, for all practical purposes, confined to inner feelings, which cannot be empirically tested, or to miracles and visions, which are not seen as common ordinary experiences and are, therefore, somewhat suspect. Few people, even those who are religious, live with a constant awareness that the world around them is inhabited by spirits that directly influence their everyday experiences. It is this living in a "natural" world which is the basis of Western secularism.

1.3 Linear Time Time, like other dimensions of the world, is linear. It extends along a uniform scale into the future and past without repeating itself. Since a person has only one life to live, he must make the most of it: the religious man by preparing for heaven, the secular man by enjoying himself. There is a sense of finality about this life, which must be lived without the benefit of a dress rehearsal, without a practice run.

1.4 Order and Immutability The world is seen as consistent and orderly—as operating according to natural laws that apply uniformly over time and space. Changes take place according to predictable processes and then only within certain limits. People do not suddenly and without explanation become demons, nor do lions become humans.

THE INDIAN WORLD VIEW

1. Maya To many Indians, the natural world has no ultimate reality. It is a world of subjective experiences—a transitory, ever-changing creation of our minds. In a chaotic, unpredictable world of experiences, order, meaning, and truth can be found only within oneself. The Ultimate Reality, or Brahman, cannot be perceived by the finite person, confined as he is to the prison of his mind. A person can gain a glimpse of it only through meditation, introspection, and the deep, innermost experiences of the self.

1.1 Relativism In the world of "maya," there are no absolutes—no sharp distinctions between "real" or objective experiences and illusions, between fact and fantasy, between absolute truth and error. Myths of the past merge imperceptibly into histories, which are subjective interpretations of events. Dreams and visions are as much a part of a man's experiential world as his "awake" life. Even right and wrong are personal interpretations of moralities that are relative to one's station in life.

1.2 Supernaturalism There is no sharp distinction between natural and supernatural. Gods and spirits are as real in everyday experiences as natural objects. Natural and supernatural explanations are freely interchanged in rationalizing daily occurrences. This blending of the supernatural and natural realms into a single framework lies at the heart of what is sometimes referred to as India's supernatural orientation.

1.3 Cyclic Time Time is a continual rerun of persons and events. The universe repeats itself in an almost unending series of epochs of prosperity and decay, of existence and nonexistence. Individuals are reborn a hundred thousand times on a thousand different levels of life. This transmigration of all things from one life to the next blurs further any distinctions that may appear to be real in this life.

1.4 Mutability and Unpredictability Things are not always what they first appear to be. The passing beggar may be a king or a demon; the lion may be a god. In folk tales, animals live and talk in a world that mirrors that of humans. In scriptures, gods and demons frequently enter the world of men in various forms. Unexplainable changes are constantly taking place on earth. It is the world to which Americans are exposed on T.V., in which Clark Kents become Supermen and Shoeshine Dogs become Underdogs.

1.5 Knowledge There exists a deep faith that the human mind, by its rational processes, can discover knowledge of the order that underlies the universe and that with this knowledge, humans can eventually control it for their own benefit. Moreover, knowledge in itself has high value. A person is often judged by his knowledge and intellectual commitment to the right ideological creeds, more than by his behavior in everyday experiences.

1.5 Wisdom Humanity's goal is to gain wisdom ("jnana")—an intuitive understanding of the true nature of reality. Unlike knowledge, which comes by rational analysis and often has little effect on a person's behavior, wisdom comes as an inner light, as a flash of insight, which completely transforms a person's life and relationships to the world. No longer bound by ignorance nor attached to this world by desire, he or she is freed to live out this life in deep inner peace and, after death, to be released from the futility of future rebirths. Like a drop of water that falls back into the ocean, so the fragment of reality in humans, the spirit, is reabsorbed and lost in the cosmic Brahman. Release, not self-realization, is the supreme end. The wise realize that in a world of maya, a person's best course of action is nonattachment and noninvolvement.

2. A Particularistic and Categorized World Americans commonly use distinct categories and dichotomies to organize experiences. They classify the world into types of objects, people, and ideas and differentiate between good and bad guys in westerns, success and failure in business, and passing and failing in school. The sciences are elaborate systems to categorize and relate experiences. For example, many Americans tend to divide living beings into different types of life: supernatural beings, people, animals, and plants. And the distinctions among them are sharp. To worship people as gods is sacrilegious. On the other hand, people cannot be killed for food, nor harnessed to a plow, as can the lower animals.

2. The Unity of All Things Human experiences are endlessly varied and fragmented, but beneath the diversity of this phenomenal world lies a single essential unity. All things are manifestations of one spirit. The result is that Indians often organize their varied experiences along continuums. Like ladders, these have many rungs, but form a single whole. Life is segmented into an infinite variety of beings: gods, demigods, spirits, demons, people, animals, plants, and material objects. But life, itself, is one. It is easy, therefore, to understand why Hindus refuse to kill animals, such as cows. It also explains why they feel it proper to worship saints, since these, like the gods, are above them in the continuum of life. Characteristically, in music, the total spectrum of sounds is divided into notes, and these into quarternotes and sixteenth notes, until the glide becomes the hallmark of Indian music.

2.1 Equality There are fundamental differences among categories within a single taxonomy or domain, but within each category things are more or less the same and equal; they are of the same kind. In the hierarchy of life, all people belong to the same category, "homo sapiens"; therefore, they are equals. The ideal society is one in which all men have equal opportunities. Every person should have the right to contract and to break relationships and the right to be respected as an autonomous person. Ideally, all people should be converted to the same religious and political point of view and observe the same customs. Integration in the universe is based on homogeneity, not on diversity.

2.1 Hierarchy Segments in any continuum are organized on the principle of hierarchy, and hierarchy is both necessary and good. The caste system is only part of a larger social order that extends up through the spirits and down through the worlds of animals and plants. Each person has a unique place in this order. All religions lead to the truth, but some are higher than others. The highest are the paths of wisdom in which the devotee gains insight into the true nature of the universe by means of meditation and asceticism. Below these are the many paths of mental devotion to the god of one's choice, and at the bottom are the paths of ritual duty—of bringing offerings to an image. Values, too, are ranked. The highest are spiritual values of release from transmigration, then the metaphysical ones of wisdom and insight, then the biological ones of health and offspring, and at the bottom, material possessions and power.

THE AMERICAN WORLD VIEW

2.2 Individualism The individuality and worth of each person is taken for granted. It is assumed that all men have inalienable rights to "life, liberty, and the pursuit of happiness." Applied to society, the stress on individualism leads to an idealization of freedom. Communism, socialism, and other economic systems, which are thought to restrict the individual, are rejected in favor of free enterprise and capitalism. Democracy, in which a man has the right to choose his rulers, is the ideal form of government. With regard to the individual, the emphasis is on self-realization. On earth, this is expressed in a search for identity and praise for the self-made man, in heaven in the ultimate self-fulfillment of the individual.

2.3 Competition In an individualistic world, all forms of life compete for resources and dominance. Therefore, people must be aggressive in their relationship to nature. Humanity "conquers space" and "beats the heat." The allopathic system of medicine is aimed at *killing* germs and *overcoming* disease. In the social order, individuals must compete for status. Their station in life should be determined not by birth, but by ability and effort.

3. Natural and Moral Management By their knowledge of natural and moral laws, people are increasingly able to control their destiny. They and not fate are primarily responsible for the engineering of the future.

3.1 Science and Technology If one wants to understand the culture of the United States, one must look at its universal education in the natural sciences, its universities, technological institutes, and research laboratories, and its industrial complexes. The Americans' commitment to science and technology goes beyond mere gadgeteering. They know that science grows even though individuals may have no personal knowledge of any of its fundamental principles, and they have faith that it can provide the grounds on which can be built a secure way of life for people.

THE INDIAN WORLD VIEW

2.2 Specialization and Interdependence Segments of a whole are also integrated on the principle of interdependence. Each caste has certain unique skills and specialized functions that are essential for the operation of the society as a whole. Each individual has certain tasks to fulfill within the family. Diversity and cooperation, not uniformity and competition, are the ideals.

2.3 Patron-Client Relationships Some people are clearly born to greater rights and responsibilities, others to service. The ideal social relationships are those that combine both the principles of hierarchy and interdependence into hereditary patron-client bonds.

3. Karma or Cosmic Law In an organic universe, in which each part contributes to the harmonious operation of the whole, all processes are governed by the law of "karma." Just as there is no distinction between natural and supernatural worlds, so there is no sharp difference between natural and moral laws. All actions are governed by karma and have both natural and moral consequences.

3.1 Samsara or Pilgrimage The condition of each life in a person's spiritual pilgrimage is determined by the actions, good or bad, of his previous lives. The fruits of one's actions are not always seen in this life. Transmigration is not fatalistic. A person's present position and the things that happen to him are determined by past deeds, but by his response to life now, he is shaping his future destiny.

THE AMERICAN WORLD VIEW

3.2 Uniform Morality and Justice People are responsible for building a society based on "self-evident" principles, such as love, equality, freedom, respect for the rights of others, and on a general humanitarian compassion for one's fellow humans. These principles apply equally to all and are the basis for legal systems. Thus, for example, war criminals are held accountable not only for the orders of their superiors or the laws of their countries, but also to universal principles of humane conduct during a conflict. The primary concern of law and morality is to mete out justice. Good must be rewarded and evil punished in this lifetime. Beyond this life, the consequence of one's actions are expressed in terms of heaven and hell.

3.3 Missionary Those who have knowledge and the truth, whether this is scientific or religious, have a moral obligation to share it with the rest of the world. All over the world, American experts are helping people of other nations to improve their educational systems, their agricultural production, their military forces, their industrial growth, and their religious destinies.

4. Self-reliance As Frances Hsu has pointed out (1972:248), the dominant value directing everyday American behavior is self-reliance. There are few fears as great as those of dependence on others and running out of money. This value has its roots in the stress of individualism, freedom, and management.

4.1 Expanding Good There has been, until recently, a belief that the world of all that is good is expanding, that there are new frontiers for people to conquer. As the geographic limits of the earth were explored, people turned their attention to the expansion of knowledge, technology, and gross national products in order to create their utopia of self-realization. People compete for what is good, but one person's advance need not come at the expense of another's fall. New opportunities are there for those who seek them.

THE INDIAN WORLD VIEW

3.2 Relative Morality Right and wrong depend for a person on his place in the universal and social orders. Consequently, there is no absolute morality. More is expected of those higher in the spiritual and caste hierarchy in terms of orthodoxy and ritual practice. "Right" lies in conformity to the cosmic order. A man who lives according to his social position and in harmony with the universe acquires the spiritual force of truth, which is moral and nonviolent. This force ("satyagraha") is ultimately superior to physical force in the establishment of a harmonious society. In a system of relative ethics, the aim of law is not justice defined in some absolute terms, but the restoration of harmony in society. Actions cannot be divided into the good and the evil, and there is no sharp difference between offender and offended. Nor is it the task of man to punish actions whose causes he can never fully understand. Final justice is meted out by the cosmic law of karma.

3.3 Inclusivism and Tolerance Cultural pluralism and ethnic relativism are inclusive—they accept a diversity of thought and action in the same world without demanding conformity to a single standard. People pride themselves in their own unique cultures. Individuals can simultaneously follow several apparently contradictory courses of action without inconsistency. Closely tied to inclusivism is a spirit of tolerance, in which each must respect the cultural differences of others and not seek to convert them to his or her own way of life.

4. Dharma or Functional Responsibility The universe and human society are organic wholes, in which each part has a unique function to fill. Only as each caste and each individual fulfills its responsibility or duty ("dharma") can the whole operate smoothly. It is wrong to abandon one's prescribed role and seek another. A person should live on the level at which he was born, and by fitting himself dispassionately into the cosmic order, fulfill the task to which he was destined.

4.1 Limited Good There exists only a limited amount of all the desired things of life, such as wealth, land, power, status, friendship, and love, and there is no direct way to increase the quantities available for all to use (Foster, 1965). Therefore, one individual's gain or advancement can only come at the expense of others. Since it is not always clear who is losing, any significant attempt by some to improve their social or economic situation is seen as a threat to all individuals, to the community as a whole.

4.2 Achievement Orientation Personal achievement, not illustrious background, is the measure of an individual's worth and social position. Hard work, careful planning, efficiency, and saving of time and effort are intrinsically good. In a predictable world, the individual is ultimately responsible for failure. For example, a man may not be able to prevent all disasters, such as accidents, illness, or death, but he can minimize their harm by means of insurance and a will. It is important, therefore, to fix blame when anything goes wrong, and the consequence of blame is guilt. Achievement is closely tied to social mobility. People should be allowed to rise to their levels of ability and not be tied down by their kinsmen or their past. The results, in part, are shallow social and geographical roots and insecurity.

4.3 Associational Groups Social groups above the level of the family are based primarily on voluntary association or contractual relationships. Status in the middle-class rests primarily in the groups a person can join. Participation in a group, however, demands involved commitment to a program and conformity to its practices. Groups must guard themselves by ostracizing the nonconformists and by segregating themselves from those inferior fellow humans who might encroach upon them from below.

4.4 Success and Progress Success and progress are unquestionably good. They are measured by the ability to produce results, such as an expanding program or growing institution, and to make a profit. The practical test for any course of action is pragmatism—Does it get results? Security for the individual comes largely through personal success. Failure leads to loneliness and a shameful dependence on others. Progress is tied to the American dream, a basic optimism, an orientation towards the future, and a stress on youth. Success is equated with superiority and right, and since Western cultures have obviously succeeded, they are superior. This sense of cultural superiority is particularly obvious in American relationships with other cultures.

4.2 Ascription Orientation Security and meaning are found in the groups to which one belongs and in the relationships one has with others, rather than in the material possessions one acquires. The building of relationships, particularly those to which one is born, is of greatest importance, for they are a measure of an individual's status and power. Because the world is not fully predictable, failure leads not so much to blame and self-accusation as to a sense of frustration. This tension is often reduced by dropping out of the situation and turning inward or by anger at the situation and turning to violence.

4.3 Jatis and Castes A person's primary ties are to his "jati," or caste, to those who are the same kind of people. Because membership is by birth, a great deal of individual variation can be permitted by the members. However, if one defies the dictates of the caste, the ultimate sanction is ostracism—to be cut off from the group.

4.4 Moksha The goal of life is not self-realization but release from the hardships of life ("moksha"). The cultural hero is the man of wisdom and insight who can rise above the troubles of this passing life and understand the significance of all things.

Basic similarities

Middle-class Americans and Indians from south Asia begin with different assumptions and therefore construct different cognitive worlds. Just how great the differences can be is illustrated by the assumptions discussed above, but a more detailed study would also show many similarities. For example, people in both societies are concerned with the problems of food, shelter, health, protection, and everyday social activities. They are interested in relatives and friends, in entertainment and the enjoyment of life. It is this fact, that there is much in common in human experiences around the world, that makes cross-cultural communication at all possible.

Anthropology and other world views

Cultural differences are found at all levels of human behavior and belief, but none seem so great or so difficult to bridge as the differences among world views. An anthropologist can study houses in another society and learn how to construct them without upsetting his own explanatory models of the world. He can discuss the structure and operation of kinship systems with the people among whom he works with a large measure of understanding and possibly even agreement. But when he studies their religious systems and world views, he faces differences that challenge his own basic postulates and raise important questions about the methods and models he, himself, is using.

Cross-cultural understanding

If people from different cultures disagree on the basic assumptions they use to organize their conceptual worlds, can they ever really understand one another? And what methods can they use when they try to do so? Suppose, for example, that a person in a different society tells us that his illnesses are due to demons, and that he has actually seen them. What are we to make of it?

Obviously, we must avoid the ethnocentric temptation to judge the person and conclude that he is ignorant and foolish, without first trying to understand him in terms of his own cultural concepts and values. But the answer to our question is not so simple. In trying to understand another culture, the outsider can observe human behavior and products, but he cannot see ideas and postulates. These he can only infer from the acts and comments of the people. There may be no informant who will, or even can, verbalize the basic assumptions of a culture, for these are not necessarily explicit ideas in the minds of the people themselves. These are the "givens" that the people take for granted, often without question or examination. If an anthropologist must depend on inference to arrive at his abstract conclusions, what do we mean when we say that he *knows* something about that culture?

Moreover, anthropologists carry their own sets of concepts. Should they describe other cultures in terms of these or in terms of the cultures' own concepts and values? As we have seen earlier, both etic and emic models are useful. But the question is, can an anthropologist, given his own cultural biases, ever really understand another culture on its own terms? And even if he does so, can he effectively communicate it to others who have not lived in-depth in that culture?

This problem of understanding can be illustrated by looking at concepts, such as maya, karma, and dharma, which, as we have seen, are basic to Indian thought. Can we translate these accurately into English? It should be clear by now that no English word has exactly the same meaning nor the same emotional associations as any one of those Indian words. To be accurate, we should use those Sanskrit terms, themselves. If we carry this thinking to the extreme, we can only understand and describe a culture in terms of its own language, but this makes cross-cultural communication and understanding virtually impossible. Each culture, then, remains a conceptual island, and, at best, we can only move from one to another.

Clearly, our understanding of another culture is only approximate, just as *its* model of the world around it is approximate. But this does not mean that we have no understanding of it at all. Careful study can give us a great many insights into another culture, and as we develop new methods for learning about the thoughts and thought processes of others, these approximations should become more accurate and easier to verify.

The problem of cross-cultural comparison will be solved only as we formulate concepts and methods of investigation that are increasingly free from the biases of any single culture. The process is a tedious one, for our biases are deep-seated. Nevertheless, a great deal of progress has already been made along this line in the field of anthropology.

Cultural relativism

The fact that cultures differ in their fundamental postulates raises the even more difficult philosophical question of what is knowledge or truth and the moral question of what is right. After we have tried to understand cultures by their own assumptions, is there any way of evaluating them by some noncultural criterion of truth or goodness?

PHILOSOPHICAL RELATIVISM? If all cultures construct models of the universe (to some extent, at least, all of them seem to provide explanations that make sense and work for the people in them), does it follow that all of these models are equally accurate maps of the external world? Does each explain reality equally well? And are they equally well adapted to the world around them?

For a concrete illustration of the problem, let us turn back to the explanations of disease. Is it true that smallpox and pneumonia are

Children's games reflect cultural values, as does this organized game in the U.S.

caused by demons? Or are they caused by viruses? Or are they produced by demons in one culture and by viruses in another? And finally, how are we going to determine which explanatory model is a better picture of the "real" world? We, in the West, might appeal to empirical facts and experiments to test these explanations. But such "proof" cannot be accepted so easily. As we have seen, in a world of maya, such "empirical facts" are thought to be often illusory and deceptive, and one turns to insights to discover truth.

The philosophical problem shows itself at several levels. On one level, the validity of our empirical observations is called into question. In the above illustration, the Western anthropologist cannot arbitrarily classify the informant's experiences of demons as hallucinations and thus not empirical; the experiences may be real to the informant. Moreover, a check with other people in the same society would show that many have "seen" demons and describe them in exactly the same terms. In short, there is an independent verification of the observations—one of the primary tests of empirical data! On what basis, then, can the anthropologist reject gods and demons as empirical realities in that culture? On the other hand, what happens to his scientific models if he accepts all such statements as empirical facts?

On another level, the validity of anthropological models is called into question. Is the Western scientific view of the world a truer picture of reality than another world view? Or are all equally true?

On the one hand, we can hold that all cultures are equally valid maps of reality. But are they? Is it true that smallpox is caused both by demons and by viruses? A social scientist, in his search for knowledge, seeks to build models that are ever more accurate statements of reality. Even when he describes people in terms of their own postulates, he does so ultimately from the vantage point of science, with the conviction that it is closer to the truth. A position of extreme philosophical relativism ultimately denies meaning to all human ideas.

On the other hand, we can hold that there is a universal cognitive order—that there is a common logic and set of philosophical principles underlying all human thought. It is necessary, here, to distinguish between human universals and philosophical absolutes. The former are similarities that can be empirically observed in all humankind—a kind of human common denominator. These include biological processes underlying perception and thought, as well as social needs, such as stimulus and security. Philosophical absolutes are judgments about reality and nonreality, about the truth and falsehood of statements that are thought to apply to all people. To assume they exist opens the door to faith in human rationality, to communication and understanding across cultures, and to meaning in human ideas. But, the question still remains, can we discover what these universal principles are, and, if so, how? This question has given rise to a great deal of scientific investigation in recent years, but it is beyond the scope of our study to look at the many answers offered.

MORAL RELATIVISM?   Cultural relativism raises a second and equally intractable question: what is right and wrong? Are there any universal moral principles that apply to all mankind, or are all values culturally relative? Bennett points out (1949:329–337) that to take an extreme position in moral relativism is to virtually deny a social humanity to all people. There is, then, no basis to condemning oppression, murder, or the liquidation of populations.

Ultimately, a position of moral relativity also leads to a denial of science itself, for science, like all world views, has a built in commitment to certain basic values and ethical principles. In the case of the social sciences, this includes a basic humanism and an honest search for truth. No scientist can tolerate the fabrication of data to support a pet theory, and few feel that their findings should be used to further human aggression or suffering.

Anthropologists, as individuals and as citizens of their societies, cannot avoid making moral judgments in their everyday lives. The

A group undergoing purification rites in Benaras, India.
Photo courtesy of Ron Wall.

same, of course, is true of their professional activities. This raises the ticklish question of whether professional associations of anthropologists should regulate the activities of members. Should anthropologists be permitted to participate in espionage or military planning?

Moral questions also confront those who seek to apply anthropology to government planning and programs of cultural change. Should anthropologists be involved in such tasks? If so, by what moral principles should they operate? On the other hand, such programs will inevitably take place, and if anthropology has something to offer in making them more beneficial or less destructive to the people affected, is it morally right for anthropologists to remain uninvolved?

Finally, in a world of growing communication and interaction, there is the problem of cultural diversity and the maintenance of world peace. Hoebel points out (1949:473–74), a "world society means a world culture with a certain measure of integration, and all present cultural systems are most certainly not compatible with each other." Therefore, "some social norms will have to give along the way. Not all can be tolerated." Some type of world consensus is needed on the

The gods Rama and Sita are carried on a temple car in a procession celebrating their marriage in India.

norms and customs that should govern international relationships if world peace is to be achieved, but the means by which such a consensus will be achieved still eludes us.

Summary

At the core of each culture, there seem to be certain basic assumptions about the natures of reality and morality. Many are implicit, because they are taken for granted and never questioned. Together, they form a more or less consistent world view that orders people's experiences and gives meaning to their lives.

A comparison of the American and Indian world views shows us how different worlds people live in can be. It also points out the methodological, philosophical, and ethical problems that arise from facing cultural pluralism honestly. A great many answers have been given to these questions, but it is beyond the scope of our study to deal with them here. Suffice it to say that in an increasingly international world, neither these differences nor the problems they raise can be ignored.

Suggested readings

Douglas, Mary.
    1970 Natural Symbols. New York: Random House. (A difficult but very useful book pointing out the correlations between general views of the supernatural and social orders.)
Forde, D., ed.
    1954 African Worlds: Studies in the Cosmological Ideas and Social Values of African Peoples. London: Oxford University Press. (An excellent collection of papers on the world views of nine African tribes.)
Herskovits, M.J.
    1972 Cultural Relativism: Perspectives in Cultural Pluralism. Frances Herskovits, ed. New York: Random House. (A reprint of a number of useful articles on the problems of cultural relativism.)
Hsu, F.L.K., ed.
    1970 Americans and Chinese: Purpose and Fulfillment in Great Civilizations. Garden City, N.Y.: Doubleday. (A comparison of American and Chinese world views and how they relate to behavior in these countries.)
Morgan, K.W., ed.
    1953 The Religion of the Hindus. New York: Ronald Press. (An interesting and useful collection of articles by seven Indian writers on the basic assumptions of Hindu thought.)
Society for Applied Anthropology
    1963 Statement on Ethics. In Human Organization, 22 (1963):237.

19

Religious structures
Dynamics in religion

Religious beliefs
and practices

A world view provides people with their basic assumptions about reality. Religion provides them with the specific content of this reality, with the things in the people's model of the universe and with relationships between these things.

Early anthropologists defined religion in terms of beliefs in supernatural beings and events. In this sense, religion stands in contrast to science and other naturalistic explanations of the world, such as some forms of Hinduism and Buddhism. But this distinction is part of the Western world view, which the anthropologist shares, and is not made by people in many other cultures.

In its broadest sense, religion encompasses all specific beliefs about the ultimate nature of reality and the origins, meaning, and destiny of life, as well as the myths and rituals that symbolically express them. In this sense, religions may or may not have gods, demons, and souls. For example, Christianity, Islam, some forms of Hinduism, and most tribal religions have supernatural beings, but some forms of Buddhism and Hinduism and scientism do not.

Religion is also based on the person's ability to transcend the self, to step "outside" of and contemplate oneself, one's fellows, and the universe. It is based on the human need to "make sense" out of human experience and find some order and significance in the whole human situation.

Religious structures

In their study of religions, anthropologists are not concerned with the truth or error of specific beliefs. This is a question of theology and philosophy. Rather, they are interested in what these beliefs tell us about the people and their culture and in how beliefs operate within the broader cultural system.

Anthropologists have used several key concepts to study religions and their place in culture and to compare them cross-culturally. Frequently, there is disagreement over how these concepts should be defined, and much of the development of anthropological theory arises out of discussions on what they mean and how they relate to each other.

Myths and rituals

People express their religious beliefs in creeds and stories and in ritual behavior. The study of these symbol systems can provide us with a great deal of insight into the ways people think and the ways they organize their cultures.

MYTHS All religions have myths or stories of cosmic origins and events and their significance for the world of here and now. These tales are often not histories or rational explanations of the natural world, nor are they meant to be. To Western minds, they may appear at times to be superstitious mixtures of fantasies and contradictions, with little in the way of a story or plot. But these are not the product of some lower order of mentality. They are fanciful and poetic commentaries on what the people think is the very basis of the world and life. Because they are based on visionary and intuitive insights into the mysteries of the universe, they must be understood as philosophies garbed in symbolic and poetic literature. As Malinowski pointed out, myths are "charters for belief" and form an integral part of culture, serving to legitimize action. Creeds setting out beliefs in rational systems are found chiefly in the great religions that developed with the rise of complex civilizations.

Anthropologists have taken different approaches to the study of myths. Some, like W.E.H. Stanner (1905–   ), look at myths as reflectors of the culture in which they are found. They are thus studied for what they convey about the way a society operates. But care must be taken to interpret myths in their historical and ethnographic contexts, for much of their meaning becomes clear only as we understand other parts of the culture of which they are a part. Moreover, there is a danger in assuming that myths accurately reflect the way people perceive reality. Myths are statements about the ultimate nature of things, not about common, everyday realities.

Other students of myths, such as A. Dundes (1934–   ), see them as giving expression to the basic psychological conflicts people have between their unconscious biological drives and the constraints of their society and culture. This might account for the fact that certain mythological themes are found in a great many cultures. For example, the tale that dry land was formed by the cultural hero from a small piece of dirt brought up from the bottom of the sea was widespread among North American Indians. In Freud's terms, this might rest in part on the desire of males to create life and valuable material from within their bodies, as women do. Since they cannot do this in normal life, they project their creative ability into myths concerning the origins of the universe.

Claude Lévi-Strauss (1908–   ), a noted French anthropologist, sees myths as logical models by which human minds try to resolve the unwelcome contradictions that are so much a part of human experience by turning to analogies at higher levels. For instance, people may seek to resolve the conflict between death and life or that between man's erotic nature and his desire for spiritual growth by depicting in myths death as the door to rebirth and erotic love for God as a spiritual expression. To this approach, Edmund Leach (1910–   ) adds the view that figures in myths are symbols with many levels of meaning and that myths, therefore, condense a great deal of information and wisdom into a compact form, which is easily remembered for transmission from generation to generation.

Cross-cultural studies, comparing myths from different cultures, reveal certain features and themes that appear to be universal or at least widely distributed in space and time. Attempts have been made to classify these themes and explain them in terms of the universal biological, psychological, and social situations that are the "givens" for all human life.

RITUALS Myths relate experiences in the form of stories. Rituals often reenact them. Both are symbolic expressions of beliefs. In its broadest sense, ritual includes all patterns of behavior, from daily greetings to rites in a temple. Religious rituals are those thought to be sacred or associated with the fundamental operations of the universe.

It is common in the West to make a distinction between ritual forms and their meanings and to value the latter over the former. This is similar to the distinction we made in Chapter 6 between the form and meaning of all symbols. But in many cultures, people do not make this distinction. For them, the meaning and the consequences lie in the act itself. For example, to many, one does not go to church in order to worship; going to church is itself an act of worship. Similarly, the bread of communion may not be seen only as a symbol of a spiritual reality but that, in fact, it becomes that reality. From this point of view, there is no such thing as an "empty ritual," and the anti-ritual views so widespread in the West make little sense to others.

Calendrical and crisis rites Religious rites can be roughly divided into those that are regular and expected events and those that arise out of unexpected crises. The former, sometimes called cyclic or calendrical rites, are part of the normal order of things. Such, for example, are the human rites of passage: birth, marriage, and death. Others relate to the cycles of nature, such as ceremonies associated with the renewal of the earth's fertility or with the harvest. Many annual festivals, such as Christmas and Easter in the West, reenact the life cycles of supernatural beings.

Calendrical ceremonies are generally performed by priests who hold religious offices. Because they can be scheduled long in advance, there is a growing sense of anticipation for the event. They are almost always observed by specific communities or societies, and when a society loses its distinctiveness, the cyclic rites associated with it die out.

Crisis or critical rites are precipiated by unforeseen events, such as plagues, droughts, wars, and other disasters. Unlike calendrical rites, these often benefit only a small group or a single individual. The ceremonies are frequently performed by diviners, medicine men, and other religious leaders, who claim to have a personal contact with the supernatural.

Rites of transition and tabus We have already seen how transitions in the social roles a person plays in life are often marked by rituals. As Van Gennep pointed out, such rituals maintain social order by arranging for an orderly separation from the old role, a transitional period in which the individual assumes a new role, and finally a reintegration into the society in his new status. The transition period is often considered sacred or thought to be fraught with spiritual dangers. In part, this seems to rest on the fact that a person in this state belongs to no clear state or category. He is a liminal or marginal person, for he lies somewhere between categories, and until his status is clear, he cannot participate in everyday life.

A somewhat analogous religious practice is "tabu," the prohibition of certain acts on pain of supernatural punishment. Mary Douglas (1921–   ) argues that acts and things that do not fit into the conceptual categories of a people are often tabu to them. For example, body excretions are not fully part of the body, nor fully detached from it. Hence, they are somehow polluting.

A more elaborate case is the Jewish dietary laws prohibiting the eating of creatures considered unclean, such as pigs, camels, fish without scales or fins, snakes, and insects. Their position, according to Douglas (1966) was ambiguous, for they did not fit clearly into the three-fold classification of life in the Old Testament: two-legged fowls that fly with wings, scaly fish that swim with fins, and four-legged animals with cloven hoves that chew the cud. By avoiding what in nature challenged God's order, the people were reaffirming their faith in that order.

Tabus may have other explanations. Supernatural power, like fire or high voltage, is potentially dangerous if not handled properly. With proper rituals and in the hands of those who know the procedures, it can benefit the user, but in the hands of the ignorant, it can be disasterous. The latter thus avoid supernaturally charged objects and places with feelings of awe and fear.

Functions and meanings Rituals play a number of important religious functions. Like myths, they often store a great deal of information to be transmitted from generation to generation. The endless repetitions and the dramatic nature of the events assure the preservation of traditional knowledge with a great deal of accuracy. In the absence of writing, rituals are particularly significant in the preservation of a culture.

But rituals do more. To the individual participant, rituals offer an opportunity to participate in the religious life of his community and thereby discover his identity in the group. Rituals also enable a person to act in the face of crisis. All people have knowledge relating to the pragmatic, technological side of life, and this knowledge gives them the possibility of planning ahead and, in a measure, of directing their future. But no matter how much knowledge they have, people cannot completely control their lives. There are unforseen accidents, unexpected turns of natural events, and mistakes in human calculations. In the face of such, people often turn to religious rituals to satisfy their need to control the future or at least do something in the time of crisis.

To the society as a whole, rituals offer an occasion for reaffirming its unity and expressing a sense of identity. The performance of a ritual itself reinforces social order and hierarchy. Leaders reinforce their roles by leading the people in worship, and the people their roles as followers, as communicants, novices, or outsiders, as men or women, in the parts they play in the ceremonies. There is a powerful message in the performance, itself.

Rituals not only dramatize the social order, they also mirror the way people perceive the total cosmic order and the way people relate to supernatural beings, to one another, and to nature. People in many societies think of the supernatural by analogy to the natural and social events of their personal experiences. God is perceived in terms of "father" or "mother," "judge," "ruler," or some other category rooted in social life. While science often builds its models by analogies to mechanical and natural things, religions often build theirs by analogies to human relations and social order.

Finally, rituals enable individuals to relate to the natural world of which they are a part. People are profoundly dependent on their ecology, on the seasonal rains, the renewed fertility of the soil and animals, the orderly cycles of sun and seasons, and the phenomena sparing them from natural disasters. Rituals are often thought to maintain this order. The rain dancer may not only be praying for rain, he may see the dance as itself producing the rain. He explains his failures as does a modern doctor when he loses a patient—to factors beyond his control or to errors in the procedure. The explanatory system itself is not questioned.

Rituals also help people relate to and influence supernatural forces and beings, often to their own advantage. The attitudes people take towards the supernatural have been the basis for anthropological discussions centering around two other terms: religion and magic.

Religion, magic, and science

People are model builders. They are blessed, and cursed, with reflection, imagination, and forethought. They can invent new ways to live and plan for the future. People are also plagued with anxieties and forebodings not only about their own lives but also about human destiny and humanity's place in the universe.

As we have noted, all people, even the most primitive, have perfectly sound empirical knowledge about some aspects of the world around them. This knowledge brings together elements of past experiences and allows people to carry out many of their practical cultural activities. Hunters know that a strong bow and the skill to use it are necessary for the kill. Craftsmen know the materials suitable for their products and the technical processes necessary to make them. Agriculturalists know the properties of the soil, the need to clean and work it, and the time and way to plant the seeds. It is the systematic gathering of such experiential knowledge in order to increase human control over life that characterizes the scientific revolution of our day. But science is more than the gathering of practical information related to everyday life. It also seeks to discover the basic processes underlying the universe and to organize experiential knowledge into broad explanatory systems that enable people to understand their place within it.

But no matter what man's knowledge and however carefully he applies it, there are uncertainties and gaps. A sudden drought or storm could wipe out the careful efforts of the farmer. Death upsets and disorganizes man's search for meaning. As Malinowski points out (1972:71), "Religion is not born out of speculation or reflection, still less out of illusion or misapprehension, but rather out of the real tragedies of human life, out of the conflict between human plans and realities."

MAGICAL ATTITUDES   Sir James G. Frazer (1854–1941) pointed out a distinction in human attitudes towards the supernatural. In some situations, people believe they control supernatural power or beings, somewhat in the fashion that scientists control chemical reactions. When the right chant is recited or the right sign is used, the supernatural power will respond in the expected way. Frazer referred to this attitude of control over the supernatural as "magical." When, for example, a south Indian villager is bitten by a viper, the snake must be caught, and the local magician must recite the following chant over the victim, seven times for each stripe on the viper's back.

> Ōm Garabaranābhava-Sarva peshāchādi gruhamulu
> Ōm, O Birthless Garavara, All evil spirits and planets
> nanu dzūchi-bhayamondi-paradzudu.
> having seen me, being afraid, may they look askance.
> Em, ksham, shaum, svaha.
> (powerful sounds).&&

Like common experiential knowledge, magic often has practical utilitarian value, relating to the problems of everyday life. It frequently fills in where technical knowledge fails. The farmer who has planted and tended his crop to the best of his ability may turn to magic to guarantee rains and ward off pests. People faced with a disease that cannot be cured by their medicines and doctors often turn to supernatural means to force a cure. (See Figure 19.1 for several examples of magical charms for practical needs.)

The test of magic is if it works, at least sufficiently well to convince the user. The Western analyst may explain the successes of magic in terms of coincidence or psychological suggestion. There are many clinically documented cases of people dying after discovering they are under a magical curse. But to the practicer, the explanation lies in the magic itself, and when it fails to produce the desired results, he does not question the system but the performance of the rite. The chant may have been recited incorrectly or the magician unpure. To return to a modern day analogy, the chemist does not reject his science when an experiment goes wrong, nor does the doctor when he loses a patient.

In itself, magic is neither good nor bad. It can be used to produce a harvest or to destroy it, to cure people or to kill them. At times, the use of magic to harm another is sanctioned by the society; a man may be expected to curse his enemy. Only when it is used in the face of social disapproval does magic become sorcery. While magicians may acquire great honor as medicine men and diviners, they are often in danger of being charged by their rivals with misusing their powers in secret.

Magic takes many forms in addition to curses and cures. The diviner reveals knowledge of some hidden or future event by mechanical means. The astrologer calculates the effects of astrological bodies on human affairs and determines auspicious and inauspicious times for various activities, including suitable times for talking to foreign anthropologists. And there is the evil eye, the malevolent force that plagues some people from birth, causing their sight to bring sickness to small children and indigestion to adults.

Figure 19.1 (opposite page) Magical charms, when properly used in a south Indian village, will automatically bring about the desired results. These charms combine powerful figures, sounds, and words. A: Yantra for a headache, including writing it on a brass plate, lighting a candle before it after it is wrapped in string, covering it with red and yellow powders, and tying it to the head. B: Yantra for assuring conception, involving inscribing it on a piece of paper or copper sheeting and tying it to the arm of the barren woman. C: Used for malaria. D: To the god Narasimha, for power and general protection. E: (For use by young men), when written on paper and tied to the arm, it will cause the woman of a man's choice to fall in love with him. (There are other charms to protect women from lecherous men who use this charm.)

Source: From *Konduru* by Paul G. Hiebert. Reprinted by permission of the Publisher, University of Minnesota Press. Copyright © University of Minnesota.

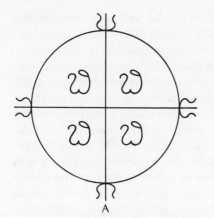

A

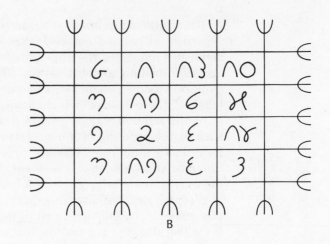

B

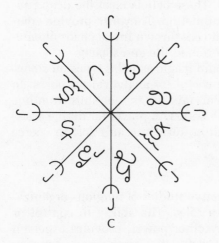

C

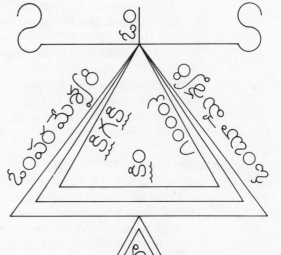

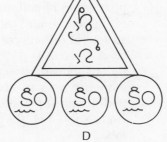

D

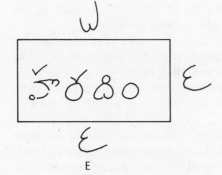

E

RELIGIOUS ATTITUDES The second type of attitude towards the supernatural pointed out by Frazer is that of religion. In religion, the believer approaches the supernatural in an attitude of subordination and supplication to spirit beings. The basic rites are prayer and worship, in which a person seeks to communicate with and gain the assistance of these beings, which have personalities much like humans.

While religion may be used in dealing with matters of everyday life, such as the ordering of human relationships and responding to crisis, its primary function is often to provide an explanatory model for the universe and humanity's place within it. For instance, a religion may not only provide believers with a course of action to prevent the deaths of their fellows, but also an explanation for the place of death and its consequences in the total order of the universe. In doing so, it often affirms that death is not real or final and that a person has an immortal soul which continues in another life. These beliefs meet the deep psychological need to deny personal annihilation. They also provide comfort and meaning to the survivors, who are thrown into a chaos of emotion that threatens the continuity of ordered life and society.

The distinction between religion and magic as polar types on a continuum of supernatural rites may be useful for analytical purposes. In practice, however, the performers often mix the two or shift from one moment to the next in use of one or the other. A prayer for divine assistance may, in a moment of desperation, turn into an effort to coerce God to act.

Shamans and priests

Much of the discussion in comparative studies of religious organizations has centered around leadership roles. The ability to control or influence supernatural power, as any other power, provides a person with prestige and authority. A useful distinction can be made between polar types of authority: shaman and priest. Both are found in all parts of the world, and the differences between them illustrate many of the structural differences between types of religious systems.

A shaman is a charismatic leader who claims to have received religious power directly through contact with the supernatural. His authority rests in his ability to convince the people of this power by performing supernatural acts and declaring the messages of the spirits. He is a prophet, the mouthpiece whereby gods and ancestors speak to men.

Shamanism is more commonly found in loosely structured societies that lack formally organized religious institutions. Ceremonies in food-gathering tribes, for example, are generally noncalendrical rites organized to cure sickness or avert disasters. Moreover, they are performed for the benefit of an individual or group within the society and, less frequently, for the community as a whole.

A priest, on the other hand, receives his authority from the office he holds in a religious organization or church, rather than from his own personal charisma. The power to influence the supernatural lies in the institution and not the person. The priest learns a body of traditional rituals from older priests, which he passes on to his successors. As a spokesman for a religious group, he is often the intermediary, who speaks to the spirits on behalf of the people.

The priesthood and organized religious bodies are generally associated with more complex societies and those with economic surpluses that can support specialists who do not produce their own food. Rituals are often public rites performed for the benefit of a whole village or community, and frequently they follow an annual ceremonial calendar. As such, they are important in maintaining the religious system and the cosmic order.

Shamans and priests are frequently found in the same culture, but in societies with highly organized churches, there is often conflict between them. To priests, with their vested interests in the bureaucracy, the shaman, with his fierce individualism, is a threat to the whole religious structure. The shaman, on the other hand, may in time develop a following, organize a cult group, and thus become the founder of a new religious organization.

Priestesses are less common than female shamans, as the centers of institutionalized religious power are usually held by men. Male dominance holds true in this, as it does in many other areas of culture in most societies.

Spirits and mana

If we turn from the structure of religious systems to their content, we find an exceedingly varied range of beliefs. However, those that deal with the nature of supernatural things can be roughly divided into two types: spirits and mana.

SPIRITS   The term "animism" was used by Sir Edward Tylor (1832–1917) for belief in spirit beings. Spirits have personalities but lack bodies; therefore they are not subject to the limitations of the material world. They are found in a great variety of forms, such as human and animal souls, witches, demons, globins, angels, and gods.

Ghosts and ancestor worship   All people face what Malinowski called the "supreme and final crisis of life"—death. While most people, if given the option, would choose to remain alive a while longer, no matter how great their difficulties, the fear of death is probably least among those who believe that life continues after death. This appears to have been the case at least for the early Christian martyrs, the Muslims engaged in "holy wars," and the sacrificial victims of the Aztecs. Death loses some of its sting when it is not seen as the extinction of being.

But if the spirits of those who die live on in some conscious form, what is their relationship to the living? Belief in ghosts is found in all cultures, and, as Frazer has convincingly demonstrated (1933–1936), in most cases ghosts are viewed with fear and dread. People often go to great lengths to insure the departure of ghosts to another world by providing them with money, possessions, and means of transportation.

Indian Muslims worship ancestors and saints.

Totemism and the A.E.F.

Ralph Linton

Many modern anthropologists discount the supposed differences in the mental processes of civilized and uncivilized peoples and hold that the psychological factors which have controlled the growth of the so-called "primitive" cultures are still at work in modern society. It is difficult to obtain evidence on this point, and a record of the development in the American army of a series of beliefs and practices which show a considerable resemblance to the totemic complexes existing among some primitive peoples may, therefore, be of interest. The growth of one of these pseudo-totemic complexes can be fully traced in the case of the 42nd or Rainbow Division. The name was arbitrarily chosen by the higher officials and is said to have been selected because the organization was made up of units from many states whose regimental colors were of every hue in the rainbow. Little importance was attached to the name while the division was in America and it was rarely used by enlisted men. After the organization arrived in France, its use became increasingly common, and the growth of a feeling of divisional solidarity finally resulted in its regular employment as a personal appellation. Outsiders usually addressed division members as "rainbow," and to the question "What are you?" nine out of ten enlisted men would reply "I'm a Rainbow." The personal use of the name became general before any attitude toward the actual rainbow was developed. A feeling of connection between the organization and its namesake was first noted in February, 1918, five to six months after the assignment of the name. At this time it was first suggested and then believed that the appearance of a rainbow was a good omen for the division. Three months later it had become an article of faith in the organization that there was always a rainbow in the sky when the division went into action. A rainbow over the enemy's line was considered especially auspicious, and after a victory men would often insist that they had seen one in this position even when the weather conditions or direction of advance made it impossible. This belief was held by most of the officers and enlisted men, and everyone who expressed doubts was considered a heretic and overwhelmed with arguments.

The personal use of the divisional name and the attitude toward the rainbow had both become thoroughly established before it began to be used as an emblem. In the author's regiment this phase first appeared in May, when the organization came in contact with the 77th Division, which had

Source: Reproduced by permission of the American Anthropological Association from *American Anthropologist,* 26 (1), 1924.

its namesake, the Goddess of Liberty, painted on its carts and other divisional property. The idea was taken up at once, and many of the men decorated the carts and limbers in their charge with rainbows without waiting for official permission. As no two of the painted rainbows were alike, the effect was grotesque and the practice was soon forbidden. Nevertheless it continued, more or less surreptitiously, until after the armistice, when it was finally permitted with a standardized rainbow.

The use of rainbows as personal insignia appeared still later, in August or September. . . . The wearing of shoulder insignia was at first forbidden by some of the regimental commanders, but even while it was proscribed many of the men carried insignia with them and pinned them on whenever they were out of the reach of their officers. They were worn by practically all members of the division when in the rear areas, and their use by outsiders, or even by the men sent to the division as replacements, was resented and punished. . . .

All the other army organizations which were in existence long enough to develop a feeling of group solidarity seem to have built up similar complexes centering about their group names. The nature of some of these names precluded the development of the ideas of the namesake's guardianship or omen giving, but in such cases the beliefs were not always the same as in the case of the 42nd Division. Many of the later organizations seem to have taken over such complexes with little change except the substitution of the namesake for that of the group from which they borrowed.

By the end of the war, the A.E.F. had become organized into a series of well defined, and often mutually jealous, groups each of which had its individual complex of ideas and observances. These complexes all conformed to the same general pattern but differed in content. The individual complexes bound the members of each group together and enabled them to present a united front against other groups. In the same way, the uniformity of pattern gave a basis for mutual understanding and tolerance and united all the groups against persons or organizations outside the system.

The conditions in the American army after these group complexes had become fully developed may be summarized as follows:

(1) A division of the personnel into a number of groups conscious of their individuality;

(2) the possession by each of these groups of a distinctive name derived from some animal, object, or natural phenomen;

(3) the use of this name as a personal appellation in conversation with outsiders;

(4) the use of representations of the group namesake for the decoration of group property and for personal adornment, with a taboo against its use by members of other groups;

(5) a reverential attitude toward the group namesake and its representations;

(6) in many cases, an unformulated belief that the group namesake was
also a group guardian capable of giving omens.

In some cases, notably the Bantu tribes of Africa, the Polynesians,
and the Pueblo Indians, ghosts are thought not to become malevolent
after death. Rather, the spirits of the dead continue as part of the society, influencing the lives of the living, favorably or unfavorably. These
ancestors are often senior members in ongoing lineages, which include
the spirits of the deceased, the living, and the unborn. Ancestors are re-
vered with festivals and offerings, and they are often thought to punish
those who violate the traditional customs of the society.

Nature worship   Humans are not the only beings thought to have
spirits. In many cultures, animals, plants, and even natural bodies,
such as the sun, moon, and earth, are seen as having souls. The sun, for
example, was worshipped in many tribes of the Americas. The Plains
Indians pitched their tepees and camps with the entrances to the east,
and their spectacular Sun Dance was performed in mid-summer, when
the whole tribe had gathered. In Polynesia and Africa, nature is associated with specific gods of the skies, waters, earth, hills, and trees.

High God worship   At the turn of this century, there was a great
deal of anthropological debate over the origins of belief in a High God.
Tylor, a cultural evolutionist, held that primitive man arrived at the
concept of the soul by reflecting on dreams and death. In dreams, people transcend their bodies and experience events outside of time and
space. In death, people leave the earth, even though their physical
bodies remain. From these observations, it was thought, early man
reached the conclusion that there are two parts to man: a material body
and an intangible soul. From this beginning, Tylor postulated (1874),
people derived the notion of spirits in other parts of nature and of
spirits above nature. The end product of this evolutionary development
was thought to be the monotheistic religions of the West.

Two decades later, Andrew Lang (1844–1912) showed that Austra-
lians, Polynesians, American Indians, and Africans had beliefs in a
High God and that these were not derived from Western monotheism.
Today we know the idea to be very widespread, particularly among
sub-Saharan African tribes and among the cultures around the Mediterranean Sea that gave birth to Judaism, Christianity, and Islam (see Lang
1898 and Schmidt 1931). In early Judaism, the High God was often seen

as distant and uninvolved in the everyday affairs of life, which were handled by lesser deities and ancestral spirits. Among the Mediterranean cultures, the High God was seen as a moral ruler, punishing evil and rewarding good.

Later, Paul Radin (1885–1963), seeking to explain the origins of the High God concept, suggested that there are two types of people in all societies: the idealists and the realists. The idealists are the mystics and philosophers, who ponder the meanings of life and seek a unified orderly explanation of the universe. They can perceive a High God in transcendent terms.

However, as Hoebel observes (1972:592), most people are materialists. "Their bellies, their health, wealth and social power mean much to them. They develop religion in terms of gods and spirits, who control the means to satisfy these needs." Most people are concerned more with their current problems than with cosmic affairs and their own ultimate destiny.

MANA   Not only are there beliefs in spirit beings but also in impersonal supernatural forces. Anthropologists have followed the lead of R.R. Marett (1866–1953), one of the first men to discuss the subject, and refer to these forces as "mana." Actually, Marett called belief in such forces "animatism," but in his discussion, he borrowed the term "mana" from the languages of Melanesia and Polynesia, a region of the world where the concept is particularly widespread.

Mana is an invisible force, which pervades the universe and is found to a greater or lesser degree in gods, men, animals, and natural objects, such as rivers, mountains, stones, and trees. But mana itself is not a personality with whom a person can communicate. It is an attribute of these objects, just as magnetism and gravitational fields are attributes of certain objects. Mana can be controlled by one who knows the formulas, but as in the case with any power, it is dangerous in the hands of those who are ignorant of its ways.

Mana helps people explain extraordinary experiences and events that cannot otherwise be explained. It also accounts for human successes. A man is successful in a fight not because he has a strong arm and a quick eye, but because he has the mana of some deceased warrior to help him. It may lie in the stone amulet tied around his neck, the tiger tooth in his belt, or the chant he recited before the battle. Similarly, a man has good crops not because he works hard—even the best workers fail at times; he succeeds because he has mana. On the other hand, mana also accounts for failures. If crops fail and weapons break for no apparent reason, it is because they have lost their mana.

Mana is often linked to tabus. Objects and persons possessing great mana are dangerous to lesser men. Among some Polynesian groups, the highest chief, his shadow, and all that he touched were full of mana and hence dangerous to commoners.

Dynamics in religion

Religious systems, like other aspects of culture, are constantly changing in response to internal social pressures, environmental changes, and foreign ideas and control. While change is a constant factor in all religions, radical or revolutionary shifts have characterized many important religious movements. A study of them can throw a great deal of light on how people and cultures function and change.

One of the significant factors in the history of the past four centuries has been the spread of European culture and colonial power over much of the world. The impact of this on tribal societies has frequently led to religious movements, in which the beliefs and values of the people have undergone radical change. The pattern, however, is not unique to our age. The movements of people and the spread of ideas and empires has characterized humanity throughout recorded history.

Faced with foreign ideas or overrun by another culture, people respond in different ways, ranging from complete acceptance to total rejection of the new ways. (See Figure 19.2.) When change is not forced on them, people are more likely to borrow ideas of technology than those of social organization or supernatural beliefs. The reason, in part, is that changes in the basic beliefs and values of a people are changes in the very core of their culture, in their world view.

Conversion and acculturation

The spread of ideas within an ethnic group is usually refered to as "diffusion." When the spread is from one ethnic group to another, the terms "assimilation" and "acculturation" are used. In both cases, however, individuals either accept or reject the new ideas for themselves. They may convert to a new set of beliefs, often reinterpreting them in terms of their old culture, or they may try to perserve their traditional beliefs as best they can. Acculturation may be defined as "relearning a new culture."

For those enculturated in one set of beliefs and values who convert to another, the process of acculturation is often lengthy. As mentioned previously, it may take generations before the converts are accepted as full participants in the new society. Moreover, converts often face internal conflicts between the old values, in which they were reared, and those they have adopted. They are often branded as traitors by others

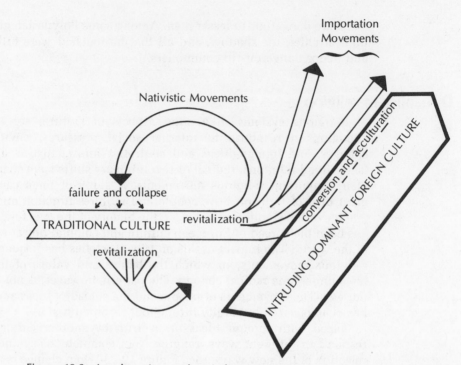

Figure 19.2 Acculturation and revitalization movements often occur after the collision between a smaller tribal culture and an intruding dominant foreign culture.

who do not convert. The transition is easiest when whole communities adopt the new beliefs.

Conversion and acculturation are never complete and instantaneous. People may embrace new ideas in dramatic movements, but they always bring with them parts of their past. The new beliefs are often stated in terms of the old thought categories. The result is a synthesis of ideas, new and old, which expresses itself in indigenous movements within the new faith.

Revitalization movements

Contemporary religious history is, to a large extent, the history of the rise and growth of new religions and messianic cults. Over 6,000 have been reported in Africa alone (Barrett 1968). Thousands of cargo cults and prophetic movements have risen in New Guinea and Oceania, and since the second world war, hundreds of new religions have appeared in Japan and the Philippines (see Worsley 1957; McFarland 1967; and Elwood 1968).

Most are revitalization movements, in which there are deliberate, organized efforts by members of a society to construct a more satisfying culture. There are usually radical differences among such movements, in terms of cultural contexts and specific beliefs, but there are basic similarities as well. Often, there are "prophets" or charismatic leaders, who bring a special revelation and start a movement, which rises suddenly, totally absorbing its adherents and giving them a whole new life-style. At the center is usually an expectation of the imminent coming of a new heaven and an earth with no sickness, poverty, or oppression. It will appear after some natural disasters, such as earthquakes and floods, and often will be accompanied by the coming of a messiah.

NATIVISTIC MOVEMENTS In some revitalization movements, the new earth is viewed as the revival of certain aspects of the people's cultural past. The present is evil and must be destroyed to usher in the golden age. Writing about nativistic movements, Ralph Linton says:

> All societies seek to perpetuate their own cultures, but they usually do this unconsciously and as a part of the normal processes of individual training and socialization. Conscious, organized efforts to perpetuate a culture can arise only when a society becomes conscious that there are cultures other than its own and that the existence of its own culture is threatened (1943:240).

A classic example of a nativisitic movement is the Ghost Dance that spread among some western American Indian tribes, which were facing economic deprivation and disease at the end of the nineteenth century (see LaBarre 1970). In 1870, Taivo, a Paiute, had a vision from the "Great Spirit" that a massive earthquake would destroy everyone but that after three days, all Indians who joined the dance would be resurrected. When this did not occur, the movement died.

It was revived twenty years later by Wovoka, a prophet who had learned some Christian theology working as a ranch hand. In an illness he had a vision of heaven and the happy reunion of the living and dead in an unending utopia. In it, God said to him that if people stopped fighting and danced the Ghost Dance, the old earth would be wiped out by an earthquake or flood, and a new one would appear.

This time, the movement spread rapidly among the Plains Indians. They felt that nature was wearing out and people becoming evil, so God would destroy the earth and replace it with a bigger one. It would slide over the old one, coming from the west. There would be a wall of flames, over which the believing Indians would be carried on sacred dance feathers, or a hurricane would kill the whites and unbelievers. Again, nothing happened, and the movement came to a sad ending when those who resisted white expansion died at Wounded Knee.

The failure of nativistic movements often leads to a breakdown of the traditional culture. People are left to fend for themselves, as individuals without the support of an integrated society. Only after some time, often generations, does a new synthesis emerge which gives the people a new sense of identity. When, for example, the Ghost Dance failed, many American Indians turned to rituals centering around peyote, mescal, and other hallucinogenic drugs, seeking to find self-knowledge and moral strength within themselves. The Red Power Movement now emerging seeks to renew the sense of American Indian identity and to regain stolen lands, not by visions but by polemics, law, and lobbies in Washington, D.C. (see Deloria, 1969).

IMPORTATION MOVEMENTS In many revitalization movements, the people seek neither to lose their identity by assimilation in a foreign culture nor to revive their past. They want a new identity, in which there is a selective combination of old values and imported riches. The result is a syncretism—a synthesis of ideas from two cultures.

The cargo cults of New Guinea illustrate importation movements. Reported as early as 1893, they have proliferated in great numbers to the present. An important theme in the more recent cults is that cargo, defined as Western material goods, such as money, canned goods, flour, rifles, and jeeps, will arrive by ship or plane for the people. After the second world war and the abundance of goods displayed by United States military forces, this theme was associated with the Americans who mysteriously departed after the war. In some cases, bamboo control towers, landing strips, and cargo sheds are constructed, and men stand ready with tin-can microphones to guide the planes to a safe landing. Those taken to see modern Australian stores, in hopes they would give up their beliefs, only return more convinced that God wants to send them the goods but that white men have stolen them on the way.

In an interesting variant, the people of the island of New Hanover tried to elect Lyndon Johnson as their president in 1964 so that they would receive the cargo. Bos Malik, their leader, told them they would have to buy Johnson, so they refused to pay taxes to the Australian administrators and collected more than $82,000 to do so. When an armed force was sent to supress the tax revolt, Malik promised that the liner Queen Mary would arrive with the cargo and with American troops to drive out the Australian oppressors. Obviously, no American troops appeared, and the revolt was crushed.

STAGES IN REVITALIZATION   When we talk of "revitalization," we are making an analogy between human societies and biological organisms. According to this analogy, societies operate to maintain the life of their members and to reduce stresses that threaten to damage or disrupt this social life in much the same way that biological processes work to maintain life and reduce stress in creatures. However, unlike cells in a body, individuals in a society are more flexible and mobile. They can and do shift from one status to another and so can maintain the essential functions of a society.

The ability of people to maintain the operations of their society depends on their ability to understand how it operates and how it relates to the environment. Each individual has his own model of how his body, personality, nature, society, and culture fit together. A.F.C. Wallace (1923–   ) has called this personal world view a "mazeway."

No two individuals share the same mazeway, not even within the same society or segment of society. Nevertheless, there must be some general agreement between people, some common world view, for them to operate within the same society and maintain its operations. When individuals or groups of people are under some kind of stress and find that their mazeways no longer can help to reduce this stress, they have two courses of action. They may choose to keep their faith in their mazeway and learn to live with the stress, or they may be willing to face the anxiety of changing their beliefs in order to reduce the stress they face. An individual's attempt to change his mazeway in order to minimize stress is called revitalization. When a number of people do so together, it is a revitalization movement.

As we have already seen in the cases of the Ghost Dances and Cargo Cults, the stresses which trigger such movements may be the conflict between their old cultural beliefs and the new world with which the people have come in contact. At other times, they arise when basic changes take place in the organization of a society. Since religious beliefs are based, in part, on analogies with human relationships, changes in the structure of a society often lead to changes in the mazeways of the people.

Individual stress and revitalization can occur when a person moves from the farm to a city and vice versa or when his status in the society changes radically. While the processes may be the same as those in a movement, the individual does not often have the support of a community of people in making such changes.

Wallace defines five stages through which revitalization movements pass. While each movement is colored by local differences in culture, the basic structure of such movements is essentially the same.

Steady state   Culture provides most people with more or less satis-

Gods Rama and brother Lakshmana (left) and Sita (right) being introduced prior to the marriage of Rama and Sita in south India.

fying ways of meeting their needs and reducing their stresses to a livable level. Changes may take place in cultural patterns, but so long as these changes do not seriously interfere with the culture's ability to meet the people's needs or leave some needs unmet, this steady state is not disturbed. There are always some people who reject normal cultural patterns or turn to some "deviant" means of coping with their circumstances. They may turn to crime or develop a psychosis. But for most people, the culture is in an ongoing steady state.

Increased individual stress   Over a number of years, the level of stress in individuals within a society may increase markedly. There may be changes in the ecology, epidemics, military defeats, political subordination, or the introduction of new ideas from without. Or there may be internal cultural tensions, as some areas of life undergo change while others lag behind. If the old cultural beliefs and behaviors can no longer deal with these stresses, people may begin to look for alternative cultural solutions to their problems. But to do so increases the stress, because people are afraid the new ways will be no better than the old and that acceptance of some new ways will undermine all of their existing beliefs and practices. There is anxiety in leaving the security of the old and familiar way of life, however imperfect it is, and striking out on a new and uncertain course.

Cultural distortion   Faced with prolonged stress and no satisfactory cultural way of dealing with it, people respond in different ways. Rigid people seemingly prefer to live with stress rather than change their ways. More flexible people may change some of their beliefs or behavior in attempts to reduce the tensions. Some people turn to alcoholism, become depressed or lazy or drop out of the society to avoid the stresses. Others turn to violence or rejection of the social and sexual norms. The result of all this is an increase in conflicts between various groups in the society, between different sets of beliefs and values, and an additional increase in the stress. In the end, people are disillusioned with their mazeways and lose a sense of meaning in life.

Revitalization   If this process of deterioration is not stopped, the society will die out or be defeated and absorbed by another society. Frequently, however, a revitalization movement, often religious in nature, brings a new set of beliefs and new ways of coping with life in a more satisfactory way, thus restoring meaning to existence and renewal to the culture.

Revitalization often begins with a charismatic leader who has a vision or insight, in which he or she sees a new mazeway, providing a new explanation to life and its possibilities. The change in the prophet may be abrupt and dramatic, leading to significant changes in his or her life-style, such as the dropping of deep-seated habits like alcoholism. It is a transformation of personality.

The message of a new world view proclaimed by the prophet on the basis of his revitalized mazeway generally provides for a new cosmic order, a destruction of the old world, a new morality, and the establishment of a utopian society. The prophet himself is the final authority in defining the message. People are converted and join the movement as followers. A few cluster around the prophet as his close disciples, and they become the leaders, who later interpret the message and institutionalize the leadership roles. Often there is opposition to the movement, and its leader must devise strategies to face the resistance.

In the life of the individual, revitalization often leads to a more active and purposeful life. When the movement attracts a large portion of the population, a social revitalization takes place. Social relationships are renewed and group action enthusiastically pursued. If the new activities help to reduce stress and restore meaning to the society, they soon become institutionalized within its structure.

New steady state   The acceptance and institutionalization of a cultural order leads to a new steady state, in which people once again can cope with their stresses and find meaning in their existence.

While many revolutionary movements fail, others succeed in achieving a cultural transformation and a new steady state. Christianity, Islam, the Reformation, Communism, and possibly Buddhism were born in revitalization movements. As Wallace points out, probably few people have lived who have not been involved at some time or other in the revitalization process.

Summary

Religious rituals and myths are symbolic expressions of the specific beliefs that people use to create their explanatory models of the world. A study of them can help us to understand the meaning people ascribe to events and things. But rituals and myths can be understood fully only within the cultural contexts in which they are found, for their meaning is tied to the culture as a whole.

Assumptions about supernatural processes vary considerably. In magic, they are seen as mechanical relationships between impersonal powers and things, in religion, as interpersonal relationships between beings. The line distinguishing the two is not always clear, and attitudes within a single ritual may vary from participant to participant and even within the same participant from one moment to the next. There is also a great deal of variation in the specific content of religious beliefs, from belief in mana and inanimate forces to belief in supernatural beings of a bewildering variety.

When religious systems fail to satisfy the explanatory needs of the people and reduce the stresses they face, the culture itself is threatened with disintegration. If, however, a prophet appears with a new mazeway, a new explanatory model that is more adequate than the old one, conversions and cultural revitalization can often take place. This, in fact, is one of the most widespread phenomena in religious movements in our day, arising, in part, from the cultural dislocation created by colonialism, global wars, and the worldwide spread of Western ideas.

Suggested readings

Geertz, C.
1968   Religion: Anthropological Study. *In* International Encyclopedia of the Social Sciences, 13:398–406. New York: Macmillan. (A good summary.)
Lessa, W.A. and E.Z. Vogt.
1972   Reader in Comparative Religion, 3rd ed. New York: Harper & Row. (A comprehensive reader; see particularly Part 3 on symbolism, Part 5 on myth, Part 6 on ritual, and Part 10 on dynamics in religion.)

Malinowski, Bronislaw.
1954   Magic, Science and Religion and Other Essays. Garden City, N.Y.:
Doubleday. (An early classic that is still significant.)
Turner, Victor.
1968   The Drums of Affliction. New York: Oxford University Press. (Important, both theoretically and ethnographically, as a detailed description
of the rituals of the Ndembu of Zambia.)

20

The arts
Entertainment

Expressive culture

People are rarely content with a purely utilitarian approach to life. They decorate their pots and baskets, embroider their cloth, paint their houses, carve their tools, and hang jewelry of all sorts on their bodies. Their houses follow architectural tastes; their evenings are spent in song and dance; their lore is full of stories, poetry, proverbs, and riddles. All reflect the human penchant for self-expression and aesthetic enjoyment. It is difficult to imagine what a society would be like without this expressive culture that pervades all areas of life—without art, music and dance, or sports and games, with un-dyed clothes, unpainted houses, and only work to break the boredom.

For purposes of study, one can divide the broad field of expressive culture into art and entertainment, although the two overlap a great deal and are more polar types on a continuum than distinct categories.

The arts

Art is an act of creation, designed to please the aesthetic senses. It is an expression of human emotions as well as ideas. The range is al-most endless: painting, carving, weaving, pottery, architecture, body decoration, drama, music, dance, story telling, literature, cake baking, flower raising, and bull fighting to name only a few. The subject matter and the ways it is expressed are as broad as human experience itself.

While all cultures have some forms of art, each has its own defini-tions of what is aesthetically pleasing and of what forms art should take. The polyphonic music of the West, in which several notes, suppos-edly in harmony with each other, are played simultaneously, is thought by people in many societies to be a terrifying discord. Many nonliterate peoples sing and play in unison. On the other hand, Ameri-cans find the four, six, or even twenty-four note scales and irregular beats of other music systems confusing or disturbing.

The comparative study of expressive arts has only just begun in anthropology. Ethnomusicologists, such as Bruno Nettl and Alan Lomax, have attempted to develop concepts and taxonomies that can be used cross-culturally, but for the most part, anthropological studies have treated art styles and their development within single cultures.

How can an anthropologist approach the study of art in view of the bewildering range and cultural diversity of its expression? Franz Boas long ago stressed the importance of art forms and the skills neces-sary to produce them. To this, Adrian Gerbrands adds the importance of the meaning of art within its cultural context (1962). These are two dimensions along which all art can be analyzed.

Form and meaning

Art is an example of man's tendency to proliferate symbols to express himself. As we have already seen, the key element of any symbol system is the linkage of forms to meanings.

Art forms in any culture are developed in styles that are accepted by certain classes or by the whole of the society. The styles are handed down from generation to generation, often by specialists who set the standards of propriety and excellence. In the United States, for example, there are traditions associated with the theater, the opera, and the symphony, as well as with various solo instruments, such as the violin, zither, mouth organ, trumpet, and piano. Moreover, within each of these traditions, there are various schools of thought, such as classical, jazz, and church music.

New art forms and styles may be created or borrowed from other peoples, but their acceptance is often a long process. For anthropologists, the study of art styles and their changes provides a great deal of insight into the development of cultures over long periods of time and into interactions among cultures.

Meaning in art is both cultural and individual. Cultures often develop their own elaborate symbol systems in connection with art. Some are overt and must be understood in order to appreciate the art. For example, in classic dances of north India, there are seven positions of the eyes, seven of the eyebrows, six of the nose, six of the cheeks, six of the lower lip, and sixty-seven of the hand, each of which conveys its own specific feeling and meaning. Other meanings may be more covert, such as the significance of certain colors and shapes in modern Western art.

But art may be more than a symbolic statement about something else. In some societies, the art symbol itself becomes the referent of the meaning. A mask used in a dance not only represents a spirit but *is* that spirit, and the wearer becomes possessed with it when he dons the mask. Dances become, not enactments of other aspects of life, but life, itself.

Art may also be intensely personal. In it, the artist may give expression to his own feelings and ideas. In this sense, he may be a prophet portraying his view of the world or proclaiming a new conceptual synthesis. However, even as he does so, his message must be understood within the symbols of his culture if it is to find acceptance by the people.

Use and function

Art can also be studied in terms of its use and function. The use is generally obvious, the specific reason for which the art is created. It may be decoration on a utilitarian object, such as a pot or basket, or it may be an object of art in itself, such as a painting. It may be used in religious rituals, in entertainment, or as a tourist commodity.

The function of art lies in its relationship to other parts of the culture. In primitive societies, ritual dances often serve magical purposes, intended to attract game or cause rainfall. They may also give expres-

Actors preparing for a drama in India.

sion to the unity of the group and the authority of its leaders. In complex stratified societies, art is often used to reinforce the high status of the elite. They alone can afford to be patrons of the arts believed to be culturally sophisticated, which are also usually nonutilitarian. They can buy the jewels and brocades, commission the works of art, and attend the theaters that become symbols of the elite.

The arts also function to store and communicate messages. This is particularly true in nonliterate societies, where much of the tribal wisdom and teachings are preserved in its arts, rituals, and folklore.

But even in complex, literate societies, the arts are important communicators of ideas and values, such as patriotism and religious beliefs. Russian and Chinese leaders are well aware of this and of the danger of uncontrolled artists and the power of culturally regulated arts to communicate political messages.

Arts and society

The relationship between art and the other aspects of culture and social organization is complex and only poorly understood. In primitive societies, with their lack of specialists, art is closely knit to other aspects of daily life. Certain members of the band or tribe develop reputations for their skills in decorating arrows or dancing, but art, as a highly specialized marketed commodity, is rare.

In complex societies, particularly urban ones, art proliferates at a great many levels, ranging from common folk art to the highly specialized skills of the professional artist. For the former, art remains an area of expression related to other areas of activity. For the latter, art may become a way of life, a speciality that can be marketed for a living. From the view of the society as a whole, art in complex societies becomes an increasingly separate institution, with its own norms, behavioral patterns, personnel, and properties.

Complex societies are characterized by many forms of highly specialized art. In the West, there are art institutions associated with classical music, the blues, country and western, rock, and a great many types of ethnic music. In each of these traditions, there are leaders who serve as models for the part-time artist. Local school orchestras look up to the city symphonies, and local rock groups imitate the superstars. The relationship and rank of these various art institutions reflects, in many ways, the overall social structure of the society.

Art in all societies expresses the basic values of the people. It is precisely for this reason that art can become the vehicle by which revolution or any other societal occurrence is expressed.

Art as a map of culture

Art is often a guide to the world view and mazeways of the people, showing us how they see their relationships to nature, to one another, and to the supernatural. Muslim art, for example, prohibited the use of human or divine figures. It thus developed elaborate and intricate designs, using plants, geometric figures, and arabic letters to fill the space. On the other hand, Indian paintings are full of gods and people in ephemeral settings that reflect the world of maya, in which there is no sharp distinction between the natural and the supernatural or between myth and history.

Gypsy women in India performing a ceremonial dance.

Changes in the world view of a society can often be studied by looking at its art. This is true with the history of the visual arts in Europe.
For the Greeks, aesthetic beauty lay in the imitation or representation
of nature. On one level, this led to a realism that has hardly been
equalled. Statues of people and animals seem nearly alive to the
viewer. On another level, nature was presented not as it is, with its im-
perfections, but in its ideal form—as the perfect human body and the
ideal architectural proportions. It was believed that visual beauty could
lead the beholder to an understanding of truth, goodness, and the
moral order of the universe.

As Christianity came to maturity in the Roman empire after the fifth
century A.D., art took on a predominantly religious theme. Because it
was thought that natural models and visual beauty might distract people from looking for inner spiritual beauty, in the same way that Adam
was deceived by the delights of the natural world, an elaborate system
of symbols was developed to represent spiritual truths. By means of
these, the nature of God was portrayed so that men might learn and

worship. The stress was on communicating a message rather than on perfecting artistic forms and techniques. In fact, irregularities and asymmetry were consciously introduced into paintings and sculptures so as to avoid naturalistic beauty that might distract the viewer and to teach him that this world was imperfect and evil. In architecture, walls were often not parallel and arches were not of uniform heights.

Medieval art stressed the inner experience, and one of its highest achievements was the Gothic cathedrals, with their lofty ceilings and stained glass windows, by which the artist transformed the outer rays of the sun into an inner illumination of the spirit. The cathedral itself was the creation of a community working in concert to give expression to its spiritual vision.

The Renaissance, with its rediscovery of the beauties of nature and the joys of this world, led to a movement in art towards naturalism. The

Women of Shambala, Tanzania grooming each other.
Photo courtesy of E.V. Winans.

Madonna and baby Jesus became increasingly human in form and size, and the halos faded away. The backgrounds began to include trees and fields. In the end, the religious message was replaced by attention to people and nature, which were appreciated for their own intrinsic values rather than for their allegorical significance. The focus shifted from message to form. Artists worked on principles of perspective and on the dynamics of light and shadow in order to create the illusion of three dimensions.

Much of modern Western art has moved towards a subjective expression of experience, of the ways in which the artist feels or perceives the world rather than what is objectively viewed. Some abstract artists stress the purely aesthetic qualities of color, line, and form in order to express beauty. Others seek to see objects from many points of view, so as to show their true nature by complex forms or to express rebellion against their culture. The diversity and complexity of modern Western art styles reflects the culture, with its complexity and the fact that it draws, for its heritage, on art styles found around the world.

How, in general, does art relate to social complexities? Alan Lomax found (1968), in studying more than 3,500 folksongs from a number of societies, that songs in simpler societies are characterized by a great deal of repetition and the use of meaningless sounds, such as "la-la-la." These societies also had fewer explicit messages, and the pronunciation of words was often slurred. It appears that music in these societies is associated more with the expression of feelings than with the communication of ideas. On the other hand, music in complex societies is characterized by a great deal of wordiness and an interest in communicating verbal information.

Entertainment

The arts give expression to humanity's aesthetic nature, but they also serve the need for entertainment, the need to avoid the boredom that threatens to make life pleasureless and purposeless. There are other areas of expressive culture, such as games and sports, that cater more directly to this aspect of human life, but as yet, anthropology has given little attention to them.

Contests and pastimes

Children's pastimes consist of a great many kinds of play, often in imitation of adult roles. In some societies, boys hunt and war and girls care for infant dolls, thereby learning and reinforcing the roles they will be asked to play in later life. In other societies, sex differences in play are minimal. Touring the countryside and sightseeing are pastimes aimed at exploring the world, practiced by children and adults alike.

Contests of skill and strength are found in most societies. Wrestling, dog sled racing, diving, rope jumping, dancing, archery, yam raising, watermelon eating and cramming people into small cars only open the list of tests of conquest or endurance. Games of skill and chance come in an almost endless variety.

Contests and pastimes often serve important functions other than entertainment. They provide people with models for participating in their culture and for practicing personal strategies for life. This can be seen in the game of Monopoly played by many middle-class American children or the game Go played by the Japanese. Some games develop group values, and other stress individualism, and in the playing of them, participants learn many of the social rules governing human interaction within that society.

American football

Entertainment forms also provide us with a great deal of insight into the ways a culture views the world. An illustration of this is American football. One of the underlying assumptions of this game is that there is a single set of absolute rules that are equally abiding on both teams and are enforced by referees, who, like little gods, rule from above, punishing with impartiality and justice those who violate the rules. It would be unthinkable to have different sets of rules for each team or to give to the team that is ahead the right to change the rules to its own advantage. It is often charged that the referees are partial in their judgments, but never with approval. The assumption is that teams must compete on equal terms within a single orderly system.

American football also portrays an explicitly structured social organization, in which the identities and roles of the members are clearly defined. Each team has its own uniforms, and each player his own highly specialized position and job. On the sidelines, the coach is often calling the plays. He cannot, however, send in one of his players as a spy, dressed in the opponent's uniform, nor should he bribe the scorekeepers.

The game is a battle between two opponents. It would be unrecognizable if there were three, four, or a dozen teams on the field, each trying to win. Moreover, the aim is to defeat the enemy, not to reach a mutual alliance. Success is measured by conquering territory until a team can enter the heartland of its opposition. When the battle lines are

Freud and Football
Child Herald

. . . Obviously, football is a syndrome of religious rites symbolizing the struggle to preserve the egg of life through the rigors of impending winter. The rites begin at the autumn equinox and culminate on the first day of the New Year with great festivals identified with bowls of plenty; the festivals are associated with flowers such as roses, fruits such as oranges, farm crops such as cotton, and even sun-worship and appeasement of great reptiles such as alligators.

In these rites, the egg of life is symbolized by what is called "the oval," an inflated bladder covered with hog skin. The convention of "the oval" is repeated in the architectural oval-shaped design of the vast outdoor churches in which the services are held every sabbath in every town and city, also every Sunday in the greater centers of population where an advanced priesthood performs. These enormous roofless churches dominate every college campus; no other edifice compares in size with them, and they bear witness to the high spiritual development of the culture that produced them.

Literally millions of worshipers attend the sabbath services in these enormous open-air churches. Subconsciously, these hordes of worshipers are seeking an outlet from sex-frustration in anticipation of violent masochism and sadism about to be enacted by a highly trained priesthood of young men. Football obviously arises out of the Oedipus complex. Love of mother dominates the entire ritual. The churches, without exception, are dedicated to Alma Mater, Dear Mother. (Notre Dame and football are synonymous.)

The rites are performed on a rectangular area of green grass orientated to the four directions. The grass, symbolizing summer, is striped with ominous white lines representing the knifing snows of winter. The white stripes are repeated in the ceremonial costumes of the four whistling monitors who control the services through a time period divided into four quarters, symbolizing the four seasons.

The ceremony begins with colorful processions of musicians and semi-nude virgins who move in and out of ritualized patterns. This excites the thousands of worshipers to rise from their seats, shout frenzied poetry in unison and chant ecstatic anthems through which runs the Oedipus theme of willingness to die for love of Mother.

The actual rites, performed by 22 young priests of perfect physique, might appear to the uninitiated as a chaotic conflict concerned only with

Source: Copyright by Thomas Hornsby Ferril, Denver, Colorado.

hurting the oval by kicking it, then endeavoring to rescue and protect the egg.

However, the procedure is highly stylized. On each side there are eleven young men wearing colorful and protective costumes. The group in so-called "possession" of the oval first arrange themselves in an egg-shaped "huddle," as it is called, for a moment of prayerful meditation and whispering of secret numbers to each other.

Then they rearrange themselves with relation to the position of the egg. In a typical "formation" there are seven priests "on the line," seven being a mystical number associated not, as Jung purists might contend, with the "seven last words" but actually, with sublimation of the "seven deadly sins" into the "seven cardinal principles of education."

The central priest crouches over the egg, protecting it with his hands while over his back quarters hovers the "quarterback." . . . Behind him are three priests representing the male triad.

At a given signal, the egg is passed by sleight-of-hand to one of the members of the triad who endeavor to move it by bodily force across the white lines of winter. This procedure, up and down the enclosure, continues through the four quarters of the ritual.

At the end of the second quarter, implying the summer solstice, the processions of musicians and semi-nude virgins are resumed. After forming themselves into pictograms, represent alphabetical and animal fetishes, the virgins perform a most curious rite requiring far more dexterity than the earlier phallic Maypole rituals from which it seems to be derived. Each of the virgins carries a wand of shiny metal which she spins on her fingertips, tosses playfully into the air and with which she interweaves her body in most intricate gyrations.

The virgins perform another important function throughout the entire service. This concerns the mystical rite of "conversion" following success of one of the young priests in carrying the oval across the last white line of winter. As the moment of "conversion" approaches, the virgins kneel at the edge of the grass, bury their faces in the earth, then raise their arms to heaven in supplication, praying that "the uprights will be split." "Conversion" is indeed a dedicated ceremony . . .

---

drawn, no player is allowed into the opponent's land. These assumptions are in sharp contrast to European football, known in the United States as soccer, in which the conquest of territory means nothing, and the enemy is all around.

Finally, there is a time limit after which the judgment is meted out, win or lose, succeed or fail. There may be a rematch at a later date, but that is another game, and scoring begins anew. There are no handicaps or rewards for the previous winner.

Despite recent challenges at the lower levels, football remains a game in which men are seen as fighting the wars and women are encouraging them from the sidelines. The heroes are those who combine physical strength and agility with mental prowess. Cooperation within the team and a killer instinct towards the opposition are rewarded.

But to understand the role of football, one must also look at the broader social context of the game: at the rivalries between neighboring towns, schools, and cities; at the recruitment and training of players; at the symbols and totemic animals associated with the teams; at the bands and cheerleaders; at the significance of the football team in a school or city; at the pre- and post-game rituals; and at the tournaments and bowl games. In this context, the game is a mirror of the American society and culture.

Similar analyses can, of course, be made for other American sports, such as baseball, basketball, ice hockey, car racing, and the like.

Summary

A great deal of human activity is given to the pursuit of pleasure, whether of the aesthetic sense or for entertainment and excitement. This expressive culture contributes a great deal to the meaning and satisfaction of life. But art and entertainment do more. They express the values and ideas of a culture and may come to symbolize the society itself. The processes by which they are created and used often reinforce the social order.

Most types of expressive culture combine a concern for form and meaning. Attention may focus more on one or the other, but rarely is either missing. In this sense, the arts and entertainment are means not only for expressing human feelings and ideas, but also for communicating these to other members of the society.

Suggested readings

Boas, F.
   1955 Primitive Art. New York: Dover. (The early classic on the anthropology of art.)

Lomax, Alan.
    1968   Folk Song Style and Culture. Washington, D.C.: American Association
           for the Advancement of Science, Publication 88. (An excellent com-
           parative approach to ethnomusicology.)

Otten, C.M.
    1971   Anthropology and Art: Readings in Cross-Cultural Aesthetics. Garden
           City, N.Y.: Natural History Press. (A reader on both theory and ethnog-
           raphy of the arts.)

Wolfe, A.W.
    1969   Social Structural Bases of Art. Current Anthropology, 10:3–44. (A crit-
           ical survey of art and its relationship to social organization.)

21

Parameters of change
Anthropological models of change

Sociocultural change

So far in this text, we have tended to look at cultures and societies as stable, integrated systems of thought and behavior. We have, to some extent, overlooked the obvious fact that all life is constantly changing. The problem is how to account for change in sociocultural models. Where does it originate? How does it occur? And how is the order and integration we observe in cultures and societies maintained in the face of constant change? These have been key questions in anthropological thought since its beginning, and the answers given reflect the different basic approaches anthropologists have taken with their data.

Parameters of change

There are a number of important variables or parameters that must be considered when we look at studies of culture change. A great deal of confusion and disagreement have been generated in the past, because social scientists have not always made clear their assumptions on these parameters. What are some of these assumptions?

Levels of analysis

Changes in cultures and societies can be analyzed on a number of different levels of generalization. At the level of the individual, we can trace changes in the lives of people as they move from one job, social class, or culture to another.

On another level, we can look at change within social groups or within societies as wholes. Jane Richardson and A.L. Kroeber, for example, made a study of changes in women's hemlines in America over a period of 300 years (Richardson and Kroeber 1940). They found that hemlines changed almost yearly, going up some years and down others. But over the three centuries, the rise and fall of hemlines followed a cyclic pattern. They moved from maximum exposure to maximum coverage and back in roughly 110 years.

Finally, we can trace the history of all of human culture at the highest level of abstraction from early societies based on hunting and gathering subsistence technologies to modern societies, many based on agriculture and industry.

Each level of generalization overlooks variations that are significant at lower levels of analysis. But each also helps us to see broader patterns that we overlook when we concentrate on the details. A scholar need not confine his study to a single level of abstraction. On the contrary, studies that deal with several levels are particularly powerful. There is a danger, however, that the analyst may take the insights and conclusions drawn from one level and transfer them to other levels, without first proving that they apply to these levels, as well.

Time

Change is a process in time, and the extent to which change takes place is often a function of the time involved. If, for instance, Richardson and Kroeber had chosen to study hemlines over a period of only ten or twenty years, they would not have discovered the larger cycles within which the yearly variations occurred. On the other hand, if they had traced the history of Western dress back to its pre-Greek origins, they would have found more fundamental changes taking place, such as the shift from draped to tailored clothing.

There are at least two ways of reckoning time. The first—and the one we have used above—is "historical time." This is calculated by placing events in a historical framework and measuring the duration of time between them. For example, we can measure the changes that took place in the United States between 1700 A.D. and the present.

A second way is to look at what Gluckman calls "structural time" (1968:220). This is the time it normally takes to complete a given social cycle. For instance, we have already seen that the "typical" individual or family goes through certain stages in the structure of a given society. For any given individual or family, this life cycle obviously takes place in historical time. But when we speak about the cycle in general, we can do so apart from history; we can use the beginning and the end of the cycle as the reference points, as well as the intermediate points of transition.

Emic and etic perspectives

From whose point of view is change to be described—from that of the analyst or that of the people he is studying? Earlier, we used the terms emic and etic to distinguish between the two.

Unless we are told otherwise, it is taken for granted that descriptions of change are given from the analyst's point of view, from an etic perspective. More recently, however, there has been a growing interest in studying change from the viewpoint of the people themselves, from the emic perspective.

Magnitude of change

How great must difference be to be considered a real change in a cultural pattern, and not simply a variation within it? Is, for example, a shift from horizontal to vertical markings on pottery designs significant, or from unglazed to glazed pots, or, for that matter, the stylistic changes in modern cars from year to year? The answer, of course, depends on the level of analysis. What appears to be a minor change at one level may be major at another. To an anthropologist looking at transportation systems in the American culture, the annual shifts of chrome in automobile design may be insignificant; but to a young motor car buff, they are watched with great excitement. Each analyst must decide which changes he will try to explain and which he can overlook.

Boundaries of analysis

Many studies of change deal with a society or with a segment of society. The assumption is that these can be treated as systems or wholes and that changes can then be explained in terms of internal and external factors. In any study of change it is necessary, therefore, to define the boundaries of the units of analysis clearly and consistently. For example, one can study the changes that have taken place in American colleges over the past ten years, but then one must define precisely who is and who is not part of a college community.

How an analyst draws the boundaries and how he views the relationships between units of his analysis and their environment play important roles in molding his theories. There has been a great deal of unnecessary confusion simply because those discussing change have not always specified the units of their analysis.

Anthropological models of change

In its brief history, anthropology has developed several important models of sociocultural change. Obviously, this has not taken place in an intellectual vacuum. Anthropologists have interacted a great deal with other social scientists, and, in part, the questions they ask and the models they build are deeply influenced by the intellectual climate of their day.

A brief sketch of some of the major theories of change can help us to see the variety of approaches taken to this question.

Sociocultural evolution

The idea of cultural evolution is by no means new. By the late eighteenth century, William Robertson had noted sociocultural similarities in widely separated parts of the world and had arranged them into three general stages, on the basis of their technological complexity. The terms he used for these stages—savagery, barbarism, and civilization—were also later used by Lewis H. Morgan. Robertson explained these similarities by likeness in environment and subsistence patterns.

Almost a century later, Marx and Engels postulated an evolution of societies through a series of stages. In the earliest societies, they said, property was held by the tribe as a whole. Only after a series of steps did it come into the hands of individuals, in the form of capitalism, which they thought would be replaced by socialism, and, finally, by Communism, which would be a kind of social utopia. Marx and Engels did not see this path as unilineal, in the sense that one stage led inevitably to another. They saw the possibility of regression, in which a society moved from one stage back to an earlier one.

According to Marx and Engels, the ultimate factors causing this development to take place were material factors—specifically, the control of economic production. In this, they rejected the view held by many earlier scientists that ideas are the prime movers in history.

Lewis H. Morgan, an American Presbyterian lawyer, and Edward Tylor, a British educator, two leading early anthropologists, proposed broad schemes of cultural evolution. Their goal was to reconstruct the total history of mankind in the most general terms in order to better understand present human conditions.

Morgan and Tylor divided human history into a series of progressive stages. We noted in Chapter 4 that Morgan traced the evolution of material culture, such as subsistence techniques and technology (1877). He was also interested in changes that took place in the social organization of families, kinship systems, and societies. Tylor was more interested in the development of religious ideas and rituals (1874). Both gathered a great deal of data, of varying accuracy, from traders, missionaries, and ethnographers around the world in order to build their theories.

Morgan and Tylor were interested not only in describing change but also in explaining it. One of the crucial questions they faced was how to explain the development along similar paths of widely separated cultures. An alternative to evolutionary schemes at their time was the contention that discoveries and inventions are rare occurrences and that diffusion is by far the most common means of people acquiring new cultural patterns.

While Morgan and Tylor recognized the importance of the diffusion of ideas, they held that the evolution of human culture around the world is a result of a series of similar independent inventions in different societies. In other words, given a certain stage in development, a society was bound to progress to the next stage. This can be explained in part, they said, by the fact that the human mind operates in much the same way in any society.

The prime movers of history, according to Morgan, were subsistence patterns. As these become progressively more sophisticated, people moved from the stages of savagery to barbarism and, finally, to civilization.

A number of criticisms were leveled against these grand theories of sociocultural evolution, but one must make allowances for the broad sweep of their coverage and the high level of generalization involved. Many details must be put aside and numerous exceptions made when broad theories are constructed.

Historical diffusionism

The end of the nineteenth century saw the rise of a group of anthropologists who rejected the broad theories of cultural evolution as undocumented speculation. The leading figure was Franz Boas, a German physicist turned anthropologist, who brought with him the strong empirical bent of the natural sciences. He stressed the need to gather facts, and more facts, before formulating a generalization, and he felt that the data then available were not adequate to formulate social laws.

Boas also criticized the evolutionists for the way in which they used the comparative method. They tended to take traits out of their cultural contexts and to use them as isolated blocks in the building of theories.

Like the evolutionists, Boas was interested in cultural history, but unlike them, he chose to work on the history of specific nonliterate peoples over relatively short periods of time. He felt that sufficient data could be gathered from intensive ethnographies, recollections of old informants, and detailed comparisons of several cultures located in a limited geographic area to trace empirically the birth and spread of various culture traits. He stressed the interrelationships of traits within a single culture and the influence the local environment had on the development of a culture.

On the question of the independent invention of cultural patterns versus their diffusion, Boas assigned a priority to neither in the absence of proof. He showed that change could be empirically documented over small geographic areas for limited periods of time. But because such studies were likely to involve the diffusion of culture rather than independent inventions, the former played a prominent part in his writings.

In the absence of written records in the tribes they studied, Boas and his students developed several tests of diffusion. 1) They assumed that the closer two cultures were geographically and the greater the flow of information between them, the greater the likelihood that cultural similarities could be explained by diffusion. 2) They assumed that the closer two cultures were in time, the greater the likelihood that similar ideas were spread by diffusion. 3) They assumed that the greater the complexity of traits shared by two cultures, the less the chance that these were the product of independent inventions. 4) Finally, they assumed that the probability of diffusion was high if traits in two societies were similar, not only in form but also in meaning and function.

Applying these tests to the study of cultural history in specific regions, Boas' disciples developed the concept of "culture area." This refers to a group of tribes within a single geographic area that share a great many culture traits, which stands in contrast to other such groups nearby. For example, one can speak of the culture area of the American Indians on the Great Plains in the 1800s or of the culture area of west Africa. In both, there are a number of tribes, yet culturally speaking, they have a great deal in common with the other tribes in the area.

In a sense, the concept of culture area is analogous to that of language area. People who speak a given language may have variations in dialects, but they have more in common linguistically than they have with others who may be nearer to them in space but speak a different language.

Culture areas are based on diffusion. It was assumed that traits spread out uniformly from a point of origin in patterns of concentric circles, and that as they spread they would tend to be less complex, because some of the details would be lost in transmission. Traits and culture complexes having the widest distribution were thought to be the oldest. The center in an area from which most traits spread was referred to as the "culture climax."

For Boas and his followers, there was no single cause that determined the course of history. They rejected the economic determinism of Marx and Engels, as well as the psychic unity of the unilineal evolutionists. They sought historical explanations for each case on the basis of empirical evidence. But in their study of particular culture histories, they have been charged with ignoring the search for general social laws, which could help us to understand mankind as a whole.

Acculturation

By the early 1930s, a number of anthropologists, such as Malinowski, Mead, and Thurnwald, were interested in what became known as "acculturation studies." Americans had a growing suspicion that the historical diffusion studies did not tell the whole story. Moreover, they were faced with the question of how to treat the American Indians, who had been driven into reservations. The British, who ruled much of the world through their colonial empire, directly faced the problems arising out of interaction between different cultures.

The focus of the new approach was on acculturation—the changes in cultures that arise from contact with other alien cultures. Because these changes are often enforced by one society on another, acculturation was seen as a distinct process, different from the processes of invention and diffusion.

One Hundred Per Cent American
Ralph Linton

There can be no question about the average American's Americanism or his desire to preserve this precious heritage at all costs. Nevertheless, some insidious foreign ideas have already wormed their way into his civilization without his realizing what was going on. Thus dawn finds the unsuspecting patriot garbed in pajamas, a garment of East Indian origin; and lying in a bed built on a pattern which originated in either Persia or Asia Minor. He is muffled to the ears in un-American materials: cotton, first domesticated in India; linen, domesticated in the Near East; wool from an animal native to Asia Minor; or silk whose uses were first discovered by the Chinese. All these substances have been transformed into cloth by methods invented in Southwestern Asia. If the weather is cold enough he may even be sleeping under an eiderdown quilt invented in Scandinavia.

On awakening he glances at the clock, a medieval European invention, uses one potent Latin word in abbreviated form, rises in haste, and goes to the bathroom. Here, if he stops to think about it, he must feel himself in the presence of a great American institution; he will have heard stories of both the quality and frequency of foreign plumbing and will know that in no other country does the average man perform his ablutions in the midst of such splendor. But the insidious foreign influence pursues him even here. Glass was invented by the ancient Egyptians, the use of glazed tiles for floors and walls in the Near East, porcelain in China, and the art of enameling on metal by Mediterranean artisans of the Bronze Age. Even his bathtub and toilet are but slightly modified copies of Roman originals. The only purely American contribution to the ensemble is the steam radiator, against which our patriot very briefly and unintentionally places his posterior.

In this bathroom the American washes with soap invented by the ancient Gauls. Next he cleans his teeth, a subversive European practice which did not invade America until the latter part of the eighteenth century. He then shaves, a masochistic rite first developed by the heathen priests of ancient Egypt and Sumer. The process is made less of a penance by the fact that his razor is of steel, an iron-carbon alloy discovered in either India or Turkestan. Lastly, he dries himself on a Turkish towel.

Returning to the bedroom, the unconscious victim of un-American practices removes his clothes from a chair, invented in the Near East, and proceeds to dress. He puts on close-fitting tailored garments whose form derives

From *The American Mercury*, vol. 40 (1937):427–429. By permission of the publisher, P.O. Box 1306, Torrance, Calif. 90505.

from the skin clothing of the ancient nomads of the Asiatic steppes and fastens them with buttons whose prototypes appeared in Europe at the close of the Stone Age. This costume is appropriate enough for outdoor exercise in a cold climate, but is quite unsuited to American summers, steam-heated houses, and Pullmans. Nevertheless, foreign ideas and habits hold the unfortunate man in thrall even when common sense tells him that the authentically American costume of gee string and moccasins would be far more comfortable. He puts on his feet stiff coverings made from hide prepared by a process invented in ancient Egypt and cut to a pattern which can be traced back to ancient Greece, and makes sure that they are properly polished, also a Greek idea. Lastly, he ties about his neck a strip of bright-colored cloth which is a vestigial survival of the shoulder shawls worn by seventeenth-century Croats. He gives himself a final appraisal in the mirror, an old Mediterranean invention, and goes downstairs to breakfast.

Here a whole new series of foreign things confronts him. His food and drink are placed before him in pottery vessels, the popular name of which—china—is sufficient evidence of their origin. His fork is a medieval Italian invention and his spoon a copy of a Roman original. He will usually begin the meal with coffee, an Abyssinian plant first discovered by the Arabs. The American is quite likely to need it to dispel the morning-after effects of over-indulgence in fermented drinks, invented in the Near East; or distilled ones, invented by the alchemists of medieval Europe. Whereas the Arabs took their coffee straight, he will probably sweeten it with sugar, discovered in India; and dilute it with cream, both the domestication of cattle and the technique of milking having originated in Asia Minor.

If our patriot is old-fashioned enough to adhere to the so-called American breakfast, his coffee will be accompanied by an orange, domesticated in the Mediterranean region, a cantaloupe domesticated in Persia, or grapes domesticated in Asia Minor. He will follow this with a bowl of cereal made from grain domesticated in the Near East and prepared by methods also invented there. From this he will go on to waffles, a Scandinavian invention, with plenty of butter, originally a Near-Eastern cosmetic. As a side dish he may have the egg of a bird domesticated in Southeastern Asia or strips of the flesh of an animal domesticated in the same region, which have been salted and smoked by a process invented in Northern Europe.

Breakfast over, he places upon his head a molded piece of felt, invented by the nomads of Eastern Asia, and, if it looks like rain, puts on outer shoes of rubber, discovered by the ancient Mexicans, and takes an umbrella, invented in India. He then sprints for his train—the train, not the sprinting, being an English invention. At the station he pauses for a moment to buy a newspaper, paying for it with coins invented in ancient Lydia. Once on board he settles back to inhale the fumes of a cigarette invented in Mexico, or a cigar invented in Brazil. Meanwhile, he reads the news of the day, imprinted in characters invented by the ancient Semites by a process invented in Germany upon a material invented in China. As he scans the latest editorial pointing out the dire results to our institutions of accepting foreign ideas, he will not fail to thank a Hebrew God in an Indo-European language that he is a one hundred per cent (decimal system invented by the Greeks) American (from Americus Vespucci, Italian geographer).

Those concerned with acculturation were interested in how one culture in contact with another could assimilate ideas from the other, on the one hand, and yet persist as an independent culture, with an identity of its own, on the other. The answer was given in terms of "boundary-maintaining mechanisms," "flexibility of internal structures," and "self-correcting mechanisms."

Boundary-maintaining mechanisms have to do with the receptivity of a culture to new ideas. Some cultures, such as the American, were thought to be "open," because they accepted new ideas and aliens readily. Others, such as the Hopi Indians in the southwest United States, were used as examples of "closed" cultures, because they resisted incursions from without.

Flexibility of internal structures refers to the degree to which alternatives are allowed within the patterns of a culture and how closely the traits are linked to one another. Autocratic systems are generally considered less flexible and less likely to change. Cultures that allow more alternatives in behavior accept and adjust to change more readily.

And, finally, in every society there are self-correcting mechanisms, which help to balance the forces of conflict and crime with forces of cohesion and togetherness. In the face of intense cross-cultural contact, the forces tending to disintegration increase; unless they are countered by mechanisms for integrating the society, it is in danger of collapse.

The conflicts that arise in the clashes of cultures we see all around us in the modern world and the forces for the reintegration of the traditional and the intruding cultures into some type of new cultural synthesis can be seen in a series of letters that appeared under the title "Tell me, Josephine," the African equivalent of "Dear Abbie." In two of these, quoted by William Mangin, young rural migrants face the dilemmas posed by Westernized city life, and Josephine tries to bridge the gap, but on the side of adapting the traditional to the modern world.*

* The following selection is from pp. 72–73, 92–93 of *Tell Me, Josephine,* edited by Barbara Hall. Reprinted by permission of Simon & Schuster. Copyright © 1964 by Barbara Hall.

Television brings a new dimension to education in Niamey, Niger. Photo courtesy of UNESCO/Studio Raccah.

Q. During the course of my marriage I find my wife belongs to a tribe which is maternal. When we divorce or one of us dies, our children will belong to her brothers. I rushed into marriage without learning of this custom.

I am afraid that if we divorce, I shall go to my village quite old and helpless while my wife's brothers will get every help possible from my children. So where should I get children to support me? My tribe does not do this.

I find some difficulty in divorcing her now, before the children come, because I love her very much and she does the same to me. But what about this awful custom? When I mention my fears she tries to bluff me by saying her brothers will let me get my children, but I don't believe it. What have you to say before I sadly act?

A. That it would be foolish to break up a happy marriage for fear of an old custom that may no longer be practiced when you are old. Do not think of divorce, many people live happily together all their lives. Also, you may die before your wife. If you are good to your children they will not desert you in your old age. Twenty years from now, these customs may have died out completely.

Q. My uncle who is a charcoal-burner was taken to Native Court and told to pay 15 pounds for damaging two virgins.

He has written to me that according to our custom I must get money for him, and send it quickly to the Northern Province or he will go to prison. This will take all my saving which I had planned to use for marriage in two years. So must I send him the money?

A. If you wish to keep tribal custom, then you are obligated to help your uncle.

If you do not care about tribal custom any more and do not intend to visit your family in the rural areas again, then no-one can make you pay. Only you can decide.

I presume that according to the same custom you will inherit your uncle's property when he dies.

Students of acculturation were interested not only in the ways cultures maintain their integration in the face of external contacts, but also in the processes by which they accept new ideas. Obviously, the first step is the diffusion of ideas from the outside. These ideas are then evaluated and selected or rejected by the recipients. The final step in the process is the integration of those ideas that are accepted into the recipient's culture.

It was found that the integration of new ideas takes place in a number of ways. In some cases, ideas are added or incorporated into the preexisting cultural system. In some, they are substituted for traditional cultural traits; for example, snowmobiles have completely replaced dog teams in many Eskimo villages. In some cases, there is syncretism, a combining of old and new ideas into patterns that are different from either. This is the case with Voodoo, which is a mixture of Catholicism and the traditional religious ideas of the West Indies, and west Africa. And, finally, in some cases, the people accept a new set of ideas but keep the new and the traditional customs separate by compartmentalizing their lives. No matter how ideas are accepted, however, they cause changes and readjustments in other areas of the culture.

Many interested in acculturation studies were concerned with contemporary world problems arising from massive confrontations between cultures due to world wars and colonialism. They felt that anthropologists should leave their ivory towers and seek to apply their understandings of culture change to alleviate these problems in

Seattle, Washington scene, circa 1890.
Photo courtesy of Photography Collection, Suzzallo Library, University of Washington, Seattle.

humanitarian ways. Not all anthropologists, however, agree with this view, and the question of using applied anthropology in programs of planned cultural change is still a matter of considerable debate.

Neo-evolutionism

In the 1940s and 1950s, there was little interest in theories of cultural evolution. However, a few anthropologists, led by Leslie White, continued to build broad models covering the total evolution of human culture. White, himself, sought to explain the development ultimately in terms of energy (1943). He saw cultures as essentially means for harnessing and using energy. As cultures develop techniques that enable them to utilize energy, they develop more complex social structures and ideological systems.

Marshall Sahlins and Julian Steward, on the other hand, turned to what has been called "specific evolution," the study of development in one or more specific cultures over a relatively short period of time. By limiting the scope of their analysis, they were able to include such factors as local environment, diffusion, and invention in their discussions. These factors had largely been ignored in the broader generalized theories of evolution.

Specific evolutionists generally see culture as an adaptive process, by which people adjust to their environments, including both their natural environment (which leads to the study of cultural ecology) and their sociocultural environment, which includes the surrounding societies offering an immediate or potential threat to the society. Little attention is given to ideology, however, or to the behavior of individuals as causative factors in the evolutionary process.

One example of the studies on specific evolution is Clifford Geertz's study (1963) of Indonesia. In the past, the Indonesians practiced two types of cultivation: slash-and-burn, and wet-rice paddy farming. The former had low productivity, with little potential for improvement. The productivity of the latter was high and could be improved markedly by greater human effort and care.

When the Dutch came to Indonesia, they turned part of the paddy land into sugar plantations. The result was an increase in population on the remaining rice lands. The people responded by increasing the rice production by more and more intensive planting, weeding, and harvesting. This continued until the farming practices developed into a highly ritualized cultivation of the land. A similar elaboration and ritualization of forms took place in the areas of kinship, politics, and religion. By contrast, areas under slash-and-burn agriculture were not subjected to the same increases in population pressure. The result was an evolution of the society into small-scale private farms that lacked the highly ritualized procedures of the wet-land cultivation.

Both general and specific evolution approaches seek to reconstruct the historical development of societies and cultures. But, as we see in this study by Geertz, specific evolution is more concerned with the study of the particular processes by which this development takes place.

Entrepreneurs and decision-making

Thus far we have looked at models that focus on changes within societies as wholes or on the total development of human culture. More recently, there has been a group of anthropologists interested in cultural change viewed from the perspective of the individual.

Homer Barnett became interested in how the innovation of new ideas occurs and how they are accepted by the people (1953). Innovation consists essentially of recombining previous ideas into new ones. An illustration of this is given by Robert Bee (1974:174–175). Imagine a young boy trying to build a toy car. He has a problem with the head-lights. The boy knows they are round, shiny things, fixed on the front of the car; this is one configuration of ideas. He remembers that tin cans are also round and shiny; this is another configuration. By analyzing the two and identifying similarities in configurations—both are round and both are shiny—he is able to substitute two empty cans for head-lights on the toy car. He does so even though their original functions were quite different.

"Analysis," "identification," and "substitution" are the three basic stages in innovation. People are constantly making such substitutions, although they are often unaware that they are doing so.

In many ways, acceptance of innovation follows the same processes. The potential acceptor first analyzes the new idea in terms of his own configurations. He identifies or matches components between the new and the old. And, finally, he decides whether or not to substitute the new for the old. The borrower never accepts an idea exactly as it is of-fered by the innovator or bringer of change. The fact is he restructures it—borrowing parts of the new idea and rejecting others, reshaping it, and possibly even changing its function. The chief difference between innovation and acceptance is that the new idea is created by the inno-vator in the former, while in the latter, the borrower modifies and rein-terprets an idea he has received from without.

It should be clear by now that Barnett is speaking of culture largely in terms of ideas that give rise to behavior rather than to behavioral pat-terns themselves. The difficulty is that it is impossible for an observer to get into the minds of other people to see what is going on. He appre-hends other peoples' ideas only indirectly.

As we have already seen, A.F.C. Wallace also used a psychological approach to culture when he introduced the concept of mazeways, the individual's unique conceptual map of the world around him. Fredrik Barth carried the idea further by investigating the rational decision-

Santa joins a Yule-tide play in India.

425

making processes of a group of people in social interaction. He showed the ways in which the decisions of one individual modify and are modified by the decisions of others in social situations (1963).

The models of Barnett, Wallace, Barth, and a number of other recent writers assume that culture is made up of individuals who make decisions, more or less rationally, from the perspectives of their own mazeways, within the alternatives open to them. Clearly, their mazeways must have much in common with the mazeways of other members of their societies if there is to be any communication and social order. It is this set of shared ideas, then, that constitutes the core of a culture.

These psychologically oriented models also assume that human beings everywhere choose a course of action that will benefit themselves the most—in other words, they try to maximize their gains. But not all people use the same set of values to judge which activities bring them the most gain. Some chose material comforts, others status or power or meaningful lives.

Finally, it is assumed that there are certain constraints that limit the alternatives open to people. These may be environment, social order, ideology, or any other limiting factor.

An example of alternatives and decision-making is given by Colin Turnbull (1968:32–33) in his description of a modern urban African. Living in two cultures and facing the tensions between them, a man chose to compartmentalize his life into two sections, living, on the one hand, in the world of modern city politics, and, on the other, in his traditional African culture. By keeping them distinct, even down to the names he used in each, he could avoid the clashes that would arise when these areas of his life confronted each other.*

> In Accra I stayed in the town household of a Kwahu family, their home residence being between Accra and Kumasi, in the depths of the countryside. In his country home the family head was a chief—*Kwame*, or "He who was born on Saturday." In his Accra house the chief became Harold, a prosperous merchant and politician. His town house was large and rambling, on two floors. He occupied the upper floor with his wife by Christian marriage and their small children. It was a magnificent apartment, with every possible luxury—including a well stocked cocktail cabinet, for the one tradition that dies the hardest is the tradition of hospitality. In this apartment lived a happy, settled, thoroughly westernized family. But downstairs lived his other family, the family of Kwame as opposed to that of Harold—all his nephews and other

appendages of his extended Kwahu family which, as Kwame, he felt obliged to support, even in Accra.

It was like going from one world to another, and I lived a completely double life with ease and pleasure in that household. Upstairs we drank whisky, danced the cha-cha and the mambo, ate bacon and eggs for breakfast and drank tea at tea time. From upstairs we sallied forth for evenings at the various smart night clubs (evening dress compulsory), or to elegant private dinner parties. But downstairs I ate *fufu* with my fingers, drank palm wine, danced *Abalabi* and learned what real family life is like.

And downstairs I learned what the African man in the modern civilized street feels like. As Harold, Kwame had made a pretty effective adjustment, and was able to live happily in Accra; as Kwame, he could live in Kwahu, without the one identity interfering with the other. But both Harold and Kwame, as separate personalities, had money in their own right: the one from business, the other from family inheritance. Downstairs the relatives did not have money and were not able to commute, so to speak, from one way of life to the other.

One of the interesting questions that arises from decision-making models of change is why some individuals tend to be more innovative, tend to take greater risks in order to explore new possibilities of gain. These people, commonly referred to as entrepreneurs, are responsible for a great many of the changes that occur in any culture. They are the first ones to try out new techniques and practices. In recent years, a great deal of attention has been given to the study of entrepreneurs and their influence on societies.

Decision-making models are a long way from the grand evolutionary schemes of Morgan and Tylor. One focuses on individuals, the other on culture at the most abstract level. One deals with short periods of time, the other with the total scope of human history. But both are similar in that they view culture as a system of human adaptation to constraints imposed by the local environment and other societies.

Summary

Change is a constant. It is also the most difficult dimension to include in models of culture and society. If we wish to avoid a great deal of confusion in discussion of change, we must specify the parameters of it. These include level of abstraction, mode of time reckoning, units of observation, and locus of observation.

Several important sociocultural models of change have been advanced in the past century. Some of the early anthropologists, trying to make sense of the total development of human culture, advanced a theory of sociocultural evolution. They sought not only to trace the sequence of stages through which all cultures have moved, but also to provide an explanation for this development in terms of subsistence patterns and technology. They found in independent invention the process to account for change.

Reacting, in part, to the speculations of these grand theoretists, the historicists tried to document change in single societies or small groups of societies over short periods of time. They stressed the importance of the diffusion of ideas.

By the 1930s there was a growing interest in situations of culture contact, a phenomena that was developing on a massive scale. A number of anthropologists turned to the study of culture contact and acculturation in order to counter the harmful effects of such contacts.

In recent years, some anthropologists have turned to the study of changes in the lives of individuals in an attempt to discover how new ideas are born and spread. They are concerned with the strategies people use in choosing between the alternatives open to them. The goal of these models is not so much to explicate the changes that take place in specific individuals as such but the universal psychosocial processes that underlie all human change.

It is now obvious that any model of society and culture must take into account not only social and cultural structures at a given point in time, but also the processes that underly change in them over time. Only with dynamic models will we understand what culture and society are all about and be able to modify them to fit our goals.

Suggested readings

Bailey, F.G.
   1969   Stratagems and Spoils: A Social Anthropology of Politics. New York: Schocken Books. (A thought-provoking book, dealing with culture from the perspective of individuals and their strategies.)
Barth, F.
   1967   On the Study of Social Change. American Anthropologist, 69:661–669. (A good introduction to the questions involved in studying cultural change.)
Bee, R.L.
   1974   Patterns and Processes: An Introduction to Anthropological Strategies for the Study of Sociocultural Change. New York: Free Press. (A useful survey of various theoretical models anthropologists have used to study change.)

Pelto, P.J.
  1973   The Snowmobile Revolution: Technology and Social Change in the
         Arctic. Menlo Park, Calif.: Cumming Publishing Company. (An inter-
         esting case study of change taking place in Eskimo culture.)
Sahlins, M.D. and E.R. Service, eds.
  1960   Evolution and Culture. Ann Arbor: University of Michigan Press. (An
         elaboration of neo-evolutionary approaches to culture change.)

The press and pull of culture
Individual strategies
Anthropology and the person

Culture and
the person

Our culture and society mold the world in which we live, but how does the individual fit into the picture? Are we the unquestioning products of our biological and cultural environments, or do we share in some way in their creation?

As we saw in the first chapters, concepts such as "culture," "society," "groups," and "norms," are products of the human mind. Combined into larger thought systems, they become the models analysts use to study a people or the model people have of themselves and their world. But whenever we reduce our experiences to categories or look for patterns in behavior in order to form generalizations, we must overlook the unique characteristics of these experiences and individuals.

The relationship between culture and the individual person must be viewed from two perspectives. On the one hand, we must look at the ways culture molds the person—as Mary Goodman so aptly puts it (1967), at the press and pull of culture. (See Figure 22.1.) On the other hand, we need to see the world from the vantage point of the individual and consider the strategies a person uses to chart a course of action in his or her unique life situations.

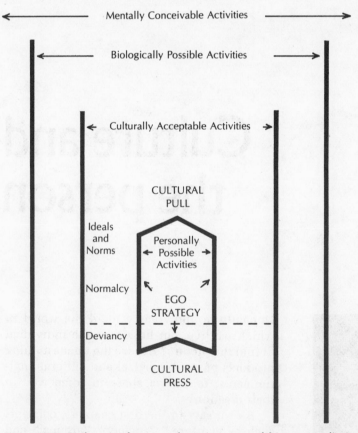

Figure 22.1 Biology, culture, and one's personal history set limits on life strategies one may choose.

The press and pull of culture

People feel the pressures of culture in two ways: as a press, which proscribes certain kinds of behavior, and as a pull, which prescribes and enculturates other thoughts and actions.

Limits set by culture

It is obvious that the physical environment sets limits on the activities of an individual. The body is bound by time and space, by size and strength, and by foods and diseases. There are a great many things one can imagine but cannot do because of the physical limitations of the body.

Physical environments also impose certain limitations on the cultural forms people create. To some extent, people can alter these limits by constructing dams, terracing hillsides, making bows and arrows, and building automobiles, planes, and computers. But man can only go so far in surmounting his natural environment and exploiting its resources. Certain physical boundaries are, of course, unyielding.

Other limits are basically biological. There are many things that are possible within the physical environment but biologically impossible or destructive. For instance, it is possible to chill or heat the body or to accelerate or decelerate it rapidly, but at some point during such a process, life ceases. Biology also determines important needs a person must satisfy, as well as basic processes by which he lives and learns. All people and cultures must take these biological boundaries, needs, and processes into account.

Within the limits of all behavior physically and biologically possible, culture sets even narrower boundaries. It is possible, for example, to walk down the street backwards or nude, but few people in an American town do so. While attempts to ignore physical and biological limits may lead to mutilation and death, continued violation of cultural norms, as we have seen, often leads to ostracism or destruction by society.

Finally, the individual's own unique history sets limits on his development. Being born in a certain social class and home and experiencing a great many unique events determine in significant ways the course of the individual's life. For some, such as the wealthy and powerful, the range of opportunities may be great, but, as we have seen, for the many poor, the restrictions of their personal lives may be great, indeed.

An Indian child resolutely guards her little treasures.

The pull of culture

While the press of culture may be more obvious, the pull is every bit as significant in the formation of the individual personality, even though the ways in which it is exerted are often less apparent.

ENCULTURATION All people are born helpless—without language, culture, or the ability to survive alone in the external, impersonal world. Yet within a surprisingly short time, the same person can be molded into an American, Dutchman, Chinese, or member of one of a thousand other societies. One of the important discoveries of the social sciences has been the crucial importance of childhood years in the formation of the human personality.

Every society has its own ways of "enculturating" its young, of teaching them its cultural ways. Ethnologists observing child rearing practices around the world have made us aware of their variety and the effect they have on producing different kinds of adults. Only recently, however, has it become clear just how important the early environmental and experiential influences are in the formation of the personality. Childhood is the period of most rapid development in such characteristics as height, general intelligence and attitudes of aggressiveness or dependence, as well as the time when foundations are laid for later development (see Bloom 1964). Moreover, it is easier to learn something new than to erase a set of learned behavior and imprint the person with another.

But how far can a culture bend and shape a person? To what extent is a child an untouched plastic form on which culture stamps its image, and to what extent is it a product of genetic codes and biologically based learning processes?

Studies on children One of the first anthropologists to be concerned with this problem was Margaret Mead, who asked the question, "Are the emotional conflicts and rebellion our adolescents face due to physiological changes that occur at puberty, or are they culturally induced?" To find an answer to this question, Mead lived for nine months in Samoa, studying fifty girls in three small villages. She found (1928) that the adolescent years were not particularly difficult for Samoan girls.

In a later study of three New Guinea tribes (1935), Mead studied the ways different cultures mold personality traits which we call masculine and feminine. She found that Mundugumor men and women were fierce and aggressive, but among their neighbors, the Arapesh, both men and women were mild and cooperative. In a third tribe, the Tchambuli, the women were powerful, aggressive, and sociable, while the men were concerned mainly with their hairdos, art, and women. She concluded that the standardized personality differences we expect to find between the sexes are largely the creations of cultures and transmitted from one generation to the next. In other words, the human being is more culturally malleable than was originally thought.

A great many studies have been made on enculturation since Mead's pioneer works. One of the best was a series of studies supervised by J.W.M. Whiting (1908–   ) in 1954–1955. Research teams were sent to conduct intensive studies of child rearing in six societies, and the results were compared. It was found that Gusii mothers of East Africa rarely cuddle or kiss their children and that the children grow up to be fearful and dependent. In later life, there is a strong hostility between the sexes, and men pride themselves in their domination over their wives. Quarreling, aggression, rape, and homicide are common in Gusii society. In contrast to this, small town New England families were found to be cooperative with members, sharing family meals and other activities. Men and women participated together in work and recreation, with little open rivalry between them.

The American family is child-centered. Francis L.K. Hsu (1963) commented that the Chinese glorify their ancestors, Hindus their gods, and Americans their children. Children are taught to be self-asserting and independent, even though, paradoxically, parents exercise considerable control over them, well into adolescent years. These personality characteristics are further reinforced in a complex society by the absence of traditional customs, the lack of extensive kinship ties, the tendency for parents to find meaning and fulfillment largely through their children and the high mobility within the society (see Goodman 1967, ch. 6).

In sharp contrast to both the Gusii and American families, Thai children learn early to fit into an orderly society, in which everyone has his place. Writing about enculturation in Thailand, Robbins Burling observed:

> Whether through indulgence or strict discipline—or, more likely, through a subtle combination of the two—Thai children do learn to be courteous and respectful at a remarkably early age. A child soon learns the differences in status among the people around him. His parents will press his palms together and hold them to his forehead to show respect for the monks, and he soon learns to raise them to his face for his parents. Just as men are ritually superior to women, so older people are superior to younger, and a child must learn the ceremonious respect due his elders. Later, he will also learn to grant the formal respect due to government officials and, above them, to royalty. Thai do not expect to associate with others as equals; everyone is seen as either superior or inferior. One cannot even speak the Thai language without indicating something about one's status, for pronouns vary with the rank of the speaker and that of the person to whom he speaks. To some extent, status is determined by birth, but because one's status at birth is attributed to the accumulation of merit in former existences, it has, in a sense, been earned. All men can look forward to the increase in status.*

Stages of life Erik Erikson (1902–) and Erich Fromm (1900–), two psychologists strongly influenced by anthropological theories and methods, have come to stress the fact that personality development continues throughout life. According to Erikson (1963), the mature person passes through eight stages. During the first year, an infant

* From page 101 of *Hill Farms and Padi Fields*, by Robbins Burling. Copyright 1965 by Prentice-Hall.

learns a sense of basic trust or mistrust of the world, particularly through his experiences with his mother. In the second year, he develops a sense of autonomy and control over himself and his environment, which allows him to stand on his own two feet. If he fails to develop this, he is left with a basic sense of inadequacy, shame, and doubt. Between the third and fifth years, the child picks up a sense of initiative and purpose, but failure to do so produces suspicion, jealousy, and a loss of imagination. The fourth stage takes the child up to about eleven years, when the child learns to work or develops a sense of inferiority.

Erikson concludes that adolescence is a time when a person must acquire a sense of identity, and adulthood a time to learn how to build intimate relationships. become productive in life, and finally develop a sense of self-integrity in the face of the prospect of death.

Based on a study of a Mexican peasant community and of western Europe in general, Fromm and Maccoby outline four major stages in the development of the personality (1970): learning to accept things from others, learning to actively take things, learning to conserve what one has, and learning to be creative and productive. They see these not as typical of each individual but as ideal types, which find varied development and expression in different peoples and different cultures.

IDEAL PERSONALITY TYPES AND NATIONAL CHARACTER Culture molds personalities in part by setting up cultural heroes, ideal characters, and role models. It tells the child not only what kind of a person he should be when he grows up, but also how he should behave as a man, a husband, a teacher, a banker, a clerk, a criminal, or a hippie.

If this is the case, one might expect people in the same culture to have similar personality characteristics. In other words, is it true that most Scotsmen are thrifty, most Germans precise, and most Frenchmen romantic?

In a classic study, Ruth Benedict (1887–1936) analyzed three cultures in an attempt to define their dominant personality types and to explain these in terms of the social organization. In her study (1934), Benedict described the Hopi Indians as invariably mild people, opposed to any show of violence or excess, keeping to the middle of the road and avoiding psychologically disruptive experiences. On the other hand, she found the Kwakiutl Indians of the northwest coast of North America to be given to excesses. According to Benedict, they were constantly trying to break through the barriers of the ordinary world, into another order of psychological experience, by means of dramatic, emotionally charged rituals. She concluded that, in fact, significantly different personality types do exist in the two cultures. Although the

The American child, like most children, learns to feed himself by trial and error.

validity of her specific conclusions has been challenged, the idea of a national character has persisted.

The second world war led to a series of studies aimed at discovering the typical personality types of the Japanese, Rumanians, Thai, and others. The purpose was to predict their responses to various military situations. Since field studies were impossible, the researchers had to depend on books, magazines, and films from these countries and on interviews with migrants to the United States (see Benedict 1946). Interest in the Japanese national character continued after the war, and field studies were made to determine the relationship between child rearing and national personality, but the results have been open to various interpretations. (For a review, see Barnouw 1973, ch. 10.)

One of the most active advocates of national character studies is Francis L.K. Hsu, an anthropologist who grew up in China, studied in London, and now teaches in the United States. Hsu suggested (1970) that national characters are formed in part by the type of relationship that is central in the family in that culture. He believes father-son relationships are most important in the Chinese kinship system and that this leads to a respect for tradition, the aged, and the ancestors. In contrast, the American family is dominated by the husband-wife relationship, which takes precedence over other family ties, hence the lack of strong traditions across generations and the stress on self-reliance among the children.

CULTURAL HEROES AND ECONOMIC DEVELOPMENT If people are influenced by their cultural ideals and heroes, how does this affect other cultural processes? In order to find out, David McClelland (1917–   ), a psychologist interested in economic development, collected children's stories in second, third, and fourth grade readers from 23 countries and compared the heroes in the stories with the rate of economic growth in each country. He found (1961) that development was most rapid in those countries where the heroes had a high motivation towards personal achievement. Since then, a number of studies have been made in different countries on the relationship between personality types and economic development (see LeVine 1966).

CULTURE AND PSYCHOLOGICAL DRIVES What impact does culture have on psychological phenomena, such as the Oedipus complex described by Freud? According to Freud, a child receives not only its nourishment but also its first pleasure and erotic sensations while suckling at its mother's breast. In time, a girl transfers her attachment to her father, but a boy wants his mother to himself. Because his father stands in his way, he has a subconscious desire to kill his father and marry his mother. Freud believed this pattern to be an inevitable aspect of the family and therefore to be found in all cultures.

In his study of the Trobriand Islanders, Malinowski found (1953) that society allowed sexual play in childhood and a general sexual license during adolescent years. In time, lovers set up more permanent family relationships. Since the society is matrilineal, a boy inherits property not from his father but from his mother's brother. Moreover, this man, rather than the father, disciplines the boy. The result, according to Malinowski, is that there is little friction between father and son, but a great deal of ambivalence on the part of a boy towards his mother's brother. He concludes that the Oedipus complex is more a product of resentment of authority than a sexual rivalry.

Since then, others have studied the Trobriand Islanders and claim

Shakespeare in the Bush
Laura Bohannan

Just before I left Oxford for the Tiv in West Africa, conversation turned to the season at Stratford. "You Americans," said a friend, "often have difficulty with Shakespeare. He was, after all, a very English poet, and one can easily misinterpret the universal by misunderstanding the particular."

I protested that human nature is pretty much the same the whole world over; at least the general plot and motivation of the greater tragedies would always be clear—everywhere—although some details of custom might have to be explained and difficulties of translation might produce other slight changes. . . .

I eventually settled on the hillock of a very knowledgeable old man, the head of a homestead of some hundred and forty people, all of whom were either his close relatives or their wives and children. . . . One day I crawled through the low doorway and found most of the men of the homestead sitting huddled in their ragged cloths on stools, low plank beds, and reclining chairs, warming themselves against the chill of the rain around a smoky fire. In the center were three pots of beer. The party had started.

The old man greeted me cordially. "Sit down and drink." I accepted a large calabash full of beer, poured some into a small drinking gourd, and tossed it down. . . .

"Ah," said the old man. "Tell us [a story]."

I protested that I was not a storyteller. Storytelling is a skilled art among them; their standards are high, and the audiences critical—and vocal in their criticism. I protested in vain. . . . Realizing that here was my chance to prove *Hamlet* universally intelligible, I agreed.

The old man handed me some more beer to help me on with my storytelling. Men filled their long wooden pipes and knocked coals from the fire to place in the pipe bowls; then, puffing contentedly, they sat back to listen. I began in the proper style, "Not yesterday, not yesterday, but long ago, a thing occurred. One night three men were keeping watch outside the homestead of the great chief, when suddenly they saw the former chief approach them."

"Why was he no longer their chief?"

"He was dead," I explained. "That is why they were troubled and afraid when they saw him."

Source: Reprinted from *Natural History*, 75(1966):28–33, with permission of Laura Bohannan. Copyright Laura Bohannan.

"Impossible," began one of the elders, handing his pipe on to his neighbor, who interrupted, "Of course it wasn't the dead chief. It was an omen sent by a witch. Go on."

Slightly shaken, I continued. "One of these three was a man who knew things"—the closest translation for scholar, but unfortunately it also meant witch. The second elder looked triumphantly at the first. "So he spoke to the dead chief saying, 'Tell us what we must do so you may rest in your grave,' but the dead chief did not answer. He vanished, and they could see him no more. Then the man who knew things—his name was Horatio—said this event was the affair of the dead chief's son, Hamlet."

There was a general shaking of heads around the circle. "Had the dead chief no living brothers? Or was this son the chief?"

"No," I replied. "That is, he had one living brother who became the chief when the elder brother died." . . . "He had also married his elder brother's widow only about a month after the funeral."

"He did well," the old man beamed and announced to the others, "I told you that if we knew more about Europeans, we would find they really were very like us. In our country also," he added to me, "the younger brother marries the elder brother's widow and becomes the father of his children. Now, if your uncle, who married your widowed mother, is your father's full brother, then he will be a real father to you. Did Hamlet's father and uncle have one mother?"

His question barely penetrated my mind; I was too upset and thrown too far off balance by having one of the most important elements of *Hamlet* knocked straight out of the picture. . . . Determined to save what I could of the mother motif, I took a deep breath and began again. . . .

"That night Hamlet kept watch with the three who had seen his dead father. The dead chief again appeared, and although the others were afraid, Hamlet followed his dead father off to one side. When they were alone, Hamlet's dead father spoke."

"Omens can't talk!" The old man was emphatic.

"Hamlet's dead father wasn't an omen. . . . It was a thing we call a 'ghost'." I had to use the English word, for unlike many of the neighboring tribes, these people didn't believe in the survival after death of any individuating part of the personality.

"What is a 'ghost'? An omen?"

"No, a ghost is someone who is dead but walks around and can talk, and people can hear him and see him but not touch him."

They objected. "One can touch zombies."

"No, no! It was not a dead body the witches had animated to sacrifice and eat. No one else made Hamlet's dead father walk. He did it himself."

"Dead men can't walk," protested my audience as one man.

I was quite willing to compromise. "A 'ghost' is the dead man's shadow."

But again they objected. "Dead men cast no shadows."

"They do in my country," I snapped. . . .

"Anyhow," I resumed, "Hamlet's dead father said that his own brother, the one who became chief, had poisoned him. He wanted Hamlet to avenge him. . . ."

This time I had shocked my audience seriously. "For a man to raise his hand against his father's brother and the one who has become his father—that is a terrible thing."

I began to get cross. "If you don't like the story, I'll stop."

The old man made soothing noises and himself poured me some more beer. "You tell the story well, and we are listening. But it is clear that the elders of your country have never told you what the story really means. No, don't interrupt! We believe you when you say your marriage customs are different, or your clothes and weapons. But people are the same everywhere; therefore, there are always witches and it is we, the elders, who know how witches work. . . . We . . . will instruct you in their true meaning, so that when you return to your own land your elders will see that you have not been sitting in the bush, but among those who know things and who have taught you wisdom."

---

that the Oedipus complex, as defined by Freud, does indeed exist, although in not so overt a form (see Roheim 1950).

THE PRESS AND PULL OF CULTURE: SOME CONCLUSIONS It is clear that culture is a powerful force in the formation of the person, both by setting limits to and models for behavior. Those reared in Western cultures often resent these pressures and regard cultural restrictions and directives as intruding on their freedom.

It should also be clear by now that no human society can exist without culturally prescribed ways of organizing life and relationships. Without models of how the world operates, shared understandings, and the predictability to which these lead, communication and social organization would be impossible. The individual would fall into despair and the society collapse into anarchy. Society and culture are essential for the person to find even the simplest conforts in life or to find meaning to existence. This does not mean, however, that he must always accept his culture as it is.

Cultures vary greatly in the degree to which they structure the lives of individuals by prescriptions and proscriptions—in the degree to which they provide people with a sense of order and security on the one hand, and allow for unique human expression and creativity and their attendant danger of disorder on the other. Moreover, they vary in what cultural patterns are enforced and how. In general, it appears that complex urban cultures offer a greater variety of acceptable behavior patterns, and that this is one factor attracting people into modern civilizations. However, these opportunities for individual expression are often bought at the price of a loss of the sense of personal security.

Individual strategies

From the point of view of the social scientist looking for broader patterns in human behavior, the individual can be viewed as part of a larger system. From the point of view of the actor himself, his society provides the arena within which he must determine a course of action, and his culture provides him the guidelines by which he can predict the actions of others and choose his own strategies.

In a few cases, behavior in a culture may be defined down to the finest detail. For example, the protocol of a formal banquet may be rigid. Not only is the table etiquette carefully defined, but also what is said and what is worn for the occasion. Similarly, a religious ritual may be carefully prescribed. Generally, however, there is some latitude permitted in behavior, and often a person can choose whether or not to participate in an activity.

The individual is capable of reflection and abstraction. He can look ahead as well as behind, formulating goals and choosing actions to achieve them. He has the capacity to hate and to love, to be a criminal or a saint, to be egocentric or altruistic. As we have seen, each also has his own understanding of the world, his mazeway or map by which he responds to the stimuli of his environment and initiates his own actions.

No two mazeways are exactly alike, just as no two cultures are the same. Yet it is only when large portions of people's mazeways are similar—when they share the same culture—that social and cultural behavior become possible. Individual creativity and expression are meaningful in a group, only as there is a great deal of common structure within which these can be mutually understood.

In analyzing the personality, Clyde Kluckhohn and O.H. Mowrer (1944) noted that there are levels of individuality, ranging from those characteristics a person shares with all other people to those which are

Table 22.1   The Individual in the Context of Life

Levels of Individuality	Antecedents and Influences			
	Biological[A]	Physical Environmental[B]	Social[C]	Cultural[D]
Universal[4]	**4A** Birth, death, hunger, thirst, elimination, etc.	**4B** Gravity, temperature, time, etc.	**4C** Infant care, group life, etc.	**4D** Symbolism, taboo on incest and in-group murder, etc.
Communal[3]	**3A** "Racial" traits, nutrition level, endemic diseases, etc.	**3B** Climate, topography, natural resources, etc.	**3C** Size, density, and distribution of population etc.	**3D** Traditions, rules of conduct and manners, skills, knowledge, etc.
Role[2]	**2A** Age and sex differences, caste, etc.	**2B** Differential access to material goods, etc.	**2C** Cliques; "marginal" men, etc.	**2D** Culturally differentiated roles
Idiosyncratic[1]	**1A** Peculiarities of stature, physiognomy, glandular makeup, etc.	**1B** Unique events and "accidents" such as being hit by lightning, etc.	**1C** Social "accidents" such as death of a parent, being adopted, meeting particular people, etc.	**1D** Folklore about accidents and "fate," etc.

Source: Adapted from Clyde Kluckhohn and O.H. Mowrer, "Culture and Personality: A Conceptual Scheme." Reproduced by permission of the American Anthropological Association from *The American Anthropologist*, 46, 1 (1944):57.

uniquely his own. They combined this dimension of behavior with the various forces that influence the individual to give us a model of the person in relationship to the environment. (See Table 22.1.) While this scheme provides us with a useful way to analyze different areas of an individual's behavior, it is important to remember that the personality is not confined only to those things that are unique to the individual, in other words, to the idiosyncratic. A person is a "whole," in some ways like all other people, in some ways like others in his society, in some ways like others who share his roles, and in some ways absolutely unique.

In anthropology, the study of how people choose their strategies—how they define their goals, how they maximize the opportunities of reaching these goals, and how they minimize dangers and failure—has only just begun. Only as these processes are more clearly understood will many aspects of life within a culture, and of cultural change be known (see Bailey 1969 and 1971).

A mother's chores may be thrust upon the very young in some cultures, such as rural India.

Anthropology and the person

Where does the study of anthropology leave us? By making us aware of the press and pull of culture in the lives of others, it makes us more aware of its effects on ourselves. Somehow, it is difficult for us to look at ourselves objectively. We are too much a part of our culture to be aware of the values and practices we so take for granted. Only as we step outside our culture by immersing ourselves in another in order to understand the world from this new perspective can we begin to look at ourselves with a measure of detachment and see the assumptions we make. It is this process that helps us deal with the ethnocentrism we all have.

No one of us, including anthropologists, can think or operate outside a culture nor live apart from a society. But strangely enough, as we become increasingly aware of the ways in which our culture molds us, we are more able to determine our responses to its pressures, to use its maps to chart a course of action, and to play a part in shaping its future. Autonomy and freedom do not lie in the absence of social laws and order, but in a knowledge of how social processes work and how they can be applied to achieve our goals.

A comparative study of societies provides us with an awareness of various cultural alternatives and their respective consequences. What types of government, family, or economic systems work, and which of them most adequately meet our needs? An awareness of cultural alternatives makes us conscious of our options.

Functional approaches point out the interdependence between various parts of culture, between a culture and its ecological environment, and between a culture and the basic psychosocial needs of human beings, which must be met if a society is to survive. Thereby it makes us more aware of the consequences of various actions. Hopefully, as our understanding of cultural processes increases, we will be able to plan changes that benefit people and lack the injurious side-effects so common in programs of planned change today.

Finally, by forcing us to come to grips with culture and cultural pluralism, anthropology forces us to develop a philosophy that can cope with human variety. Perhaps in doing so, it can help us break from the narrow parochialisms of our past and give us a sense of the international nature of humankind. In the long run, the greatest contribution of anthropology is to our understanding of ourselves and our world.

Suggested readings

Barnouw, Victor.
   1973   Culture and Personality, rev. ed. Homewood, Ill.: Dorsey Press, 1973. (A general review of the field, methods used, and some of the recent issues.)
Benedict, Ruth.
   1934   Patterns of Culture. Boston: Houghton Mifflin. (A classic, which is still relevant to the discussion of national character.)
Erikson, Erik H.
   1963   Childhood and Society, 2nd ed. New York: W.W. Norton. (A provoca-

tive study of the development of human personality through various stages.)

Fromm, Erich.
1964   The Heart of Man. New York: Harper and Row. (A useful book on Fromm's view of the personality.)
Mead, Margaret.
1949   Male and Female. New York: William Morrow. (A summary of the relationship between culture and personality in seven primitive societies and the U.S.)
Middleton, J. ed.
1970   From Child to Adult: Studies in the Anthropology of Education. Garden City, N.Y.: Natural History Press. (A book of readings on ethnographies and theories of enculturation.)
Whiting, B.B., J.W.M. Whiting and R. Longabaugh.
1975   Children of Six Cultures: A Psycho-cultural Analysis. Cambridge, Mass.: Harvard University Press. (An up-to-date analysis of the impact of child rearing on the formation of the personality.)

Bibliography

Achebe, Chinua
    1969   No Longer at Ease. Greenwich: Fawcett Publications.
Aginsky, B.W.
    1940   An Indian's Soliloquy. American Journal of Sociology. 46:43–44.
Apter, D.
    1965   The Politics of Modernization. Chicago: University of Chicago Press.
Bacon, E.
    1958   Obok: A Study of Social Structure in Eurasia. Viking Fund Publication in Anthropology, No. 25. New York: Wenner-Gren Foundation.
Bailey, F.G.
    1969   Stratagems and Spoils: A Social Anthropology of Politics. New York: Schocken Books.
    1971   Gifts and Poisons: The Politics of Reputation. Oxford: Blackwell.

Banton, M.
  1968   Voluntary Associations: Anthropological Aspects. International Ency-
         clopedia of the Social Sciences. 16:357–362.
Barnett, D.
  1968   Schism and Renewal in Africa: An Analysis of Six Thousand Contem-
         porary Religious Movements. London and Nairobi: Oxford University
         Press.
Barnett, H.G.
  1953   Innovation: The Basis of Culture Change. New York: McGraw-Hill.
Barnouw, Victor
  1973   Culture and Personality. Revised Edition. Homewood, Ill.: Dorsey
         Press.
Barth, Fredrik
  1961   Nomads of South Persia. New York: Humanities Press.
  1963   The Role of the Entrepreneur in Social Change in Northern Norway.
         Bergen: Scandinavian University Books.
  1967   On the Study of Social Change. American Anthropologist. 69:661–
         669.
  1969   Ethnic Groups and Boundaries. Boston: Little, Brown and Company.
Bee, R.L.
  1974   Patterns and Processes: An Introduction to Anthropological Strategies
         for the Study of Sociocultural Change. New York: The Free Press.
Befu, H. and L. Plotnicov
  1962   Types of Corporate Unilineal Descent Groups. American Anthropol-
         ogist. 64:313–327.
Belshaw, C.S.
  1965   Traditional Exchange and Modern Markets. Englewood Cliffs, N.J.:
         Prentice-Hall.
Bendix, R. and S.M. Lipset
  1966   Class, Status and Power: Social Stratification in Comparative Perspec-
         tive. 2nd Edition. New York: The Free Press.
Benedict, Ruth
  1934   Patterns of Culture. Boston: Houghton Mifflin.
  1946   The Chrysanthemum and the Sword; Patterns of Japanese Culture.
         Boston: Houghton Mifflin.
Bennett, J.W.
  1949   Science and Human Rights: Reason and Action. American Anthropol-
         ogist. 51:329–337.
Berlin, Brent and Paul Kay
  1969   Basic Color Terms: Their Universality and Evolution. Berkeley: Uni-
         versity of California Press.
Berne, Eric
  1964   Games People Play. New York: Grove Press.
Biederman, Paul, Ed.
  1967   Economic Almanac: 1967–1968, Business Factbook. National Indus-
         trial Conference Board. New York: Macmillan.

Bierstedt, Robert
    1970   The Social Order. 3rd Edition. New York: McGraw-Hill.

Bloom, B.S.
    1964   Stability and Change in Human Characteristics. New York: John Wiley and Sons.

Boas, Franz
    1940   Race, Language and Culture. New York: The Free Press.
    1955   Primitive Art. New York: Dover. First published in 1929.

Bock, P.K.
    1969   Modern Cultural Anthropology. New York: Alfred A. Knopf.

Bohannan, Paul
    1967   Law and Warfare: Studies in the Anthropology of Conflict. Garden City, N.Y.: Natural History Press.

Bohannan, P. and J. Middleton, Eds.
    1968a   Kinship and Social Organization. Garden City, N.Y.: Natural History Press.
    1968b   Marriage, Family and Residence. Garden City, N.Y.: Natural History Press.

Bolinger, D.
    1968   Aspects of Language. New York: Harcourt Brace Jovanovich.

Boulding, K.E.
    1964   The Meaning of the 20th Century: The Great Transition. New York: Harper and Row.

Bowen, Elenore Smith
    1964   Return to Laughter: An Anthropological Novel. New York: Doubleday Anchor Book.

Bradley, Charles C.
    1968   Human Water Needs and Water Use in America. In Environments of Man. Jack B. Bresler, Ed. Reading, Mass.: Addison-Wesley.

Brain, Robert
    1969   Friends and Twins in Bangwa. In Man in Africa. Mary Douglas and Phyllis Kayberry, Eds. London: Travistock.

Brown, Robert
    1963   Explanation in Social Science. London: Routledge.

Bruller, Jean (pseudonym, Vercors)
    1953   You Shall Know Them. Translated by Rita Barisse. Boston: Little, Brown and Company.

Bryson, Lyman, et al.
    1954   Symbols and Values: An Initial Study. New York: Harper.

Bureau of Census, U.S. Dept. of Commerce
    1970   Census of Population: Marital Status.

Burling, Robbins
    1965   Hill Farms and Padi Fields: Life in Mainland Southeast Asia. Englewood Cliffs, N.J.: Prentice-Hall.
    1970   Man's Many Voices: Language in Its Cultural Context. New York: Holt, Rinehart and Winston.

Casagrande, J.B., Ed.
　　1960　In the Company of Man: Twenty Portraits by Anthropologists. New York: Harper and Row.
Chalmers, D.M.
　　1965　Hooded Americanism: The First Century of the Ku Klux Klan, 1865–1965. Garden City, N.Y.: Doubleday.
Chambliss, W.J.
　　1969　Crime and the Legal Process. New York: McGraw-Hill.
Chapple, E.D. and C.S. Coon
　　1942　Principles of Anthropology. New York: Holt.
Chase, Stuart
　　1954　Power of Words. New York: Harcourt Brace.
Chaudhuri, Nirad C.
　　1968　The Autobiography of an Unknown Indian. Berkeley and Los Angeles: University of California Press.
Chomsky, N.
　　1957　Syntactic Structures. The Hague: Mouton.
　　1965　Aspects of the Theory of Syntax. Cambridge, Mass.: M.I.T.
　　1968　Language and Mind. New York: Harcourt, Brace and World.
Clifton, James A., Ed.
　　1970　Applied Anthropology: Readings in the Uses of the Science of Man. Boston: Houghton Mifflin.
Cohen, R. and J. Middleton, Eds.
　　1967　Comparative Political Systems. Garden City, N.Y.: Natural History Press.
Cohen, Yehudi A.
　　1964　The Transition from Childhood to Adolescence: Cross-cultural Studies of Initiation Ceremonies, Legal Systems and Incest Tabus. Chicago: Aldine.
　　1968　Man in Adaptation: The Biosocial Background. Chicago: Aldine.
Dalton, George, Ed.
　　1967　Tribal and Peasant Economies. Garden City, N.Y.: Natural History Press.
　　1968　Primitive, Archaic and Modern Economics: Essays of Karl Polanyi. Garden City, N.Y.: Doubleday.
　　1971　Economic Development and Social Change: The Modernization of Village Communities. Garden City, N.Y.: Natural History Press.
Deloria, Vine, Jr.
　　1969　Custer Died for Your Sins: An Indian Manifesto. New York: Macmillan.
　　1974　Behind the Trail of Broken Treaties: An Indian Declaration of Independence. New York: Delacorte Press.
Douglas, Mary
　　1966　Purity and Danger. London: Routledge and Kegan Paul.
　　1970　Natural Symbols. New York: Random House.
Druberg, J.
　　1935　The "Best Friend" among the Didinga. Man. 37:101–102.

Drucker, P. and R.F. Heizer

    1967   To Make My Name Good: A Reexamination of the Kwakiutl Potlatch. Berkeley: University of California Press.

Dundes, Alan

    1962   Earth-Diver: Creation of the Mythopoeic Male. American Anthropologist. 64:1032–1051.

Dyson-Hudson, N.

    1963   Karimojong Age System. Ethnology. 3:353–401.

Eisenstadt, S.N.

    1956   From Generation to Generation. New York: The Free Press.

    1970   Readings in Social Evolution and Development. Elmsford, N.Y.: Pergamon Press.

    1971   Social Differentiation and Stratification. Glenview, Ill.: Scott, Foresman.

Elwood, D.

    1968   Churches and Sects in the Philippines. Dumaguette: Silliman University Press.

Ember, C.R. and M. Ember

    1973   Anthropology. New York: Appleton-Century-Crofts.

Erikson, Erik H.

    1963   Childhood and Society. 2nd Edition. New York: W. W. Norton.

Evans-Pritchard, E.E.

    1937   Witchcraft, Oracles and Magic among the Azande. Oxford: Clarendon Press.

    1940   The Nuer. New York: Oxford University Press.

Forde, Daryl, Ed.

    1954   African Worlds: Studies in the Cosmological Ideas and Social Values of African Peoples. London: Oxford University Press.

Fortes, M.

    1949   The Web of Kinship among the Tallensi. London: Oxford University Press.

Fortune, R.F.

    1932   Sorcerers of Dobu: The Social Anthropology of the Dobu Islanders of the Western Pacific. London: Routledge.

Foster, G.M.

    1965   Peasant Society and the Image of the Limited Good. American Anthropologist. 67:293–315.

Frazer, James G.

    1911–1915   The Golden Bough: A Study in Magic and Religion. 12 Vols. 3rd Ed. London: Macmillan.

    1933–1936   The Fear of the Dead in Primitive Religion. 3 Vols. London: Macmillan.

Fried, Morton

    1967   The Evolution of Political Society. New York: Random House.

Fromm, Erich

    1964   The Heart of Man. New York: Harper and Row.

Fromm, Erich and Michael Maccoby

1970　Social Character in a Mexican Village: A Sociopsychoanalytic Study. Englewood Cliffs, N.J.: Prentice-Hall.

Geertz, Clifford

1963　Agricultural Involution. Berkeley and Los Angeles: University of California Press.

1968　Religion: Anthropological Study. *In* International Encyclopedia of the Social Sciences. 13:398–406. New York: Macmillan.

1972　Religion as a Cultural System. *In* Reader in Comparative Religion. W.A. Lessa and E.Z. Vogt, Eds. 3rd Edition. New York: Harper and Row.

Gerbrands, A.A.

1962　The Art of the Asmat, New Guinea. New York: New York City Museum of Primitive Art.

Gibbs, James L., Ed.

1965　Peoples of Africa. New York: Holt, Rinehart and Winston.

Glick, Paul C. and Robert Parke, Jr.

1968　New Approaches in Studying the Life Cycle of the Family. *In* Selected Studies in Marriage and the Family. R.F. Winch and L.W. Goodman, Eds. 3rd Edition. New York: Holt, Rinehart and Winston.

Gluckman, Max

1949　Malinowki's Sociological Theories. Rhodes Livingstone Papers No. 16. New York: Oxford University Press.

1964　Closed Systems and Open Minds: The Limits of Naïvety in Social Anthropology. Chicago: Aldine.

1968　The Utility of the Equilibrium Model in the Study of Social Change. American Anthropologist. 70:219–237.

Goldschmidt, Walter R.

1954　Ways of Mankind. Boston: Beacon Press.

1965　Theory and Strategy in the Study of Cultural Adaptability. American Anthropologist. 67:402–408.

Goodenough, Ward H.

1963　Cooperation in Change. New York: Russell Sage Foundation.

1970　Description and Comparison in Cultural Anthropology. Chicago: Aldine.

Goodman, Mary

1967　The Individual and Culture. Homewood, Ill.: Dorsey Press.

Goody, J.R., Ed.

1958　The Developmental Cycle in Domestic Groups. Cambridge: Cambridge University Press.

Gudschinsky, S.C.

1964　The ABC's of Lexicostatistics (Glottochronology). *In* Language in Culture and Society. D. Hymes, Ed. New York: Harper and Row.

Hall, Edward T.

1959　Silent Language. Greenwich, Conn.: Fawcett.

Hambly, W.D.

1927　The History of Tattooing and Its Significance. New York: Macmillan.

Hammel, E.A. and W.S. Simmons, Eds.
   1970   Man Makes Sense: A Reader in Modern Cultural Anthropology.
          Boston: Little, Brown and Company.
Hammond, Dorothy
   1972   Associations. A McCaleb Module in Anthropology. Reading, Mass.:
          Addison-Wesley.
Hammond, Peter B.
   1971   An Introduction to Cultural and Social Anthropology. New York:
          Macmillan.
Harris, Marvin
   1968   The Rise of Anthropological Theory. New York: Thomas Y. Crowell.
Harris, T.A.
   1967   I'm O.K.—You're O.K. New York: Avon Books.
Hayakawa, S.I.
   1964   Language in Thought and Action. 2nd Edition. New York: Harcourt
          Brace Jovanovich.
Henry, Jules
   1963   Culture Against Man. New York: Random House.
   1973   Pathways to Madness. New York: Vintage Books.
Herskovits, Melville J.
   1958   Cultural Anthropology. New York: Alfred A. Knopf.
   1966   Cultural Dynamics. New York: Alfred A. Knopf.
   1972   Cultural Relativism: Perspectives in Cultural Pluralism. Edited by
          Frances Herskovits. New York: Random House.
d'Hertefelt, Marcel
   1965   The Rwanda of Rwanda. In Peoples of Africa. James L. Gibbs, Ed. New
          York: Holt, Rinehart and Winston.
Hiebert, Paul G.
   1969   Caste and Personal Rank in an Indian Village: An Extension in Tech-
          niques. American Anthropologist. 71:434–453.
   1971   Konduru: Structure and Integration in a South Indian Village. Min-
          neapolis: University of Minnesota Press.
Hodge, R.W., et al.
   1966   Occupational Prestige in the United States: 1925–1963. In Class,
          Status and Power. 2nd Edition. R. Bendix and S.M. Lipset, Eds. New
          York: The Free Press.
Hoebel, E.A.
   1954   The Law of Primitive Man: A Study in Comparative Dynamics. Cam-
          bridge, Mass.: Harvard University Press.
   1972   Anthropology: The Study of Man. 4th Edition. New York: McGraw-
          Hill.
Homans, G.C.
   1950   The Human Group. New York: Harcourt, Brace and World.
Homans, G.C., and D.M. Schneider
   1955   Marriage, Authority and Final Causes: A Study of Unilateral Cross-
          Cousin Marriage. New York: The Free Press.

Hsu, Francis L.K.

    1963   Clan, Caste and Club. New York: Van Nostrand.

    1970   Americans and Chinese: Purpose and Fulfillment in Great Civilizations. Garden City, N.Y.: Natural History Press.

Hughes, Charles, Ed.

    1972   Make Men of Them: Introductory Readings for Cultural Anthropology. Chicago: Rand McNally.

Hymes, D. Ed.

    1964   Language in Culture and Society: A Reader in Linguistics and Anthropology. New York: Harper and Row.

Inkeles, A. and P.H. Rossi

    1956   National Comparisons of Occupational Prestige. American Journal of Sociology. 61:329–339.

Jarvie, I.C.

    1968   Limits to Functionalism and Alternatives to It in Anthropology. In Theory in Anthropology. R.O. Manners and D. Kaplan, Eds. Chicago: Aldine.

    1973   Functionalism. Minneapolis: Burgess.

Jorgensen, J.G. and M. Truzzi, Eds.

    1974   Anthropology and American Life. Englewood Cliffs, N.J.: Prentice-Hall.

Josephine

    1964   Tell Me Josephine. Edited by Barbara Hall. New York: Simon and Schuster.

Kinsey, Alfred C., et al.

    1953   Sexual Behavior in the Human Female. Philadelphia: W.B. Saunders.

Kluckhohn, Clyde

    1959   Common Humanity and Diverse Culture. In The Human Meaning of the Social Sciences. Daniel Lerner, Ed. New York: Meridian Books.

Kluckhohn, C. and W. Kelly

    1949   The Concept of Culture. In The Science of Man in the World Crisis. Ralph Linton, Ed. New York: Columbia University Press.

Kluckhohn, C. and O.H. Mowrer

    1944   "Culture and Personality": A Conceptual Scheme. American Anthropologist. 46:1–27.

Kochman, Thomas

    1975   Towards an Ethnography of Black American Speech Behavior. In Cultural and Social Anthropology. P.B. Hammond, Ed. New York: Macmillan.

Korbzybski, Alfred

    1933   Science and Sanity: An Introduction to Non-Aristotelian Systems and General Semantics. International Non-Aristotelian Library Publishing Company.

Kroeber, A.L.

    1909   Classificatory Systems of Relationship. Journal of the Royal Anthropological Institute of Great Britain and Ireland. 39:77–84.

1948 Anthropology. Revised Edition. New York: Harcourt Brace Jovanovich.

LaBarre, W.
1970 The Ghost Dance: Origins of Religion. Garden City, N.Y.: Doubleday.

Landis, P.H.
1965 Punitive vs. Therapeutic Justice. *In* Towards a Sociology of Culture in India. T.K.N. Unnithan, et al. New Delhi: Prentice-Hall of India.

Lang, Andrew
1898 The Making of Religion. London: Longmans, Green and Company.

Leach, Edmund
1961 Rethinking Anthropology. London School of Economics, Monographs on Social Anthropology, No. 22. London: Athlone.
1967 The Structural Study of Myth and Totemism. Association of Social Anthropologists, Monograph 5. London: Travistock.

Lemarchand, Rene
1970 Rwanda and Burundi. New York: Praeger.

Lerner, Daniel, Ed.
1959 The Human Meaning of the Social Sciences. New York: Meridian Books.

Lessa, W.A. and E.Z. Vogt, Eds.
1972 Reader in Comparative Religion. 3rd Edition. New York: Harper and Row.

LeVine, R.A., et al.
1966 Dreams and Deeds: Achievement Motivation in Nigeria. Chicago: University of Chicago Press.

Lévi-Strauss, Claude
1963 Structural Anthropology. New York: Basic Books.
1969 The Elementary Structures of Kinship. Revised Edition. Boston: Beacon Press.
1969 The Raw and the Cooked. New York: Harper and Row.

Lewis, Oscar
1963 The Children of Sanches: Autobiography of a Mexican Family. New York: Random House.

Lewis, Sinclair
1950 Babbitt. New York: Harcourt, Brace, Jovanovich.

Linton, Ralph
1943 Nativistic Movements. American Anthropologist. 45:230–240.

Little, K.B.
1965 West African Urbanization: A Study of Voluntary Associations in Social Change. New York: Cambridge University Press.

Llewellyn, K.N. and E.A. Hoebel
1941 The Cheyenne Way: Conflict and Case Law in Primitive Jurisprudence. Norman, Okl.: University of Oklahoma Press.

Lloyd, P.C.
1966 The New Elites of Tropical Africa. London: Oxford University Press.

Loeb, E.M. and J.O.M. Broek
1947 Social Organization and the Long-House in Southeast Asia. American Anthropologist. 49:414–425.
Lomax, Alan
1968 Folk Song Style and Culture. Washington, D.C.: American Association for the Advancement of Science, Publication 88.
Lynd, R.S. and H. Lynd
1929 Middletown, a Study in Contemporary American Culture. New York: Harcourt, Brace and Company.
1937 Middletown in Transition: A Study in Cultural Conflict. New York: Harcourt, Brace and Company.
McClelland, D.C.
1961 The Achieving Society. Princeton, N.J.: D. Van Nostrand.
McFarland, H.N.
1967 The Rush Hour of the Gods: A Study of New Religious Movements in Japan. New York: Macmillan.
MacIver, Robert and Charles Page
1949 Society: An Introductory Analysis. New York: Holt, Rinehart and Winston.
McLuhan, Marshall
1964 Understanding Media: The Extensions of Man. New York: McGraw-Hill.
Mair, Lucy
1974 African Societies. London: Cambridge University Press.
Malinowski, Bronislaw
1922 Argonauts of the Western Pacific. London: Routledge.
1931 Culture. In Encyclopedia of the Social Sciences. 4:634–642. New York: Macmillan.
1945 The Dynamics of Culture Change. New Haven, Conn.: Yale University Press.
1953 Sex and Repression in Savage Society. London: Routledge and Kegan Paul.
1954 Magic, Science and Religion, and Other Essays by Bronislaw Malinowski. Garden City, N.Y.: Doubleday Anchor Books.
1972 The Role of Magic and Religion. In Reader in Comparative Religion. 3rd Edition. W.A. Lessa and E.Z. Vogt, Eds. New York: Harper and Row.
Mandelbaum, David
1970 Society in India. 2 Vols. Berkeley and Los Angeles: University of California Press.
Mangin, William, Ed.
1970 Peasants in Cities: Readings in the Anthropology of Urbanization. Boston: Houghton Mifflin.
Marett, Robert
1909 The Threshold of Religion. London: Methuen and Company.

Marshall, Lorna
   1967   !Kung Bushman Bands. *In* Comparative Political Systems. R. Cohen and J. Middleton, Eds. Garden City, N.Y.: Natural History Press.
Martinson, F.M.
   1960   Marriage and the American Ideal. Dodd Mead and Company.
Marx, Karl
   1967   Capital, 2 Vols. New York: International Publishers. First English edition, 1887.
Marx, K. and F. Engels
   1959   Basic Writings on Politics and Philosophy. L.S. Fever, Ed. Garden City, N.Y.: Doubleday.
   1970   The German Ideology. C.J. Arthur, Ed. New York: International Publishers. First published, 1932.
Mauss, M.
   1954   The Gift: Forms and Functions of Exchange in Archaic Societies. New York: The Free Press.
Mead, Margaret
   1928   Coming of Age in Samoa. New York: William Morrow.
   1935   Sex and Temperament in Three Primitive Societies. New York: William Morrow.
   1949   Male and Female: A Study of the Sexes in the Changing World. New York: William Morrow.
   1956   New Lives for Old. New York: Mentor Books.
Merton, Robert K.
   1968   Social Theory and Social Structure. Glencoe, Ill.: The Free Press.
Michels, Robert
   1949   Political Parties: A Sociological Study of the Oligarchical Tendencies of Modern Democracy. Glencoe, Ill.: The Free Press.
Middleton, J.D., Ed.
   1970   From Child to Adult: Studies in the Anthropology of Education. Garden City, N.Y.: Natural History Press.
Middleton, J.D. and D. Tait, Eds.
   1958   Tribes Without Rulers. London: Routledge.
Miller, S.M. and T. Fox
   1965   Occupational Stratification and Mobility: Intra-Country Variations. Studies in Comparative International Development. 1:1–10.
Mitchell, W.E.
   1963   Theoretical Problems in the Concept of Kindred. American Anthropologist. 65:343–354.
Mitford, Jessica
   1963   The American Way of Death. Greenwich, Conn.: Fawcett Publications.
Morgan, K.W., Ed.
   1953   The Religion of the Hindus. New York: Ronald Press.
Morgan, L.H.
   1877   Ancient Society, or Research in the Lines of Human Progress from Savagery, through Barbarism to Civilization. New York: Holt.

1954   League of the Ho-dé-no-sau-nee, or Iroquois. 2 Vols. New Haven, Conn.: Yale University Press. First published in 1851.

1965   Houses and House-Life of the American Aborigines. Chicago: University of Chicago Press. First published in 1881.

Murdock, George P.

1949   Social Structure. New York: Macmillan.

1967   Ethnographic Atlas. Pittsburgh: University of Pittsburgh Press.

Murphy, R.F. and J.H. Steward

1956   Tappers and Trappers: Parallel Process in Acculturation. Economic Development and Cultural Change. 4:335–355.

Nadel, S.F.

1957   The Theory of Social Structure. London: Cohen and West.

Nair, Kusum

1962   Blossoms in the Dust, the Human Factor in Indian Development. New York: Frederick A. Praeger.

Nettl, Bruno

1964   Theory and Method in Ethnomusicology. New York: The Free Press.

Nida, Eugene

1960   Message and Mission. New York: Harper.

Niehoff, Arthur H., Ed.

1966   A Casebook of Social Change: Critical Evaluations of Attempts to Introduce Change in the Five Major Developing Areas of the World. Chicago: Aldine.

Norbeck, Edward

1974   Religion in Human Life: Anthropological Views. New York: Holt, Rinehart and Winston.

Odaka, K. and S. Ikuta, Eds.

1965   Proceedings of the International Symposium on Social Stratification and Social Mobility in East Asian Countries. East Asian Cultural Studies. Vol. 4, Nos. 1–4.

Olsen, Marvin E.

1968   The Process of Social Organization. New York: Holt, Rinehart and Winston.

Otten, C.M.

1971   Anthropology and Art: Readings in Cross-Cultural Aesthetics. Garden City, N.Y.: Natural History Press.

Ottenberg, Simon

1968   Double Descent in an African Society: The Afikbo Village Group. Seattle: University of Washington Press.

Pavalko, R.M.

1971   Sociology of Occupations and Progessions. Itasca, Ill.: F.E. Peacock Publishers.

Pelto, P.J.

1973   The Snowmobile Revolution: Technology and Social Change in the Arctic. Menlo Park, Cal.: Cummings.

Pfeiffer, John E.

1972   The Emergence of Man. 2nd Edition. New York: Harper and Row.

Plotnicov, Leonard
    1967   Strangers to the City: Urban Man in Jos, Nigeria. Pittsburgh: University of Pittsburgh Press.
Pospisil, L.
    1972   The Ethnology of Law. A McCaleb Module. Reading, Mass.: Addison-Wesley.
Postman, Neil and Charles Weingartner
    1969   Teaching as a Subversive Activity. New York: Delacorte Press.
Radcliffe-Brown, A.R.
    1922   The Andaman Islanders. Cambridge: The University Press.
Radcliffe-Brown, A.R. and D. Forde, Eds.
    1950   African Systems of Kinship and Marriage. London: Oxford University Press.
Radin, Paul
    1927   Primitive Man as Philosopher. New York: D. Appleton.
    1937   Primitive Religion: Its Nature and Origin. New York: Viking Press.
Rattray, R.S.
    1923   Ashanti. Oxford: Clarendon Press.
    1927   Ashanti Law and Custom. Oxford: Clarendon Press.
Read, K.E.
    1965   The High Valley. New York: Scribners.
Richardson, J. and A. L. Kroeber
    1940   Three Centuries of Women's Dress Fashions: A Quantitative Analysis. Anthropological Records. 5:111–154.
Riordan, William L.
    1963   Plunkitt of Tammany Hall. New York: E.P. Dutton.
Roach, M.E. and J.B. Eicher, Eds.
    1965   Dress, Adornment and the Social Order. New York: Wiley.
Robertson, William
    1812   The History of America. Philadelphia: J. Broien and T.L. Plowman.
Roheim, Geza
    1950   Psychoanalysis and Anthropology, Culture, Personality and the Unconscious. New York: International Universities Press.
Ross, Ralph
    1962   Symbols and Civilization. New York: Harcourt Brace Jovanovich.
Sahlins, M.D.
    1960   Evolution: Specific and General. In Evolution and Culture. M.D. Sahlins and E.R. Service, Eds. Ann Arbor, Mich.: University of Michigan Press.
Schmidt, W.
    1931   The Origin and Growth of Religion. Translated by H. Rose. New York: Lincoln MacVeagh
Schneider, D.M.
    1968   American Kinship: A Cultural Account. Englewood Cliffs, N.J.: Prentice-Hall.
Schusky, E.L.
    1965   Manual for Kinship Analysis. New York: Holt.

Service, E.R.

    1962   Primitive Social Organization: An Evolutionary Perspective. New York: Random House.

Simmons, Leo W., Ed.

    1942   Sun Chief: The Autobiography of a Hopi Indian. New Haven, Conn.: Yale University Press.

Singer, M.

    1968   Culture: The Concept of Culture. International Encyclopedia of the Social Sciences. Vol. 3. New York: Macmillan.

Skeat, W.W.

    1966   Malay Magic: An Introduction to the Folklore and Popular Religion of the Malay Peninsular. New York: Barnes and Noble.

Social and Economic Statistic Administration, Bureau of Census, U.S. Department of Commerce.

    1970   Census of Population: Marital Status.

Spencer, R.F.

    1952   The Arabian Matriarchate: An Old Controversy. Southwestern Journal of Anthropology. 8:478–502.

    1959   The North Alaskan Eskimo. Smithsonian Institute, Bureau of American Ethnology Bulletin No. 171.

Spindler, George D., Ed.

    1970   Being an Anthropologist: Fieldwork in Eleven Cultures. New York: Holt, Rinehart and Winston.

Spradley, J. and G. McDonough

    1973   Anthropology Through Literature. Boston: Little, Brown and Company.

Stanner, W.H.E.

    1963   On Aboriginal Religion. Oceania Monographs, No. 11. Sydney.

Steward, Julian H.

    1955   Theory of Culture Change. Urbana, Ill.: University of Illinois Press.

    1968   Cultural Ecology. In International Encyclopedia of the Social Sciences. Vol. 4. New York: Macmillan.

Swadesh, Morris

    1952   Lexico-statistic Dating of Prehistoric Ethnic Contacts. Proceedings of the American Philosophical Society. 96:453–462.

    1971   The Origin and Diversification of Language. Edited by J. Sherzer. Chicago: Aldine, Atherton.

Terkel, Studs

    1967   Division Street: America. New York: Pantheon Books.

Thomas, Elizabeth M.

    1958   The Harmless People. New York: Vintage Book Series.

Thrower, Norman

    1966   Original Survey and Land Subdivision: A Comparative Study of the Form and Effect of Contrasting Cadastral Surveys. Association of American Geographers, Monograph Series, 4. Chicago: Rand McNally.

Thurnwald, Richard C.

    1916   Bánaro Society: Social Organization and Kinship System of a Tribe in

Interior New Guinea. Lancaster, Pa.: American Anthropological Association.
1932   The Psychology of Acculturation. American Anthropologist. 34: 557–569.
de Tocqueville, Alexis
1966   Democracy in America. A New Translation by George Lawrence. New York: Harper and Row. First published in 1835.
Toffler, A.
1970   Future Shock. New York: Random House.
Turnbull, Colin M.
1961   The Forest People: A Study of the Pygmies of the Congo. New York: Simon and Schuster.
1968   The Lonely African. New York: Simon and Schuster.
Turner, Victor W.
1968   The Drums of Affliction. Oxford: Clarendon Press.
Tyler, Stephen A., Ed.
1969   Cognitive Anthropology. New York: Holt, Rinehart and Winston.
Tylor, E.B.
1874   Primitive Culture: Researches into the Development of Mythology, Philosophy, Religion, Language, Art and Custom. 2nd Edition. 2 Vols. London: John Murray.
1888   On a Method of Investigating the Development of Institutions Applied to the Laws of Marriage and Descent. Journal of the Royal Anthropological Institute of Great Britain and Ireland. Vol. 18.
Union Bank of Switzerland
1975   Business Facts and Figures. May.
United Nations Statistical Office
1972   Statistical Yearbook, 1972.
1975   Monthly Bulletin of Statistics. April.
United States Bureau of Census
1973   World Population: 1973; Recent Demographic Estimates for the Countries and Regions of the World.
United States Department of Commerce
1974   Statistical Abstracts of the U.S.: 1974.
Unnithan, T.K.N., et al.
1965   Towards a Sociology of Culture in India. New Delhi: Prentice-Hall of India.
van den Berghe, S.L.
1965   Africa: Social Problems of Change and Conflict. San Francisco: Chandler.
van Gennep, Arnold
1960   The Rites of Passage. Chicago: University of Chicago Press. First published in 1909.
van Peursen, Cornelis
1972   Phenomenology and Analytical Philosophy. Pittsburgh: Duquesne University Press.

Wallace, A.F.C.

1956   Revitalization Movements. American Anthropologist. 58:264–281.

1961   Culture and Personality. New York: Random House.

Warner, W. Lloyd

1960   Social Class in America. New York: Harper and Row.

Warner, W.L., W.C. Bailey, et al.

1949   Democracy in Jonesville, A Study in Quality and Equality. New York: Harper.

Warner, W. Lloyd and P.S. Lunt

1941   The Social Life of a Modern Community. New York: Yale University Press.

Warner, W.L. and L. Srole

1945   Yankee City Series. Volume 3. New Haven, Conn.: Yale University Press.

Weber, Max

1947   The Theory of Social and Economic Organization. Translated by A.M. Henderson and T. Parsons. New York: Oxford University Press.

Wells, H.G.

1905   A Modern Utopia. London: Chapman and Hall.

West, James

1945   Plainville, U.S.A. New York: Columbia University Press.

Westermarck, E.

1922   The History of Human Marriage. 5th Edition. New York: Allerton Book Company.

White, Leslie A.

1938   Science is "Sciencing." Philosophy of Science. 5:369–389.

1940   The Symbol: The Origin and Basis of Human Behavior. Philosophy of Science. 7:451–463.

1943   Energy and the Evolution of Culture. American Anthropologist. 45:335–356.

1959   The Evolution of Culture. New York: McGraw-Hill.

1964   Energy and Tools. In Culture and Social Anthropology: Selected Readings. P.B. Hammond, Ed. New York: Macmillan.

Whiting, B.B., J.W.M. Whiting and R. Longabaugh

1975   Children of Six Cultures: A Psychocultural Analysis. Cambridge, Mass.: Harvard University Press.

Whiting, J.W.H., et al.

1966   Field Guide for a Study of Socialization. New York: J. Wiley.

Williams, Glanville

1945–1946   Language and the Law. Law Quarterly Review. pp. 61–62.

Winch, R.F. and L.W. Goodman, Eds.

1968   Selected Studies in Marriage and the Family. New York: Holt, Rinehart and Winston.

Wolfe, A.W.

1969   Social Structural Bases of Art. Current Anthropology. 10:3–44.

Worsley, P.

1957   The Trumpet Shall Sound: A Study of Cargo Cults in Melanesia.
London: Macgibbon and Kee.

1967   The Rush Hour of the Gods: A Study of New Religious Movements in
Japan. New York: Macmillan.

Yalman, Nur

1971   Under the Bo Tree: Studies in Caste, Kinship and Marriage in Interior
of Ceylon. Berkeley and Los Angeles: University of California Press.

Index

Names appearing in capitals refer to authors cited in text.

alism, 345, 348; of nation-states, 272, 345–48; of the neolithic era, 97–98, 101; of nomadic communities, 96, 265–67; and norms, 15, 245, 318–23, 332, 356, 367; and the Oedipus complex, 439, 442; and ownership, 71–75; pariahs, 285–86; peasant, 92; and personality types, 437–39; and politics, 322, 335–52; and the population explosion, 101–3, 105; "primitive," 69; and property, 246–47, 298–99, 305; and the quality of life, 105; and race, 277; relationships in, 139–55, 323, 368; and religion, 163, 356, 371–94, 415; and resources, natural, 105–9, 217, 337; and revitalization movements, 388–94; and rites, 160–70; and rituals, 372–76, 399, 400, 415; roles in, 139–55, 185, 197; and science, 4–5, 298, 376–78, 380; and society (see society): sodalities, 244; space, the sense of, 34–35; and stages of life, 436–37; and the state, 343–48; and status (see status); and symbols (see symbols); tabus, 323, 375, 386; time, sense of, 34–35, 412–13; of towns, 267–68; and transportation, 100; in tribes, 266, 268, 272, 279–80, 340–43; universals in, 20–21, 28, 78, 195, 322–23, 366, 374; and values, 50, 277–79, 336, 387, 401; and world views, 33, 355–68, 391, 393, 402

culture area, the, 417
culture climax, the, 417
culture heroes, 439
culture lag, 28–29
culture shock, 39–41
custom, 27, 318–23
cyclic time, 358

data, field, 47–53, 68, 117 (see also empirical observation and the observer)
"Death of Amara, The" (Bohannan), 171–72
death rites, 169–70
decision-making, 336, 424–27
descent, principles of, 222–23, 231–34
description, in cultural anthropology, 62–68

determinism, economic, 414–15, 417
diachronic studies of language, 130, 132
differentiation: social, 302–3; technological, 301–2
diffusion, 388, 416–17
discrimination, 184
distortion: in communication, 125–25; cultural, 392–93
distribution: of cultural traits, 67; of resources, 337
divorce, 207
double-descent, 231–34
DOUGLAS, MARY, 375
dowry, the, 206
DUNDES, A., 373
duolocal residence, 217
dyads: descent, 208; marriage, 198–203, 206–7; mother-child, 209
dysfunctional traits, 79, 85
DYSON-HUDSON, N., 250

ecology, cultural, 89–109
economic determinism, 414–15, 417
economics: and castes, 284; and change, 310–11, 314; and distribution systems, 303–10; hierarchies in, 286; organization of, 297–315; and property, 298–99; reciprocity in, 303–5; and redistribution, 305–7; and status, 286, 288
education, 191, 288–89
elites: political, 352; social, 290–91
emic models, 51–53, 67, 286, 365, 413
empirical observation, 7 (see also data, field and the observer)
enculturation, 197, 434–37
endogamy, 199, 202, 279, 285
energy resources, 107–9
ENGELS, FRIEDRICH, 417
entertainment, 399, 404–8
entrepreneurs, 424–27
environment, 91, 298, 356, 433
ERIKSON, ERIK, 436
ethnic groups, 129, 182, 279–86 (see also race)
ethnic "osmosis," 279
ethnocentricity, 38–39, 47, 363
ethnographic approaches, 53–59
ethnography, the new, 51–53
ethnomusicology, 398
ethnoscience, 51, 129–30

etic models, 50–51, 53, 67, 179, 286, 363–64, 413

evolution, cultural, 69–70, 414–16, 423–24

exogamy, 198

explanation, in cultural anthropology, 10, 69–86

expressive culture, 397–408

extended families, 214–16

extensions, marriage, 213

family: conjugal-natal, 207–17; and culture, 195–217; definition of, 197; extended, 214–16, 265–66; nuclear, 208–9; patrilineal extended, 265–66; and polygamy, 209

family planning, 103

father, sociological, 163

"Feast of Love, The" (Marriott), 56–57

feedback: in communication, 136; role, 149

feudalism, 307

fictive marriage, the, 214

folk systems, 47–49

food-gathering societies, 94—96

food-producing societies, 96–101

food-synthesizing societies, 100–1

football, American, 405, 406–9

formalization, 254–56

forms: artistic, 398–99; cultural, 28–29

FOSTER, GEORGE, 265

FRANKLIN, BENJAMIN, 13–14

fraternal polyandry, 210

FRAZER, JAMES G., 377, 381

FREUD, SIGMUND, 439

"Freud on Football" (Herald), 406–7

FROMM, ERICH, 436, 437

functionalism, 70–86

functions: of art, 399–401; latent, 84–86; of rituals, 375–76

funeral rites, 169–70, 173

GEERTZ, CLIFFORD, 14, 22, 356, 424

generalization, in cultural anthropology, 5–8, 55, 64, 68, 235

geographic groups, 93, 261–72

GERBRANDS, ADRIAN, 398

ghettoes, cultural, 40

Ghost Dance, the, 389, 391

ghost worship, 381–82

GIDDINGS, FRANKLIN, 179

glottochronology, 132

GLUCKMAN, MAX, 78, 148, 183

"going native," 52

GOODMAN, MARY, 432

gossip, 183, 265

government, 97–98, 191, 267, 339–59 (see also politics)

grammar, 128–29

GRIMM, JACOB, 130

GRIMM, WILHELM, 130

gross domestic product per capital (GDPC), 108–9

group marriages, 211

groups: associational, 362; boundaries of, 183–85; castes, 182; dynamics of, 181–86, 188–89; ethnic, 129, 182, 279–86; geographic, 261–72; interaction among, 279; kinship, 221–40, 266, 341–42; societal, 179–80, 223, 275–93; stable, 182, 184; statistical, 178–79; territorial, 267

HALL, EDWARD, 34

health measures, modern, 102–3

HERALD, CHILD, 406

hierarchy, 96, 283, 286, 359

high god worship, 385–86

historical diffusionism, 416–17

HOEBEL, E.A., 291, 318, 319, 320, 323, 324, 367, 386

holistic approaches, 20–25, 71

horizontal roles, 152–53

horizontal social mobility, 189

horticultural societies, 98–99

housing, 71–74, 76, 91–93, 216–17

HSU, FRANCIS L.K., 436, 439

hunting cultures, 92, 94–96

ideal personality types, 437–39

identity: class, 287; ethnic, 278–79; group, 180, 181–82; personal, 161–62

ideologies, 310, 338

"image of the limited good," 265

incest, 198

Indian village law, 326–31

Indian world view, 35–37, 356–63

"indiscriminate" survey system, the, 71

individuality, 75–76, 360, 443–46

industrial societies, 92, 99–100

initiation rites, 164–66

institutions, social, 177–92, 253–57

interclass mobility, 293
international governments, 349

jajamani system, the, 306–7
JARVIE, I.C., 78
jural law, 319–20

karma, 360
KAY, PAUL, 10
kindred, the, 224–25
kinship systems, 196–203, 206–17,
    221–42, 266, 341–42, 415
kinship terminologies, 234–40
KLUCKHOHN, CLYDE, 120, 443
KROEBER, A.L., 237, 238, 412
kula ring, the, 304–5

LANG, ANDREW, 385
language: areas, 417; and cultural anthro-
    pology, 125–30, 132–35, 417;
    diachronic studies of, 130, 132; and
    ethnic differences, 129; and ethno-
    science, 129–30; silent, 34–35;
    and symbol, 144; synchronic studies
    of, 125–30; transformational model
    of, 129
language barriers, 47
latent functions, cultural, 79, 84–86
law: and cultural anthropology, 4–5, 311,
    318–32, 360; Cheyene, 325–26; crim-
    inal, 322; Indian village, 326–31;
    jural, 319–20; social, 311
LEACH, EDMUND, 373
leadership: and art, 400; charismatic, 322,
    393; political, 336, 339; in stable so-
    cieties, 96, 267, 340
LEE, DOROTHY, 119
"legal culture," 339
levirate, 203, 212, 213
LÉVI-STRAUSS, CLAUDE, 201, 372
LEWIS, OSCAR, 311
LEWIS, SINCLAIR, 186, 187
lineage, 226–227, 231, 277
lineality, 235
linear time, 358
linguistics: anthropology of, 22, 121;
    comparative methods of, 130, 132
LINTON, RALPH, 141, 383, 418
LLEWELLYN, KARL, 318, 319, 320, 323
LOMAX, ALAN, 398, 404
Lord's Prayer, The, three versions, 131

MacIVER, ROBERT, 190
magic, 376–78, 380, 399
MALINOWSKI, BRONISLAW, 70, 75, 198,
    305, 373, 377, 381, 417, 439
mana, 386
MANGIN, WILLIAM, 420
manifest functions, cultural, 79
MARETT, R.R., 386
marriage, 48–49, 95–96, 166–69,
    197–203, 206–14, 222–23
MARRIOTT, McKIM, 56–57
MARX, KARL, 286, 288, 310, 311, 314,
    414, 417
material culture, 29–30, 33, 61–68, 185,
    186, 191, 337
mating, 166–68, 197, 222–23
matriclans, 228, 232, 233
matrilineage, 227, 231
matrilocal residence, 217
maya, 358, 364, 365
mazeways, personal, 391, 393, 425, 426,
    443
MEAD, MARGARET, 417, 435
media, of distribution, 303–10
medium, of communication, 125–30,
    132–35
megalopolises, 270
MERTON, ROBERT, 79
message, in communication, 122,
    135–36
"metes-and-bounds" survey system, 71
MICHELS, ROBERT, 255
minorities, 285–86
MITFORD, JESSICA, 173
models: for action, 356; of change,
    414–27; comprehensive, 25; concep-
    tual, 157–73; culture as a, 28–29;
    decision-making, 427; emic, 51–53,
    67, 179, 286, 364, 413; entertainment
    as, 405; etic, 50–51, 53, 67, 179, 286,
    363–64, 413; evaluation of, 12–13,
    14–16; evolutionary, 69–70; explana-
    tory, 356; interaction of, 25; multiple,
    22–23; person-environment, 444;
    psychological, 426; scientific,
    365–66; for social participation, 405;
    transformational, of language, 129;
    world views, 355–68
monarchies, 344–45
monogamy, 207, 211
moral relativism, 366–68

MORGAN, L.H., 62, 64, 65, 69, 70, 198, 234, 414, 415, 427
mother, sociological, 162
mother-child dyad, 197
MOWRER, O.H., 443
multiplex roles, 148–50
MURDOCK, GEORGE P., 206, 235, 237, 238, 287
MYRDAL, GUNNAR, 185
myths, 372–76, 401

names, 162, 255
national character, 437–39
nationalism, 345, 348
nation-states, 272, 345–48
nativistic movements, 389–90
"Natural History of a Kiss" (Pike), 26–27
nature worship, 385
neo-evolutionism, 423–24
neolithic era, 97–98, 101
neolocal residence, 217
NETTL, BRUNO, 398
new ethnography, 51–53
NIDA, EUGENE, 120
nomadic communities, 96, 265–67
norms, 15, 245, 318–23, 332, 356, 367
nuclear families, 208–9

observer, cultural anthropologist as, 5–11, 47, 50 (see also data, field and empirical observation)
occupational status, 288
Oedipus complex, 439, 442
oligarchies, 255
"One-hundred per cent American" (Linton), 418–20
organization: economic, 297–315; political, 335–52
"osmosis," ethnic, 279
ownership, 71–75

paired relationships (see dyads)
parallel cousins, 200, 202
pariahs, 285–86
patriclans, 228, 232, 233
patrilineage, 231, 277
patrilineal extended family, 265–66
patrilocal residence, 217
"Peace Corps Backlash" (Buchwald), 104–5
peasant societies, 92

personality types, 437–39
personhood, 2–4, 431–36
philosophical relativism, 364–66
physical anthropologists, 22
PIKE, E. ROYSTON, 26
plow agriculture, 99
PLUNKETT, GEORGE, 350
points of view, anthropological, 19–41
politics: and ideologies, 338; and leadership, 336, 339, 352; organization of, 335–52; and parties, 347; and power, 336; processes of, 322, 349–59; and resource allocation, 337 (see also government)
polyandry, 209, 210, 213
polyethnic societies, 280–82
polygamy, 209, 210
polygyny, 209, 210
population explosion, 101–3, 105
POSPISIL, LEOPOLD, 320, 321, 323
potlatch, 305
POWERS, STEPHEN, 62
preferential marriages, 200–3
prescribed marriages, 200–3
prestige, social, 185, 186, 252
priests, 280–81
"primitive" culture, 69
progeny price, 203
property, 246–47, 298–99, 305 (see also ownership)

race, 277 (see also ethnic groups)
RADCLIFFE-BROWN, A.R., 70, 76, 167
RADIN, PAUL, 385
ramages, 226
rank, 141, 189 (see also status and stratification)
RATTRAY, R.S., 231
receiver, in communication, 122, 124–25
reductionism, in cultural anthropology, 305–7
relationships: cultural, 139–55; international, 368; legal, 323
relativism, cultural, 364–68
religion: and acculturaltion, 388; and culture, 163, 356, 371–94, 415; dynamics in, 386–94; and science, 376–78, 380; in society, 191, 356, 415; and technology, 387; and world views, 371
residence, types of, 217

resources, natural, 105–9, 217, 337
revitalization movements, 388–94
revolution, urban, 97–98
RICHARDSON, JANE, 412
rites: birth, 160–63; calendrical, 374;
    crisis, 374; death, 169–70; funeral,
    169–70, 173; initiation, 164–68; mar-
    riage, 166–69; of passage, 160–70
    (see also rituals)
Rites de Passage, Les (van Gennep), 160
rituals, 372–76, 399, 400, 415 (see also
    rites)
ROBERTSON, WILLIAM, 414
roles: cultural, 139–55; in cultural
    anthropology, 142–44; and marriage,
    197; and social stratification, 185–86,
    188–89
role conflict, 143–44
role confusion, 153–54
role expectations, 146–48
role feedback, 149
role pairs, 145–51
rules, cultural, 48

sanctions: legal, 320–21, 332; social, 265
SAPIR, EDWARD, 33, 121
"Savages, We Call Them" (Franklin),
    13–14
science, 4–5, 298, 376–78, 380
secret societies, 251–52
sender, in communication, 122–24
serial monogamy, 48, 207
sex: and kinship systems, 235; and social
    groups, 248–49
"Shakespeare in the Bush" (Bohannan),
    440–41
shamans, 251, 380–81
silent languages, 34–35
SIMMONS, LEO W., 204
simplex roles, 148–50
slavery, 291–92
social classes, 286–93
social elites, 290–91
social groups (see groups)
social institutions, 177–92
social laws, 311
social mobility, 189
social programming, 144
social stratification, 185–86, 188–89
"social zones," 35
socialism, 415

societal groups, 179–80, 223
society: age grades in, 249–51, 342; and
    the arts, 398–404; authority in, 185,
    186, 246; and boundaries, class,
    292–93; and bureaucracies, 100,
    346–47; and caste systems, 182,
    282–85, 287–88, 339, 362; and
    change, 30–32, 77, 310–11, 314,
    411–27, 444; and clans, 228, 229,
    232, 233, 341–42; classes in, 286–93;
    control, 265, 377–78; and culture
    (see culture); and customs, 27,
    318–23; death rites, 169–70;
    decision-making, 336, 424–27; defi-
    nition of, 33; differentiation in,
    302–3; discrimination in, 184; and
    economics, 286, 288, 297–315; and
    education, 191, 288–89; elites in,
    290–91; entrepreneurs in, 424–27;
    ethnic groups, 129, 182, 279–86; ex-
    tended families, 214–16; families,
    195–217, 265–66; food-gathering,
    94–96; food-producing, 96–101;
    food-synthesizing, 100–1; functions
    in, 79, 84–86, 375–76, 399–401;
    funeral rites, 169–70, 173; gossip,
    183, 265; and government, 97–98,
    191, 267, 339–59; groups in (see
    groups); hierarchies in, 96, 283, 286,
    359; horticultural, 98–99; hunting,
    94–96; identity, 161–62, 180, 181–82,
    278–79, 287; and ideology, 310, 338;
    and the "image of the limited good,"
    265; and incest, 198; individuality
    in, 75–76, 360, 443–46; industrial, 92,
    99–100; initiation rites, 164–66;
    institutions in, 177—92, 253–57; and
    kindred, 224–25; and kinship
    systems, 196–203, 206–17, 221–40,
    266, 341–42, 415; and law, 4–5, 311,
    318–32, 360; leadership in, 96, 267,
    322, 339, 340, 393, 400; and magic,
    376–78, 380, 399; and marriage,
    48–49, 95–96, 166–69, 197–203,
    206–14, 222–23; models of (see
    models); monarchies, 344–45; and
    myths, 372–76, 401; and names, 162,
    255; nationalism in, 345; nation-
    states, 272, 345–48; nomadic com-
    munities, 96, 265–67; norms of, 15,
    245, 318–23, 332, 356, 367; oligar-

chies, 255; pariahs in, 285–86; peasant, 92; and politics, 322, 335–52; polyethnic, 280–82; prestige in, 185, 186, 252; and property, 246–47, 298–99, 305; rank in, 141, 189; revitalization movements in, 388–94; rites in, 160–70; rituals in, 372–76, 399, 400, 415; roles in, 139–55, 185, 197; and science, 4–5, 298, 376–78, 380; secret societies in, 251–52; and sex, 235, 248–49; and sodalities, 244; stateless, 340–43; and states, 343–48; statistical groups in, 78–79; status in, 85, 139–55, 162–63, 245–46, 250; stratification in, 185–86, 188–89, 287–89; and symbols (see symbols); tabus in, 323, 375, 386; towns, 267–68; tribes, 266, 268, 272, 279–80, 340–43
sociological father, 163
sociological mother, 162
sodalities, 244
sororate, 212, 213
space, sense of, 34–35
specialization, 96, 101, 254, 264–65, 300, 301, 309–10, 360
"specific evolution," 423–24
SPENCER, ROBERT, 280
stable groups, 182, 184
stages of life, 436–37
STANNER, W.E.H., 373
stateless societies, 340–43
statistical groups, 78–79
status: achieved, 151–52; and age, 250; and art, 400; ascribed, 151–52, 277; and clothes, 85; concept of, 141–42; economic, 286, 288; multidimensional, 290; occupational, 288; social, 85, 139–55, 162–63, 245–46, 250 (see also rank and stratification)
"status cluster," 143
STEWARD, JULIAN, 423
stratification: class, 287–90; economic, 288, 310; educational, 288–89; ethnic, 287–88; in society, 185–86, 188–89 (see also rank and status)
stratigraphic approaches, 22
subsistence levels, 93–101, 415
substitution marriage, 211–13
suburbs, 269–70
suitor service, 203

"Sun Chief: The Autobiography of a Hopi Indian" (Simmons), 214–5
supernaturalism, 358, 376
survey systems, 71
symbols: ambiguity of, 120; arbitrariness of, 116–17; artistic, 399; and behavior, 144; and communication, 118, 125; and concepts, 125, 117; and cultural anthropology, 113–37; ethnic, 278; and experience, 120; of hierarchies, 283; and ideals, 118–19; institutional, 255; and kinship terminologies, 234–40; and language, 144; meaning of, 118; money as, 308; and perception, 119–20; personal, 117; and social stratification, 182, 185–86; written, 133–34
synchronic studies of language, 125–30
systems: of belief, 310; caste, 287–88; classification of, 65, 67; of distribution, 303–10; the jajamani, 306–7; kinship, 221–40; legal, 317–32, 338–39; political, 338–39; technological, 356

tabus, 323, 375, 386
taxonomies, 67, 168
technology, 90, 92–97, 100–1, 298–303, 337, 356, 387, 415
territoriality: ethnic, 280; governmental, 343
THURNWALD, RICHARD, 34–35, 164, 412–13
time: sense of, 34–35, 412–13; types of, 358
"Totemism and the A.E.F." (Linton), 383–85
towns, 267–68
"township-and-range" survey system, 71
transformational model of language, 129
transition rites, 375
transportation, 100
tribes, 266, 268, 272, 279–80, 340–43
TURNBULL, COLIN, 426
TYLOR, EDWARD, 415, 427

unilateral kinship systems, 223, 226–30
universals, cultural, 20–21, 28, 78, 195, 322–23, 366, 374

values: and art, 401; cultural 277, 336; in

30008